Leo Strauss on Hegel

I0085889

The Leo Strauss Transcript Series

SERIES EDITORS: NATHAN TARCOV AND GAYLE MCKEEN

The Leo Strauss Center
The University of Chicago
HTTP://LEOSTRAUSSCENTER.UCHICAGO.EDU/

VOLUMES IN THE SERIES

Strauss on Nietzsche's Thus Spoke Zarathustra
Edited by Richard L. Velkley

Introduction to Political Philosophy
Edited by Catherine H. Zuckert

Leo Strauss on Hegel
Edited by Paul Franco

Leo Strauss on Hegel

Edited by Paul Franco

THE UNIVERSITY OF CHICAGO PRESS
Chicago and London

The University of Chicago Press, Chicago 60637
The University of Chicago Press, Ltd., London
© 2019 by The University of Chicago
All rights reserved. No part of this book may be used or reproduced in any manner whatsoever without written permission, except in the case of brief quotations in critical articles and reviews.
For more information, contact the University of Chicago Press, 1427 E. 60th St., Chicago, IL 60637.
Published 2019
Paperback edition 2021
Printed in the United States of America

30 29 28 27 26 25 24 23 22 21   1 2 3 4 5

ISBN-13: 978-0-226-64068-6 (cloth)
ISBN-13: 978-0-226-81678-4 (paper)
ISBN-13: 978-0-226-64071-6 (e-book)

DOI: https://doi.org/10.7208/chicago/9780226640716.001.0001

LIBRARY OF CONGRESS CATALOGING-IN-PUBLICATION DATA

Names: Strauss, Leo, author. | Franco, Paul, 1956– editor.
Title: Leo Strauss on Hegel / edited by Paul Franco.
Other titles: Leo Strauss transcript series.
Description: Chicago ; London : The University of Chicago Press, 2019. | Series: The Leo Strauss transcript series
Identifiers: LCCN 2018061749 | ISBN 9780226640686 (cloth : alk. paper) | ISBN 9780226640716 (e-book)
Subjects: LCSH: Hegel, Georg Wilhelm Friedrich, 1770–1831. Vorlesungen über die Geschichte der Philosophie. | History—Philosophy. | Philosophy, German.
Classification: LCC D16.8.H49 S77 2019 | DDC 901—dc23
LC record available at https://lccn.loc.gov/2018061749

Contents

Note on the Leo Strauss Transcript Project

Leo Strauss is well known as a thinker and writer, but he also had tremendous impact as a teacher. In the transcripts of his courses one can see Strauss commenting on texts, including many he wrote little or nothing about, and responding generously to student questions and objections. The transcripts, amounting to more than twice the volume of Strauss's published work, add immensely to the material available to scholars and students of Strauss's work.

In the early 1950s mimeographed typescripts of student notes of Strauss's courses were distributed among his students. In winter 1954, the first recording, of his course on natural right, was transcribed and distributed to students. Professor Herbert J. Storing obtained a grant from the Relm Foundation to support the taping and transcription, which resumed on a regular basis in the winter of 1956 with Strauss's course "Historicism and Modern Relativism." Of the 39 courses Strauss taught at the University of Chicago from 1958 until his departure in 1968, 34 were recorded and transcribed. After Strauss retired from the university, recording of his courses continued at Claremont Men's College in the spring of 1968 and the fall and spring of 1969 (although the tapes for his last two courses there have not been located), and at St. John's College for the four years until his death in October 1973.

The surviving original audio recordings vary widely in quality and completeness; and after they had been transcribed, the audiotapes were sometimes reused, leaving the audio record very incomplete. Over time the audiotape deteriorated. Beginning in the late 1990s, Stephen Gregory, then the administrator of the university's John M. Olin Center for Inquiry into the Theory and Practice of Democracy funded by the John M. Olin Foundation, initiated the digital remastering of the surviving tapes by Craig Harding of September Media to ensure their preservation, improve their audibility, and make possible their eventual publication. This remastering received financial support from the Olin Center and a grant from the Division of Preservation and Access of the National Endowment for the Humanities. The surviving audiofiles are available at the Strauss Center website: https://leostrausscenter.uchicago.edu/courses.

Strauss permitted the taping and transcribing to go forward, but he did not check the transcripts or otherwise participate in the project. Accordingly, Strauss's close associate and colleague Joseph Cropsey originally put the copyright in his own name, though he assigned copyright to the Estate of Leo Strauss in 2008. Beginning in 1958 a headnote was placed at the beginning of each transcript, which read: "This transcription is a written record of essentially oral material, much of which developed spontaneously in the classroom and none of which was prepared with publication in mind. The transcription is made available to a limited number of interested persons, with the understanding that no use will be made of it that is inconsistent with the private and partly informal origin of the material. Recipients are emphatically requested not to seek to increase the circulation of the transcription. This transcription has not been checked, seen, or passed on by the lecturer." In 2008, Strauss's heir, his daughter Jenny Strauss, asked Nathan Tarcov to succeed Joseph Cropsey as Strauss's literary executor. They agreed that because of the widespread circulation of the old, often inaccurate and incomplete transcripts and the continuing interest in Strauss's thought and teaching, it would be a service to interested scholars and students to proceed with publication of the remastered audiofiles and transcripts. They were encouraged by the fact that Strauss himself signed a contract with Bantam Books to publish four of the transcripts, although in the end none were published.

The university's Leo Strauss Center, established in 2008, launched a project, presided over by its director, Nathan Tarcov, and managed by Stephen Gregory, to correct the old transcripts on the basis of the remastered audiofiles as they became available, transcribe those audiofiles not previously transcribed, and annotate and edit for readability all the transcripts including those for which no audiofiles survived. This project was supported by grants from the Winiarski Family Foundation, Mr. Richard S. Shiffrin and Mrs. Barbara Z. Schiffrin, Earhart Foundation, the Hertog Foundation, and contributions from numerous other donors. The Strauss Center was ably assisted in its fundraising efforts by Nina Botting-Herbst and Patrick McCusker, staff in the Office of the Dean of the Division of the Social Sciences at the university.

Senior scholars familiar with both Strauss's work and the texts he taught were commissioned as editors, with preliminary work done in most cases by student editorial assistants. The goal in editing the transcripts has been to preserve Strauss's original words as much as possible while making the transcripts easier to read. Strauss's impact (and indeed his charm) as a teacher is revealed in the sometimes informal character of his remarks. Sentence fragments that might not be appropriate in academic prose have been kept; some long and rambling sentences have been divided; some repeated clauses or words have been deleted. A clause that breaks the syntax or train of thought may have been moved elsewhere in the sentence or paragraph. In rare cases sentences within a paragraph may have been reordered. Where no audiofiles survived, attempts have been made to correct likely mistranscriptions. Brackets within the text record insertions. Ellipses in transcripts without audiofiles have been preserved. Whether they indicate deletion of something Strauss said or the trailing off of his voice or serve as a dash cannot be determined. Ellipses that have been added to transcripts with audiofiles indicate that the words are inaudible. Administrative details regarding paper or seminar topics or meeting rooms or times have been deleted without being noted, but reading assignments have been retained. Citations are provided to all passages so readers can read the transcripts with the texts in hand, and notes have been provided to identify persons, texts, and events to which Strauss refers.

Readers should make allowance for the oral character of the transcripts. There are careless phrases, slips of the tongue, repetitions, and possible mistranscriptions. However enlightening the transcripts are, they cannot be regarded as the equivalent of works that Strauss himself wrote for publication.

Nathan Tarcov, Editor-in-Chief
Gayle McKeen, Managing Editor
August 2014

Editorial Headnote

Strauss's course was taught in a seminar form. He began class with general remarks; a student then read aloud portions of the text, followed by Strauss's comments and responses to student questions and comments. The text assigned for this course was G. W. F. Hegel, *Philosophy of History*, translated by J. Sibree (New York: Dover Press, 1956). When the text was read aloud in class, this transcript records the words as they appear in Sibree's translation. Original spelling has been retained. Citations are included for all passages.

The course had sixteen sessions. Since audiotapes for all sessions have survived, this transcript is based upon remastered audiotapes. Minor changes to the transcript are not noted. For example, we have corrected inaccurate noun-verb agreement, rectified peculiar word order, and inserted prepositions or connecting words in the interest of readability.

A version of the transcript showing all deletions and insertions will become available on the Leo Strauss Center website two years after print publication of this transcript and can be made available upon request meanwhile for the same price as the printed version. The original transcript may be consulted in the Strauss archive in Special Collections at the University of Chicago Library.

This transcript was edited by Paul Franco, with assistance from Jordan Goldberg, C. C. DuBois, Gayle McKeen, and William Wood. The index was prepared by Derek Gottlieb.

Introduction to the Transcript of Leo Strauss's 1965 Course on Hegel's *Philosophy of History*

Paul Franco

In the winter quarter of 1965, Leo Strauss offered a course on Hegel's *Philosophy of History* at the University of Chicago. It was the second time Strauss had offered such a course—the first time was in the autumn quarter of 1958. No audiotapes survive for the 1958 course, and the original transcript of it is in a somewhat fragmentary condition. Audiotapes for the 1965 course, on the other hand, do survive, and therefore it has been possible to reconstruct a relatively complete transcript of it. It is this latter transcript that follows, supplemented where helpful by passages from the 1958 course transcript in notes.[1]

It is fortunate that we have access to these courses. Hegel is one of the few great philosophers that Strauss did not write about at any length over the course of his career. There are, of course, numerous references to Hegel in Strauss's published writings, some of them quite intriguing. But more often than not, Hegel is treated as a domino in Strauss's schematic history of modern political philosophy and of the genesis of historicism. The courses he taught at the University of Chicago reflect a much deeper engagement with Hegel on Strauss's part, and one that is surprisingly sympathetic to the great nineteenth-century thinker.

Before taking up the content of these courses, I would like to briefly survey Strauss's engagement with Hegel in his published writings.[2] There are three principal contexts in which Hegel's name comes up in Strauss's writings: in connection with his studies of Hobbes in the 1930s; in his debate with Alexandre Kojève in *On Tyranny*; and in his account of the "three waves" of modern political philosophy. Let me begin with the Hobbes-Hegel connection.

During the 1930s, Strauss was deeply engaged in the study of Hobbes's political philosophy. This is evidenced not only in his 1936 book, *The Political Philosophy of Hobbes*, but also in a number of unpublished writings on Hobbes that have been printed in Strauss's *Gesammelte Schriften* and recently translated into English.[3] As is well known, Strauss's interest in Hobbes stemmed from a desire to investigate the roots of modern political philosophy with a view to critiquing it and reopening the quarrel between the ancients and the moderns.[4] As part of this investigation, Strauss seems to have envisaged writing a comparative study of Hobbes and Hegel.[5] This intention received expression in a footnote in Strauss's Hobbes book, where he wrote: "M. Alexandre Kojevnikoff and the writer intend to undertake a detailed investigation of the connexion between Hobbes and Hegel."[6]

The context of this footnote is a comparison between Hobbes's principle of the fear of violent death and Hegel's account of the origin of self-consciousness in the master-slave dialectic. For Strauss, the fear of violent death in Hobbes plays the same foundational role with respect to modern moral and political philosophy that radical doubt in Descartes plays with respect to modern metaphysics. Like radical doubt, the fear of violent death springs from distrust of nature rather than grateful acceptance of it, and it leads to an effort to actively control nature rather than to mere contemplation of it. According to Strauss, Hegel agrees with Hobbes on this foundational point when he locates the origin of self-consciousness in the slave's fear of violent death in his life-and-death struggle with the master. For both Hobbes and Hegel, bourgeois morality is ultimately grounded in the vanity-quelling fear of violent death.[7]

The other connection Strauss draws between Hegel and Hobbes relates to the latter's turn to history in his translation of Thucydides. This turn to history, Strauss claims, was motivated by Hobbes's interest in the application of moral precepts. Reason by itself is incapable of getting human beings to obey moral norms; historical examples are needed to make obedience easier. This same conviction of the impotence of reason and rejection of the morality of obedience ultimately underpin Hegel's philosophy of history, according to Strauss. From Hobbes to Hegel, the problem of applying moral norms and guaranteeing the actualization of the best regime becomes the focus of modern political philosophy.[8]

As it turned out, Strauss and Kojève never wrote their projected comparative study of Hobbes and Hegel.[9] They did, however, collaborate almost two decades after the publication of *The Political Philosophy of Hobbes* on a book that allowed Strauss to engage more fully with Hegel's philosophy, or at least Kojève's idiosyncratic version of it. *On Tyranny* (1954) began life as a commentary by Strauss on Xenophon's short dialogue *Hiero*. Strauss used this dialogue to show how Xenophon employed a socially responsible rhetoric that allowed him to reveal certain truths to a small minority of philosophers while hiding them from the majority of ordinary citizens. This rhetoric, he said, was "based on the premise that there is a disproportion between the intransigent quest for truth and the requirements of society."[10] This premise was also bound up with the purpose of the dialogue: to contrast two different ways of life, the political life and the philosophical life, and to show the superiority of the latter by pointing to the self-sufficiency of the wise man versus the political ruler's need for love.[11]

It is precisely this radical disjunction of philosophy and politics, theory and practice, that Kojève criticizes in his response to Strauss. The philosopher, he argues, plays a crucial role in positively influencing political reality and in bringing about the "universal and homogeneous state" that constitutes the Hegelian end or goal of history. Kojève rejects what he sees as Strauss's "Epicurean" idea of the philosophical life as isolated from society and devoted to the quest for purely theoretical truth. Such an idea rests on a "theistic" conception of Being as immutable and eternally identical to itself. This conception, however, goes out the window once one accepts Hegel's radically "atheistic" position that "Being itself is essentially temporal." Then the philosopher must flee the "isolation of the garden" and "participate in history" in order to reveal Being. The only way for him to establish his truths is through "social and historical verification." To retreat into solitude, as Strauss suggests, leads inevitably to solipsism.[12]

In his response to Kojève, Strauss makes a number of revealing comments about Hegel. In the first place, he repeats the point he made in *The Political Philosophy of Hobbes* that Hegel incorporates the modern rejection of the morality of obedience initiated by Hobbes: "Kojève's or Hegel's synthesis of classical and Biblical morality effects the miracle of producing an amazingly lax morality out of two moralities both of which make very strict demands on self-restraint." Doubting the efficacy of reason to bring about obedience to moral norms, Hegel continued and radicalized the "modern tradition that emancipated the passions." Strauss once again compares Hegel's teaching in the master-slave dialectic to Hobbes's doctrine of the state of nature. Though Hegel's teaching is certainly more sophisticated than Hobbes's, it still starts from the false Hobbesian assumption that "man as man is thinkable as a being that lacks awareness of sacred restraints or as a being that is guided by nothing but a desire for recognition."[13]

The second fundamental point about Hegel—or Kojève's version of him—that Strauss makes in his response concerns the end or goal of history. Kojève famously describes this end in terms of the "universal and homogeneous state," that is, the nonnational and classless state. Strauss wonders whether such a state, where no struggles remain and there is nothing left to do, does not rather resemble the state of Nietzsche's "last man" and point toward the destruction of humanity.[14] This is a criticism that Strauss comes back to again and again in his correspondence with Kojève,[15] and we will see it appear in his courses on Hegel as well. Kojève himself seems to concede this point to Strauss, and as time went by he described the end-state in ever more ironic, less utopian terms. Thus he writes to Strauss: "In the final state there naturally are no more 'human beings' in our sense of an *historical* human being. The 'healthy' automata are 'satisfied' (sports, art, eroticism, etc.), and the 'sick' ones get locked up."[16]

Strauss concludes his response to Kojève by reprising the grand contrast between classical and modern political philosophy that overarched his Hobbes book. Whereas classical political philosophy held that the actualization of the best regime depends on chance, modern political philosophy seeks to guarantee the actualization of the optimal social order by lowering the goal for man. Whereas the "classical solution supplies a stable standard by which to judge any political order," the "modern solution eventually destroys the very idea of a standard that is independent of actual situations."[17] It is this interpretation of modern political philosophy as an inexorable slide from the realistic lowering of standards to the historicistic abolition of them that dominates the last set of writings by Strauss that I want to consider.

In "What Is Political Philosophy?" and "The Three Waves of Modernity," Strauss divides the history of modern political philosophy into three stages or "waves" and considers Hegel under the rubric of the second. But the thinker who dominates Strauss's discussion of the second wave is Rousseau. Already in *Natural Right and History*, Strauss argued that by positing freedom rather than rationality as the distinctive character of man, "Rousseau may be said to have originated the 'philosophy of freedom'" that came to fruition in Kant and Hegel.[18] In "What Is Political Philosophy?" and "The Three Waves of Modernity," he stresses how Rousseau's doctrine of the general will destroyed the possibility of appealing from positive law to natural law and thus led to the complete collapse of the *ought* into the *is*, the ideal into the actual. In this way, Rousseau advanced the movement begun by Machiavelli and Hobbes that sought "to guarantee the actualization of the ideal, or to prove the necessary coincidence of the rational and the real." Hegel's turn to the philosophy of history represents a further step in this realistic process of lowering standards as a means of guaranteeing the actualization of the right order:

> The actualization of the right order is achieved by blind selfish passion: the right order is the unintended byproduct of human activities which are in no way directed toward the right order. The right order may have been as loftily conceived by Hegel as it was by Plato, which one may doubt. It certainly was thought by Hegel to be established in the Machiavellian way, not in the Platonic way: it was thought to be established in a manner which contradicts the right order itself. The delusions of communism are already the delusions of Hegel and even of Kant.[19]

Such a passage might lead one to believe that Strauss approaches Hegel in much the same way that Karl Popper did in his 1945 polemic *The Open Society and Its Enemies*, in which Hegel, along with Plato, is treated as a precursor of twentieth-century totalitarianism. But this is not at all the case. In a scathing review of John Wild's 1946 book *Plato's Theory of Man*, for example, Strauss sharply criticized Wild's totalitarian interpretation of Hegel, arguing that "Hegel is so far from being a 'totalitarian' that he rejects Plato's political philosophy precisely because he considers it 'totalitarian.'" Hegel criticizes Plato for lacking an awareness of the modern principle of "subjective freedom," which holds that the "individual as such has an infinite value."[20] When we turn to Strauss's courses on Hegel, we find him repeatedly denying that Hegel is any sort of totalitarian thinker or deifier of the state. More generally, he insists that Hegel is a profound thinker who deserves to be treated with the utmost respect. In one place, for example, he states: "I am not a Hegelian, and I do not believe that one can say that history is rational. But on the other hand, one must not underestimate the immense intellectual power which was Hegel's and by virtue of which he brought to light many very interesting things" (chapter 7, 163).

The text Strauss chose for his courses on Hegel's political philosophy was *The Philosophy of History*. He says he chose this text rather than the *Philosophy of Right*, even though the latter was published by Hegel himself, because Hegel is much more accessible in his spoken lectures than in the written works he published during his lifetime. (The same might be said of Strauss.) He also claims that Hegel's teaching in the *Philosophy of Right* "is essentially related to his philosophy of history, and one understands his political philosophy proper . . . better if one views the historical matrix out of which that philosophy emerged" (chapter 1, 18). For both courses, Strauss used John Sibree's English translation of *The Philosophy of History*, the only one available until quite recently, but he frequently corrects the translation and introduces passages from Georg Lasson's German edition, which contains transcribed material that is not found in Sibree's translation.[21]

One of the first questions that confront any reader of Hegel's *Philosophy of History* is what the relationship is between philosophy of history and empirical history. To what extent is Hegel's philosophy of history based on an a priori logic or metaphysics that has little to do with the history written by professional historians? Hegel himself denies that the philosopher of history simply ignores empirical history: "we must take history as it is, and proceed historically, i.e., empirically," eschewing "a priori fabrications."[22] And Strauss backs him up on this point. He is at pains throughout his lectures, and often in the face of student skepticism, to bring out Hegel's empirical procedure. As he puts it early on in this 1965 course: Hegel is "one of the most empirical philosophers . . . Precisely by looking at history as it was, and no arbitrary constructions and monkey business, will the reason of history appear" (chapter 1, 37). "Empirical" here, of course, does not mean that the philosopher of history simply or passively receives the facts without exercising subjective discrimination or judgment. Even the ordinary historian, Hegel tells us, "brings his categories along with him, and sees his data through them."[23] Strauss concurs. Every historian has to distinguish the important from the unimportant, and this in no way detracts from his objectivity (chapter 4, 94; see also 1958: 5, 6).[24]

How does Hegel distinguish between the important and the unimportant in his philosophical account of history? Strauss claims that Hegel "regards as most important what a human society regards as most important," what it bows down to (1958: 5). Again and again in these lectures, Strauss points to the primacy of religion in Hegel's understanding of various societies and cultures. In order to understand a society as it understood itself, Hegel looked at what the members of that society looked up to or bowed down before: "A nation is what it is by virtue of what it looks up to, what it regards as the highest, as the divine" (chapter 9, 208). In his discussion of Hegel's interpretation of the Greeks, Strauss articulates the central premise of Hegel's empirical approach to history: "I remind you of the fact that Hegel asserts more than once what we can call the primacy of religion. In other words, the core of a culture is religion" (chapter 11, 249). It is this emphasis on the primacy of religion that ultimately distinguishes Hegel's approach to history from Marx's. Whereas "Marx understands man as primarily a needy being in the sense of bodily needs . . . Hegel understands man as the deferential being" (chapter 6, 153).

Related to the question of Hegel's empiricism is the question of his fairness to non-Western cultures. In his discussions of Africa, China, and India, Hegel is perfectly comfortable making judgments about their relative value in the overall scheme of history. The students in Strauss's courses, similar to students today, raise many questions about this aspect of Hegel's philosophy, and Strauss addresses them head on. He refers to certain present-day liberals who assert that all cultures are equal, but he finds this position self-contradictory in that most past cultures have not been liberal (chapter 3, 72–73). In the sixth session of this 1965 course, Strauss probes this liberal relativist position more deeply, asking after the standard by which Hegel judges various cultures. He argues that it is above all with a view to science and political liberty, two things that remain highly regarded even today by many people, that Hegel judges cultures to be superior or inferior. These are not arbitrary standards, though Strauss acknowledges that they—especially science—no longer have the manifest authority they once possessed in the past. Nevertheless, he urges skeptical students not to dismiss Hegel too quickly: "the same fairness to which China and India have claim, Hegel too has claim" (chapter 6, 136).

As part of this obligation to treat Hegel justly, Strauss is particularly concerned to refute the charge that Hegel is some sort of racist. Yes, he believed that Protestantism was more congruent with the modern rational state than either Catholicism or Judaism, but this does not mean that Catholics or Jews (or Chinese or Hindus) can be excluded from becoming members of such a state. Strauss hammers this point home in a particularly compelling way. That Hegel had nothing to do with racism, he argues, is demonstrated by the fact that "a famous constitutional lawyer in Germany," namely, Carl Schmitt, "who became a Nazi himself for deplorable reasons," announced that Hegel died when Hitler came to power on 31 January 1933 (chapter 6, 137). Strauss alludes to this statement by Schmitt at several points in his lectures, always as a way of discrediting any attempt to link Hegel with fascism or totalitarianism.

Apart from questions of method and approach, Strauss pays particular attention in his lectures to what Hegel calls the "means of spirit" and the goal that is achieved by those means. With respect to the means by which history progresses, Hegel famously focuses on the crucial role of passion and self-interest. In his earlier writings on Hegel, as we saw, Strauss laid strong emphasis on this aspect of Hegel's philosophy of history, connecting it with the conviction of the impotence of reason, the rejection of the morality of obedience, the emancipation of passion, and the preoccupation with actualization that characterizes modern political philosophy more generally. Toward the beginning of this 1965 course, he remarks on the convergence between the *is* and the *ought*, the amoral and the moral, in Hegel's philosophy: "Order comes out of disorder, without being intended: this is, one can say, the simple formula of Hegel's philosophy of history." It is a formula that extends to history in general the invisible hand argument Adam Smith used to analyze the laws of economics (chapter 1, 26). Toward the end of the course, in a lengthy digression on "the very notion of a philosophy of history," Strauss comes back to this idea that Hegel adopted Adam Smith's economic teaching in his philosophy of history, showing how the rational order emerges naturally out of individuals pursuing their self-interested desires. This was all part of the modern quest to guarantee the actualization of the best regime. Whereas the traditional view had been that the actualization of the best regime required "severe self-sacrifice" and therefore depended on chance, the modern view as articulated by Hegel held that the best regime resulted from the indulgence of desire. The rational and the actual thus necessarily coincided (chapter 13, 298).

Even here, though, Strauss adds some nuances in his lectures that are not present in the broad brush strokes of his earlier published writings. For example, in connection with Hegel's discussion of world-historical individuals like Alexander the Great, Caesar, and Napoleon, who brought about the rational end by acting on their "morally bad passions," Strauss points out that Hegel's treatment is not nearly as tough as Machiavelli's: "Strange as it may sound, I believe you will gradually see that Hegel's conception of the world-historical individual is more moral than that of Machiavelli. I think, in a way, he moralizes the hero and thus brings about this union between the universal and the particular" (chapter 2, 57–58; see also chapter 3, 75).

There is a very interesting discussion of the morality/immorality of the world-historical individual in the 1958 course. In connection with Hegel's notorious comment that the world-historical individual "must necessarily trample on many an innocent flower, crushing much that gets in its way,"[25] Strauss considers the question whether Hegel would have excused the actions of the Communists and Nazis under this principle. He is doubtful that he would have. He first points out that Hegel "would never have defended" Napoleon's illegal execution of some individual (unfortunately the text is garbled) that violated international law. He continues: "But let us take the 'murder,' as they say now, of twenty million peasants by Stalin—innocent flowers, we understand. What about that? Hegel could not argue from a moral point of view in the strictly moral sense, but I think he would take a broad political view and say that a regime that establishes itself in this way, against such powerful resistance, and at a certain point numbers become meaningful . . ." (1958: 4). Here the text breaks off as the recording reel is being changed, but the clear implication seems to be that Strauss does not think that Hegel's notion of the world-historical individual can be used to justify the actions of Stalin or Hitler.

Strauss is not entirely unsympathetic to Hegel's somewhat hardboiled attitude toward self-righteous moralism in politics. He calls Hegel "the most powerful critic of the moralistic attitude toward the great political issues" (1958: 4). The high-water mark of such moralism was achieved in the eighteenth century with the philosophies of Rousseau and Kant (chapter 3, 73–74). Hegel's criticism of it consists, first, in pointing out that the moral individual's protest against the immorality of the historical process amounts to a contemptible desire that virtue be rewarded in this life. Second, Hegel argues that if the moral individual were really consistent, he would desire the destruction of the immoral order in which his virtue flourishes. The virtuous senator in the Roman Republic, say, Cicero, should see the destruction of the republic as a "perfectly legitimate treatment of a rotten regime" (1958: 5). Finally, Hegel criticizes the "schoolmasters" and valet psychologists who condemn the world-historical deeds of an Alexander the Great or a Caesar simply because they were motivated by the desire for glory. In support of Hegel, Strauss alludes to Plato's more profound treatment of this issue in the *Republic* through the relationship of Socrates and the ambitious young Glaucon. He also seems to endorse Hegel's impatience with political moralizing by referring to the hypocritical pacifism of the British Labour Party in the 1930s. He concludes that "one cannot say that Hegel is an immoralist. In spirit he is very far from that." Significantly, however, he adds that "Hegel is helped [. . .] by his certainty that a radical breach of law, what we call a revolution, is the victory of the higher concept of justice over a lower concept of justice. In the moment this premise becomes doubtful, one will become somewhat hesitant to accept Hegel's proposition" (1958: 5).

From Hegel's discussion of the means of spirit, Strauss turns to his analysis of the end or goal that is achieved through those means, namely, the rational state. And as I have already pointed out, he categorically denies throughout his lectures that Hegel can in any way be described as a totalitarian thinker or one who deifies the state. The clearest expression of this view comes when Strauss responds to a skeptical student:

> Perhaps you are a victim of those people who call Hegel a deifier of the state and a precursor of totalitarianism, which is simply not true. Hegel accepted the constitutional monarchy of the nineteenth century, which was quite authoritarian but the opposite of totalitarian. The freedom of the economic sphere was taken for granted. It had to be protected, of course, by prohibitions against fraud, the protection of property, and so on. That was clear. In this sense, Hegel is a liberal. (Chapter 8, 192)

In the 1958 course, Strauss makes a similar point in response to a student who asks Strauss to clarify his claim that Hegel would never have accepted either communism or National Socialism as falling within the rationality of history. Strauss replies that Hegel's belief in the rights of man implies that "a fair and independent judiciary is absolutely essential to a civilized and respectable state," and such an institution cannot exist in either a communist or a fascist regime. "Hegel was in this sense a constitutionalist." Strauss adds that Hegel also "admitted natural right" and affirmed that the principles of property, the inviolability of the person, and so forth "are things which do not depend on human arbitrariness or legal enactment but are truly natural, rational principles," even though they have not always been known as such. "Hegel is not a relativist; on the contrary, he is a big bogey for all relativists—you know, the absolutist par excellence!" (1958: 4).[26]

As the statements in the previous paragraph show, Strauss does not characterize Hegel's political philosophy simply in terms of what it is not. In addition to not being a totalitarian or deifier of the state, Hegel is said to be a liberal, a constitutionalist, and a believer in natural right. The two attributes that Strauss comes back to again and again in his lectures to characterize Hegel's political philosophy are the rights of man and an educated, independent civil service: "If one wants a single formula indicating what Hegel's philosophy of right stands for, it would be 'rights of man' plus a wholly independent civil service" (1958: 10).[27] With respect to the rights of man, we have already seen Strauss mention Hegel's support of the right of property and the inviolability of the person. He also emphasizes Hegel's commitment to religious liberty, at one point calling him "amazingly liberal" in this regard (1958: 5).

While Hegel was a liberal in his defense of the rights of man, his belief that government should be run by a trained bureaucracy showed that he was no democrat. Strauss brings out this antidemocratic aspect of Hegel's political philosophy by looking carefully at Hegel's critique of "liberalism" in the final pages of *The Philosophy of History*. Against a government presided over by an educated civil service, Hegel argues that "liberalism"—by which he really means democracy—sets up "the atomistic principle . . . which insists upon the sway of individual wills; maintaining that all government should emanate from their express power, and have their express sanction." Hegel believes that this illicit extension of the rights of man into the political sphere will lead to "agitation and unrest," the solution for which will have to be worked out in the future.[28] Strauss comments on this passage that it "is probably the strongest statement in favor of the view that Hegel still sees unsolved fundamental problems" (chapter 16, 351–53).

We may doubt that democracy necessarily poses the problem for constitutional government that Hegel suggested it did. But Strauss points to another difficulty in Hegel's doctrine of the state that may not be so easily resolved. Not surprisingly, given Strauss's philosophical preoccupations, it concerns the relationship between the state and religion, the theologico-political problem. As we have seen, Strauss lays great emphasis on the fact that Hegel regards religion as the fundamental phenomenon in understanding a society, any society. This goes for the modern rational state as well, which rests on the religious foundation of Protestantism. By emphasizing the religious basis of the state, Hegel diverges from liberal secularism and has far more in common with the classical notion of the regime as relating to the "spirit of the whole society" (1958: 4). And yet, as we have also seen, Hegel is "amazingly liberal" when it comes to granting citizenship to various religious groups: Catholics, Jews, even Quakers and Anabaptists. It is true that in the *Philosophy of Right* Hegel argues that the state should require citizens to belong to some religious community, but it need not be concerned with which specific one.[29]

This, for Strauss, constitutes a major ambiguity in Hegel's teaching. On the one hand, Hegel seems to suggest that religion, specifically Protestantism, is a crucial bond for the modern state. On the other, he seems to discount its importance by granting citizenship to non-Protestants. Hegel would perhaps suggest that reason in the form of philosophy can take the place of religion as the binding force of society, but this clearly applies only to a few gifted individuals. What happens to the vast majority of nonphilosophical citizens? In his 1958 course Strauss asks: "how do these people that can partake of reason only via religion still partake of reason when religion is no longer there as the most socially potent force? Think of the simple fact that if the newspaper takes the place of the daily prayer, it empties the society completely. I think there is no provision for that grave problem in Hegel or in anything which is today inspired by Hegel" (1958: 5).

Strauss treats the theologico-political problem in Hegel at even greater length in this 1965 course, which only shows how seriously he took it. Once again, he underlines the primacy of religion in Hegel. But unlike other societies—ancient Greece, for example—the modern state is indifferent to the specific religion of its members. Strauss again alludes to the *Philosophy of Right*, where Hegel says that the state should require every citizen to be a member of a religious community and yet be indifferent as to which specific one. There is a contradiction here, which Hegel tries to resolve by suggesting that philosophical insight might replace religion, but this does not do much for the nonphilosophical many. Because they cannot shut out the disenchanting aspects of modern culture, the common people gradually lose their naïve faith, but they have nothing to replace it.

> They surely do not have the comfort of Hegelian philosophy. Hegel cannot do more than shrug his shoulders. He knows that sooner or later the circles of property and culture-think will affect the simple people. The circles of culture and property cannot always stop conversation when a maid enters at a dinner ... So the common people will gradually be affected by what is going on among their betters, but they don't become philosophers or anything like philosophers. They are in a difficult situation, a discord. Hegel has no comfort for us at this point. (chapter 13, 300)

The "discord" Strauss points out here raises serious questions about the claim that the political order described by Hegel is the simply rational order. Strauss says there is only one contemporary thinker he knows of who continues to argue on behalf of the Hegelian state: Alexandre Kojève, "who wrote probably the best book on Hegel in this generation." But Strauss makes clear that Kojève radically transforms Hegel in his interpretation. The "universal and homogeneous state" that Kojève describes is only half-Hegelian, the rest is Marx. The state articulated in the *Philos-*

ophy of Right is neither politically universal nor socially homogeneous.[30] Strauss concedes that a "case can be made that what Hegel meant is, under the radically changed circumstance of the twentieth century," something like what Kojève describes: "abolition of war and poverty and hard work, and within that society the possibility of a genuine philosophy." Nevertheless, he still does not think that Kojève's universal and homogeneous state resolves the grave problem raised above concerning the absence of a social bond in the modern state stemming from the decline of religion (1958: 5, 7; see also chapter 12 below).

Apart from his conception of the universal and homogeneous state, Kojève is perhaps best known for his controversial notion of the "end of history." This notion plays a huge role in Strauss's lectures, though without being attributed to Kojève. In this 1965 course, he mentions it in the first lecture in connection with the famous passage from the preface to the *Philosophy of Right* on the owl of Minerva, a passage Strauss says will serve "as a kind of motto for this course." The implication of this passage, according to Strauss, an implication drawn by Spengler in *The Decline of the West*, is that modernity represents the "final stage" of history, after which "nothing of any importance can come. There may be a spreading . . . But no fundamental change, no creation, is possible anymore." Insofar as Hegel's philosophy represents the most comprehensive self-understanding of modernity, it is the "final doctrine." Strauss cautions that this does not make Hegel arrogant; almost all great philosophers have "laid this claim to finality."[31] Nevertheless, the belief in an absolute moment in history when all contradictions have been reconciled constitutes "the most controversial thing in Hegel's philosophy of history" (chapter 1, 29–31).

Responding to a student, Strauss acknowledges that it is a question— "the crucial question"—whether Hegel actually believed that his philosophy and the social order of his time constituted the end or peak of history. But in both the 1958 course and the 1965 course, he generally answers that question in the affirmative. Perhaps the most commonly adduced piece of evidence that Hegel did not believe history had come to a definitive end is the passage in the introduction of the *Philosophy of History* about America as the "land of the future."[32] Strauss brings this passage up on several occasions, but he denies that it suggests that any "new principle of fundamental importance" will emerge in America (chapter 4, 100–101; chapter 5, 122; see also 1958: 5, 6).[33] He also in several places registers his difference with R. G. Collingwood on this point (chapter 14, 316; see also 1958: 4, 5, 10).[34]

Perhaps the most fascinating aspect of Strauss's discussion of the end of history in these lectures is the ambiguity he detects in Hegel's under-standing of it. For Hegel, a people is at its most vital when it is not fully conscious of itself, when it does not yet know its distinctive work. When a people does finally become self-conscious in a reflective way, reverence ceases, self-interest emerges, and decay or corruption sets in. In this way, Strauss argues, Hegel seems to agree with Rousseau's analysis in the *First Discourse* that science and moral and social corruption go together. This is what is implied in Hegel's famous saying that the "owl of Minerva takes flight with the coming of the dusk": philosophic understanding appears on the scene only when a civilization is in decline. Hegel suggests this applies not merely to past philosophies but also to his own in relation to modern Europe. As he did in his discussion of Hegel's understanding of the relationship between the state and religion, Strauss shows that He-gel's "view of the human order . . . is not as harmonious as it is frequently presented." The good, the beautiful, and the true do not necessarily all go together: "The development of man's most important desire and, ac-cording to Hegel, his highest desire, the desire for knowledge . . . is not possible under the same conditions under which society has really flour-ished" (chapter 2, 55–56).

Strauss's elaboration of this ambiguity in Hegel's understanding of the end of history has a distinctly Nietzschean, or even Spenglerian, ring. Indeed, references to Spengler's *Decline of the West* abound in Strauss's discussion. For Hegel, the end of history means that all the fundamental problems have been solved; there remain no fundamental tasks. In this sense, the peak of history is also a going down or decline. This is the ominous meaning of the owl of Minerva passage. The twilight in which philosophical wisdom appears is the twilight of nihilism. It is the dawn-ing of Spengler's "Faustian culture" and Nietzsche's "last man." It is the "end of all meaningful life." Strauss finds this implication of Hegel's no-tion of the end of history so problematic that he wonders whether "Hegel was fully aware of what he clearly implied: that with fulfillment, with the completion of world history, there is now the beginning of a final decay, a final corruption of mankind." He says that "this is really the great prob-lem of Hegel: What is the end of history, and what does this mean? Is it possible to live on that basis? One could say that this was the beginning of Nietzsche's criticism of Hegel" (1958: 3, 5; see also below, chapter 11, 253, chapter 13, 301–2).

It was Nietzsche's criticism of the Hegelian end of history that Strauss raised against Kojève in his debate with him in *On Tyranny*, and it is hard not to think of that debate in connection with Strauss's discussion of the end of history in his lectures. Despite the note of criticism, Strauss still credits Hegel with an awareness of the fundamental tension between knowledge and political life—the tension so forcefully articulated by Rousseau in the *First Discourse*—that eludes lesser thinkers. Strauss says Marx, for example, unlike Hegel, completely disregarded this crucial complication in Rousseau's teaching. He adds: "I think one cannot mention Marx and Hegel in the same breath as far as these questions go, because Marx is infinitely less philosophic than Hegel was" (1958: 3).

The respect for Hegel as a thinker that comes through in this passage and, indeed, throughout Strauss's lectures is one of the things that make them particularly worth having. Of course, such respect does not imply agreement. In keeping with the more critical posture found in his published writings, Strauss insists in these lectures that he is not a Hegelian (again, see below, chapter 7, 163).[35] Nevertheless, he does not take his primary purpose in the classroom to be to critique Hegel but to give students an appreciation of a major modern thinker—"the outstanding philosopher of the nineteenth century"[36]—comparable in stature to Plato, Aristotle, and Kant. Strauss's exemplary understanding of the primary task of the teacher is nicely captured in the following statement from the 1958 course: "But what . . . I am not a Hegelian; I do not defend my own position; but we must try to understand what Hegel means" (1958: 6).

One of the principal appeals of these lectures is what they reveal about Strauss as a teacher, in particular his patience, generosity, humanity, and humor. With respect to the latter, at the beginning of one class session, he commends the paper of a student—a Mr. Reinken, who also has the responsibility here of reading aloud the passages from *The Philosophy of History* that Strauss wished to discuss—for being "very delightful. You were the first one, I believe, whose paper was accompanied by enjoyment." He follows this with one of the great understatements of all time: "When reading Hegel himself, one is not induced to smile. So it is from a non-Hegelian point of view that the smiling comes in" (chapter 15, 327). Those who remember the Tareyton cigarette commercials from the 1960s will appreciate Strauss's colloquial encapsulation of the master-slave dialectic: "The slave is the one who just gives in, who rather switches than fights; and the master is the one who rather fights than switches" (chapter 14, 307). I will resist the temptation to pile up more examples, leaving it to the reader of these lectures to find the buried treasures on his or her own.

A word about the text. Because the course was a "seminar,"[37] Strauss's initial remarks generally take off from the specific student paper that opens each class period. He then comments on specific passages from *The Philosophy of History*—read aloud by Mr. Reinken—and responds to student questions arising from his commentary. The only exceptions to this procedure occur in the first class session, where Strauss gives a general introduction to Hegel's philosophy of history, and in the thirteenth session, where he delivers an almost uninterrupted lecture on "the very notion of a philosophy of history." In a few places, noted in endnotes, I have deleted unproductive or largely inaudible exchanges with students. Where appropriate, I have added supplementary material from the 1958 course transcript in the endnotes.

1 Preliminary Considerations

Leo Strauss: I believe we do not have to give long reasons why we should study Hegel in our capacity as political scientists. It suffices to mention the name of Marx. And Marx, or at least Marxism, is a legitimate subject of political science however narrowly conceived. There is another reason or objective which has very much to do with the scope of political science. Political science was always understood to deal with the political community, the commonwealth, or to use a term which came to the fore in modern times, with the state. But the state is no longer now generally taken as the comprehensive theme of reflections on human society. As you all know from practice, the term which is now in vogue, which means the whole of a society, is *culture* rather than state. Now this change is from a clearly political orientation to one which is transpolitical, finding as it were the root of the political in something superpolitical, and Hegel has very much to do with that, as we will . . . see.

I chose Hegel's *Philosophy of History* and not his *Philosophy of Right* despite the fact that the *Philosophy of Right* was published by Hegel himself, and so there we have Hegel himself unquestionably, while the *Philosophy of History* is lectures given by Hegel and as Hegel more or less improvised them while he went in different years. And out of what his students—and apparently very intelligent students—jotted down, the original editors put together these lectures, and the more recent editor gave quite a very different version of Hegel's lectures because he had found or considered lecture notes which had not been known or considered by the first editors.[1] But precisely the fact that that is a lecture and not a book is, in the case of Hegel at any rate, a great help, because Hegel is an unusually difficult writer and in his lectures he is much more easy to follow than in the works which he published himself.

In addition, there is this other reason why we should study his *Philosophy of History*: Hegel's political philosophy proper as presented in the *Phi-*

losophy of Right is essentially related to his philosophy of history, and one understands his political philosophy proper as philosophy of right better if one views the historical matrix out of which that philosophy emerged, and that exactly we find in the lectures on the philosophy of history. One can say Hegel was the first to make the understanding of the history of political philosophy an essential ingredient of political philosophy itself. But in the past the situation was generally like that, say, of the relation of the history of physics to physics today. You can be a first-rate physicist without being versed in the history of physics. I mean, you will have heard some names, like Newton and so on—that goes without saying—but this of course cannot be called the history of physics. Now Hegel makes the history of political philosophy a form of political philosophy. Think of Locke: there is no concern with the history of political philosophy; he fights certain individuals who were very powerful in his time and who he thinks were fundamentally wrong, like Filmer, but to go back behind that and give, as it were, a reasonable survey of the history of political philosophy is of course in no way his concern.

I suppose you all know the fact that Hegel was born in the year 1770 and died in the year 1831. These dates are not altogether negligible, because there are other dates with which they are connected. I mention three which are crucial for Hegel. In 1781, Kant published his *Critique of Pure Reason*. In 1785, a man probably unknown to all of you, a German writer [LS writes on the blackboard] published a book on the doctrine of Spinoza.[2] This was a very big splash and had very great importance for Hegel. And though Jacobi is not comparable to Kant in any way, he gave a very important turn to speculation in Germany at the time and to Hegel in particular. And the third date is known to all of you: 1789, the French Revolution. These are the minimum facts one must know if one wants to understand Hegel.

Now I will speak about Kant and Spinoza in a very provisional way, only to that extent to which it is necessary to have some answers for Hegel. Now Kant is very famous up to the present day as a critic of metaphysics. So is, of course, David Hume. But we must consider the peculiarly Kantian features, because they alone determine Hegel. According to Kant, man is faced with a fundamental alternative: either a rationalism or an empiricism; or more precisely, either the dogmatism of pure reason (or Platonism) or empiricism (or Epicureanism). I hope I didn't mix you up by the many "or's" I used; the two alternatives are clear. Dogmatism of pure reason is Platonism; empiricism classically represented by Epicureanism.

Now this is an undeniable fact that we find throughout the ages, this alternative which we can loosely call that between spiritualism and materialism. But Kant sees the situation in a new way. I give you first his diagnosis of these two alternatives. First, the world has a beginning in time and is limited in space. The reverse, the world has no beginning in time and no limit in space. Secondly, the thinking self is indivisible and therefore indestructible. Against that, the Epicurean view: everything within the world is divisible and perishable. Thirdly, the spiritualistic view: we are free in our actions. The others say our actions are fully determined by nature or fate. And finally, the first school says there is a highest cause of the world, whereas the others say there is nothing beyond the natural things and their order. I do not think that it is a question whether this is a historically correct view. We know that Epicureans of course did not admit that everything within the world is divisible: the atoms are not divisible. So Kant construed, as one could say, the two alternatives—as it were, he presented the two ideal types rather than the two historical types, which is of course perfectly legitimate.

Now the situation according to Kant, and which distinguishes him from his predecessors, is that he says that—very crudely stated—both alternative positions are demonstrable, in other words, not that neither has demonstrated his position so that you could then still say that maybe in a generation from now someone will come up and establish either Platonism or Epicureanism. Now Kant says each of these schools *proves* its thesis. So what is the conclusion? The demonstrations must be based on a fundamental defect. They may be formally correct as demonstrations, but based on a fundamental defect. And therefore no demonstration is possible. I add one important point in Kant's analysis of these two opposed positions. The Platonist position—which would of course also include Leibniz in modern times and generally speaking the spiritualistic philosophy—this position is favorable to morality and religion and therefore fundamentally popular. I mean not that it is easy, such that everyone can read Leibniz, but the thesis of Leibniz appealed to the masses and the state. The other position is unfavorable to religion—I mean Epicureanism, it always has this reputation—and Kant draws a conclusion which is quite remarkable: this materialistic-atheistic position can never become popular. This is one of the gravest historical errors which Kant surely . . . But this shows how different the situation at the end of the eighteenth century was from what it became in the nineteenth century.

But what is Kant's solution? The assertions of empiricists—ah yes, Epicureans, we must not be very squeamish—are true of the phenomenal world, of anything which can occur to us in ordinary life or in science. We can distinguish the phenomenal world from another world: the things that have an existence in themselves outside of our thoughts, what Kant frequently calls "the thing in itself" or also the "noumenal" world. So in other words, atheistic-materialism is the only way in which we can proceed in trying to understand, say, the growth of a tree, a thunderstorm, or whatever it may be. But it is also clear that this is absolutely limited to all attempts at finding our bearings or explanation. It is not *simply* true, it is not true of the things in themselves. The assertions of dogmatism, of Platonism, are true but they cannot be theoretically established, demonstrated. But they are true only in practical intent, as postulates of practical reason.

The moral law is the only thing within them which cannot be understood as part of the phenomenal world, according to Kant. Now if you understand the moral law according to Kant, we are left to demand the existence of God and the immortality of the soul on moral grounds, and we can do that because empiricism, or Epicureanism, has nothing to say beyond the phenomenal world. In all study of phenomena, we must assume that every action of men is a form of necessary cause, i.e., that man's not responsible. I mean, the fact that a man committed a murder was due to his temperament, his I.Q., his environment, problem home and so on—you know the whole rigmarole. But as moral beings we *know* that we are under the moral law and hence that we are free to obey it and also to disobey it, and therefore that men's actions must be understood as right or wrong, as due to the right or wrong use of their freedom. And for that use of their freedom they are fully responsible. The good or evil action cannot be traced beyond the act of freedom, which is the beginning. He chose, say, to commit murder; you cannot trace it beyond that without destroying the responsibility. It is *the* starting point and not the result of previous causes.

Kant surely claimed to have refuted metaphysics by refuting the two kinds of metaphysics, spiritualism and materialism. And to repeat, Kant does much more than say that neither of these two antagonists proved his point. Then the issue would still be open: maybe some greater spiritualist or materialist will come up in the future and solve it. No, Kant has shown that the demonstrations are valid demonstrations, and therefore something is wrong in the very question.

Now let me leave it at this point about Kant and say a few words about Spinoza. Spinoza was not very well known at that time, and the first man who spoke highly of Spinoza and not as a character—that had been done before, that business that he was an honest man—but of his intellect and of the solidity of his doctrine, that was Jacobi, who was an opponent of Spinoza but who felt that Spinoza's doctrine is the culmination of human reason. If human reason follows its own laws, then it will arrive at Spinoza's doctrine, the denial of a personal God, the denial of immortality, the denial of freedom. Now Spinoza's doctrine has the form of a deductive system, like Euclid's work, starting from definitions, axioms, etc., which are simply presupposed. And Spinoza doesn't give you any reason why he gives these definitions or . . . and therefore one can say Spinoza starts in a dogmatic way. This led to the demand of those who were attracted by Spinoza in one way or the other after Kant that this cannot be done. These very premises, or whatever the true premises are, are themselves in need of deduction. One must truly begin from nothing. Spinoza's metaphysics, now, is neither materialistic nor spiritualistic. There are two attributes of God or nature, called by him extension and cogitation, which are irreducible to each other. Soul cannot be reduced to matter, and matter cannot be reduced to soul, and they are attributes of the one substance, i.e., God. All particular things—me, this, etc.—are modes of an attribute of God. Now this [LS points at something] is clearly a mode of the attribute of extension, because it is an extended thing; but if I feel pain, this is clearly a mode of the attribute of thought, of cogitation. All particular things are modes of an attribute of God, yet the highest form of the knowledge of God, which Spinoza calls intuitive knowledge, is knowledge of the singular things or events *as* modes of God. In other words, if you know God in himself you know God much less than if you understand, say, this thing, or this event, the room, as a consequence of other modes, of a given attribute of God. God's full being, one can say, is in the particulars—the singular things, as Spinoza says—in God's developed stage and not insofar as he is transcended or undeveloped.

Spinoza asserts the strict necessity for everything; and in this respect, he clearly belongs to the Epicurean-empiricist camp. What does he do with freedom? Spinoza replaces the distinction between free and necessary by the distinction free and compelled. You may remember that Hobbes's *Leviathan* does something of this kind. So in other words, if you do something freely, this is as necessary as if you do something under compulsion. What does this mean? The free acts are as necessary as the compelled or compulsory ones. A thing is free if it exists by virtue of the necessity of its nature alone and is determined to act by itself alone. In this sense, of course, God alone is free. But we act as distinguished from our being acted upon if something takes place within us or outside of us, if this event which happens either within us or outside of us can be clearly and distinctly understood as following from our own nature. Our mind acts, as distinguished from being acted upon, insofar as it has adequate ideas, insofar as it has clear and distinct knowledge. In a word, freedom is necessity, but a special kind of necessity, understood necessity. Freedom, one can also say, is self-determination, but self-determination as distinguished from indetermination. Your nature, your innermost being, determines you; the action is determined. This is freedom. Now after these few remarks about Spinoza, I will try to give a very provisional statement of what Hegel is about.

Hegel starts from the assumption that philosophy is the quest for the substance, for the single substance of which everything else is a necessary attribute or mode, in such a way that its flowing or emerging from the substance can be clearly and distinctly understood. That substance is what Kant meant with the thing in itself. Kant has proven that the thing in itself is not knowable. That what [which] is knowable, Kant said, is only the phenomena, which are only *for* the thinking subject, not in themselves, the phenomena which are constituted by the activity of the subject. But what about that activity of the subject?, Hegel asks. The activity of the subject which produces the phenomena is not itself a part of the phenomenal world, because it produces phenomena. The activity of the subject both in building up the phenomenal world and the moral law, this is the thing in itself, according to Hegel. So in other words, Kant has discovered the true thing in itself without being aware of it. What Kant calls the transcendental activity of the ego, that is the thing in itself. Hegel has a simple formula for that: the substance—I mean, that which Spinoza was seeking, single substance—is the subject.

So by this combination of Kant and Spinoza, Hegel, and also some of his German predecessors, brought forth a new kind of metaphysics which cannot be mistaken for the pre-Kantian metaphysics, as I sketched them along Kant's lines before. The first ground or grounds, we can say, is not transcendent, as God or the Epicurean atoms are; it is not outside of man. The chief theme of this metaphysics is the life of the human mind, and it is primarily, to use a book title of Hegel's, phenomenology of the mind. Understanding the life of the mind—this is not the whole, but the most important part, one can say, of this new metaphysics.

Now before I go on, I would like to see whether I have made myself understood. Now please be frank. Were you able to follow this very crude presentation of what Kant effected or claimed to have effected, and of what Spinoza did on the other hand, and how this was combined in Hegel's mind? Yes?

Student: You describe Hegel as arriving at the conclusion that somehow Kant had not understood properly the thing in itself. I didn't quite understand what the two factors were that came together in Hegel's mind.

LS: Well, we have the phenomenal world, the only world we know empirically. But this world, according to Kant, is constituted by acts of the thinking ego, I mean not the habitual desires of this or that individual, but by reason following its essential laws. Now where is reason? Where does reason belong? Is reason a part of the phenomenal world? It is not, it cannot be. Why not—and that is not clear in Kant—why not simply say this is the thing in itself?

Student: That's what Hegel does.

LS: Yes, in a very simplified statement. So in other words, Kant had the thing in itself, so to speak, in his hands and did not recognize it; and this he combined with Spinoza by saying that this reason, or to use a more general term here, the subject, is the substance. If you understand the substance in the way in which Spinoza understood it as consisting equally of extension and cogitation, then you won't understand anything that Kant had said. Mr. Reinken?

Mr. Reinken: Two questions, or two statements. First, when Kant and later Hegel speak of this reason, the subject, do they mean the average common reason of the actual human race, rather than the reason of some other being?

LS: Well, that is a great question, one of the most difficult questions regarding Hegel. In one sense, it surely does not mean merely human reason. Hegel speaks of God all the time, and there is a divine reason effective in everything, in nature as well as in history. But the great question, which cannot so easily be settled by quotation, is whether this reason which is effective in everything is self-conscious reason, or does reason reach its self-consciousness only in man? That is the question. And there is a great ambiguity regarding this point in Hegel. Do you understand this? I mean, the average reason, that is not of very great importance because it is so often wrong; we would always have to say reason proper, following its own laws. I mention one point in passing: there is something Kant and Spinoza have in common, although they are very antagonistic to each other—Kant was very antagonistic to Spinoza. Spinoza's chief work, what now would be called his metaphysical work, has the title *Ethics*. I mean, people who wrote about God and his attributes, etc., didn't call their books *Ethics*. Kant for his part taught the primacy of *practical* reason. Theoretical reason is limited to the phenomenal world, and the most important question, how shall I live, is wholly beyond theoretical reason according to Kant. But the primacy or supremacy of practical reason, this will be preserved in Hegel. Hegel makes, as it were, the paradoxical attempt to integrate Kant's primacy of practical reason into an again-theoretical philosophy. Hegel's philosophy is a theoretical philosophy, but it integrates the whole of practical philosophy into the theoretical framework. That is, in a way, the secret of his philosophy of history, but we will come to that later.

Now I will give a few other points in order to prepare ourselves for Hegel. For Kant, as already in a way for Spinoza, morality or goodness is no longer the perfection of human nature in the ancient and Thomistic sense. That is out, for different reasons. Kant's reason can be stated very simply as follows: if morality were the perfection of human nature, we would already know that human nature is good. Only then can its perfection be good. How do we know that? We cannot presuppose that; therefore we have to make an entirely different beginning.

According to Kant, morality is not deducible from anything else. According to the traditional views, morality is deducible from something else: from human nature, or from God, or in another way. In Kant, this is impossible because if morality were deducible from something, then its laws would not be categorical, to use a Kantian term: act in such and such a way . . . don't ask questions. That is categorical, because otherwise it would be: act in such and such a way *in order to*. Then you can raise the question, but maybe there are other ways in order to get that "in order to" which don't have to be moral. So morality has no support beyond reason itself. Is then morality completely alien to everything that is? Is there not some necessity or some support? And here is where the postulates of God and the immortality of the soul come in. We do not know that God exists, we do not know that the soul is immortal, but we must postulate the existence of God and the immortality of the soul if we do not wish to despair of morality. Morality belongs to the noumenal world. Only through

God and morality can there be a proper proportion between morality and happiness. Here in this life we do not find the proper proportion of things, the prosperity of the wicked and the misery of the just. That cannot be. That can only be if there is a just judge of the universe and life after death. The moral commands must be understood as commands which carry with themselves promises and threats. This Kant still presupposes.

Now Hegel disagrees with that entirely. He rejects the concern with the reward of virtue altogether. He's a fine man who says he wants to be rewarded for having helped his brother in need or having saved the life of a child, and so on. Hegel criticizes the concern with the reward on moral grounds; hence there is no longer for Hegel a way from morality to the future life in the sense of the life after death. This is out for Hegel. But there is the other thing in Kant already which becomes more important in Hegel. We must be morally concerned. One could say the concern with a reward is extramoral, because a truly moral man does not wish to be rewarded, is not concerned with being rewarded. But we must be morally concerned with the existence of the social order in which morality is not persecuted. Is this not our moral duty, to be concerned with the society in which morality is not persecuted? Because if it is, there is a conflict of duties: of the duty to obey the civil law and the duty to obey the moral law. As moral beings we are obliged to wish for such a state of things that this conflict does not exist, or to hope for it, the moral hope. There must be a necessity somehow compelling the amoral lawgiver to give laws compatible with morality. There must be a kind of convergence between the *is*, what the lawgiver or the lawgivers do and so on, and the *ought*, the moral law. Now this is the meaning of Kant's philosophy of history. Extramoral things, like in the natural traits and the ever-increasing costs of war — not yet the atomic bomb but just the plain budget — make it more and more inevitable that government should be republican and not monarchic, and therewith the rule of law within the states and between the states. Even if there is no way from morality to the postulate of a future life, there is a necessary connection between morality and the vision of the political future, of the future of men on earth. It is very interesting that Kant's philosophy of history was not presented by Kant in his great systematic works. There the postulate of the immortality of the soul is central. But this he did in some occasional writings. We will discuss them in the next quarter. But they are very important and crucial for the understanding of what Hegel did after him. There was, as it were, a conflict which one can study in the late eighteenth century: What is more important, the moral order after life or in the earthly future? We can say philosophy of history won out by virtue of the acceptance of the second alternative. We will see that later.

In Kant, the convergence of the *is* and the *ought* [LS writes on the blackboard] is something in which we must believe, for which we must hope. One cannot be truly moral if one does not hope for the future of morality. For Hegel this convergence is a fact, something demonstrable. There is no longer any *chance* which would completely upset all apple carts, so to speak, or, in other words, there is no longer an inscrutable providence. Hegel speaks of providence, as you will have seen, but it is a scrutable providence. There is an order, a moral order in history, but this moral order is in all interesting cases perfectly lucid to us. So a scrutable providence reigns. One speaks of a necessary convergence between the *is* and the *ought*, between the amoral—not necessarily antimoral—and the moral. More generally of disorder and order. The extramoral world, the world of the phenomenal, is a world of moral disorder, not only to-day where we know this from well-known facts mentioned by the president yesterday,[3] but at all times the world was not a very orderly place. Order comes out of disorder without being intended: this is, one can say, the simple formula of Hegel's philosophy of history. When Alexander invaded Persia, he didn't dream that a society based on the rights of men would be established millennia later; nevertheless, he worked for it without knowing it. More generally stated, order comes out of disorder without being intended. Now this thought was quite familiar to people in Hegel's time—as already in Kant's time, by the way. The greatest example is the cosmogony of the modern age. The planetary system—how did it emerge out of some world or whatever it might be understood to be? Then we have this wonderful system, the sun and the stars, and the fixed stars and so on . . . Coming closer to home, we have what Hegel calls the system of wants, which had been analyzed by Adam Smith. He also had order coming out of disorder. Everyone thinks of himself alone, no one of the common good, but precisely this brings about the common good. If the baker and candlestick maker would think of the common good, he would ruin these beautiful economic laws which make society run.

Now what was understood of, say, cosmogony and economics, and perhaps also some other spheres, is enlarged by Hegel to the whole of history. In the whole course of history no one thinks of establishing the rational order. And for the very simple, important reason that no one can know it in advance. How could Alexander the Great have had an inkling of the rational order if his teacher Aristotle believed that there are men who are by nature slaves, i.e., something incompatible with the natural order? So men have said they move toward it blindly, and yet this blind movement has an order, an even order, toward this rational order. The process produces both the rational order and the awareness of the rational order. I mean, after all, it could be thinkable, could it not, that men had known at all times the end, but it was not possible to execute, to achieve the end for a variety of reasons until, say, in Hegel's time. But they could not even have *known* it. The historical actors do not consciously strive for the end, and in this respect, the historical process resembles a natural process. What do the parts of our body or of an animal body do when they tend towards something? There is no conscious striving there. So the historical process is in a way like a natural process, an organic process, and that is indeed the case according to Hegel. But this has one very grave implication. If the historical process is like an organic process, there must be a peak. In all growth there are limits. There is a German proverb: It has been arranged that the trees won't grow into heaven. So there must be a term of the growth. And what follows, may I ask, after a being has reached the term of his growth? Let us say decay—let us not speak unnecessarily of death, and so decay.

Now I ask you, Mr. Reinken, to read here something from Hegel's *Philosophy of Right*, a passage which we will need as a kind of motto for this course. Well, no, I could read it myself. On page 227, that is, from the preface to the *Philosophy of Right*.[4] Here Hegel had opposed throughout the preface the philosophers who want to teach the state, i.e., the government, what they should do, and that is not the function of political philosophy. "To say one more word about preaching what the world *ought* to be like: philosophy arrives always too late for that. As *thought* of the world, it appears at a time when actuality has completed its developmental process and is finished, completely. What the conception teaches, what philosophy teaches, history also shows as necessary: namely, that only in a maturing actuality the ideal appears and confronts the real. It is then that the idea rebuilds for itself this same world in the shape of an intellectual realm, comprehending this world in its substance. Then philosophy comes, and when philosophy comes, it paints its gray on gray. A form of life has become old, and this gray on gray cannot rejuvenate it, only understand it. The owl of Minerva begins its flight in the dusk." Minerva is the goddess of wisdom. Wisdom appears when dusk is coming, after the historical process. Let us take a simple example, Greece, a very great society for Hegel. When does philosophy come and deal with Greek society? When the decay had come, after the sophists and so on, as Hegel puts it . . . So this is the crucial point, it seems, in Hegel. We must check on that.

Hegel's *Philosophy of History* deals not merely with Greece or Rome or the Far East or the Middle Ages but with modernity, and even the completion of modernity, which according to Hegel could not take place prior to the French Revolution and after the taming of the French Revolution by Napoleon. But what of the task of the future? . . . except the theoretical task, to understand. Spengler wrote his *Decline of the West* during the First World War. I think it came out for the first time in 1917. This was a sensational thing, a book with the title, the setting or going down of the West. But he only said with a certain nasty harshness, one could say, what Hegel had meant: that modernity, if we mean by modernity the development, say, roughly since the Reformation, is the final stage, and after that nothing of any importance can come. There may be a spreading, say, the South American republics may function or may not function, but . . . and so on. But no fundamental change, no creation, is possible anymore. This seems to be at least one strand in Hegel's thought. Whether it is the only one we will have to consider.

Now at this point I thought I should mention a right to be given: again I invite discussion because I cannot assume that I make everything clear to everyone. Yes?[5]

LS: . . . practical philosophy becoming speculative, i.e., theoretical, and this applies surely to Hegel. Now he would not deny that this has a great practical use. I mean, Hegel hoped that he could convince some of these foolish democrats that it is much better to be ruled by a benevolent king and by a high-class permanent civil service than by a tyrannous demagogue. He hoped. But the question to that extent was of course meant to be practical; but it was much more a defense, and a defense through understanding, through proving the reasonableness of what already existed. Such a defense of an established order, even if meant to be purely theoretical, is bound to have practical consequences. I mean, to the extent to which Hegel convinced people, he decreased the power of the revolutionary movement; and after all, out of his loins, so to speak, came the Hegelian Left, as it is called. You know there was the splitting of the school: the Hegelian Right, which was conservative and identified itself with the established order; and then there was the Hegelian Left. The most famous of the Hegelian Left was of course Marx, who broke with

Hegel radically. But Marx says somewhere that according to Hegel the philosopher comes always *post festum*, after the festival, when everything is over.[6] And what Marx wanted is that the philosopher should change the world. As he put it on another occasion, "hitherto the philosophers have only interpreted the world (i.e., theoretical), but what is important is to change the world."[7] So Marx's philosophy, if we can still call Marx's doctrine a philosophy, is the reaction to Hegel and therefore practical, but in a very different way to that in which Aristotle's *Politics*, for example, was practical.

Student: . . . could not possibly apply to the practical philosophers . . .

LS: No. In other words, don't look for any innovations or any fundamental change. I mean, Hegel surely would have been opposed to the senseless privileges of the Prussian nobility which still existed in fact, because you want the best men to be in the highest positions regardless of whether they are noblemen or commoners. But this was no longer a fundamental change because the principle was readily admitted. A career as a French prime minister at that time was a career open for the talents, i.e., not according to birth. Yes?

Student: You said that modernity for Hegel was the final stage, that means the peak? Would that then mean that the philosophy that mirrors modernity would be the culmination of philosophy for Hegel?

LS: Sure. But this required still a very enormous theoretical effort: Hegel's own philosophy. In Kant, the philosophy of history is one of an infinite progress in the future, i.e., that the rational order will never be truly established, only to ever greater approximation. This required a complete revamping of Kant's doctrine and this synthesis with Spinoza of which I spoke at the beginning. But beyond Hegel there may be quite a few subordinate questions, both theoretical and practical, which are not settled—that goes without saying—but no radical reorientation. It's the final doctrine.

This sounds very strange to us, but we must not forget that the philosophers generally speaking, surely in modern times but to some extent also in ancient times, laid this claim to finality. Let us take—not to speak of Descartes—Aristotle, who did not visualize that his notion of the cosmos and of man within the cosmos, and therefore also of virtue and vice and what a good order is, could possibly be turned down as radically insufficient.[8] So we find in Hegel this so-called historical awareness—in Hegel's words, as we will read, "the individual is the son of his time,"[9] and by that he means of course not only the man in the street but also the philosopher. Hegel was the first to face this difficulty: If the philosopher is the son of his time, how can he have found the eternal truth? And Hegel's general answer is: He can, if he lives in the moment in which time as it were coincides with eternity.

Student: History and philosophy coincide like the ought and the is. If the ought and the is converge, would it be proper to say that philosophy and history converge?

LS: Not quite. This is a very insufficient statement, because that would presuppose that the truth is known to philosophy at the beginning, which is not the case.

Student: So far you have interpreted Hegel without mentioning his dialectic at all.

LS: No, I did not.

Student: You interpret him as saying that there is an endpoint in history. Or am I right? Not only that there is a peak, but that there is an endpoint. Do you think that looking at Hegel's dialectic offers you a way of getting out of this interpretation? Because I don't see that.

LS: But that was the issue between Khrushchev and Mao. Khrushchev said we have now the final society, i.e., the society without contradictions, but Mao denies this. And Mao denies not only that present-day Russia is paradise, which is easy to deny, but he denies that there could ever be a society without contradictions. And there is a Marxist justification for that. Marx calls the whole history of mankind as we know it, or believe to know it, the *pre*-history. The history begins only with the universalization of communism. But history means, of course, change. But I suppose what Mao must mean is that contradictions which occur after the establishment of communism are radically different from the class conflicts, that kind of contradiction which existed in all historical society. Did I answer your question? Because I forgot it.

Student: My question is, what exactly are you saying that Hegel had in mind? If you say that history is going to stop, then the dialectic will stop.

LS: Yes, but there is no difficulty there, if all contradictions are reconciled, if Hegel's key word is "reconciliation."

Student: Every outcome, every move to a different level which reconciles the contradictions that existed before . . .

LS: Yes, but for Hegel this is exactly the point, that there is a final and absolute reconciliation, in which there is no longer any fundamental task for the human race. But I'm perfectly open, we will discuss this question. I think it is, in a way, the crucial question, because it is the most controversial thing in Hegel's philosophy of history. Did he or did he not believe in the finality of his doctrine and of the social order as in substance established in his time? Yes?

Student: According to Hegel, the men of the past could not understand the end toward which they were striving; the end became available only in Hegel's time. How was it possible for men who were found, say, at the end of certain eras, say, Plato and Aristotle, to have even any rightful claim to be philosophers at all?

LS: To which Hegel answers: They were philosophers of the first order. But what is a philosopher? A philosopher is a man who *seeks* wisdom, and they were all men who sought wisdom, but only now is philosophy capable of getting rid of the distinction between the quest for this and the conquest.

Student: But what is it then that makes the quest for wisdom come at the end of an era? I mean, it is possible to see that wisdom itself could not come until the whole historical cycle has completed itself. But what is there which according to Hegel would cause philosophy to rise at the end of the Greek period of history as opposed to the middle of it, if all philosophy is a quest for wisdom?

LS: There is some element of truth in that, that people are more given to thinking, wondering, questioning, in times of crisis than in times when everything is obviously—in their opinion, that is—in order. I believe that the last English philosopher of the first rank, David Hume, published his *Treatise of Human Nature* in 1740. In 1745 the second Pretender came to Scotland and was defeated,[10] and the order which had been coming gradually from the Puritan Revolution and finally established in 1688 was now settled. So the old issue between hand and pen on the one hand and the archbishops and lords on the other was now absolutely settled. Naturally one had not settled the question of how far the masses had the say in government—you know, the rotten borough[11] question, the whole question of reform, then in the nineteenth century the question of social legislation. But these were no longer issues of that fundamental character as those which had come in from the sixteenth century on. I mean, to say that the greatest names in English philosophy—Bacon, Hobbes, Locke, Berkeley, Hume—being located there can be said to have something to do with the fact that this was *the* social crisis of England. Whereas in Germany the great development of philosophy came much later, because the crisis began to touch Germany only with the approach of the French Revolution and of course after it. There was Leibniz before, but Leibniz was a unique figure. I say this only in order to defend Hegel against you. I don't say that one can say this simply on the basis of induction.

Mr. Shulsky: Can you explain how some philosophers who seek to sell programs seem to come before the events you describe? Hobbes, Locke for instance—they talk about innovations, they were innovative. The situation occurred later rather than before.

LS: I do not know what Hegel would say, but I am somewhat fearful that he might say they were not philosophers of the first order. The contempt for British philosophy is a very powerful tradition in Germany; and then a Frenchman, one of these germanified French thinkers, visited Schelling—Schelling was the friend and later in a way a competitor of Hegel, eclipsed by Hegel—and spoke to Schelling about Locke. Schelling simply said: "Je méprise Locke"—"I despise Locke." That was all. I believe this is an important part of the story. English philosophy of course had some influence, but not in the period of the greatest development of German philosophy. After the German idealistic philosophy had lost its power over the public mind, which was roughly around 1840 to '48, then the English and French came over quite strongly, and John Stuart Mill was a big figure in Germany, say in 1860 to '70. But with the recovery of Kantianism, that was finished. I am just trying to guess what Hegel would think of them. But the point which you take is of course absolutely correct. They initiated. I mean, one cannot possibly deny that there was not this terrific cooperation of science and technology before. Bacon and Descartes demanded it. Yes?

Student: You said that Hegel began with the quest for the substance of which all else is a necessary attribute or mode and that the activity of the subject produces the thing in itself. Am I correct in saying that this statement has some logical overtones? And if it does, would that be . . .

LS: In Hegel one can say everything has a logical overtone. But no, let me say only this: don't pay too great attention to this. What I said about this prehistory of Hegel—Kant and Spinoza—was a deliberately provisional statement to link, to lead up to this new kind of thinking. If you have any difficulty, forget about it. The main point I want to make is only that this famous formulation of Hegel's, "the substance is the subject,"[12] points directly to Spinoza, because there is only one substance, etc.; and on the other hand, there was the subject coming to this position through Kant. Because it was Kant, not Descartes, whose notion of the subject became decisive for Hegel. Just forget about it. Don't pay too much attention. You probably have no teaching experience, and as a teacher one has to lead up from all parts of the horizon to something, and one is not always successful. Teaching can never become a scientifically conducted affair. Yes?

Student: May I ask a question about the meaning of the word "subject" when you use it? Ordinarily, we think of subject as opposed to object, and substance as opposed to procedure. Would here Hegel say that subject is the substance? I'm confused.

LS: No, the substance, say, the core, that out of which everything else must have proceeded and through which everything else must be understood, is *the* subject. The subject, say, the Cartesian *ego cogito*, the Cartesian ego which thinks, but with only this difference: in Descartes, there is at least some lack of clarity as to whether the thinking ego is not itself a substance like the old soul-substance. This is wholly out in Kant, and therefore Hegel chose as subject that which organizes, orders the sensations into an ordered world, that which is, which legislates to itself a moral life. However, these two things of the ego may be connected: that is the substance. This needs a long commentary, as someone pointed out before. There is a question of what about God: Is not God that subject? That we should have said the substance is God, which would have been a very familiar assertion, or at least a much more familiar assertion than what Hegel said.

I would like to mention only one point regarding the relation of Hegel's political philosophy to his philosophy of history. One can say that Hegel's political philosophy, which he presented in his *Philosophy of Right*, answers the question of the right political order—and the political order is always right—whereas his philosophy of history answers the question of how the right political order became actual and known. You see these additional considerations here. Then the question is: Why does Hegel need such a supplement to political philosophy as, say, Aristotle or Locke did not need? What was the Aristotelian answer to the question of how the good social order has become actual, or Plato's?

Mr. Reinken: In speech.

LS: But that is not actual. Is it actual, in the first place? Is it actual, and if it becomes actual, how does it become actual? Chance. That's out in Hegel. I mean, that's the negative condition of the whole philosophy of history, that chance doesn't play any significant role. And what about its having become known; how does the just order become known?

Mr. Reinken: Aristotle sat down and thought about the nature of man.

LS: But still, he had to have some guidance. I mean, the expression "the nature of man" is not sufficiently clear.

Mr. Reinken: The constitutions of the bad cities.

LS: That doesn't let us know about the good city. On the basis of what can you distinguish between the good and bad regime? I give you a very simplistic answer which is of course also from Plato. He had his knowledge of what is by nature right; whether all men have such knowledge to a sufficient degree is very uninteresting. But at any rate, it is possible for man to know what is by nature right in Plato. Now this natural right doctrine developed later, after Aristotle, into a doctrine of natural law, especially in the Middle Ages. This was the answer to how is the good order known: fundamentally because it presupposes the natural order. But here a new question arose in the sixteenth century and later especially—Vico was a good example which we study on occasion: Can there be a natural law if it is not duly promulgated? The Patagonians, to take an extreme case—can man be obliged to act according to natural law if he hasn't the slightest inkling of its character? And so the question of promulgation in a way, of course, in Vico's works becomes the backbone of the whole thing: the proof that natural law as ordinarily understood, especially by these princes—Grotius, Selden,[13] and Pufendorf—this natural law could not have been known until very high in the . . . And therefore it becomes necessary to know: How did these more or less benighted men build up their societies, how did they find their bearing? And then he makes his final distinction between the three stages—divine, heroic, and human societies—but this is already a kind of philosophy of history in Vico, so that, in other words, the immediate, entering wedge for philosophy of history is the question of the promulgation of natural law. Which does not create a grave difficulty if one accepts the biblical account; it was promulgated to our first ancestors, and through their faults this awareness was lost and therefore it is no longer a question of the first order, but it is only a grave question from a practical point of view. How can you be harsh on these poor savages who don't have any recollection of these things anymore and act on their dim lights? It's obviously an important practical question. But the theoretical question aside, the tacit premise of the whole thing is of course that the biblical account of the origin of man and of humans as a whole is no longer literally accepted. Yes?

Student: I was going to ask if a body of logic is a premise of Hegel's philosophy of history, and if it is, what work?

LS: That is a very good question. It is hard to answer that question. But negatively it can be stated as follows. Hegel's *Logic* has, so to speak, nothing to do with what is ordinarily understood by logic. It has much more to do, if one wants to use an illustration, with Plato's doctrine of ideas. You must not forget that the establishment of logic as a separate discipline is post-Aristotelian; you cannot presuppose that in Plato and still less in earlier thinkers. Now, what is Plato concerned with? I give you some textbook answers now. The truly *being* beings are the ideas. The ideas can be perceived only by the pure mind, not by the senses. They are eternal, unchangeable, and always the same, identical with themselves. I mean, what this sounds like to begin with is absolutely fantastic assertions. The usual answer is of course that Plato hypostatized concepts, and the concept of a mode, not to mention a more dignified animal, is really unchanged. And it's also not mystical. You can see modes, but you cannot see *mode* on its own. And Plato, by unbelievable and incredible stupidity which is sufficiently excused by the low development of the human mind at the time [laughter], hypostatized concepts. Let us not quarrel with that. Now, Plato sketches in the seventh book of the *Republic* a pursuit which he regards as the highest of which man is capable, and that he calls dialectics. This is somewhat ambiguous. Why Plato calls it dialectics I must now postpone, though we may have occasion to bring it up. Now, this dialectics has to be with ideas and nothing but ideas. It moves, as it were, from one idea to another until it has exhausted the whole realm of ideas, and then it reaches the highest idea, that to which all ideas owe their being ideas as well as their knowability. And that he calls the idea of the good, or the good.

Now Plato never presented this dialectics of the ideas. He gives a sketch of it to some extent, and a very comical sketch to boot, in the dialogues called *Sophist* and *Statesman* and so on, but no Platonic system is ever presented. Hegel's *Logic* is that. One can say Hegel presents in the *Logic* what Plato calls the highest generality of being, the greatest *genera* of being, the *megista gene*. He presents them systematically and exhaustively, and shows then in the following parts of his system, which can be called the philosophy of nature and philosophy of the mind, how these ideas—I use the Platonic expression, not the Hegelian—why the whole realm of ideas necessarily externalizes into nature on the one hand and mind on the other hand. In the mind alone really the true perfection is reached. That is of course Plato. Socrates calls this, by the term peculiar to him, a flight into the *logoi*: into the speeches, the accounts, the conditions. That is a very hard thing, let us leave that open. But obviously "logic" is derived from *logos*, and you can therefore understand that in a sense it is possible to call the rhetoric of the ideas the "logic," but surely not in the sense of the rules of thinking and this kind of thing.

Student: Where is Hegel's speculative philosophy contained? Is Hegel's speculative philosophy in his *Logic*?

LS: Yes, and in his philosophy of nature and his philosophy of the mind. He wrote a book, a kind of compendium for students, the *Encyclopedia of the Philosophical Sciences*. There you have the whole presented theoretically. The word which is applied in the textbooks to Hegel, at least it was when I was a student, is "panlogism." Hegel surely is the most radical rationalist that ever wrote.[14] Nothing is accepted as given; everything must be understood as necessary by seeing its genesis. This is the process of the dialectic. For example, if you take Spinoza's *Ethics*, it is as rational externally as Euclid's *Elements*, but where does he get his axioms and definitions? We must begin from scratch. In this sense, Hegel is much more radical than Descartes with his universal doubt. Hegel begins freely, from nothing in a sense. He begins, for some reason, his *Logic* with being as distinguished from nothing. He could as well have begun it with nothing, and it would have led—I mean, one would have to rewrite the beginning of his *Logic*, but it would have led then from nothing to being and becoming and so forth. That is a claim of Hegel that he has achieved perfect clarity about everything—I mean, not about the contents of the person, of his neighbor, and of this kind of thing in which only pickpockets are interested, but all things of any importance to a human being. This he claims. All data are as it were transformed into evident necessities, and they too as data . . . I mean, obviously we have the observed facts, the world, but we don't understand, we don't know the causes, we don't understand the necessity. And that there is such a thing as the world, we all know that. But do we understand it as necessary? No. We take it as given. There is another formula which Hegel uses for his logic, which is of course somewhat ambiguous but still of some help. The *Logic* describes God as he is prior to the creation of the world. The two branches of his creation are nature and the human mind. But this creation must be understood as a necessary progress. It is free only in the sense that God creates creatures without any compulsion. Necessity is only within it, but otherwise . . .

Student: Would it be inaccurate to say that Hegel rejected any ordinary ways of thinking. For example, there is a sense in which Hegel rejected the principle of contradiction; but the principle of contradiction is used in our ordinary reckoning and in reasoning, and so forth, is not—

LS: What Hegel only means is that if you dig deeper, then the principle of contradiction won't be helpful. On the other hand, Hegel would never say that Mr. Berman has glasses and from now on . . . On the other hand, Hegel is, in a way—and we will find this in his *Philosophy of History* very clearly—one of the most empirical philosophers, at least according to his claim, that I am aware of. Precisely by looking at history as it was, and no arbitrary constructions and monkey business, will the reason of history appear. We will have a number of opportunities, I have no doubt, to illustrate—because more is not possible—the character of Hegel's thought . . . his other writings. Let us now call it a day until Thursday.

2 Reason in History and the Nature of Spirit

Leo Strauss: Now, as Mr. Bruell rightly saw, the original history—consider Herodotus as an example—and the philosophic history of Hegel have something very important in common over against what we may loosely call academic history.[1] And how can we state this as simply as possible? What is characteristic of men like Thucydides and Herodotus?

Mr. Bruell: They represent the spirit of their times.

LS: The spirit lives in them. To state it very simply, they *belong*. And therefore, when Thucydides speaks, the spirit of Athens speaks through him regardless of whether he wishes to convey it or is aware of it or not. Now reflective history does not belong, the reflective historian does not belong. For example, take a simple case. A man who writes a history of the fourteenth century today is obviously not a fourteenth-century man. There is some alienness between the student and the subject matter. And why does a philosophic historian belong? He too belongs, yes? After all, he as the philosophic historian will write about the fourteenth century as well, but he is not a fourteenth-century man.

Mr. Reinken: He understands the phenomena of spirit, the fact that these are developments of spirit.

LS: In other words, the philosophic historian deals with that in the fourteenth century which is still present and which will always be present, namely, that which forms a part of the spirit as a whole in its completion. This is very roughly why Hegel thinks that there is such a profound connection between this wholly nonphilosophic original history and the truly philosophic history over against that half-philosophic reflective history. This corresponds very much to Hegel's spirit as a whole, this kind of particular preface. Now there is of course one minor difficulty regarding this which Hegel did not develop. You must never forget that this is not an elaborated book. These are lectures. You mentioned only Thucydides and Herodotus, but he gives some other examples. Let us limit ourselves to the classical ones for simplicity's sake.

Mr. Bruell: Seneca and Caesar.

LS: Ja, but what is the difference? Let us take Caesar, a particularly clear case. What is the difference between Caesar and Herodotus? The most obvious difference?

Mr. Bruell: Caesar was a general.

LS: And Herodotus?

Mr. Bruell: No.

LS: So the Persian wars, which are in a way the peak of Herodotus, Herodotus did not participate in. And he was not in *charge*. It is not quite clear what Hegel thinks it means to belong. Does it mean to be a member of the society, or does it mean to be politically active on a higher plane? Now, from the latter point of view, say, Churchill would be an eminent example in our age—and to some extent also de Gaulle, only Churchill is much more historic than de Gaulle is, and Hegel would say that this is much more relevant for understanding the twentieth century, what has happened there, than the laborious productions of the academic historians and so on. But this is not entirely cleared up, because the statement in this generality as he makes it on one or two occasions, that the original historians are statesmen and generals, is refuted not by Thucydides but by Herodotus.

Mr. Bruell: In connection with that statement that the ancient historians were generals, he says the situation in our time is completely altered. But I don't understand. He doesn't seem to develop that.

LS: Yes, but what he has in mind is that the professors have taken over. I mean, it is of course not literally true. Napoleon wrote his memoirs on St. Helena and so on, but generally speaking today, as you know, every general writes, gives his account, and whether they are very relevant I don't know. I have never studied them except on a few occasions. Yes, Mr. Bruell?

Mr. Bruell: Is that what he means by saying that our culture is essentially comprehensive and immediately changes all events into historical representations?

LS: Yes, one could. This is in Hegel's mouth an ambiguous statement. It could also refer to the bookish character of the nineteenth century compared with the Greeks and Romans, who were much less bookish.

Now there is another point which I would like to take up right away. Hegel makes it clear that what he is presenting in this book is based on speculative or theoretical philosophy. Speculative or theoretical philosophy proves that, stated simply, reason rules the world. But still, what does philosophy of history do? Is it simply based on Hegel's metaphysics, or is it not meant to carry conviction to some extent by itself? You refer to that.

Mr. Bruell: In one place he says that it proves the thesis, but not in terms of absolute proof but in accordance with the facts.

LS: What does that mean? One can perhaps say that we proceed here historically, empirically, that is to say, without presupposing altogether this metaphysics' truth. How does he proceed there? Let us try to illustrate. There is some reason to assume that Greece played a considerable role in the history of the human mind. But Hegel is still not primarily concerned with the philosophers but with what the Greeks did in other respects, especially politically. How would he find that out? I mean, why does he then prefer, say, Herodotus and Thucydides to modern historians of Greece?

Mr. Bruell: Because they do represent that spirit.

LS: So in other words, the gist of Greekness is directly available to us if we linger, as he puts it, with Homer too of course, but especially with Thucydides and Herodotus; and this is infinitely more important than to know this or that detail regarding dates, tribute rates, the number fallen in a given battle, and who was the grandmother of that general, and so on. And here we have the gist of the . . . Now, and what Hegel has in mind really is that if we would read, say, one hundred books—if I may use a very popular notion, great books of these various societies or cultures—and would linger with them and also consider the sequence in which they were written, then this picture of the progress of reason or freedom would emerge without doing any violence to the facts. To that extent, it appears to be empirical. We must see this at greater detail.

Student: When he speaks of Thucydides, he says that . . . speeches are not the original speeches, and he says Thucydides is only reflecting the whole spirit of the society. Is he using that as a proof of what you just said, that he so reflected that Thucydides was able to make up the speech?

LS: But they were all Greeks and therefore they are of course all of a fundamental unity of culture, if I may use this term, which is perfectly compatible with great variety and even antagonisms within it. And what Thucydides does is to present to us a great variety within Greekness; and he does this for some reason especially in the form of speeches which he has at least written, composed, even if he had heard the gist of the speeches from some reporters, or maybe he had heard the speech himself.

Student: Does he say that Thucydides did not have to reflect upon this in order to be able to create this?

LS: No, reflection has a stricter meaning in Hegel. I mean, he knew that Thucydides and Herodotus were very thoughtful men. But reflection is not identical with thought; reflection is a certain kind of thought, and it is a kind of thought which, let us provisionally say, does not belong—that you are outside. I mean, therefore, say natural science generally speaking would belong to the sphere of reflective thought. But every thought which presupposes that we belong is not really reflection, because there is always the conscious presence of the thinking ego, which is essential. How can I describe it more simply for present purposes? You know the distinction between intellect and reason, that's a traditional Aristotelian distinction: the intellect, which grasps the essences; and reasoning, *ratio*, ratiocination which links up. Now something like that distinction is implied by Hegel, only the terminology is completely changed. The lower is called understanding, *nous*, *intellectus*, and the higher is called reason. That has very much to do with Kant, but it is in an entirely different medium, the reassertion of the old distinction between understanding and reason. The key point is this: reflection is simply controlled by the principle of contradiction, and reason is dialectical, i.e., thinks through contradiction. So reflection has this very narrow sense, you see, and it is also that, as you see, reflection means a certain questionable distance from the object, implies abstraction, merely abstract thought. Now, there is this remark which . . . that when he says that in a sense one cannot learn anything from history.[2] The passage has often been quoted. Now there is a point. Burke says already before Hegel that from history much political wisdom may be learned as habit, not as precept. Now the vulgar view is that you can learn wisdom as precept. Hannibal did this and this at Cannae;[3] therefore, if you want to have a victory like Hannibal's, you have to do what Hannibal did. You know all the rest. Burke has already denied that because fundamentally . . . the circumstances differ in each case but yet we are helped in our understanding by observing how different wise action looks in different circumstances. This kind of flexibility we surely can acquire through well-conducted historical readings.

Now I do not remember what the immediate context was in which I began to speak of this. Now these people who think they can derive precepts from history; a very good example, superficially at least, would be Machiavelli's *Discourses on the First Ten Books of Titus Livy*. He reads Livy, and then he says he draws lessons, recipes, from what he saw. If you want to establish a commonwealth, you must stand alone. You can read almost any of these 142 chapter headings of the *Discourses*—they have this character. This is what Hegel regards as something very inferior because of its abstraction: it doesn't see the connection. And the key point for Hegel is, as Mr. Bruell brought out, that all political action takes place within a specific culture, to use a present-day term, and therefore the rules, the recipes, are not transferable from one culture to another. In other words, something which works well in culture A might be fatal in culture B, etc. So to repeat, reflective means abstract, lacking the concreteness which either the immersion in your society has, say, Thucydides, or the universality again that is also again concrete.

Student: So then reflection is neither understanding nor reason.

LS: No, I think from Hegel's point of view it would be called understanding in this limited sense, I mean in the limited sense in which it is lower than reason. Understanding is essentially nondialectical. Hegel occasionally uses the expression the "rigid" or "stiff" understanding, "either-or" without seeing the transition, the radical change from one to the other, what he calls truly speculative thinking. Well, some of these points will surely become clearer as we go. Now there is one point I think which we should state right away, and merely as a thesis, so that we never forget it and try to understand it. On pages 9–10 of your edition, it is made clear that *the* premise which he presupposes in these lectures on the philosophy of history is—let me see, near the beginning, where he speaks of reason. We can leave this term here, without discussing its relation to God. Read this sentence, please.

Mr. Reinken:

[Reason] is substance, as well as infinite power; its own infinite material underlying all the natural and spiritual life which it originates, as also the infinite form—that which sets this material in motion.[4]

LS: Let us leave it at that. And let me keep in mind only one point. The premise is the omnipotence of reason. And you can also say this is simply a somewhat unusual statement for the omnipotence of God. But the key point is this: reason—and this is surely no longer compatible with ordinary theology—is both the form and the matter. That reason should be the form, this wasn't always so. But that reason should also be the matter, that everything is rational—this is exactly what people mean when they speak of Hegel's panlogism. And we must gradually try to understand this to begin with wholly unintelligible assertion: there is nothing outside of reason, nothing which is not rational.

Now Hegel starts first by a reference to what he has shown elsewhere, and since we have not read that, we simply have to regard this as a mere assertion and forget about it, hoping, however, to get some illustration of this paradoxical assertion as we go. But Hegel knows that you cannot merely make assertions and say: As I have proven elsewhere. He must appeal to something which the readers or hearers know, and therefore he reminds them of their religious faith. On page 13, line 15 following. Let me first say this: one thing is clear, that you all have learned at home or in Sunday school . . . that there is divine providence as the wise government of the world, that is what I say, only I will show you the wisdom of the government, and it is better to show it to you than merely to assert it, which is of course a very complicated method. Now let us go on here.

Mr. Reinken:

> But a difference—rather a contradiction—will manifest itself, between this belief and our principle—

LS: So Hegel does not beat around the bush. I mean, he does not say: My view is identical with the religious view. There is a difference, there is even a contradiction, a contrariety between them. Yes.

Mr. Reinken:

> just as was the case in reference to the demand made by Socrates in the case of Anaxagoras's dictum. For that belief is similarly indefinite; it is what is called the belief in a general providence, and is not followed out into definite application or displayed in its bearing on the grand total—the entire course of human history. But to *explain* history is to depict the passions of mankind, the genius, the active powers, that play their part in the great stage; and the providentially determined process which these exhibit constitutes what is generally called the "plan" of providence. Yet it is this very plan which is supposed to be concealed from our view: which it is deemed presumption even to wish to recognize.

LS: So in other words, the ordinary view is that belief in providence includes, as it were, a prohibition against prying into providence, and for Hegel this proposition is in no way valid. Yes?

Mr. Reinken:

The ignorance of Anaxagoras as to how intelligence reveals itself in actual existence was ingenuous. Neither in his consciousness, nor in that of Greece at large, had that thought been farther expanded. He had not attained the power to apply his general principle to the concrete, so as to deduce the latter from the former. It was Socrates who took the first step in comprehending the union of the concrete with the universal. Anaxagoras, then, did not take up a hostile position towards such an application—

LS: No, Socrates did not take this polemical position. This is ambiguous because in German he uses the personal pronoun, the third person "he," and it is the translator's business to find out who the "he" is. But this is not important for us now. Go on.

Mr. Reinken:

He, then, did not take up a *hostile* position towards such an application. The common belief in providence *does*; at least it opposes the use of the principle on the large scale, and denies the possibility of discerning the plan of providence. In isolated cases, this plan is supposed to be manifest. Pious persons are encouraged to recognize in particular circumstances something more than mere chance; to acknowledge the guiding hand of God, e.g., when health has unexpectedly come to an individual.[5]

LS: Hegel says: Well, here there is, as they say, providence, and why not in the fate of large societies in order to grasp whole historical processes? What is spoken here incidentally of Socrates, the union or reconciliation of the concrete and the universal, this gives us a hint of what Hegel means by saying that reason is both the form and the matter. The concrete too, and not only the forms, the categories or however you call it, are rational and must be understood as rational. And in connection with his attempt to show that what he is doing is only to do consistently what is implied in the Christian or the Western religious tradition and therefore it shouldn't be paradoxical—it is paradoxical, you say, that everything is rational, but it is not paradoxical to say that God has created everything wisely. And you admit he says, this . . . 2 and 2. And now put 2 and 2 together, and you arrive at my view. Yes?

Student: But isn't there a further difference in that in some cases, for instance in the books of the prophets in the Old Testament, certain political events are attributed to providence—the Babylonian captivity and so forth—and he seems to have a different notion that there has to be a reason which is ruling in the world throughout to a specific end, rather than simply reasonable things happening to favored nations.

LS: But I think Hegel would simply say: Well, what the Old Testament prophets say is all right, but what about God? Does he not also govern the Persians, the Babylonians, the Greeks, and so on, and must we not also seek for his wisdom there? I mean, speaking still ad hominem. You know what that means, on the basis of the opinions of people other than himself.

Now on page 15 in the center, let me raise the question: What then is the plan of providence in world history? I see now that may not be . . . I will read on. Has the time come to understand that plan? In other words, the plan could not always be understood, but sooner or later the time will come. A religious man might say: at the end of time, it would become clear. But Hegel finds his judgment day, so to speak, could come during history. And then he goes on, and that is in your edition. I would like to observe only the following general points. In the Christian religion, God has revealed himself, i.e., has given men to know what he is, so that he is no longer hidden.

Mr. Reinken:

In the Christian religion, God has revealed Himself, that is, he has—

LS: He appeals again to something which everyone knows. Now what does it mean, God has revealed himself?

Mr. Reinken:

in other words, He has given us to understand what He is, so that He is no longer a concealed or secret existence. And this possibility—

LS: That of course is what the Christians would no longer admit, that there does not remain any longer a mystery, a divine mystery, but this is Hegel speaking. Revealed religion is a religion in which everything is revealed, especially regarding God. Yes.

Mr. Reinken:

and this possibility of knowing Him, thus afforded us, renders such knowledge a duty. God wishes no narrow-hearted souls or empty heads for His children, but those whose spirit is of itself, indeed, poor, but rich in the knowledge of Him, and who regard this knowledge of God as the only valuable possession. That development of the thinking spirit which has resulted from the revelation of the Divine Being as its original basis, must ultimately advance to the intellectual comprehension of what was presented in the first instance to feeling and imagination. The time must eventually come for understanding that rich product of active reason which the history of the world—[6]

LS: Yes, so this is clear. And now here's something which is not in your edition, which I will translate to you. "Now the peculiarity of Christian religion is that with it that time—the plan of providence is . . . has come. This constitutes the absolute epoch in world history."[7] The absolute epoch in world history is the epoch in which the plan of God becomes known. But in the original version, in the New Testament texts, this was not yet in the form of reason. Now, in and through Hegel it has become rationally clear; therefore the absolute, the consummation of the absolute epoch, and therefore we can say the absolute epoch simply, is here, is Hegel's. In Hegel, the plan of history has become clear, so that it can be taught rationally in classrooms, which could not be said before. So let us keep in mind this expression "the absolute epoch." Hegel lives in the absolute epoch, and he will later explain quite clearly what the reasons are why one can say that, say, around 1820 or thereabouts, the absolute epoch of world history has come.

We must read the most important passages. We have a lot of things we will postpone. We are confronted with this question which we cannot solve for the time being; we will find some passages which will help. Reason is the form and the matter, and therefore there is nothing which is not rational. This needs a very long footnote, and the footnote is Hegel's *Logic*, you can say. But we must limit ourselves to the remarks which Hegel makes here. Now the difficulty is indicated, for example, on page 16 at the beginning of the third paragraph.

Mr. Reinken:

It must be observed at the outset that the phenomenon we investigate—universal history—belongs to the realm of spirit. The term "world" includes both physical and psychical nature. Physical nature also plays its part in the world's history, and attention will have to be paid to the fundamental natural relations thus involved. But spirit and the course of its development is our substantial object. Our task does not require us to contemplate nature as a rational system in itself.[8]

LS: Now let us stop here for one moment. The spirit of which Hegel speaks here and which we can loosely say is identical with reason, this spirit is understood in contradistinction to nature. And therefore this is the problem of Hegel: to prove, I mean to show, that spirit and the spiritual or the intellectual is rational is not so terribly difficult, but what about nature? He speaks, in a passage which is not here, even of the *opposition* between nature and spirit. How does spirit, which is in itself a potentiality, acquire its content? That is another way of stating the question: How does form cause the matter? On page 17, paragraph 3, "The nature of the mind, or spirit."
Mr. Reinken:

The nature of spirit can be understood by a glance at its direct opposite, matter.

LS: In other words, here the simple reaction would be, Hegel cannot possibly say that matter is spiritual or, more generally stated, that reason is the form and the matter. Here is an obvious obstacle, but not for Hegel, as we will see. Go on.
Mr. Reinken:

As the essence of matter is gravity, so, on the other hand, we may affirm the substance, the essence of spirit, is freedom.

LS: Apart from everything else, I think it is a beautiful and suggestive combination. Matter is related to spirit as gravity or heaviness to freedom, to wind. Matter is not wind. Good. Nietzsche used this then later in his *Zarathustra*, when he spoke of the spirit of heaviness as the one which . . . spirit of heaviness, because our spirit can be heavy, as we know, and this is the spirit which . . . which is opposed to all creativeness. But let us go on. Yes.
Mr. Reinken:

All would readily assent to the doctrine that spirit, among other properties, is also endowed with freedom. But philosophy teaches that all the qualities of spirit exist only through freedom, that all are but means for attaining freedom, that all seek and produce this and this alone. It is a result of speculative philosophy that freedom is the sole truth of spirit. Matter—

LS: That means that spirit is in no way compelled by any other thing. Freedom, not compulsion; it acts only through its own impulses, laws, whatever you call it. Yes?
Mr. Reinken:

Matter possesses gravity in virtue of its tendency towards a central point. It is essentially composite, consisting of parts that exclude each other. It seeks its unity, and therefore exhibits itself as self-destructive, as verging toward its opposite and indivisible part. If it could attain this, it would be matter no longer; it would have perished. It strives after the realization of its idea.[9]

LS: That's the key point here. So in other words, matter points by itself towards spirit. Matter following its own logic would destroy itself as matter and become spirit. Matter is for Hegel essentially self-contradictory, which doesn't mean that it doesn't exist. And this fundamental contradictoriness will come only in the mind, because the mind does not have this radical self-contradictoriness that wishes something which by reaching it would cease to be mind. There is another passage which is not in your translation which I would like to read to you, where he says, as it were, in passing: "If the divine essence were not the essence of man and nature, it would be an essence which would be as nothing."[10] I mean, in other words, the transcendence of God as it is usually understood has here become very questionable. God is what he produces, and this can be roughly divided into nature and mind, nature and man.

There is one point about which you have not spoken, Mr. Bruell, and I don't blame you for that because the matter was so enormous. There is something called mind. By the way, the difficulty is due to the fact that the German word which Hegel uses, Geist, means both "mind" and "spirit," and therefore sometimes one says mind, and sometimes spirit. It is very hard to translate it by the same term all the time. So there is the doctrine of the mind which becomes relevant for the understanding of history by an intermediate thought. I mean the mind—let us speak of the divine mind, and there is of course also the mind of man, i.e., the mind of individuals—but this would not be of any help for the understanding of history. There is an intermediate thought which enables Hegel to make his philosophy of the mind the basis of the philosophy of history. And what is that?

Mr. Bruell: Is it the world-historical figures, the heroes?

LS: No, not yet. There are folk-minds. The universal mind, if I may say so, realizes itself through folk-minds, through a kind of collective minds and not simply through individuals. This is here rather suddenly introduced, but it is obvious that without this concept of the folk-mind there would be no possibility of giving an account of history in terms of mind. History has to do primarily with political societies—states, empires, kingdoms—but this is for Hegel not enough. The political life is a part of a larger whole. This thought is today extremely popular, of course; at that time it was only beginning. What is now called culture Hegel calls the specific mind, the folk-mind. These are the true subjects of history, not political history only as an ingredient of it. One can perhaps state it as follows: History is rational . . . because it is a work or activity of the mind. But the mind is historical because it is collective mind, folk-mind, and therefore the mind embodied in the historical ages. The rule which Hegel gives here is this: that every folk-mind goes through a cycle, from a beginning through a peak to its decay. And this is a necessary process. There will be no chance; no traffic accidents, as it were, will prevent the completion of such a cycle. When a given folk-mind has reached its end, has realized itself fully, then the mind goes over, the world mind goes over to another nation which begins where the preceding nation left off and had to leave off. And nation number one then ceases to be of any interest. It is of great interest to the people who belong to that nation but not to the objective observer. Take a country like Portugal, which played a very great role once, had a high development. Today it is not in the forefront anymore, to put it mildly. One could give other examples, too.

Now there is one passage which I thought I should read. Very important passages of the book are missing. The folk-mind, this is the key point. It's hard to say how to translate the German word *Volk*. The simple translation into English would be "nation," but they see the inadequacy of that word and therefore translate it by "folk." We have to read it as that. A community surely of language and culture, and also naturally of descent. That is clearly implied. These nations have a nature in the sense that for some they belong to a certain climate and other conditions. Hegel will speak of that later. But more specifically, their nature is their fundamental disposition. But dispositions atrophy if they are not actualized. And the actualization means, according to Hegel, they are *posited*, as it were. This folk makes itself responsible for what it does. And this is not merely an irrational process without choice and freedom, so a man or a nation is what he is not by nature but by his action or his choice. This is developed at great length.[11]

So while there is something like nature, this nature becomes relevant only by actions of the will, by actions of the mind. And through this transformation it ceases to be natural and becomes spiritual. As something spiritual, the folk-mind cannot die out, but it becomes the matter for a higher principle embodied in another people. So here we have at least the partial answer to the question: Why can reason be both form and matter? Because the earlier stages of the mind are matter for the higher stages, and the great question is of course when that which is not mind at all, loosely called matter simply, how can this also be mind in a manner? He has given an indication only by the general remark about matter and its essential contradictoriness which we have read. The process leading from one folk to another is rational, which means nothing is lost. The essence of a folk-mind is preserved. This is naturally crucial, because if something important is lost, one cannot speak simply of progress as a change, but maybe what was lost was much more important than what has been acquired since.

The folk-mind, we can say, if this is of some help for later discussion, is the mediation between nature and mind. There is one passage which I must read to you, unfortunately also not in your translation. He discusses here the transition from one folk-mind into another. He says: "The universal mind never dies, but the folk-mind which belongs to universal history must come to the knowledge of that which is its work, it must reach the point where it thinks itself."[12] The folk-mind, in other words, is fundamentally not conscious of itself. But at a certain stage it acquires consciousness of itself, it knows truly its work. Previously it didn't know that its work was itself. Say laws coming down as Antigone says[13] are imposed on the Greeks, and at a certain stage people come to see they are our laws, we make them. This thinking, this reflection no longer has any respect of the immediate, meaning here Antigone and this law which comes from she-doesn't-know-where and she bows reverently to it. But from a certain moment on, this reverence ceases: there takes place a separation of the subjective mind, the individual, from the universal mind, which expresses itself in these generally accepted views and values, etc. The individuals retreat within themselves, are no longer above all citizens, and strive for their own purposes. Think of Alcibiades, of whom Hegel surely thought. Alcibiades, what did he care for Athens? Athens was for him an opportunity, and if that opportunity ceased to be an opportunity, he betrayed her and went to Sparta. We have already noticed that this is the corruption, the decay of the people. Everyone makes his own purposes according to his passions. At the same time, however, while the mind, the spirit, withdraws within itself, thinking becomes now a reality by itself, an independent reality, and the sciences emerge. The sciences emerge with this liberation or emancipation of the individual, which is identical with the decay of the folk-mind, of the common spirit. Hence sciences and the corruption or destruction of the people are always connected with each other. Did you ever hear such a proposition?

Student: Sounds like Rousseau.

LS: Rousseau, especially in the *First Discourse*, the *Discourse on the Arts and Sciences*. So you see this is accepted by Hegel: the sciences and moral and political corruption go together. This is very important for a reason which I indicated last time. Does anyone remember?

Mr. Reinken: The owl of Minerva.

LS: Can you spell it out?

Mr. Reinken: That historical understanding comes when we have hit the peak.

LS: Not necessarily so, but in the proper sense and also simpler. What is true here of the Greeks is also true of Hegel's time. This consciousness, this full consciousness of the modern Western mind achieved in Hegel is connected with the corruption of modernity. The owl of Minerva, as Hegel has rightly called it, begins its flight in the dusk.[14] Yes?

Student: Hegel however says that Aristotle liberated Alexander the Great from his particular inclinations and allowed him to become a great man, through . . . teachings, and he says that Alexander embodies the spirit of Greece in some way.

LS: Yes, but on the other hand, of course he was the great figure of Greece. Hegel's truly Greek spirit of Athens is out at that time, and you get what later came to be called Hellenism, which prepares in a way the Roman Empire. That's something else, because the question of Alexander will come up later. There are more remarks which we have not read, unfortunately. At the end, the mind arrives at full consciousness. Full consciousness will not mean that you can explain every detail of the funny dream you had . . . but in the important respects you—

Student: Would Hegel have to accept the corruption of modernity, or would you say there is something fundamentally different about his own philosophy that would enable him to write at a period when things weren't corrupt, the reason being that there is no more corruption, there is nowhere else for the world spirit to go in modernity, it's reached the end?

LS: Yes, but why does he make this remark about the owl of Minerva when he speaks of his doctrine and the function of his philosophy in modern Europe? I mean, if it had occurred here only, then one could say: Well, hitherto it always happened that when a culture broke down and reached its fulfillment, then disintegration follows accompanied by the possibility of self-understanding. But now, in this fortunate time of Hegel that is no longer the case. But unfortunately he wrote the passage about the owl of Minerva in his introduction to his *Philosophy of Right*, i.e., in connection with *modern* thought.

Student: Well if that's so, then would that be incompatible with saying history has reached an end?

LS: No. I mean, that is a very dark question because it is hard to know what Hegel thought of the beginning and the end of the human race. That is one of the amazing things in Hegel, that one simply doesn't know what he thought about that. I mean, he discusses very briefly the question of the species, animal species, somewhere in the *Encyclopedia*—I always think of the social sciences, you see how much of a social scientist I am—*of the Philosophical Sciences*; and then he simply says: Well, this question of taxonomy has utterly nothing to do with the question of the order of coming into being. But after all, if the universe is not eternal, the question of the genesis of the species is very important. It is impossible to say. It is unbelievable, you can say, but here we are: Hegel did not discuss this question. Therefore, whether the human race was likely to last for millions or billions of years, or only a few hundred years—

Student: But in order for Hegel to be right, the spirit should have reached—[15]

LS: —an order based on the recognition of the rights of man, but not democratic. This is the right order and the only sensible order: all problems are solved in it. There is no reasonable possibility of protesting it. There are plenty of unreasonable possibilities; for example, a high official who is not appointed to the position which he would like is of course disgusted and would perhaps try to do all kinds of things, but he has no leg to stand on. There is no longer a publicly defensible principle in the world to which a man can appeal against the truth as presented by Hegel in his *Philosophy of Right*. This is the point.

And there are of course great difficulties, because there was a great social question not yet so powerful in Germany in Hegel's time, but it became of course very powerful with the industrialization of Germany and the problem of democracy connected with that. But we are concerned only with what Hegel explicitly said. We must try to understand how it is possible that someone should have made this apparently preposterous assertion. Mr. Shulsky?

Mr. Shulsky: Could he be somehow asserting that the immanent corruption of modern political institutions wouldn't really matter very much, because there being no further stage, you could exist with a corrupt political order. It would not be threatened, it would go on . . . status.

LS: No. Let us assume that, after all, there are certain built-in resistances against political corruption. I simply mean that people get fed up with it, and then there will be some kind of revolution which of course is no longer an interesting revolution. I mean, no principles are at war . . . the French Revolution, but it is only a return to the principles already codified in Hegel. This kind of thing, is that what you mean?

Mr. Shulsky: No, more something along these lines: that the Greek world as it was more or less viewed, once everybody began to take an individual look at the laws, they didn't accept them; while in the modern world, presumably we can go on with everyone taking his individual view and not taking the political view because we're not threatened in the same way the Greek world was by someone coming after us.

LS: But the Greeks did not know that, of course.

Mr. Shulsky: No, but I'm saying, how can he say we're at the end of history in modern times?

LS: I suppose he must have thought something of this kind, that there is a kind of plateau we have reached and this will of course expand. He was wondering what was going to happen in this country and in Russia. But he didn't know. But I think in the spirit of his philosophy one could say this rather would spread to America as well as to Russia, but there is no evidence. Yes?

Student: I understood you to say that once . . . set down there remains no rational way to a restoration, perhaps irrational attempts at . . .

LS: Yes, people simply did think of people as a kind of Western cowboy who finds this modern life, where crime is allegedly taken care of by public authority and everything is done in an orderly manner, very dull. Such people would like to do these things, and they might have some success because there is a time when crime is not properly taken care of by the official authorities. But gradually people come to see that it is impossible to leave this to the arbitrary will of individuals, and there will be a revamping of the police systems and also a change in the laws. But these are not fundamental things. They can be very important to the individuals involved, but no new principle can ever emerge. When we come to the book we will see that every epoch of which Hegel speaks has a principle of its own, which was an entirely new principle at the time. There is no longer a place in the world for a new principle; there is plenty of space for spreading and for the ever more adequate embodiment of the final principle. I mean, think of penal law, how terrible that still was in many respects 130 years ago and how there was plenty to do there. But this is only a further elaboration, there is nothing of fundamental interest.

Student: My question is, how can one say that, given Hegel's understanding of the rational as I understand his understanding of it, how can you say that an idea is irrational, when as an idea after all it is rational?

LS: Which idea?

Student: Any one of these so-called irrational tendencies.

LS: No, Hegel says it is not an idea *because* it is irrational—say, a kind of Gary Cooper romanticism, or a Clark Gable, or whatever. That is not an idea because it is not rational; it is a childish dream which has a certain appeal to some grown-up people but it is a childish dream. And of course also, because it is not rational, it has no power. And there can be occasionally some affair somewhere in a western town perhaps or village or hamlet, but that would be easily stopped, and even if it creates an uproar for a couple of years by some strange combination of circumstances, it has no future. You have heard the expression, "that has no future." That is what he means. There is nothing which has a future except—I will state it inoffensively—the constitutional state, run by a civil service, and of course preferably (and that can easily be done) by a very responsible and highly educated civil service. And if people think they can do without a good civil service and without a properly trained one, then Hegel will say that after a short while you will notice that this doesn't work as well because it is not in accordance with the spirit of this time. Yes?

Student: You said before that the . . . relationship between corruption and the rise of science. Is it correct to assume, or to understand, that the rise of science is possible because the major political problems have been solved, according to Hegel?

LS: In a way, yes, and only because they have been solved is it possible to give the theory of it.

Student: I don't understand then the relationship between the solution and the rise of science and corruption.

LS: That is a longer process. He is speaking here of a much broader phenomenon. I think he is here thinking primarily of what happened in Greece. There was this order, this old order, culminating in a way in the victory in the Persian War, and then gradually, in pragmatic terms, Greece becomes much more powerful and wealthy. Then public tasks no longer have this grand compelling character, and there begins this movement towards a . . . as seen in the Spartan war; and in this, and especially during the preparation for war, there we see a disintegration beginning. The ultimate reason is not the harshness of the war but the absence of such compelling public tasks, wholly public tasks, one could almost say, as the defense of Greece against Persia. And in connection with this, some individuals think it is wonderful to have a stable of racing horses and to win in Olympia each time, such as Alcibiades—and of course, since he was a very clever man, also to have conversations with Socrates and other people. And others who simply don't like this playboy existence at all, and they say: No, we stay with Socrates and talk with him from morning to evening about what virtue is, what courage is, what education is, and whatever it may be, and yet no longer truly participate in the life of the *polis*. Individualists, yes, but this individualism is of course the condition of science in the widest sense of the term.

So for Hegel science is most important. Philosophy is science. His great work has the title *The Science of Logic*. And yet, as it were, you can't eat the cake and have it. The time in which the German cities were flourishing, late Middle Ages up to the . . . perhaps—Hegel would never use this example; I use it only from the point of view of social health—in that time science would have been absolutely impossible. In other words, Hegel's view of the human order—we will see other examples of that later—is not as harmonious as it is frequently presented in the Hegelian tradition, that you get the good and the beautiful and the true all at the same time in the same manner. That is not so, according to Hegel. The development of man's most important desire and, according to Hegel, his highest desire, the desire for knowledge, demands a price. I mean not merely this price, which goes without saying, the infinite effort . . . but it is not possible under the same conditions under which society has really flourished. But there are quite a few objections to this interpretation of Hegel. Let us be open and see what we find out. I would like to see on page 20 at the beginning of the second paragraph.

Mr. Reinken:

> The question of the means by which freedom develops itself to a world conducts us to the phenomenon of history itself. Although freedom is primarily an undeveloped idea, the means it uses are external and phenomenal, presenting themselves in history to our sensuous vision.

LS: In other words, the end of history is not visible, strictly understood. What is visible, I mean what we observe and what we hear about, is what in the light of the end appears as means. And that is what ordinary historians speak about, but they do not speak about it as means; they speak about these battles, these revolutions, these restorations, or what have you. Yes, go on.

Mr. Reinken:

> The first glance at history convinces us that the actions of man proceed from their needs, their passions, their characters, and talents, and impresses us with the belief that such needs, passions and interests are the sole springs of action, the efficient agents of this scene of activity. Among these may perhaps be found aims of the liberal or universal kind—benevolence it may be, or noble patriotism. But such virtues and general views are but insignificant as compared with the world and its doings. We may perhaps see the ideal of reason actualized in those who adopt such ends and within the sphere of their influence; but they bear only a trifling proportion to the mass of the human race, and the extent of that influence is limited accordingly. Passions, private aims, and the satisfactions of selfish desires are on the other hand, most effective springs of action. Their power lies in the fact that they respect none of the limitations which justice and morality would impose on them; and that these natural impulses have a more direct influence over man than the artificial and tedious discipline that tends to order and self-restraint, law and morality.[16]

LS: Yes. So what we see first, I mean, as unsophisticated people just reading the report, is that these big actions and transactions are the actions of individuals; and then we see there are good guys and bad guys, and the one we like and the other we detest. In other words, we study their motives: was he public spirited or was he just a man concerned with his own self-aggrandizement? Generally stated, we study their passions. Now Hegel says that from the higher point of view these passions are the means for the world-historical process and that the usual moralistic view, as Hegel calls it, is not very helpful, because sometimes a man was very good and politically of a high order and yet in an outlying district, so to speak, of no importance for the history of the world. And then another man of very dubious morality who was however at the right place at the right time and could use the proper levers, he was concerned with his self-aggrandizement without any question, and yet the situation was such that he could not aggrandize himself but by doing a public service of the first order and bringing about the transition from principle A, which had become obsolete, to principle B. Hegel's direct experience is of course Napoleon, but he's thinking also of Alexander the Great and of Caesar and of some other people. So the end is the rational end: the good or true or just society, however you call it. But the means through which it is brought about are the passions of men and partly, to say the least, the morally bad passions. We will see that Hegel's view of the passions and of these world-historical individuals is not quite as tough as that of Machiavelli. I think Hegel is pointing forward in the direction of Carlyle much more than back in the direction of Machiavelli. This is . . . unfortunately not sufficient.

Now here he says at the end of the passage Mr. Reinken read, the passions are in a way natural, the virtues are artificial due to conscious discipline. This old issue of nature and convention is here still alive, only for Hegel it is different: what is natural is lower than what is brought about by the mind and the intellect. And Hegel has to answer this question: What do the passions, which are always selfish, have to do with the universal end? That is the proper place to start, and this is a more specific formulation of the same problem which, generally stated, means that reason supplies both the form and the matter. In a manner, reason is effective in these terrible warriors and tyrants and makes them what they are. It was not Napoleon, God knows what went on in . . . this occasion. But it was not merely Napoleon with this particular . . . affairs and whatever, but something in Napoleon which is responsible for that new civil code, the Code Napoléon, and for this complete change in civil law which he talks about, and other matters. Strange as it may sound, I believe you will gradually see that Hegel's conception of the world-historical individual is more moral than that of Machiavelli. I think in a way he moralizes the hero and thus brings about this union between the universal and the particular.

Now let me explain things by one word again. Hegel reminds us of the belief in providence, and he says: What I will do is really to prove what everyone asserts, that there is a divine government of the world. In the coming of modern times and the modern rationalism, the English poet Pope had written a poem which has the purpose "to vindicate the ways of God to man."[17] And Hegel says, as it were: I shall vindicate the ways of God in history to man, and this means one crucial point, because what is so shocking and what seems to contradict so much the belief in a wise government of the world when we look at history? Answer: the terrible evil with which it abounds, physical evil as well as moral evil. The victory, temporary or sometimes more than temporary, of terror—think only about the Roman emperors in Tacitus. Just read a few chapters from time to time, and there you see what absolute beasts could hold human beings in thrall. There is no possibility, it seems, of saying a good word about them. But Hegel wants to: the vindication of providence means the justification of evil. That is crucial. So if we may play fast and loose with these general terms form and matter, somehow corresponding to the difference of good and evil, evil is as necessary for the final perfection as good. And in a more immediate sense it is even more important, because these great revolutionary changes are brought about by men whom we in our unsophisticated and healthy mood would call evil rather than good.

Mr. Shulsky: Doesn't that again raise the question of what happens in modern times when there are no more big changes? What purpose would evil serve then?

LS: This is the point. This is obviously the same question. How did Hegel think things would go from here? But fundamentally there can no longer be a revolution, except a replica of the French Revolution, say, if they would make a revolution in what is now Yugoslavia, which at that time was Turkish. If that could be assured, Hegel would probably say it was quite good. I don't know, but I suppose so. But still, what is new is only an expansion of the thing.

Mr. Shulsky: What about the problem of the people in modern times in the states which are modern? They are still the same; they still have the same passions, but now these passions no longer have a purpose, because there is nothing to which they can be the means.

LS: That's very good, because the final order is found, because if some-one has a passion and expresses it in a manner not conducive to the common good, then he will become an ordinary criminal; and if the criminal police and the courts do their duty, he will be taken care of. Now of course Hegel is not so much concerned with vulgar passions leading to sex, and murder even, but he is concerned with these great passions, the great political ambitions. They can also be very dangerous, of course; there are always laws for high treason, *lèse majesté*, and so on. Something to worry about. But the fundamental problems are solved. There are always loose ends around, but this is not a philosophic problem.

Mr. Shulsky: This seems to punch a few holes in his vindication of providence, because if he wants to explain why there is evil, he does it by saying evil serves a purpose, and it's a good purpose.

LS: Yes, but the question why there should be passions of the non-world-historical kind is not discussed here. But I suppose one could explain why an animal-like man must have these passions. You know, I suppose it would be quite good if people of different sexes loved one another. You cannot get that without making some allowance for the passion of genesis: the possibility of genesis implies love. I think he would also follow to some extent on Adam Smith regarding what he calls society as distinguished from the state or, to put it harshly, on Mandeville: private vices, public benefits.[18] I mean, if there were not people who were unreasonably eager to get richer and richer, this would lead to very great damage for the economy. It is relatively simple to vindicate private passions and was done long before Hegel. But here we are concerned with private passions on a world-historical level.

3 The Actualization of Spirit in World History

Leo Strauss: Now Mr. Hewitt, you spoke chiefly of this *Moralität/Sittlichkeit* business.[1] I'll use the German terms for the time being. What is the purpose of this discussion in Hegel? It didn't become clear, and I believe that was the reason why it was so hard to follow you. Why is this issue important?

Mr. Hewitt: My knowledge of the issue is limited to this text.

LS: I think this becomes perfectly clear from the discussion, maybe partly from what we discussed last time. I do not remember now so clearly, but I think it also becomes clear from what we read today. Mr. Bruell, do you remember why this question is so very important for Hegel? I mean very obvious things, without going into any deep things. He wants to present a philosophy of history, and there is one great, massive obstacle, very popular and well known. What is the common view of history, I mean at that time? Or throughout the ages, even but . . . no longer today perhaps.

Mr. Bruell: The objection is that philosophy would present a process opposed to history, that it would force—

LS: Oh, no, that is not a popular argument if it is based on philosophy.

Mr. Reinken: That history is just a long tale of misery.

LS: Yes, Hegel wants to show that history is rational. And the ordinary view is that history is not rational at all, rather a long tale of misery. But there is also great prosperity in history. So what is the key point?

Mr. Shulsky: Well, it seems to be a recollection of crimes.

LS: So the prosperity of the wicked and the misery of the good. Now wicked and good: this is a simple moral distinction, and therefore Hegel is confronted with the problem of morality. To what extent is morality in this simple sense the vantage point for judging of history? And therefore the distinction which Hegel made on other grounds, between morality and *Sittlichkeit*, comes in. Hegel grants, as it were, that the simple moral man is right in his judgment on history, but he questions his competence. You have to have a broader view of morality than the simple moral man. This is the key point, the purpose of the discussion. Now as for the distinction itself, it is hard to see how one could translate it conveniently into English. Sibree doesn't make any suggestions?

Student: He just uses "morality" all the time. The one point where Hegel speaks of both *Sittlichkeit* and *Moralität*, he translates *Moralität* as "morality" and *Sittlichkeit* as "ethics."

LS: That is a merely verbal help. Then you have to define what it means. Yes?

Mr. Shulsky: Well, sort of like mores or the French *moeurs*.

LS: Yes, but if you would say the "ethos" of the society it would be slightly better than to speak of "mores." One could also suggest that one translates *Moralität* by subjective morality and *Sittlichkeit* by objective morality—I mean just as a help, but this also needs some discussion. But what is Hegel thinking about?

Hegel's primary conception of morality is derived from Kant. It is really, you can say, his formulation of the Kantian notion. According to Kant the only thing of absolute worth is a good will, and this good will consists in respect for the moral law, or the law of reason. Kant thought that this purely formal thing, the mere respect for the moral . . . For Kant, this moral law means more specifically: Act in such a manner that the maxim guiding you, with a view to which you act, is susceptible of universalization. Now what does this mean? You have the maxim to get along in the world by hook and by crook. I do not mention any individual among you but an indeterminate individual. And then Kant says: How do I know that this is immoral? Answer: I try to give it the form of universal law. Everyone ought to get along in the world—everyone, not only you who want to have a special exception made for yourself—everyone is obliged to get along in the world by hook and by crook. And then Kant says: Then you see that this is impossible, as this is a self-contradictory proposal. But if a man has a maxim to help his neighbors and then you try to universalize that, then you see this works. Hence it is a moral maxim.

That's a very crude statement, but sufficient for the present purpose. And this is what Hegel denies. Hegel says: Why this good will? This fundamental integrity, as one might call it, is indeed essential to goodness, but it is unable by itself to produce any content. I mean, it excludes mere brutish self-assertion. If someone takes a very nasty content, but doesn't regard himself as an exception but says everyone should do it—

for example, a criminal says, I want to engage in racketeering—this of course presupposes that the majority of people don't do it, because otherwise the whole plan, the whole maxim wouldn't work. So this is indeed precluded by morality in the Kantian sense. But on the other hand, think of all kinds of very beastly moralities taught by so-called intellectuals, and not with a view to their aggrandizement because then they wouldn't write these books, they would keep it secret and act on it, of course. But then these things can be preached—the master's morality—as universal morality, of course not valid for everyone (you have to be a master for that) but surely without any regard to persons. And Hegel says that there must therefore be something else which cannot be produced by the individual conscience legislating for itself, and this is, let us say, morality in the objective sense. That is what is embodied in the institutions and ethos of a given society. So Hegel says that if we make this distinction, then we can get rid of the difficulty created by the prosperity of the wicked and can have a nonmoralistic but in a deeper sense moral view of world history. That is what he is driving at.

Now Hegel sometimes uses here phrases which do not remind one directly of Kant and the strict Kantian ethics but something broader. When he speaks in this passage to which you referred of the peasant or herdsman, a simple fellow who has never heard of Kant or even of ethics—honest people, they exist at all times. And let us take such a view; I mean, they exist in all kinds of societies, without a doubt, even if there are cannibal societies, even there there is a difference between honest men and other people. They only believe that cannibalism is a perfectly good thing, but not by virtue of any corruption. They are as honest as anyone in our societies. But that has to do with the defectiveness of their objective morality. Is this clear?

Mr. Hewitt: I don't think he gets out of it that clearly.

LS: Let us first try to explain it relatively independently of what Hegel himself says. Now in other words, Hegel means by morality, we can say, simple honest decency without any regard to its content. And now he says: If you take morality in this sense, history is indeed a terrible spectacle at first glance. Not quite, because he will say immediately: If this honest man takes himself seriously, then he will not be concerned with reward for virtue, and then what is the prosperity of the wicked and the misery of the good? It should be of no interest precisely if he is honest. He has no right to speak of it. But the more important consideration, as I said before, is that the important point is not this merely formal honesty, which means in effect you are a nice guy acting according to the principles of your society. But the important question is: What are the principles of your society? What is the substantive morality? And this substantive morality changes. The Greek morality is not the morality of the Middle Ages, and that is not that of our time. Now this change of the moralities, this is the most highly moral thing in the world, and this is brought about by the revolutionaries—I use a non-Hegelian term. And the revolutionaries, with their crimes, they are the most important men in the world from the highest moral point of view, even if they do all kinds of lousy things, where the simple man says they are disgusting because of the kinds of things they do. This is indeed deplorable, Hegel says, but he doesn't count compared with the revolutionary. This is roughly what he is driving at. Now let us return to the discussion. Did you want to say something?

Mr. Shulsky: This final way of getting over the difficulty by saying that whatever the world-historical people do is sort of okay in a certain sense because they're advancing the more important progress of the idea, this really leaves the distinction of *Moralität* and *Sittlichkeit* completely, doesn't it? They're not operating in the sphere of *Sittlichkeit* or in *Moralität*.

LS: No, they are; I mean their concern or that to which they are dedicated is *Sittlichkeit*. But not because morality in that sense doesn't change: there are always honest people, people who do not prefer their own selfish interests to the interests of the society to which they belong and so on. This exists always. And that is always respectable, but it is not enough. Let me say this simply in this way: The moral man, in an older language but not entirely meaning what Hegel means to say, this man is a law-abiding man, and law-abidingness is always a fine thing. But we cannot avoid the question: By which law does he abide? If this is a law favoring cannibalism, it is inferior to a law which forbids cannibalism, and even which establishes effectively the dignity of every man. And that makes all the difference. And if he is a revolutionary, he is not law-abiding, but a lawbreaker. Law-abiding I equate now with morality.

Student: But with *Sittlichkeit*.

LS: Yes, but by breaking the law, by being a criminal in this sense, he brings about a higher level of *Sittlichkeit*, of morality in the full sense of the word. Yes, Mr. Bruell?

Mr. Bruell: What about the case where from the simple point of view he wouldn't seem to be bringing about a higher level but a lower level? For instance, the story of Cyrus, the corruption of a Sparta into an Oriental despotism.

LS: But Hegel would simply say this is a wrong interpretation of what happened, this was a fiction of . . . But Alexander the Great would be an example. And Alexander the Great, by destroying the *polis* in a way, by depriving it of its life, brought about the Hellenization of the non-Greek world, and that was a great progress. Although he did terrible things, killed his best friend, you know—

Mr. Bruell: I'm not concerned with that, but suppose—

LS: You should be concerned.

Mr. Bruell: My question is not concerned, but it was directed to the fact that perhaps what he was trying to instill was better.

LS: But Hegel denies that. That is his "optimism," that the historical process is progressive, and if something is destroyed it deserved to perish. Hegel admitted that in a way classical Greece was something which has never been restored, but nevertheless, pagan as a whole, it deserved to perish because something much better came out of it: modern Europe. Yes?

Student: What about the question of Antigone and the opposition between piety to the gods and piety to the state or law-abidingness?

LS: Yes. This is a long question which Hegel will take up in the section on Greece. We will come to that. This dialectic, the family and the *polis*, is essential to the *polis*, and this is the ultimate reason why the *polis* is destroyed. The insolubility of the Antigone problem, of the family . . . We will come to that. Did you want to ask a question?

Student: I wanted to ask the same question.

LS: I see. Now I wish to remind you briefly of what we discussed last time, and we also have to look at a few passages in last time's assignment. Now the key assertion, to repeat, is that history is a rational or reasonable process. Now there are three ways in which Hegel lays the foundation for that. First, the omnipotence of reason has been proven, according to Hegel's claim, by Hegel in his *Logic*, in his philosophy. This is presupposed. Secondly, Hegel says that this omnipotence of reason is granted by all his students or listeners because it is implied in the belief in providence. And thirdly, the reasonable character of history will be proven *a posteriori*, empirically, in the philosophy of history.

Now the difficulty is this. Reason has to do with universals, with universal ends. History has to do with particulars: nations, conflicts among nations, individuals, their deeds and sufferings. Now this conflict or divergence between the universal and the individual is mediated to some extent by the nation. The nation is something universal, something common, comprehensive, compared with the individual. A nation is constituted by a national mind, the folk-mind, but still it is something particular: the French mind, the . . . mind. But each folk-mind is a part, or facet, or stage of the mind, the world-mind, and this is therefore a reconciliation between the universal and the particular. As regards the individuals in particular, without knowing it they or some of them bring about the work of the world-mind, and that is the doctrine of the world-historical individuals.

This is not in the translation, but Hegel says somewhere here in the original, "the unmoved mover," using the language of Aristotle.[2] The eternally unmoved infinite is . . . and then we have history. What is the connection? The unmoved mover has no consciousness of itself. Consciousness presupposes individuality, the finite ego. But the ego primarily wills itself, its own satisfaction and happiness, its own finite ends; and the question is therefore the way in which the individual is led from his finite ends to the universal absolute. Let us turn to the translation, page 28, in the center. One moment. That was from last time, we did not finish it.

Mr. Reinken:

> This union of the two extremes—the embodiment of a general idea in the form of direct reality, and the elevation of a specialty into connection with universal truth—

LS: That is only the reverse side of the first. How can the individual with his finite, narrow ends become, in a way, the absolute mind by understanding the whole? And the other way round, how can the unmoved mover become conscious of itself?

Mr. Reinken:

> is brought to pass, at first sight, under the conditions of an utter diversity of nature between the two, and an indifference of the one extreme towards the other. The aims which the agents set before them are limited and special—

LS: "Finite" is what it says.

Mr. Reinken:

> but it must be remarked that the agents themselves are intelligent, thinking beings.

LS: Yes, "knowing, thinking beings." So in other words, he wants only to satisfy his interests, say, in food or shelter, nothing else. Very fundamental. But he has intelligence, he thinks about the means of getting food or shelter. And this very fact that he uses intelligence, if only in a very instrumental sense, for these finite purposes, this has infinite consequences because the universality of intelligence itself, of any thinking however instrumental, has infinite consequences.

Mr. Reinken:

> The purport of their desires is interwoven with general, essential considerations of justice, good, duty, etc.—

LS: So in other words, this fellow who is only concerned with food and shelter has to live together with others who also want food and shelter, and then the question arises inevitably sooner or later: Is he entitled to get this piece of food or to find his shelter here or there? By this very fact he is concerned with right, although always only incidentally: he is primarily concerned with food. But the consideration of right is a universal consideration. He has some crude notion of justice, but this crude notion of justice by its dialectics will lead eventually to the full notion of justice. Yes?

Mr. Reinken:

> for mere desire—volition in its rough and savage forms—falls not within the scene and sphere of universal history. Those general considerations which form at the same time a norm for directing aims and actions, have a determinate purport; for such an abstraction as "good for its own sake" has no place in living reality. If men are to act, they must not only intend the good, but must have decided for themselves whether this or that particular thing is a good. What special course of action, however, is good or not is determined, as regards the ordinary contingencies of private life, by the laws and customs of a state. And here no great difficulty is presented. Each individual has his position; he knows on the whole what a just, honorable course of conduct is. As to—[3]

LS: Simply by being a member of society, he learns it from childhood on: this is to be done and this not to be done. Of course there are criminal parents, negligent parents, but they are the exceptions. And therefore, generally speaking, that is so. But here there is something which he omitted: "Every individual is the son of his nation, on a determinate stage of the development of that nation. No one can jump over, or disregard, the spirit of his nation as little as he can disregard or free himself of the earth on which he lives."[4] Let us turn to page 29 in the translation, second paragraph.

Mr. Reinken:

> It is quite otherwise with the comprehensive relations that history has to do with. In this sphere are presented those momentous collisions between existing acknowledged duties, laws and rights, and those contingencies which are adverse to this fixed system, which assail and even destroy its foundations and existence, whose tenor may nevertheless seem good, on the large scale advantageous, yes, even indispensable and necessary. These contingencies realize themselves in history. They involve a general principle of a different order from that on which depends the permanence of a people or a state. This principle is an essential phase in the development of the creating idea, of truth striving and urging towards consciousness of itself. Historical men, world-historical individuals, are those in whose aims such a general principle lies.[5]

LS: Yes, let us stop here. So in other words, in a way it is necessary that the customary morality, the only morality known to the people in question, be questioned, not merely by argument, but by deed. In a sense, this is the deepest crime, a much deeper crime than an ordinary crime, because an ordinary crime does not make doubtful the established order. But the revolutionary, as distinguished from an ordinary criminal, questions the law as a whole and not merely this particular law, if it is even correct that a criminal *does* question a given law. The ordinary murderer does not say that the provision against murder should be abolished but only that he wants to get away with murder. But a revolutionary questions the law as a whole and tries to replace it by another law which he claims to be better, a higher right; but this higher right cannot be accepted except by a break of a radical kind.

Now here is where heroes come in. The crucial conclusion which Hegel draws here is this: that the passions animating the historical heroes are not immoral because they are in the service of that higher right; for the purpose of their passion and of the idea of the universal is the same. The historical hero identifies himself with the great public task. He does not merely abduct that task in order to serve his thirst for immortal fame in the way he looks around for which alignment might be most conducive not merely now but to his immortal fame; rather, he identifies himself with it. Even if Napoleon, for example, sided with the French Revolution or certain versions of the French Revolution only because this was the only thing which promised him great success—obviously, if he had taken the side of the *ancien régime*, he would have been guillotined, or at any rate he wouldn't have become the success he was—so even granting that originally this was a merely calculating identification, it couldn't remain that; he had to identify himself wholeheartedly. In other words, the historical hero is characterized by a passion, but he is a passionate partisan of a cause, and that distinguishes him from the mere climber. Now here the objection arises that the world-mind, so to say, uses human beings as means. When Napoleon or Caesar have fulfilled their function they are just thrown out. Napoleon goes to Helena, no one cares. Caesar is murdered by Brutus and Cassius, it doesn't mean anything. But they have fulfilled their function. This is what he calls the ruse of reason. Now is the use of human beings as means not immoral? Does the world-mind not act immorally? Let us see, page 33, paragraph 2.

Mr. Reinken:

> But though we might tolerate the idea that individuals, their desires and the gratification of them, are thus sacrificed, and their happiness given up to the empire of chance to which it belongs, and that as a general rule, individuals come under the category of means to an ulterior end, there is one aspect of human individuality which we should hesitate to regard in that subordinate light, even in relation to the highest, since it is absolutely no subordinate element, but exists in those individuals, as inherently eternal and divine. I mean morality, ethics, religion. Even when speaking of the realization of the great ideal aim by means of individuals, the subjective element in them—their interests, and that of their cravings and impulses, their views and judgments, though exhibited as the merely formal side of their existence—was spoken of as having an infinite right to be consulted. The first idea that presents itself in speaking of "means" is that of something external to the object, and having no share in the object itself. But merely natural things—even the commonest, lifeless objects—used as means must be of such a kind as adapts them to their purpose; they must possess something in common with it. Human beings least of all sustain the bare external relation of mere means to the great, ideal aim. Not only do they in the very act of realizing it make it the occasion of satisfying

personal desires whose purport is diverse from that aim; but they share in that ideal aim itself, and are for that very reason objects of their own existence, not formally merely, as the world of living beings generally is, whose individual life is essentially subordinate to that of man and is properly used up as an instrument. Men on the contrary are objects of existence to themselves as regards the intrinsic import of the aim in question.[6]

LS: I think we can stop here. The main point should have become clear. Man is as it were an end in himself, Hegel says. But how and why? Surely his nose is not an end in itself. He is an end in himself only by virtue of the divine which is in him, and this is not treated as a means in this use of the individuals by the world-mind, because this divine is a new idea, the new cause: the divine. In other words, the great actors are sacrificed. This is another way of putting the objection: their virtue is not rewarded; hence, no providence. Hegel's answer is in page 34 in the second paragraph.
Mr. Reinken:

In contemplating the fate which virtue, morality, even piety experience in history, we must not fall into the litany of lamentations that the good and pious often, or for the most part, fare ill in the world, while the evil-disposed and the wicked prosper. The term "prosperity" is used in a variety of meanings—riches, outward honor, and the like. But in speaking of something which in and for itself constitutes an aim of existence, that so-called well or ill-faring of these or those isolated individuals cannot be regarded as an essential element in the rational order of the universe. With more justice than happiness—or a fortunate environment for individuals—it is demanded of the grand aim of the world's existence that it should foster, nay, involve the execution and ratification of good, moral, righteous purposes.[7]

LS: And this of course is done in fact. I mean, a higher cause is victorious. And these people who say the good are not rewarded, they are very immoral, because they want to have a reward for their virtue, instead of regarding their virtue as its own reward. Yes?
Mr. Shulsky: Could we just go back a minute to this idea of the use of human beings as means? He says actually the human beings have to have some share in the end towards which they're being used. Doesn't that contradict what he said in other places about the passion of the

world-historical individual? He does seem to be used as a means. He even uses the example of the wind or the fire which is used to make a building, which keeps out the wind and which is fireproof, as the example of what happens to the passions of men when they're used in such a way as to frustrate their purposes.

LS: Which purposes? The irrelevant part of the purposes. Napoleon wished to continue ruling France after he had done his work. Absolutely uninteresting . . . Who cares? But the main point, the Code Napoléon, his new legislation: that was finished, and that stayed.

Mr. Reinken: So he says the good that men do lives after them.

LS: Absolutely. That's what Hegel means in a somewhat unorthodox manner. But as for your objection at the beginning of your statement, namely, more from the point of view of the simple decent man, of the simple honest man—how did you put it? He is, as it were, discredited completely by the world-historical person. Hegel would deny it. He would simply say that he doesn't know that his view of justice is simple-minded, he doesn't know the implicit dialectics; but if he understood what he wants, the victory of right comes about although in a manner in which he would not recognize. By the way, there is something of Plato in that. Here is a very crude notion of justice, say, justice consists in leaving everybody what belongs to him, in giving to everybody what belongs to him. Very simple-minded, of course, but to some extent a very sound view. But difficulties arise there. To take the simple Platonic example: If you give a madman the gun of which he is the rightful owner, is this a just act? No. Then you have to make a distinction here. Just action is not only to give everybody what is his property, but also if there is a reasonable certainty that he will use it well or can use it well. And once you begin, an enormous field develops, and Hegel says when we think that through, no holds barred at any point, then we arrive eventually at the notion of justice codified by Hegel in his *Philosophy of Right*, which is the true order, the just order, and this could never have come into being except by all these revolutions which have taken place throughout history.[8] So in other words, the simplest peasant or herder somewhere in Mesopotamia—no one knows where—what he ultimately wanted without knowing it has now become actual. So he is not disavowed, although he would not recognize the full actualization of what he meant by, say, even sacrificing his children to Baal, which would be wholly incompatible with the rational order of things. But what did he mean by that, ultimately? That there is something higher than the individual, higher than man, which can demand the sacrifice of one's own son—yes, the greatest sacrifice. To some extent that is true, only not in this simplistic way that you sacrifice a child.

Student: Isn't this a question which can only arise from past events too, the relationship between individuals and the world spirit as means and the user? At the present time you couldn't say that the state is committed to sacrifice individuals for the sake of future development. This doesn't legitimize that sort of thing.

LS: Yes, but why?

Student: Because there is no future stage.

LS: Yes. All problems have been solved: the order now existing is just, and therefore this can only be a crackpottish and therefore simply criminal affair. That's the reason. Although violence could go on—I mean, that is after all the Marxist point, and not only but especially the Marxist point: that the order presented by Hegel's *Philosophy of Right* is not the just order, and therefore—

Student: . . . to sacrifice individuals—

LS: Sure.

Student: This is the Marxist—

LS: Yes, no question. And they don't even take this trouble which Hegel took to justify it before the forum of ordinary moral spirit. But they could perhaps say that Hegel did it. You must read Hegel, as Lenin said; study Hegel's *Logic* and then you will become a Marxist-Leninist. Whether it is so simple is another matter. On page 37 in the translation, line 9 following. That is the sentence to which we refer frequently.

Mr. Reinken:

> The religion, the morality of a limited sphere of life—that of the shepherd or a peasant, for example—in its intensive concentration and limitation to a few perfectly simple relations of life, has infinite worth, the same worth as the religion and morality of extensive knowledge and of an existence rich in the compass of its relations and actions. This inner focus, this simple region of the claims of subjective freedom, the home of volition, resolution and action, the abstract sphere of conscience, that which comprises the responsibility and moral value of the individual, remains untouched and is quite shut out from the noisy din of the world's history, including—

LS: You see, he can speak in an almost Kantian manner of the absolute worth of the good will of the individual, as you say. I don't question that.

Mr. Reinken:

including not merely external and temporal changes, but also those entailed by the absolute necessity inseparable from the realization of the idea of freedom itself. But as a general truth, this must be regarded as settled, that whatever in the world possesses claims as noble and glorious, has nevertheless a higher existence above it. The claim of the world spirit rises above all special claims. These observations — [9]

LS: So in other words, the right of the world-mind transcends all particular rights, we can say, like the right of that simple herder and peasant. His good will has an infinite value. Hegel grants that. But precisely if we take his morality seriously, we know that he cannot be interested in a reward for his honesty. Therefore, if he complains about strange things going on in the world — there simply *is* injustice, think of some poor peasant in the Ukraine, and you know this — if he was a decent man, his decency remains unimpaired. What happens now is something much more important. I don't know whether Hegel would have gone so far as to defend the action of Stalin and similar . . . but still there is surely this problem of whether world-historical action can be measured by the standards of private morality, because *Moralität* is the same as private morality.[10] Yes, Mr. Shulsky?

Mr. Shulsky: Presumably what has absolute value about this peasant or this shepherd is the good will and the decency with which he approaches the moral problem, not his particular views. Those presumably would change as history marches on.

LS: Yes, and he simply could not be expected to have thought through these complicated questions. This is simply for him a traditional morality, and ordinary morality is always traditional morality, which is incompetent to question the sufficiency of the tradition.

Mr. Shulsky: In other words, to change the tradition you might have to get rid of him in a violent manner, but that's not saying that he wasn't a good man.

LS: Yes, sure.

Mr. Bruell: Isn't there a greater question of justice involved than the question of the peasant: all the people who existed before Hegel's time, because in a way they were deprived of the opportunity for the future?

LS: But something of this kind is hard to avoid, if you speak of progress in any sense. You have to say that all moralities, all cultures as we say now, that are or ever were are equally good, which is very hard to defend. You know, there is a certain kind of present-day liberal who in effect says that, if not in so many words. This is hard to do for the very simple reason that since most cultures were not liberal, if they say they are as good as a liberal culture, they seem to contradict themselves. So I think one has to make a choice. We all have to do that. And therefore Hegel cannot be blamed because he says the morality of secularized Christianity is the highest above all else, and the proof he claims he will give here. I'm sorry, I've neglected you.

Mr. Hewitt: This was on the same thing. If you say the morality of the peasant or the fisherman or whatever is of infinite value—not necessarily in his judgments or anything like that, that doesn't affect him, but in his attitude—how can the world spirit still be above what he calls infinite here?

LS: This is a repetition of Kant's notion of morality. He says: I see what you mean and I bow down to these simple people who are honest people. There is something very high in that, but it is not the only thing which is high. Even Kant himself, Hegel could say, got into trouble because these simple people of good will are so good and so decent because of their innocence. They are not truly tempted; and as Kant puts it, the trouble with innocence is that it is so easily lost. [Laughter] Therefore it is not enough to be innocent and to be obedient and law-abiding, but you need knowledge or principles. These alone can confirm it. Therefore his whole moral philosophy is necessary to buttress this simple goodness which left to itself would not be good enough. So Hegel could argue here on a Kantian basis, because Kant in a way admits the insufficiency of the simple good will.

Mr. Hewitt: So in a way "infinite" is a way of expressing very high goodness, which is nevertheless still not the highest—

LS: Surely in Hegel it is not meant as literally as in Kant. In Kant it has the simple point which it also had in Rousseau. Obviously for both men, and for many more men, but among the greatest especially for these two men, there was a deep experience, a feeling of humiliation, as it were, which they as men of the mind—and what brilliance, what depth—had when confronted with the simple artisan or peasant who has nothing to do with the marvels of the understanding but is an honest man. That was a terrific thing. I mean, we still can understand that, I believe, and in a way one could understand it at all times. But it took on this crucial philosophical point only in the eighteenth century, in the context in which it seemed to be necessary to ascribe the highest worth to morality in order to be entitled no longer to ascribe it to religion, i.e., to positive religion. If we call the view according to which moral virtue is the highest "moralism," this is the peculiarity of the eighteenth century. The Stoics said something different, although it sounds like that for the very simple reason that for the Stoics part of what virtue is is the virtue of physics and logic: it shows it is not simply identical to moral virtue. But in the eighteenth century, beginning already earlier, moral virtue was regarded as the one thing needful by some very outstanding thinkers—the most famous are surely Rousseau and Kant—and this is questioned by Hegel. Hegel of course is in this sense an old-style philosopher in that the highest is thinking rather than morality: thinking is somehow based on morality, but morality itself is not the highest. But the view that moral virtue is the one thing needful reached the level of philosophical teachings in the eighteenth century and especially in Kant, but Kant himself admitted that he got the decisive impulses in this respect through Rousseau, so we have to mention Rousseau here too. There are others, but the general tendency in these centuries was to find a way out from positive religion—the simple usual explanation is the religious wars, conflict—to find a common basis that all men of good will could agree upon. And for some time of course it was said morality plus natural religion: natural religion as distinguished from revealed religion. But then the great question came, especially raised by Kant: Which comes first? Is our concept of God not in itself dependent on our concept of justice, morality? Can we worship a God who is not just? But then we have to know what justice is: morality. Kant has thought this through more than anybody else. Yes?

Student: On the question of rewards, if I could return to the previous question that we read on the other page: in asking the question about whether the universal idea was doing something immoral to the world-historical figures, you said no, because the greatest things in them were carried on. I was wondering, what about men of lesser vision, men who didn't intend to overthrow the whole order? Like those Caesars after Caesar, whose entire ambitions were realized, when we compare them with Caesar, whose lower ambitions were not realized.

LS: Let's see, whom did you mean now? Do you mean Marcus Aurelius, or what? I mean, the good emperors or the bad emperors?

Student: A bad emperor, let's say Nero.

LS: But you know what happened to him. The moral man in the simple sense cannot be displeased with it, because Nero was—

Student: Let's say a bad man, let's say a tyrant who . . .

LS: There were quite a few.

Student: Now would there be any, did Hegel ever consider why . . .

LS: He would simply say: You are a moral man; why are you concerned with a reward for virtue? And there is a remark, I forgot where, of utter contempt for people who want to be rewarded if they have helped their friend or saved their brother or mother from a terrible situation—what disgusting people! Also if you can't stand the thought that crooks of the first order are prosperous, if it is a matter of general public decency, why don't you vote for the right candidates and see that laws and perhaps also the judicial procedures are changed so that these racketeers don't have the power they have now? That's the sensible thing. But when you go beyond that, is it not some hidden envy of their yachts and dames and so on? [Laughter]

Student: Still Hegel was saying more, Hegel was saying that specifically for the world-historical figures, they should not have their private ambitions satisfied, whereas all others—

LS: No, Hegel only raises this question. This is an objection made by others which Hegel has to meet. He sees no difficulty in that, that there are these great individuals, the heroes who bring about these epoch-making changes and have their satisfaction in bringing about these changes but then are thrown on the rubbish heap of history. That's it. Trotsky said that.

Student: Then there's no particular reason why the world-historical figures should suffer these things and not a petty tyrant.

LS: But only in the case of the world-historical heroes is Hegel confronted with this simplistic popular criticism. If the tyrants are thrown in the dust-heap, like Nero, everybody's satisfied with that, there is no question; but that a man who should have brought about the most salutary changes should then be discarded, that seems to be shocking. Yes?

Student: I don't think that Hegel denies that these heroes are immoral in the ordinary sense of that word. He doesn't meet the objection by saying that they are moral in the ordinary understanding of moral. In this passage we discussed, it doesn't appear to me that he has said that these men are not immoral in the ordinary sense of that term. He speaks of the valet.

LS: No, that is true. In other words, he moralizes them much more—not only than Machiavelli but also than Plato would have done. That is quite true, and he prepares Carlyle's hero worship[11] obviously by this point. It's true. But I think that it is implied in what he says. After all, he knew the crimes which Napoleon had committed.

Student: . . . he may have said were not crimes.

LS: No, I think Hegel would have judged that they were crimes, but that they are not at the same level and that it is a kind of pedantry to measure them. But as a statement of the valet—it speaks as much from my interpretation as from yours—the valet knows the weaknesses of the hero, including the moral weaknesses. All the seamy side of his life—it has a seamy side, we know that. Why does it not also include all the things which at least from a moral point of view are criminal? But this is not the true thing of the hero.

Student: But more than that, it's a question of the problem of the state, which requires immoral acts; and this the valet could not overlook as being immoral, although he might have overlooked intemperance, for example.

LS: Yes, but still the form of the statement is of course more Machiavelli's notion—Romulus killing his brother Remus, this kind of thing, you mean. But in Machiavelli's construction this man is concerned only and fundamentally with his own selfish advancement, his immortal glory; and then he figures out the only way to become immortal is to do services to others which will always be remembered. But he does not identify himself with his services in the way in which he does according to Hegel. In other words, if you mean that Hegel moralizes the hero beyond Machiavelli, I would agree with that. Is this what you meant?

Student: Well, partly.

LS: I'm speaking now from a Khrushchevian point of view. He sits there in his well-built house—

Mr. Reinken: But that's what sets the seal on Khrushchev's individual accomplishment. Russians are beginning to behave like people.

LS: Oh, I see. That's another way of putting it. But still, I wonder whether this is a situation which is according to his own desires. Yes?

Student: Would it be correct to say that Hegel's teaching with respect to history undermines the kind of primitive virtue that he professed to admire?

LS: No, one could put it this way: speaking from Hegel's point of view, he puts it into its place. It is not the highest.

Student: In his point of view, I can see that, yet it strikes me that his reducing, in a sense, of the simple idea of problems through history, however correct it may be, still is an unedifying teaching from the standpoint of the simple man.

LS: Oh, yes, there is no doubt about that.

Student: In that sense, it could be immoral.

LS: Sure. In other words, it could be edifying for the simple man only in the last stage of the development, where his simple morality is now substantially identical with true justice. But one could also say the earliest simple men are not hurt by it because they are dead, and in their times they had already accomplished it. Now let us go on and see whether we can make some progress.

Now history is the actualization of the purpose of reason in and through the individuals. But history presents itself primarily as political history, as the fate of states. This needs some qualification because the state depends on religion. This is a thought which is developed in the sequel; and religion is the fundamental phenomenon, and the relation between religion and the state is now the subject. What is your result regarding which comes out on top, religion or the state?

Student: Well, religion is necessary because morality is the bond of the individual to the state, and he denies the proposition of those who say the religion presupposes the state.

LS: Yes, so religion is the fundamental phenomenon?

Student: Yes.

LS: But does it mean that it is the highest phenomenon? I mean, we are speaking now only of religion and the state.

Student: No, because it is unconscious.

LS: Yes. Now anticipating what follows later, I would say that religion is the fundamental phenomenon, and religion—specifically speaking, Christianity, the absolute religion, in which God has become man—is the union of God and man. Now Hegel's philosophy is the central Christian dogma in its rational form which, in a nonrational form, is Christian religion as such. So in the final secularization of Christianity, which is the fulfillment of Christianity, there the state is surely absolutely necessary. Whether religion as religion is crucial is an open question; we will discuss some passages from the *Philosophy of Religion* later on. This I would like . . . But what is the state is a discussion here: a certain kind of union between reason and the individual. In and through the state the individual becomes himself, i.e., free. Why? Yes?

Student: The state frees him from his own subjectivity, from being bound to his own purely natural life.

LS: Yes, but how does this come out? I mean, the primary phenomenon is desire, and there is a certain kind of desire which we call will. Will is reasonable desire, rational desire—desire in accordance with reason.

But what is a desire in accordance with reason? As we have learned from Rousseau or Kant?

Student: Generalized desire.

LS: Generalized desire. The *volonté générale*, the general will. In merely desiring, for food or whatever, I am not free because I'm pushed and pulled by my stomach, and by some molecules, and whatever it may be. I do not determine myself; I am determined by my stomach. To be free means not to desire but to will; and I will only if I obey the law, the law which is generalized desire, no longer simple desire. Therefore, the state is the actualization of freedom, and not as the people in the eighteenth century thought, that freedom precedes the state. The alternative view is the state of nature. Men are free prior to entering civil society and not after. Hegel rejects that and has asserted sympathy for the so-called patriarchal society, which antedates the state. In the patriarchal society, we overcome merely selfish desire, and dedication to the whole is to be found there.[12] But why is Hegel not satisfied with the patriarchal society? Yes?

Mr. Hewitt: Because that's not a self-conscious society?

LS: Yes. It is so to speak instinctive rather than rational.

Mr. Hewitt: Is he thinking primarily of China or of the Chinese?

LS: No, I think he has in mind certain theories about patriarchal societies advanced by some romantics.

Mr. Hewitt: Well, I was thinking the kind of relationships he talks about within the family sounds like traditional Chinese.

LS: That could be. There will be a long discussion of China later. Yes, these passages were discussed by you; the fundamental distinction between the state on the one hand, and religion, art, and philosophy on the other. Religion is primary but religion is not the highest. The highest is philosophy.

Mr. Hewitt: There's a difficulty in regard to those distinctions at one point. He talks of religion or of philosophy and art being developmental— they build up what came before, whereas a political constitution does not depend on what came before. It's unique.

LS: I remember that you quoted that, and I didn't remember the passage in Hegel. Do you know where it is?

Mr. Hewitt: Yes, page 47 in our text, in the middle of the page.

LS: That is a discussion of patriarchal society?

Mr. Hewitt: No, he's talking about the constitution. This underlined passage.

LS: Ja, I remember. On page 47. What does he mean by that?

Mr. Hewitt: What I got out of it is that science and art develop continually through history, but political things don't, they're proper to a given age and people.

LS: Could it not be that Hegel means something more limited? Imitators of Greek art, German philosophy, poetry, give something very different, say, from the French Jacobins who tried to imitate ancient Romans. Hegel is speaking on this rather external level; that the imitation of ancient art and philosophy is something more defensible than the imitation of ancient political institutions because in the ancient political institutions, to take the most simple example, slavery was allowed, and the Jacobins didn't think of reintroducing slavery. That's a completely different thing, whereas on the level of art and philosophy, it has a greater possibility. I don't say that this suffices, because underlying that is Hegel's fundamental distinction between the kinds of mind: there is a subjective mind, the subject of psychology; the objective mind, that is the state and society; and the absolute mind, religion, art, and philosophy. Hegel cannot possibly have deified the state, because the state is on a definitely lower level than religion, art, and philosophy.[13] That's clear. It is surely connected. Mr. Shulsky?

Mr. Shulsky: What I got out of that was the idea that as philosophy develops, the principles which have been transcended are still part of philosophy, because otherwise one wouldn't understand the higher principles. But since the state is just the latest principle, each stage is the principle of the state, you couldn't look back to the previous states and try to imitate them, whereas in philosophy, in order to understand this succession, you have to understand the Greek philosophy as the Greeks do it and then transcend it.

LS: But in a way you say more clearly what I tried to say, namely, this: when we speak of political things, we think primarily of action. And when we think of philosophy, to take the clearest case, we think of thinking. Now in the sphere of action, an imitation or reactivation of classical antiquity is absurd; but in the sphere of thinking, a reactivation of classical antiquity is absolutely essential if we want to understand our own thought. On this page—this is not in the translation—he refers to Montesquieu.[14] Now Montesquieu was more responsible than anyone else for the notion of the folk-mind. Therefore it is very important to emphasize what Hegel does not do. For Montesquieu, the folk-mind is the product of n factors: climate, population, character, nature of the territory, the fates of that particular nation, and so on. So the folk-mind is a product. For Hegel it is the origin of everything else in the nation, and therefore Hegel's meaning is radically different. But the practical conclusions are not so very different, against the traditional notion of political philosophy as Mr. Hewitt points out. It is impossible to treat the political constitution, the political order of a country, in isolation from its spirit, a spirit expressing itself especially in its religion, and therefore the classical notion—at least the apparently classical notion—that the political question can be treated in isolation is fundamentally wrong.

Mr. Shulsky: Could you just comment on the relation of this to Aristotle's notion of the regime, which also goes beyond the simple state? I mean, certainly he didn't say there was a state and then that everything else was part of it.

LS: Sure, but what is a regime? I mean, every society is a multitude of human beings. But this multitude of human beings is as such the matter, the *hyle*, and it is given a form by the regime. Aristotle uses the example of fifty men, and they are now used as a tragic chorus, and tomorrow it is a comic chorus. They are the same men: the matter is the same but these are two essentially different choruses, two essentially different societies, because they are ordered differently, with a view to a different purpose. So if you have a multitude of men, they may be ordered—let us take the simplest example, in a linear manner—each man counts as much as everybody else: democracy. And you can have it in a pyramidal form, going up to one head; this would be monarchy, and aristocracy would be something in between. And you can make all kinds of subdivisions. Now the regime is characterized by the quality or the characteristics of the group of the kind of men who set the tone of that society in broad daylight. I mean, not like the people in Hollywood now, who in a certain sense can be said to set the tone of the society, but the people who actually set the tone by ruling, by giving the laws. And so the form is inseparable from the end. The kind of men is characterized by that to which they are dedicated. If they are oligarchs, then they are dedicated to wealth, and this gives the society its character. If they are aristocrats—I take the deceptively simplistic formula—they are dedicated to virtue, and the end of the society which they control is virtue. Is this what you meant?

Mr. Shulsky: Yes.

LS: Now where does Hegel come in? I discussed this question in a different way—but it is fundamentally the same question—in my course on Comte.[15]

Mr. Shulsky: The question then becomes—certainly Aristotle wouldn't have thought that you could just change things by simply changing the government, where you could deliberate on the best form of government, that would be unrelated to what we might call now the culture. This was the Hegelian—

LS: But there is no concept of culture in Aristotle. For better or worse, it doesn't exist.

Mr. Shulsky: Well, put it this way. Hegel seems to be arguing directly against the idea that you could simply construct a government regardless of what the people think.

LS: Aristotle would grant that, of course.

Mr. Shulsky: Aristotle would grant that, too, so there's at least that much in common.

LS: Yes, but still there is a very profound difference. Yes?

Mr. Hewitt: Well, there seems to be a peculiarly modern notion here, that you can have political constitution in the abstract. Hegel seems to be talking against that.

LS: Sure. In other words, against certain simplistic men like Tom Paine, Aristotle and Hegel are in agreement. Therefore we are now concerned with the difference between Aristotle and Hegel. Yes?

Mr. Shulsky: Well, put it this way. Could you formulate the differences as being this: that for Aristotle, you have a regime which one way or another you enforce on the society and that sets the whole tone, so it's the constitution of the regime that is the important thing, and things follow from that?

LS: Not quite, but there must be a certain aptitude of the matter; if not, it wouldn't work. No, that is not the fundamental difference. I mean, surely Hegel is, you can say, more quietistic, more passivistic than Aristotle, but this is only a difference of degree, not an essential difference. What is the fundamental difference? When Aristotle speaks about such things as the city and the regime, there is a broader background which is not necessarily of importance within the moral-political considerations but is somehow there; and without it, Aristotle could never have written the *Ethics* and the *Politics*. What is it?

Mr. Shulsky: The idea of the specific aim of the regime.

LS: No, that is intrapolitical; but we're speaking from the broader, the more comprehensive—

Mr. Reinken: Last time the answer was natural right.

LS: This is also too limited, because natural right is itself a political part.

Mr. Hewitt: There is a single Greek culture.

LS: Oh no! That is modern and wholly unancient.

Student: The natural ends of man?

LS: Beyond that, nature as a cosmos. And in Hegel there is no cosmos; you can say there is no cosmos proper. The material universe, as it is called, is of no great importance for Hegel, but the place—I speak now provisionally—of *physis* or cosmos is taken in Hegel by the historical process. Therefore the cultures, if one uses post-Hegelian terms, are the Hegelian or Comtean or modern substitute for *physis*. That is the question. Let me state it somewhat differently, more precisely perhaps. The classical notion of *physis*, of nature, is inseparable from the concept of *nomos*. I know that this is not the textbook version which says that this is an invention of the sophists, but this is simply not true of *nomos*, of man-made establishments, conventions, and they are understood here as fundamentally arbitrary. Now of course it was admitted there is an indefinite variety of such *nomoi*, but no particular order in that. One could perhaps try to say why the Persians conceive of their gods in this way and the Egyptians in that way, how is it connected; one could do it, but this wouldn't do away fundamentally with the arbitrary character. Now what Hegel implies, if I try to state it now in classical terms, is that the sequence of the *nomoi*—China, India, etc.—this is the true *physis*, the absolute. In other words, that is the simplest form. There is therefore a radical change of course in the approach to political things.

Mr. Shulsky: But then presumably this way in which we use a culture or a civilization nowadays is different from Hegel because somehow the center has been taken out, there's no longer the spirit which guides everything but sort of an amorphous mass.

LS: Yes, you can say that. It is perhaps a bit harsh. But I would put it this way. For Hegel, what we now call culture has a definite hierarchy, and religion has the central position. But the present-day view of a culture is egalitarian. There are *n* elements—morality, economics, mores, laws, government, arts and crafts, skills, I don't know what, the language structure I suppose also—*n* things. And one has no right whatever to say one of these elements is more important or interesting than the other, except from the purely subjective point of view. Some people like art more than they like technology and so they will study the arts, but in themselves they are all equal. This egalitarian conception is now certainly prevailing.

Mr. Shulsky: Certainly post-Hegelian.

LS: The difficulties can easily be seen because you cannot delimit a culture anymore. You have to speak of subcultures, and the line between a culture and a subculture is not always kept. They speak of the cultures of juvenile delinquents in Chicago; there may be a different one in Boston or in St. Louis. In other words, it becomes ever more meaningless; the connection between culture and the noblest things which it originally had is lost. And then, I do not know how I get . . . and there are *n* cultures and they are from the point of view of social science absolutely equal, because any preference would be subjective. That was not yet so in Hegel. And this notion developed in the nineteenth century more and more and is now absolutely . . . I have not studied the anthropological literature, but I believe that Ruth Benedict[16] plays a considerable role in making the concept of culture so popular. *Patterns of Culture*, I believe, is the book. It is required reading in our College, if I'm not mistaken, and still a basic work. Now in her case it is very clear. As she says in her preface, if I remember well, her whole thought was due to stimulation by Spengler in his *Decline of the West*. It is interesting, whatever you may say against Spengler—and many things can be said against him—Spengler's folk meant only high cultures; I forgot how many, six or eight. Whereas in Ruth Benedict, any culture is a culture—in other words, two different North American tribes of Indians, the one gentle and the other savage, which is a favorite example of hers, which is of course a sign that the concept of high culture is lost. And the consequence is that you have to use strictly superficial distinctions now, like preliterate and literate, not to say underdeveloped and developed. They have found a new one: emerging and nonemerging. It is very interesting to see how here the strictly scientific motivation, no value judgments, goes along with a democratic, i.e., value-inspired motivation not to hurt anybody's feelings. There is no doubt that this is part of the story, but it is very strange, this preestablished harmony between strict scientific objectivity and an extreme version of democracy. It gives food for thought.

Now I have expatiated a bit about things different from Hegel, but since we have no access to Hegel—or to anything, for that matter, if we do not think about ourselves and our opinions—this kind of reflection is not extraneous to our study. I hope you are aware of that.

4   Historical Understanding and the Folk-Mind

Leo Strauss: [in progress]—you mentioned at the end,[1] America the land of the future is indeed crucial to us, as we shall see later. Because if this is Hegel's last word, then he has to be understood as some people do understand him, that Hegel does not claim the end of history has come. Only since we cannot know anything about the future must we therefore stop in the present. We will take this up later. I would like to raise another question. You began by stating to us Hegel's criticism of simple empiricism, the idea that you can just look at things without any preconceived notion. In the late nineteenth century, people spoke of a science without any presuppositions. Now I think today this notion is generally dropped, but empiricism simply understood would be a science without any presuppositions except those which arise while we look at the fact. And in this connection there was a switch from this notion, from this criticism of simple empiricism to a criticism of the wrong kind of generalities. Some people say morality is always the same, and epic poetry is to be found in India as well as in Greece and the difference is therefore not important. What is the connection between the two criticisms?

Mr. Shulsky: Well, the first, he says that when people allege the criticism of philosophic history as insinuating an idea, they are taking the basis that no ideas at all . . .

LS: Yes, and how do we go on from here to the criticism of these false generalities?

Mr. Shulsky: Well, this again I think goes back to our earlier statement that the essential part of history—that it is an idea that reveals itself in successive stages—is proved already; and this is the essential way in which we must look at history, and these other ways of looking at it will yield nothing. But this is a result of the *Logic*.

LS: But since Hegel promises to some extent that he would prove his philosophy of history independently of the *Logic*—

Mr. Shulsky: Well, that's coming in the sequel, though, when he shows that this is the principle—

LS: But he would have to give us an inkling of how he proceeds. And it is absolutely in the spirit of Hegel to have such a kind of empirical procedure. How would this come about? Now as to the question which I just raised, the connection is probably this: these people say they proceed strictly empirically, but because it is impossible to understand anything without concepts, the result is simply that they will get the wrong kinds of concepts, and in particular such concepts which do not make allowance for diversity and see only the things which you find everywhere and which will never make you understand history, i.e., variation, difference, change. But how could one proceed empirically? Hegel says that freedom, in this full sense in which he means it, is the key. Now what is behind that? I mean, what very simple reasoning is behind that, without going into all the subtleties?

Mr. Shulsky: That reason is the most potent force in the world and hence would have to be revealed in the world's history.

LS: Yes, but perhaps somewhat more precisely, the essence of man is freedom, and therefore if we look at human affairs, history, we have to look at it from the point of view of freedom. What is the traditional definition of man?

Mr. Shulsky: That he is a composite of reason and of passions which are unreasonable.

LS: What is the simple sentence which has been quoted throughout the ages?

Student: A political animal.

LS: A rational animal. And therefore we have to look at rationality, because animality as such would not explain it, because otherwise there would also be a history of horses, rats, microbes, and so on, which is not likely to be the case. But as for the replacing of rationality by freedom, is this the invention of Hegel? Does anyone know that? There was a very famous man prior to Hegel who explicitly attacked the definition of man as a rational animal and said, no, the specific difference is not rationality but freedom.

Student: Rousseau.

LS: Yes. Do you know where?

Student: The *Second Discourse*.

LS: Yes, thanks. I mean whatever Rousseau meant by it, but at first glance surely that seems to be the basis for what Hegel has in mind. But let us assume that we do not know that man is a free being; maybe he is distinguished by rationality or something else. If we would proceed in a purely empirical manner, because Hegel is somehow trying that, how could one do that without making any assumptions outside of the subject matter, being loyal to the phenomena which we are studying and not distorting them from a point of view alien to them? How would one have to proceed? Yes?

Mr. Shulsky: You would have to try to understand each successive society as it understood itself, at least in terms of its own philosophy and its religion, and then—

LS: Yes, but how do you proceed? That is not so simple. I mean, people do that today with, how do you call it, Gallup polls and other questionnaires of sorts, which it is true you cannot address to dead people. Nor can you address them to people who are not—that the governments do not permit you to, and this would have been the case in most societies of the past. But how can you do that—I mean, which is probably not sufficient but which is surely an objective beginning?

Mr. Shulsky: Well, of course this is already in a way using his theory, but not in any crucial way. You would have to look at those men in the society who, coming so to speak late in the development, were the ones who reflected on the whole development and hence thought the spirit of their own age and put it into writing.

LS: Yes, as he says, if you want to know what Greece—read Thucydides. All right, that is a very good example. But if you read Thucydides, you learn a lot about Athens and Sparta and many more things. But about one thing you learn almost nothing, except a little bit.

Mr. Reinken: The Greek mind?

LS: Yes, but I mean something more special. What according to Hegel is the most important thing by which the folk-mind is what it is?

Mr. Shulsky: Consciousness of freedom.

LS: No, more fundamental.

Mr. Reinken: Religion.

LS: Religion. What do you learn of Greek religion from Thucydides? Well, if you read him, study him very thoroughly and listen to every overtone, you learn a bit. But otherwise you don't learn anything because that is exactly the meaning of the book, to show that the Peloponnesian war, in contradistinction to the Trojan war, took place without any divine interference. And Thucydides even suggests that this is the key to the Trojan war: as little as Athena and Zeus, or Apollo for that matter, interfered in the Peloponnesian war, when he was an eyewitness, as little did the gods interfere in the Trojan war. That was a Homeric, a poetic adornment, that was not . . . wouldn't be good enough. But we have already the answer implied. I mean, but of course one can say, prior to study, why should religion be the fundamental phenomenon? So there must be a more elementary consideration which Hegel does not bring out but which he implies. I think this is the premise in a simpler manner: we understand a man or a group of men if we look in the first place at what they look up to, to what they are dedicated. They will of course fall short of it, that goes without saying, but still this gives the hint, gives us the best clue to what they are: what they will, what they esteem, or, to use the language of the present day, what their values are. So we have to begin from that, and this is not a very difficult thing because it is written large everywhere—the law books, the official documents, written or unwritten, that does not enter into it—that can easily be found out. I have been told by a student of Chinese things that the Chinese travelers who wrote books about the neighboring barbarians, as they called them, asked the people they visited first: How do you bow to your kings? This is a more special version of that. Men have to bow to something, and of course they would bow to their kings.[2] But how? But we have to generalize that properly. You see these Chinese travelers were in a way quite thoughtful men, and that . . . are dedicated. And if there should be people who are not dedicated to anything, a possibility which Hegel will discuss—we will see that next time—they are in a way not yet human beings. There are such individuals or maybe even societies, but the world-historical nations, as Hegel calls them, they have all dedicated themselves to something. And by this they even tacitly admitted Hegel's philosophy of history, because since these things changed—I mean, Zeus was out at a certain time along with his whole family—then it is in the logic of their submission that they must go over from Zeus to another worship, although the empirical Greece didn't do that, but this is a minor thing.

This is very roughly what Hegel has in mind. We do not say that this and this is the most important—economics, relations of production, or art or . . . No, we ask the people themselves: What do you regard as most important? And we do not make simple statistics and ask some people who are perhaps too foolish to understand our question; we ask the most intelligent and the most authoritative men, the men who are most entitled to be regarded as spokesmen for that society. Then we are as objective and as empirical as we can be. And what Hegel claims, then, if we look at these nations, these cultures as they are called today, and get this massive information about these things, then we will see that without our manipulating the evidence, these answers order themselves into a certain sequence which is intelligible. This is Hegel's assertion at least. But the starting point, I think, is empirical. Yes?

Student: But isn't our conception of an intelligent man that he is not like a common man? We wouldn't be studying the aspirations of the common people by studying the aspirations of the intelligent men.

LS: That depends. Do you believe that if, say, a Homer says that Zeus is the father of gods and men, the common men would say: No, but Heracles is the father of gods and men? Of course not. In other words, there would be no difference. But the common man might sometimes have difficulties in understanding such a question. Take a very simple case. Let us assume there is still—there is no longer, I suppose—a small island in the South Seas, and an anthropologist comes to study the people there to find out about their mores and about their way of thinking and so on. Can these people understand that? I mean, they could understand someone coming to them in order to trade with them or because he has been guilty of murder in his homeland and has to escape and find refuge with them, and other motives of the same kind. But that someone should come only in order to find out what they think, that they simply would never understand. The mere fact that the anthropologist enters the island changes the island to the extent to which this is understood, because then the whole framework is in a way destroyed by the realization of such a possibility: to understand a very simple question which the common man could answer but which he might not be able to understand as it is meant, but the more reflective man would understand that. It is only in this sense that I mean it. Yes?

Mr. Shulsky: I think, though, there's the point that if you wanted to apply this principle to modern-day America, it would get more difficult because there you would find more people who would say that their values are such, but of course the common man is only interested in money. It would be more difficult to get at the basis of what they all—

LS: There is no question that a society which is constituted by the official knowledge or admission that there is such a thing as science is a different society. But where do we find that? I mean, we are so spoiled by the many centuries of the Western world. But even if we look at earlier Greece or, for that matter, earlier Rome, how distrusted and misunderstood the people were who said we want to understand and nothing else.

Today that is taken for granted: every boy and girl learns it in the first grade of elementary school. Don't ask me how well he understands it, but he at least has some awareness, intelligibility or familiarity. But nevertheless, although it is the case most familiar to us, it is a very special case because society is not defined as such by the presence within it of theoretical men, but only if you use a very loose word like intellectuals. And say a shaman in Siberia is fundamentally the same as what a professor is in the United States now, and that is I think still based on a profound misunderstanding of what science is. Yes?

Student: Isn't there a problem involved in maintaining on the one hand that the way to understand past ages is to understand what people in them looked up to, and on the other hand to maintain, first of all, that most of the people of the age, people who actually carried things out, were actually unconscious of what they were doing was leading to, that the world-historical heroes had more limited motives than what we see they accomplished, and even that the philosophers who came at the end of the age could not see really what all this was leading to? Is it really possible to understand people of an age as they understood themselves, and on the other hand to say that they really didn't understand what they were accomplishing?

LS: That is another question, whether it is possible to understand other people, another society, as they understood themselves. For Hegel there is no question that it is possible. Let us disregard it. We may take up this question on another occasion, but for Hegel it is taken for granted. But otherwise, if we disregard then this issue which falls outside of Hegel, I do not see your difficulty. For example, regarding the Greek gods: this antedates the philosophers by far. Speaking from an older point of view than that of Hegel, we have Homer and Hesiod and the tragic poets. Here we can know what goes on; the presupposition of these works is that this is not a specialty of the poets, but something that all their listeners knew as a matter of course. What does the figure of Apollo or Athena mean in Homer and so on, if these are not figures of which everyone knew in a way? Homer might have known more about them and might have been able to tell stories about them which not every Greek could tell—I take this for granted—but that there were such beings and that they had fundamentally these characteristics which they have in Homer, that was, I think, presupposed. I see no difficulty there. I mean, I think that Plato meant something else by Athena and Zeus than the ordinary Greek men. But how do we know that? Answer: by reading Plato. And here it is clear from the context that this is already something which is no longer commonly accepted or popular; it is very true that Socrates was condemned for not accepting the gods as the city understood them. This is also a simple fact of history, there is nothing subtle in that. I mean, there are many, many questions of the greatest subtleties which arise on that basis, but the proposition itself, I believe, is simple and commonsensical. I would be grateful if you gave me an example which obstructs this attempt so to speak at the beginning.

Student: Maybe I'm bringing in something which is beyond the question simply of whether Hegel will understand these people on the basis . . .

LS: No, that would be a question which we would have to consider, whether Hegel manipulates the evidences. If he does that, that is too bad, but then he is disloyal to his own intention. But the question is that this evidence is not a far-fetched thing. They found digging up somewhere an inscription which throws an entirely new light on the Greek gods, but Hegel is not interested in that and he makes this perfectly clear. Because if it were such a far-fetched thing which could only be brought out by this particular thing, it would not have been a public power in Greece. In other words, how far these gods were already of Oriental origin, that is not relevant; for the Greeks, they were the gods on Olympus and worshiped by the Greeks above all, although the other nations also knew of them in a way, having other names for them and so on. One has to stick to that first. It is not so difficult, I mean, it is surely not far-fetched for Hegel. Now is there any other point? Mr. . . . .

Student: Mr. Strauss, doesn't this presuppose at least in a historical context that the way to understand another people or the evidence that this person would take is necessarily written evidence?

LS: Yes, I believe so. Or at least written either by the people themselves or written down when there was still time. Let us assume there is an illiterate tribe, and some literate traveler goes there and tells us the answers which he received to his questions. This we would accept. Yes, there is this virtue of writing that cannot well be denied, that this is the only way in which these things are accessible to later ages which are not connected through an oral tradition with the people concerned.

Student: The apparent problem, at least in my mind, is that these then become essentially public statements. They are sort of common property.

LS: Yes, public, therefore this makes them easily accessible.

Student: This makes them easily accessible to the historian. How valid is this understanding first of all of an individual and secondly of a group of individuals by their public statements?

LS: All right. That is naturally a question which we must raise, but one could say that one has the right to raise this question only after it is made clear what the explicit opinions and public opinions were. If you find out, say, in Egypt or Mesopotamia or wherever that you had a certain teaching regarding the gods, and then you find out—also of course by written evidence, how else could you?—that the priests had a secret teaching in which they regarded this public teaching as sheer opium for the people, then we have to take cognizance of that. That goes without saying. That is clear, but this needs proof. The primary thing, clear as the day, is that this was what the Egyptians and Mesopotamians believed, held, and we have to start from that, even as a psychoanalyst must start from the manifest content of dreams before he can interpret them. Even a Marxist must start from the manifest superstructure, laws or whatever they may be, before he can find out how this is related to the true thing, the substructure, the infrastructure. That is clear. But we must start from the manifest by all means; from the known we must go to the unknown, proceed to the unknown and not the other way around. I once heard of a psychoanalytical writer who tried to explain the fact of sexual desire by the fact—he was speaking only of the man—that they desired to return to their mother's womb, which is a beautiful example of explanation of the known by the unknown [laughter] because the whole psychoanalytic theory would not be possible if there were not sexual desires in the first place. I mean desires of a male man for a female human being; that is the absolute starting point. But if this has to be explained by such an inferred desire for grown-up men to return to their mother's womb, then anything goes. [Laughter]

There is a passage for last time's assignment which we have not discussed, to which we should pay an attention. It is in page 57 of the translation. What Hegel says here about the beginning of history, Mr. Hewitt, you remember, what is the point which he makes here?

Mr. Hewitt: He makes the point that history begins with the state and not with the individual man or even with family-societies or clan-based societies.

LS: No, that is not the main point here in this first part when he refers here to Schelling and Schlegel;[3] people have asserted the existence of a primitive people from which all science and art, has only been . . . This original nation antedates the human race proper and is eternalized in the old myth under the image of gods: in other words, there was a perfect beginning. This is the view which Hegel attacks. The beginnings are imperfect. Now Hegel of course mentions here only some theories of contemporaries, but it has a much broader bearing naturally. Yes?

Mr. Shulsky: The Bible, the old biblical account.

LS: The biblical account? Surely not Adam and Eve, with perfect knowledge and in addition perhaps divine graces, but Hobbes rather—the Hobbean men, rather, are at the beginning. That is absolutely crucial. Otherwise, how could the whole history be a history of progress? This point we must at least mention. Then let us turn to page 63, line 4 from bottom.

Mr. Reinken: "Here we need adopt one of history's logical results, viz., that every step in the process—"

LS: Can you begin before, when he speaks of logic? A little bit before?

Mr. Reinken:

> The logical, and as still more prominent, the dialectical nature of the idea in general, viz., that it is self-determined, that it assumes successive forms which it successively transcends, and by this very process of transcending its earlier stages, gains an affirmative and, in fact, a richer and more concrete shape—this necessity of its nature and the necessary series of pure abstract forms which the idea successively assumes is exhibited in the department of logic.

LS: Yes, but in the German it is "in logic," not the department of logic. But in this case one seems to know that this is a correction by Hegel's son, and Hegel himself wrote "in philosophy." So in other words, this somewhat schoolmasterly departmentalization is not Hegel's work. So this fundamental character of the idea of the concept is known in philosophy, and here meaning the philosophy of history. We have to accept only this. Go on.

Mr. Reinken:

> Here we need adopt only one of its results, viz., that every step in the process, as differing from any other, has its determinate peculiar principle. In history this principle is idiosyncrasy of spirit—

LS: That is a bit too fancy: "the peculiarity of the spirit, the people." In other words, there Hegel has shown that there is an order of concepts, let us say, in the logic, the order of concepts which follow each other necessarily, and this of course does not immediately concern us here. But one thing we must accept is that there is an order, a necessary order, and the necessary order we have to do with in history is the necessary order in which the folk-minds follow each other.

Mr. Reinken:

> peculiar national genius. It is within the limitations of this peculiarity that the spirit of the nation, concretely manifested, expresses every aspect of its consciousness and will, the whole cycle of its realization. Its religion, its polity, its ethics, its legislation, and even its science, art and mechanical skill all bear its stamp.

LS: In other words, science too is a part of the folk-mind. Strictly understood, that would mean there is no universal science. Greek science is not modern science. Yes?

Mr. Reinken:

> These special peculiarities find their key in that common peculiarity, the particular principle that characterizes a people; as, on the other hand, in the facts which history presents in detail, that common characteristic principle may be detected.

LS: In other words, say, a treaty, a battle, are things which occur everywhere, but Greek treaties, Greek battles are somehow Greek, and Babylonian battles—to some extent even the things which go through everywhere will be affected by the peculiar spirit of the people within which they take place.

Mr. Reinken:

> That such and such a specific quality constitutes the peculiar genius of a people is the element of our inquiry which must be derived from experience and historically proved.

LS: So in other words this cannot be taken over from any preceding discipline, like logic and such. So in other words, here we are on our own and cannot refer to Hegel, to the *Logic*, but what is the difficulty here? I mean what is the problem, how do we proceed empirically?

Mr. Reinken:

To accomplish this presupposes not only a disciplined faculty of abstraction, but an intimate acquaintance with the idea. The investigator must be familiar *a priori* (if we like to call it so) with the whole circle of questions to which the principles in question belong.[4]

LS: And so on. And as he explains later, to state it differently, however empirically we wish to proceed—and we want to proceed empirically—we must be able to distinguish between the important and the unimportant, the essential and unessential, and mere *empeiria* doesn't tell us anything. Things don't run around with a tag, "I am essential" or "I am unessential." [Laughter] So therefore there is no *empeiria* without preceding principles of relevance, without preceding concepts. So in other words, philosophy of history cannot be simply independent of philosophy, but this is only here stated in a very general way. One must have some awareness of the essential, and here he speaks of the fundamental ambiguity regarding the essential. It is differently understood by intelligence, *Verstand* in German, and by reason, in German *Vernunft*. The lower form of understanding is based on, starts from the fact that there is an unchangeable human nature, which on a certain level is true. For example, there could not have been any human life without such things as the memory, and there is no reason to assume that the memory differs in the different cultures. And therefore if there is a psychological study of the memory, this would be equally valid for all cases. But this is a lower level of understanding. The higher level is based on the insight that it is of the essence of human nature to change. Man is always thinking, one can say, but he is not always thinking the same. The content of his thinking radically changes, and it is with this content that we are concerned. Therefore Hegel calls this "concrete" versus the abstract way in which we disregard the content when we analyze, for example, processes of retention, processes of reasoning, without consideration of the content. In other words, for the *Verstand*, for the lower, the content comes from elsewhere. As you see very clearly in formal logic, rules of reasoning are here, but the content must come from elsewhere. I mean, formal logic doesn't tell you that the syllogism which is impeccable in form is wrong in matter. Take any simple foolish formally correct syllogism: "All geese roar; all men are geese; hence, all men roar." See? And obviously both premises are materially wrong. Formal logic doesn't tell you that. But *Vernunft* in Hegel's sense produces its content as well as the form. Let us turn to page 65 in the second paragraph.

Mr. Reinken:

A similar process of reasoning is adopted in reference to the correct assertion that genius, talent, moral virtues, and sentiments, and piety may be found in every zone, under all political constitutions and conditions, in confirmation of which examples are forthcoming in abundance. If in this assertion the accompanying distinctions are intended to be repudiated as unimportant or nonessential, reflection evidently limits itself to abstract categories and ignores the specialties of the object in question, which certainly fall under no principle recognized by such categories.[5]

LS: This is another illustration. Hegel doesn't deny that this is true. This is correctly said, that genius, talent, moral virtues and sentiments, etc., can be found everywhere. But the differences are here disregarded: the differences, what is the object of the genius, of moral virtues, talent and so on in different cultures, this is what truly counts. Now one form of this disregard of the concrete, the changing, is moralism, the belief that there is a universally valid moral law in the light of which all human actions have to be judged, a law as accessible to a Chinese as to a Westerner or anyone else. That moral law is formal. It does not determine the content. For example, it is compatible with slavery, with serfdom, or with the denial of the legitimacy of either slavery or serfdom. You can be an honest slave owner, you can be an honest feudal lord with serfs, you can be an honest and loyal free laborer. And you can be an honest slave, you can be an honest serf, you can be an honest wage earner; it is unaffected by that, and yet does it not make ultimately a moral difference whether there is an institution of slavery and of serfdom, or the denial of both? The fully moral content is brought about by action which may be action against the moral law—we have discussed this subject—against the formal law. On page 62 in your translation, will you read that?

Mr. Reinken: "Universal history" after these remarks?

LS: May I see? Here, 66. I'm sorry.

Mr. Reinken: Bottom of the page.

We may fairly decline on this occasion the task of tracing the formalism and error of such a view and establishing the true principles of morality or rather of social virtue, in opposition to false morality—

LS: And what is this? Social virtue is *Sittlichkeit* in German. We have discussed this difference last time. Yes?

Mr. Reinken:

For the history of the world occupies a higher ground than that on which morality has properly its position, which is personal character, the conscience of individuals.

LS: Yes. He says "private," which is a *Privatgesinnung*, private moral sentiment. It is ethically private, not public, because if it were public then the content would come in, the content of the morality of the social order in which it takes place. Yes?
Mr. Reinken:

their particular will and mode of action. These have a value imputation, reward or punishment proper to themselves. What the absolute aim of spirit requires and accomplishes—what Providence does—transcends the obligations, and the liability to imputation and the ascription of good or bad motives, which attach to individuality in virtue of its social relations. They who on moral grounds, and consequently with noble intention, have resisted that which the advance of the spiritual idea makes necessary, stand higher in moral worth than those whose crimes have been turned into the means—under the direction of a superior principle—of realizing the purposes of that principle. But in such revolutions, both parties generally stand within the limits of the same circle of transient and corruptible existence. Consequently, it is only a formal rectitude, deserted by the living spirit and by God, which those who stand upon ancient right and order maintain. The deeds of great men, who are the individuals of the world's history, thus appear not only justified in view of that intrinsic result of which they were not conscious, but also from the point of view occupied by the secular moralist. But looked at from this point, moral claims that are irrelevant must not be brought into collision with world-historical deeds and their accomplishment. The litany of private virtues—modesty, humility, philanthropy, and forbearance—must not be raised against them.[6]

LS: And so on. I think we have discussed this last time. But it was necessary to read this passage. Now let us turn to page 69 in the second paragraph, where he begins to speak of philosophy.
Mr. Reinken:

Philosophy also must make its appearance where political life exists; since that in virtue of which any series of phenomena is reduced within the sphere of culture, as above stated, is the form strictly proper to thought.

And thus for philosophy, which is nothing other than the consciousness of this form itself—the thinking of thinking—the material of which its edifice is to be constructed is already prepared by general culture. If in the development of the state itself periods are necessitated which impel the soul of nobler natures to seek refuge from the present in ideal regions—in order to find in them that harmony with itself which it can no longer enjoy in the discordant real world, where the reflective intelligence attacks all that is holy and deep, which had been spontaneously inwrought into the religion, laws and manners of nations, and brings them down and attenuates them to abstract godless generalities—thought will be compelled to become thinking reason, with the view of effecting in its own element, the restoration of its principles from the ruin to which they had been brought.[7]

LS: Yes, "to bring about in its own element the restoration or the healing of the corruption to which it has brought itself." Does this not remind you of an earlier passage which we have discussed, but somehow at variance with it? Originally, thinking unconsciously produces these laws and orders and religion, and then these gods are no longer worshiped. They were in the good old times, and thinking has something to do with that corruption. Thinking produces these gods, and yet thinking also endangers them. And then there is a third stage in which another kind of thinking, a less abstract, less formal kind of thinking puts a stop to that dissolving, disintegrating thinking and therewith saves the old order on a higher level. This is what Hegel here suggests, and I mean, do you know of any historical phenomenon which would particularly illustrate what Hegel means?

Mr. Bruell: The writing of history had that same sort of development.

LS: That is true, absolutely, but a specific historical phenomenon?

Mr. Reinken: The Bourbon Restoration and . . . and putting Europe back together after the French Revolution?

LS: Perhaps, but there is no philosophy involved. Yes?

Student: Greece and fifth-century Athens at the time of Socrates.

LS: And what about the dissolving thought at that time?

Student: Well, I don't know which side to attribute it to, but say that the sophists would be the—

LS: Yes, and the restoring on a higher level?

Student: Well, the restoring on the higher level of thought would be Socrates.

LS: Yes, I'm sure that he thought of that when he wrote these lines. So
we have read before that the sciences belong to the age of corruption. You
remember when he almost literally restated Rousseau's famous thesis?
But here there seems to be a difference between what he said before, and
this is very important for Hegel's own view of his own work. There was
the European order, and this meant for Hegel not only Christianity in
general but Protestant Christianity in particular. And then there came
the equivalents of the sophists, who were they?

Mr. Reinken: The *philosophes?*

LS: No, they were very inferior men compared to Hegel, to those who
Hegel has in mind.

Mr. Shulsky: The Enlightenment.

LS: The Enlightenment. Voltaire was the greatest man, surely. And
then they destroyed the traditional Christian belief in its Protestant version, and then what does Hegel do? He restores it, indeed not in the way
in which Luther and orthodoxy understood it—in other words, for Hegel's view, the verbal inspiration and miracles are of no interest whatever,
but the central dogma, God having become man, speculatively understood, that's what Hegel also says. Yes?

Student: In this paragraph it says thought turning upon itself and being . . . Does he view thought as the corrupting element itself, or as a
manifestation of . . .

LS: No, it has a contribution of its own to make.

Student: For example, for the sophists and perhaps the Enlightenment, it could be argued that at least they, if not Hegel and Socrates,
were in part existent because of certain historical events in the state at
the time.

LS: Sure, and therefore there was something apart from the sophists,
ancient or modern, which was responsible for the decay. I mean, let us say
the consequence of the religious wars, or whatever you might think of
which brought about a corruption, and this corruption was continued in
a different way by the writers of the Enlightenment, who partly used this
corruption as an argument against the old and established order. There is
no difficulty whatsoever. But the question is this: if what Hegel suggests
here is true, true philosophy puts an end to corruption, contrary to what
seemed to be suggested in the earlier passage. But in another series of
these same lectures, when he speaks of the corruption of the people, he
mentions together the sciences and philosophy: in other words, not only
abstract thought, which is fundamentally what we ordinarily mean by

scientific thought, but also philosophy. The times of instinct-like action of a nation are the times of its virtues so that, in other words, philosophy as philosophy cannot stop the corruption simply. It can show the impossibility, the stupidity of the Enlightenment, but it cannot completely stop that. That has very much to do with the meaning of the owl of Minerva. That is the question. You know, according to this passage here, there would be no owl of Minerva but it would be a restoration with a new day beginning now. That is the difficulty. Yes?

Mr. Shulsky: He says more specifically later on that this restoration is only in fact perfected in thought. Socrates and Plato produced the good city in thought—

LS: Yes, in that case he says it. Socrates and Plato could only as it were distill the highest and greatest of Greekness and hand it over to the future, but they could not put a stop to the decay of the *polis*. This is clear, but the interesting question is: What about Hegel? In other words, is Hegel another Plato and Aristotle, as he in a way claimed to be, who arrives at the time when the West has arrived at its dusk? That's the question. Or is this the new dawn for the West? Could philosophy open up a new period for the same people or for the same culture? That is the question. Yes?

Mr. Shulsky: It's interesting to see that many of the things he attributed to the corruption of the West—he talks about the Enlightenment and the abstract type of understanding, the formal understanding—are things that have continued and are forceful now; I mean the idea of democracy itself as opposed to what should have been the true principle of our age, of a monarchy. So at least what has happened in fact has been that the decay in a sense has continued despite the restoration of the true principle.

LS: It is perfectly legitimate to use facts which have happened after Hegel against Hegel, because he is a philosopher of history. I do not deny that. But even if we take only his doctrine and do not demand from him hindsight, even then this question which I raised arises. The Enlightenment, one can say, from Hegel's point of view is a caricature of Christianity, while the Christianity as attacked by Voltaire is a caricature to some degree. Hegel presents the true Christianity, the distilled essence of Christianity. The question concerns the historical significance of this Hegelian work regarding the Christian world from this point of view. In other words, does he do for the Christian world what Plato and Aristotle did for the Greek world, or is it radically different? It depends on the implication of this very pregnant phrase "The owl of Minerva begins its flight in the dusk." We may perhaps take up here right away a passage which occurs at the end of today's assignment, and which has very much to do with that. On page 86, the second paragraph.

Mr. Reinken:

> America is therefore the land of the future, where in the ages that lie before us, the burden of the world's history shall reveal itself—perhaps in a con-test between North and South America. It is a land of desire for all those who are weary of the historical lumber room of old Europe. Napoleon is reported to have said: "*Cette vieille Europe m'ennuie.*" It is for America to abandon the ground on which hitherto the history of the world has de-veloped itself. What *has* taken place in the New World up to the present time is only an echo of the Old World—the expression of a foreign life; and as a land of the future, it has no interest for us here, for as regards history, our concern must be with that which has been and that which is. In regard to philosophy, on the other hand, we have to do with that which (strictly speaking) is neither past nor future, but with that which *is*, which has an eternal existence—with reason; and this is quite sufficient to occupy us.[8]

LS: Now in the original there is also the sentence: "The philosopher has not to do with prophesying," i.e., with the future.[9] He has only to do with what is accessible to him, the present or the past, and hence one could say—and some people have said—Hegel does not mean to say that this is the complete account of world history as finished, but only as knowable now, say, around 1825 or thereabouts. "America is the land of the future"—there are certain other remarks in a letter about Russia reminiscent of the famous statement by Tocqueville about the American-Russian antago-nism of the future.[10] But the question is: Was this of any importance to Hegel? I think one can definitely say no. A little bit later, unfortunately not in the translation, he says: "The totality consists in the union of the three principles, and this union takes place in Europe."[11] These principles of which we have spoken before—the African, the Asian, and the Euro-pean principles. For America, only the principle of not being completed and not becoming completed would remain, i.e., no principle of any fun-damental importance. In other words, Hegel doesn't claim to predict or foresee what will happen after his death, especially in the United States

or, for that matter, in Russia, but no new principle of fundamental impor-
tance will emerge. I think there is no doubt that this was Hegel's view.[12]
Now let us then return to the other point. Page 75, paragraph 3.
Mr. Reinken:

> It is not of the nature of the all-pervading spirit to die this merely natural
> death; it does not simply sink into the senile life of mere custom, but, as
> being a national spirit belonging to universal history, attains to the con-
> sciousness of what its work is; it attains to a conception of itself. In fact,
> it is world-historical only in so far as a universal principle has lain in its
> fundamental element, in its grand aim: only so far is the work which such
> a spirit produces a moral, political organization. If it be mere desires that
> impel nations to activity, such deeds pass over without leaving a trace; or
> their traces are only ruin and destruction.

LS: He thinks of Genghis Khan here or, say, what has been going on
for many centuries in central Africa. There is no principle involved. Hence
it is not world-historical.
Mr. Reinken:

> Thus it was first Chronos—Time—that ruled; the Golden Age, without
> moral products; and what was produced, the offspring of that Chronos,
> was devoured by it. It was Jupiter—from whose head Minerva sprang, and
> to whose circle of divinities belong Apollo and the Muses—that first put a
> constraint upon time, and set a bound to its principle of decadence. He is
> the political god, who produced a moral work—the state.[13]

LS: He, namely Zeus, and this is an interpretation of the myth of
Chronos and Zeus. Let us see the sequel of that myth on page 78, second
paragraph, when he speaks again of Zeus. Here.
Mr. Reinken: On page 77.

> Zeus, therefore, who is represented as having put a limit to the devouring
> agency of Time, and stayed this transiency by having established some-
> thing inherently and independently durable—Zeus and his race are them-
> selves swallowed up, and that by the very power that produced them—the
> principle of thought, perception, reasoning, insight derived from rational
> grounds, and the requirement of such grounds.

LS: "The demand for such grounds, the demanding of such grounds."
So in other words, Hegel takes here the continuation of the myth, the
continuation not taught by the Greeks. Chronos was succeeded by Zeus,
and that is the order of the world now prevailing. That's what the Greeks
thought. But what happened afterward? Zeus himself has been swal-
lowed up. Go on.

Mr. Reinken:

> Time is the negative element in the sensuous world. Thought is the same
> negativity, but it is the deepest, the infinite form of it, in which therefore all
> existence generally is dissolved; first finite existence—determinate, limited
> form: but existence generally, in its objective character, is limited; it ap-
> pears therefore as a mere datum—something immediate, authority—and
> is either intrinsically finite and limited, or presents itself as a limit for the
> thinking subject, and its infinite reflection on itself.[14]

LS: Now let us try to understand that. A world-historical people, say,
like the Greeks, has a universal principle, mythically expressed in the
Olympian gods. And this principle of a nation objectivates itself in the
laws and in the thoughts of such a nation. These objectivations are not
primarily known to be objectivations but to be simply absolute. And Antigone refers to these laws which she must obey or the gods; they are not
objectivations of the Greek spirit, they are self-subsistent beings. But then
these objectivations are corroded by thought; and the culmination of this
is that they are as it were taken back by the spirit into itself. The spirit
becomes aware of having caused them, created them, and when this has
taken place a transition to another folk-mind happens.

This is roughly Hegel's scheme. The question is: Does this go on and
on forever, that every nation, every culture in its spirit objectivates itself
and then comes to realize the nonabsoluteness of these objectivations and
the new production takes place? Does this go on indefinitely? Now unfortunately this passage is not in the translation. I will try to translate as
well as I can.

> This going on, this sequence of stages, seems to be a process in infinity,
> according to the notion of perfectibility, a progress which remains eter-
> nally away from the goal. Nevertheless, while in the progress toward a new
> principle, the content of the previous stage is grasped in a more general
> manner, in a more thoughtful manner. This much is certain, that the new

Gestalt, the new shape which this takes on in a new nation, is neverthe-less determinate; but against thought, against concept, no limited *Gestalt,* no limited shape, can remain firm. If there were anything which concept could not corrode, not digest, then there would be the highest tornness, thought confronted with an absolute irrationality, misery. Yet, even if that were so, it would be only thought which comprehends itself, i.e., the very irrationality is thought, is understood. For only thought is that which is in itself limitless, and all actuality is determined. And thus even the tornness would cease, and mind would be satisfied in itself.[15]

There is an implication that every culture has a specific character, and having a specific character means there is a limited character. Greece is not Mesopotamia, that is what he means by *Gestalt:* as it were, visibly different and opposed to the other. Can this go on and on? Must there not be a definite shape which can no longer be corroded? This would then be the full externalization, the full actualization of the mind, the final culture which from one point of view is just one culture among many with spe-cific features. From an external view, you can just enumerate *n* cultures, of which the final culture is one. But if you understand what is going on, you see this is the final culture.

Well, to give a somewhat more popular example, Spengler's book is very well known in our age, and I believe even those among you who have never read it have been confronted with this famous picture which Spengler draws: the *n* different—not many, seven or eight—high cul-tures which ever existed; what we call Western culture, and what he calls Faustic culture, is only one of these. And just as all these cultures have this cyclical movement (which by the way corresponds in a sense to what He-gel says: there is also a beginning, a flowering, and then a contraction as it were at the end), but yet there is a difference—Spengler only does not reflect on this as much as Hegel does—but there is one radical difference between the Faustic culture and all other cultures, and that is that only in the Faustic culture do you find such an understanding of history, such an understanding of culture. Only in the Faustic culture do you find the self-consciousness of culture. This is, let us say, the unconsciously Hege-lian thought in Spengler. Therefore, the Faustic culture is a final culture; and therefore, whereas after all the other cultures which were a new one emerged, this is no longer possible. After the exhaustion, the mind has found full satisfaction by becoming fully clear about itself.

Now in the sequel we must at least try to understand what this is about, why this discussion of geography has a very crucial meaning. Hegel asserted that there is such a thing as a rational history because there are folk-minds. The rationality of history is guaranteed by the fact that the carriers of history are folk-minds and therefore parts of the universal mind. But there is another side to that: there is an obvious connection between the visible—the nations—and nature. The very name "nation," derivative from *nasci*, from which nature is also derived, intimates that: for example, the connection between folk-mind and the climate, the nature of the territory, the nature or characteristics of the people—whether we call that "race" or not doesn't make any difference. Now let us assume, according to a more common view, that the folk-mind is to some extent at least the product of nature. There would be no rationality of history, because nature does not have the rationality which the mind has. That is the importance of this discussion. Hegel has therefore to show, while admitting the connection between nations and nature, that this does not make the nation simply a function of nature. Did you want to say something?

Mr. Bruell: I understood earlier that Hegel had maintained that the rationality would be shown in nature as well as in history.

LS: Yes, but that is not as simple and wouldn't be helpful for the purpose. Now, how does Hegel show that? I mean, Hegel admits there is such a connection, and there are limited cases which are clear. If the climate is too hot or too cold, no development of the higher faculties of man will take place, so only the moderate zone is of any importance here. But how does Hegel show in a very simple way the relative unimportance of climate or nature? The maximum which nature offers is opportunities, but it never exerts a compelling influence. So there couldn't be a high culture in Greenland or in equatorial Africa, for example. But there was a very high culture, say, in Asia Minor, the coasts of Asia Minor, at the time of Homer. Is the climate of Asia Minor a sufficient explanation of the Homeric poems, to put it very simply? That is the question which Hegel discusses. How does the argument develop?

Mr. Shulsky: Obviously not, because there hasn't been that type of poetry since Homer's time and the nature has remained the same.

LS: Yes, surely, this is the simple proof that there cannot be a determination. But nevertheless, Hegel says that while there is no dependence of mind on nature there is a certain correspondence, and the example which he discusses especially is the difference between the river valley cultures and the coastland cultures. And the fact that the European culture in its original form comes from coastal countries around the Mediterranean, whereas the great Asiatic cultures are river valley cultures, is of some importance. Hegel, in other words, sees a certain correspondence between the greater flexibility, the greater freedom of European development and this maritime character of the geographic condition. The thing which is so strange to us but has to do with this notion of correspondence is that Hegel asserts that the New World—America and of course also Australia—is new not only in the sense that it is new to the Old World, the Europeans, but that it is new in an absolute sense. Read this, it is very strange. Where is that? 81, top.

Mr. Reinken:

> Their geological antiquity we have nothing to do with. I will not deny the New World the honor of having emerged from the sea at the world's formation contemporaneously with the old; yet the Archipelago between South America and Asia shows a physical immaturity.[16]

LS: And so on. Yes, and he speaks also about the weakness of American crocodiles and other beasts; and Alexander von Humboldt, who had seen them in the Amazon River and so forth, assured people in Germany that they are quite respectable.[17] This is one of the famous weaknesses of Hegel. But the other point which he makes is of somewhat greater interest, but of course the interpretation is a long question: that the American natives, the inland Indians, compared even with the Negroes of whom Hegel had no high opinion, that they were unable to coexist with the whites whereas the Negroes at least learned to work, and so on. In the case of such a great man as Hegel, one must wonder what the question is which he has in mind, however inadequate his answer may be. One can perhaps say this: How does it come about—that's the question which Hegel answers—that there was no phenomenon like Confucius or Buddha in America? There was no such cultural phenomenon of the highest order. Apparently Hegel didn't know anything of Aztec and Inca culture, but still, in all fairness this is not comparable to Hindu and Chinese culture. And this is a relative justification of Hegel's atrocious assertion that the American continent and its native population would not have had any message for the older continent, whereas the older continent, and not only its Christian but even its Indian and Chinese parts and perhaps some other parts, would have had a message for America. This is surely a fact which is not altogether unworthy of thought. And if you read the statement from this point of view and forget about the crocodiles, we will look at it, I believe, more adequately.

So next time we will come to his discussion of Africa and begin the discussion of China. Is there any point which you would like to raise? Yes, Mr. Glenn.

Mr. Glenn: Hegel is an interpreter of history, and in so doing he understands himself to be rebuilding at a higher level Christianity, which in principle has been destroyed by the Enlightenment.

LS: Let me put it this way: Christianity as understood by the orthodoxies or by the theologians.

Mr. Glenn: All right. Now the difficulty is for one who is not persuaded that orthodox Christianity is no longer of validity. How can a person like that approach the study of Hegel, because Hegel seems to be subversive of Christianity? You understand?

LS: Yes, that was the reason why he was so attacked already in his lifetime. You can find many references, explicit or implicit, to that fact . . . And he was called at that time a pantheist—that was the word they used—and after his death, the then-Prussian government called a former friend of Hegel, a fellow philosopher, Schelling, to the University of Berlin in order to counteract the dragon-seeds of the Hegelian pantheism. No, that was clear. But I believe one can say that Hegel's philosophy of history is fantastic, and that this is not merely an accident, I mean due to certain defects of Hegel's presentation, but the reason is probably that history is not a rational process. This is very easy to say, it is very commonsensical to say, but the difficulty is this: Hegel had some empirical evidence for asserting that the historical process is rational, and that empirical evidence is the fact of progress. Or is this not a fact? Because if there is progress, then it has gone on, on the whole, rationally. I mean, maybe it was not so rational that we could figure out the superiority of Hindu religion to Chinese religion as Hegel thought, this kind of thing. But fundamentally there is a progressive process, and that seems to be a sign of rationality. Is this not correct to say that progress in a limited sense is obviously a fact? For example, men's ability to move quickly from one place to another: there is obviously an enormous progress that has been made in this and many other things, above all in science. Yes?

Mr. Shulsky: But couldn't it be that some fields of endeavor are by their very nature progressive? I mean, if you're just talking about the number of facts one knows, as long as these things aren't lost, all you can do is add to the store. In other words, when we know how to go ten miles an hour, if we discover how to go fifteen miles an hour, that's added to it, and as long as this isn't forgotten, you're always adding to this. In these restricted realms, there's not much problem about progress. It's the only way the thing could go. You couldn't all of a sudden have to go slower than before.

LS: Yes, but what does belief in progress mean, in contradistinction to this restricted progress of which you speak?

Mr. Shulsky: A belief in the progress of the basic philosophic ideas.

LS: What about social-political progress?

Mr. Shulsky: In a way that's what can equally be questioned and what was being questioned, and what he was fighting against by saying you have to look at the content of these societies and not merely the external things.

LS: But still, Hegel said the rights of man are formally recognized and have become the basis of the legal system and the whole social order in the Western world. Is this not a great progress compared with relatively humane societies in earlier times which did not have a formal recognition of such rights of man? This is, I think, a major point in Hegel's reasoning. But what about that?

Mr. Bruell: I was going to ask you if there were principles that have bearing on politics which one could appeal to, and on the basis of those prefer a city as the best form of political life?

LS: But Hegel would simply say that the society which regarded it as a possible right to enslave human beings is morally inferior to a society which denies that right.

Mr. Bruell: Yes, but if that statement itself were questionable—

LS: But who questions that? That's the point.

Mr. Shulsky: But even not questioning that, though, it's true that there has been progress in the idea that the right of the individual has been made the basis of our society, but maybe we have paid a price for that in the quality of life of society, so it's not progress.

Strauss: One doesn't have to go so far. One simply has to mention what happened after Hegel in Hegel's own country to the rights of man. And how do the rights of man look today, the prospects? That depends so much on whether the West has the capacity to survive. So in other words, not only are there limited progresses, as you stated, technological and so on, but even if there are genuine progresses in important spheres, the question arises: Will these progresses go on? Will they go on? And then there would be in retrospect, say, a thousand years from now, a progressive period—say, for two or three centuries in the West, followed by another night. How can we exclude that?

Mr. Shulsky: Couldn't this be in a sense tied in with the fact that while there was certain obvious progress which was manifest and people could see, there was a decay that was more subtle, that people couldn't see?

LS: The basis of this optimism, as it were, was stated very clearly by Kant in one of his minor writings when he, speaking of the French Revolution, says that these things cannot be forgotten.[18] In other words, say, the destruction of the Bastille in 1789 cannot be forgotten. But the question is: Is this true? I mean, it may still be written down in the histories and transmitted from generation to generation, but will it be a living memory which makes it absolutely certain that there will be no Bastilles anymore? That is a different proposition. And I believe that Hegel could assume that the majority of his listeners and readers would have no doubt of the fact of progress, and progress in the decisive matters, of course. But we have not yet discussed the question of progress regarding philosophy. We must take this up at a proper occasion.

5   Africa and China

Leo Strauss: Your last remark[1] leads very far and I suggest we postpone it. I shall also disregard your clear summary of the survey which Hegel gives in this lecture, because this will be repeated at much better length when he comes to the particular cultures like China, India, and so on. Now there is one point which we should clear up regarding Africa—and of course we must disregard entirely the present situation or, for that matter, any problems of the Negroes in this country. For the Africans, you said there is nothing higher than man, and this is the natural man. And therefore this man has no sense of the dignity of man. Where is the connection? I mean, if nothing is higher than man, that would seem to be a very high sense of the dignity of man. How does Hegel explain this apparent difficulty?

Student: It seems to me his explanation is that man gains dignity only if he has something to look up to. There has to be something higher than his own being; and in looking up to something, then he can have respect for his own being. But if he can't look up to a higher being, then he can have no respect for his own being.

LS: In other words, if there is nothing higher than man, then man is just an animal species like any other, and we could speak of the dignity of dogs, monkeys, and so on and so forth, and also of the dignity of man. Man needs something. I mean, if man is not given the dignity by something higher than himself, then he has no dignity—that is the biblical formula, created in the image of God, and in Hegel's formula it would be reason. Reason is something which is not merely a faculty of man, but which in a way rules the whole; that is indeed this point. What Hegel said about the Negroes is easy to understand: that they come to participate through slavery in, say, Phoenician culture, or the culture of Islam or Christianity, and therefore cease to be natural men as they were in Africa. But still there is some difficulty which came out also in the discussion of China. If everything depends on man's recognizing something higher than man and bowing to it, this happened in China already.

But this is obviously not sufficient. What is the other movement, the ingredient which is also required?

Mr. Bruell: That part of that something be contained in man himself.

LS: Yes. In other words, there must be some reconciliation between this highest and man. Again, the Christian theological formula is that God has become man, which Hegel interprets in his manner. But of course one can also state it in this form: that the final man, so to speak, has a sense of the dignity of man because he is self-legislative. In other words, he is not merely subject to a law handed down to him from on high, but he legislates for himself, imposes a law upon himself, whereas a natural man does not impose any law. In the earlier stages, men obey laws as handed down, say, the laws of the Greeks when Antigone speaks of these laws. But eventually, man recognizes that these laws are in fact self-imposed but not known to have been self-imposed, and the eventual stage is that man knows that he obeys laws which he knows, and then the full reconciliation is achieved. This is roughly what he has in mind. I think we leave it at that.

Student: China somehow is in history and somehow it is not in history. Somehow it's beginning, yet somehow it doesn't participate; that is, it participates in the spiritual and yet it doesn't participate in the movement.

LS: What is the empirical basis for this statement? I mean, it is clear to what extent it belongs to history, because here man is subject and bows. But there is the other side, which he expressed by saying that China in a way does not belong to history.

Student: Well, there are a number of quotes. The first thing is, he says Africa is outside of history because it doesn't participate in movement. Then he makes several remarks about China to the same effect that China and India lie, as it were, still outside the world's history. That's on page 116.

LS: Ja, but what does he mean by that?

Student: I took him to mean that as a matter of fact they're static. That is, they do participate in the spirit, in freedom, in some way, but nonetheless there's no movement in those worlds.

LS: Yes, but what about, say, Persia, which is different in this respect? Which empirical facts does he have in mind when he makes these distinctions?

Student: They have the same type of government now that they had when they began. There's been no change, the same type of regime.

LS: We know that, but on the other hand, I believe that he has in mind also and very importantly the fact that there was no influence of China and India on the West, whereas there was some such influence of Persia, if only because of the rule of the Persians over the Jews, which created some unity; on the other hand, in Hegel's time, in the case of India, there was already to some extent an influence of the West on the East. And of course this is now much more visible, especially in China, because Marxism is, as we all know, of Western origin; and therefore there is a difference between those cultures which in a way helped to bring about the West and those which did not. And this is, I think, indicated by Hegel in this manner.

There are a number of other passages which are also of great importance, which unfortunately are not in the translation. Here is the sentence: "As soon as man appears as man, he is in opposition to nature. Only by this fact does he become man. The Negro presents natural man" and so on.[2] So in other words, the opposition to nature makes man *man*. I mean, that is not true of any other being, even if that being, like a spider, for example, or ants, creates edifices of some sort, there is no opposition to nature. The opposition to nature makes man *man*. Man is a being which transforms nature, a thing which plays a very great role then in the Marxist doctrine. So he transforms nature, and whatever we are concerned with in every stage except the lowest is that man transforms an earlier transformation: say, the Romans transformed their Greek heritage, but this Greek heritage is already a transformation of nature, or rather a transformation of an earlier culture, say, Oriental culture, and so on. And the peculiarity of the first and lowest cycle would be that there is not yet a preceding transformation, that some transformation starts here. And this is what Hegel has in mind when he says that reason is both the form and the matter of history, because the matter is already a transformation of nature and the beginning is indeed this, the Negro. The Negro presents natural man in his whole wildness and uncontrolledness. He is the immediate man, meaning that no mediation between him and nature has taken place. There is nothing in this character we find which reminds of the human. So we find in Africa altogether that which one has called the state of innocence, the unity of man with God and nature. Now this is a very strong stand, that cannibalism and atheism is a state of innocence, for this is a state of unconsciousness of oneself. This first natural state is a bestial state. Paradise . . . is in Greek "the zoo," the animal garden where man has lived in a bestial state and was innocent, and man is not supposed to be innocent, but responsible. So now is this whole presentation, the . . . natural man is man in the state of innocence. But now this is very much changed towards the beginning. This is surely a radical transformation of the biblical view, the perfect beginning we spoke of last time. But it is not only directed against the ordinary biblical view, it is also meant against a philosophic view. I mean, what is the natural man? Where do we hear of the natural man?

Student: Locke, Rousseau.

LS: Rousseau more obviously, in the *Second Discourse* especially. And Rousseau had of course said that the natural man is a stupid animal, and man is both prerational and presocial, but that was all. Hegel gives a much more specific delineation of the natural man. This bestial state, this savage state was a great theme of Hobbes's, as you will remember. But what is the difference between Hegel's description of natural man, man in the state of nature, and Hobbes's . . .

Student: In the state of nature for Hobbes, you at least have a sense that they can come together and form a contract.

LS: Yes, so in other words—

Student: They're not completely natural.

LS: Well, this is natural. But their naturalness enables them to act to bring about an artifice called the Leviathan. And why not the Negroes, according to Hegel's description? Would they be able to do that?

Student: No.

LS: And why not?

Student: They lack reason and they lack freedom, I mean, the ability to form the . . .

LS: Yes, but how can this state be depicted more concretely? Because I believe something depends on it. Yes?

Student: According to Hegel, man in the state of nature was not conscious of himself, therefore he could not be . . . into . . .

LS: Very well, this very simple calculation: my life is threatened by the war of everybody against everybody, and that is true of everybody else, so we all have a common interest. That establishes why that is a thought absolutely beyond the people concerned. Man in the state of nature, Hegel as it were replies to Hobbes, is wholly incapable of leaving it. He must undergo a very long civilizing process before he could do what Hobbes says he does: establish a state, and especially a reasonable state. Or in the words of Marx, the educator himself must be educated; and that cannot be done by any educator but, because the educator would already have been educated, must be done by some historical process—in a rational process, say, in a department of education or something like this—which could not take place here. Now let us turn to page 93 in the translation, towards the bottom of the page.

Mr. Reinken: Five lines from bottom.

> Religion begins with the consciousness that there is something higher than man. But even Herodotus called the Negroes sorcerers.

LS: Now there is something omitted which is of some importance. "This form of thinking is not present with the Negroes. The character of the African shows the first opposition of man to nature." There is such an opposition because otherwise they would not be human. "In this state he has this notion: he and nature being opposed to each other, but he as ruling over the natural—this is the basic relation of which we have the first relation, the oldest testament, from Herodotus. We can express their religious principle in the proposition which Herodotus stated in Africa, all are sorcerers."[3] Yes?

Mr. Reinken:

> Now in sorcery, we have not the idea of a God, of a moral faith. It exhibits man as the highest power, regarding him as alone occupying a position of command over the power of nature.[4]

LS: In other words, this crudest form of religion, or prereligion rather, sorcery, has of course one crucial character. It is something that is distinctly human. Monkeys have no sorcerers. And therefore here the opposition between man and nature, which according to Hegel is of the essence of man, shows itself on this stage. They do not have any religion because they do not know of anything higher than man. And when he speaks of sorcery later on, explaining that—I believe these passages are not in the translation—he says: "They do not call on God in this sorcery activity. There is no higher power which they address, but the men concerned believe that they cause this effect by themselves. In a word, man regards himself for the highest which here can command."[5] By the way, I cannot of course go into the question, the main reason being my incompetence, of whether Hegel's notion of African religion is true or not. I remember having read a book by Professor Eliade[6] of our Divinity School which suggests an entirely different notion of the Negro pantheon—I mean very different from this notion which Hegel has. I cannot go into it, but that goes of course for all the parts, when he speaks about China and India and so on. We would have to ask people who know this subject matter whether the information which Hegel had was in any way sufficient.

Student: Would you comment on these different editions? Karl Hegel's preface to this edition says that this is the second edition based on Hegel's manuscripts and that this is corrected and revised somewhat by lecture notes. This is not the first edition.

LS: The main point is this: I do not know the whole history. I could read to you here the statement, which would take too much time. But the most important event, as far as I know, is this. About ten to twenty years ago, a German scholar, Hoffmeister, went over the whole material of new lecture notes which have been discovered since and revised the whole edition, but unfortunately he did this only for the first part of the *Philosophy of History*.[7] Then he died. So for this first part we have a much better and richer edition, but not for the whole; and I mean this unfortunate accident is of use to us only today, because next time I have to fall back on the older edition which has been more or less literally translated in the edition which you use.

Student: Your edition has never been translated, then.[8]

LS: No. So sorcery is the control of nature. Technology is the control of nature. What is the difference between sorcery and technology? Don't answer that technology works and sorcery doesn't. I mean, as far as the possibility goes, this working of the one and not working of the other is a consequence of a more fundamental defect. What does technology do which sorcery does not?

Mr. Reinken: It inquires into the possible; that is, he has to know what the laws are which the things effect.

LS: Both the sorcerer and technology vanquish nature. But, as Francis Bacon put it, the scientist vanquishes nature by obeying her in the first place,[9] and this obedience, this recognition of something objective, that is according to Hegel's analysis lacking in the sorcerer, and this is probably the reason why the one works and the other doesn't work. And if sorcery works, it may be due to entirely different things, especially if it is an effect on wide-eyed human beings. There is however an objection to this interpretation of Negro religion, on page 94, second paragraph.

Mr. Reinken: Just above the middle.

The second element in their religion consists in their giving an outward form to this supernatural power, projecting their hidden might into the world of phenomena by means of images.

LS: I would like to say that here there is not the word "supernatural" in the German original, but it may have occurred a bit before. I wonder whether it was there, because if it is supernatural, there would be a recognition of something higher. Yes?

Mr. Shulsky: I have a German edition from which this is translated, and it's just here *Macht*.

LS: *Macht*, the same. You see, so it's even—look, I have found another thing in the translation. There is also in this translation, in such a crucial point, on page 81 in your translation at the top—I noticed this by accident. I'm very sorry, that was also a mistake. But surely here we have cleared it up now. So there is nothing of supernatural, that would seem to run counter to everything Hegel said. So how do we read it then?

Mr. Reinken:

an outward form to this power, projecting their hidden might into the world of phenomena by means of images. What they conceive of as the power in question is therefore nothing really objective, having a substantial being and different from themselves, but the first thing that comes in their way. This, taken quite indiscriminately, they exalt to the dignity of a "genius"; it may be an animal, a tree, a stone, or a wooden figure. This is their fetish—a word to which the Portuguese first gave currency, and which is derived from *feitizo*, magic. Here, in the fetish, a kind of objective independence, as contrasted with the arbitrary fancy of the individual—

LS: In other words, here is another being, the fetish, to which the sorcerer seems to bow, which he seems to recognize. Yes?

Mr. Reinken:

seems to manifest itself; but as the objectivity is nothing other than the fancy of the individual projecting itself into space, the human individuality remains master of the image it has adopted.[10]

LS: More literally translated, "the individual arbitrariness objectivates itself in the fetish" and so on; therefore it never reaches the independent. As he puts it a bit later, their god always remains within their power, establishing and opposing arbitrarily, and therefore they are never raised above their arbitrariness. In a word, there is no relation of dependence in this religion, and therefore it is not in any real sense of the word religion. The objectivity always remains subject to arbitrariness. The substantial always remains within the power of the subject. This is a religion of the Africans, it doesn't go further. There is indeed here a superiority of man above nature—this is here somehow recognized—which a dumb animal could never have, but in the manner of arbitrariness. Let me just say that they know the arbitrary and accidental will of man which is higher than the natural, and by this very fact they are human and not monkeys. Now let us turn to page 95, the second paragraph, as regards the relation of man to man.

Mr. Reinken:

> But from the fact that man is regarded as the highest, it follows that he has no respect for himself; for only with the consciousness of a higher being does he reach a point of view which inspires him with real reverence.

LS: Let me see. This would require a higher and absolute value which man would have himself, and this absolute value man could not simply give himself; it must have been given to him. Therefore there can be no dignity of man. Yes?

Mr. Reinken:

> For if arbitrary choice is the absolute, the only substantial objectivity that is realized, the mind cannot in such be conscious of any universality. The Negroes indulge therefore that perfect contempt for humanity, which in its bearing on justice and morality is the fundamental characteristic of the race. They have, moreover, no knowledge of the immortality of the soul, although specters are supposed to appear. The undervaluing of humanity among them reaches an incredible degree of intensity. Tyranny is regarded as no wrong, and cannibalism is looked upon as quite customary and proper.[11]

LS: And then he gives some examples of cannibalism. So in other words, we do not have to read the daily papers, we can find it already here. But then he makes a very strange statement; I do not know whether it is in the translation: "Human flesh is used not so much as food, but on the occasion of festivals, many hundred prisoners are tortured, decapitated, and the body is returned to him who has captured him; and this capturer divides the corpse up."[12] Now this is very interesting. Is this in the translation? No. Because it is quite interesting that in spite of their savagery they know that man is not like any brute; and by that he means, by the way, they do not eat human flesh in the way they eat the meat of cows or goats and so on or something. The peculiar character that the eating of human flesh is part of the celebration and also the other things to which he refers later, that the eating of the heart of an enemy is meant to give powers which they do not expect after eating the heart of a chicken or of a lion. In a way they are aware that man is something special, but of course this awareness can never reach solidity because of the reason given. Yes?

Mr. Shulsky: But isn't this something of a purely animal characteristic, too? I mean, a certain awareness of a difference between—lions do not attack each other.

LS: Yes, but lions do not eat lions—the higher animals, let us say. And man is this fantastic beast which, while being higher, can also be so much lower than the animals, in other words, because he has this wider range. I mean, he is not regulated by instinct and so on, in the way in which the animals . . . again a passage which is not in this translation. Then he speaks about slavery among the Negroes, which of course follows when there is no recognition of the dignity of man and therefore no objection whatsoever to slavery: "The lesson which we draw from this condition of slavery with the Negroes, and only a side of which is interesting to us, is this, which we know from the idea that the state of nature is the state of absolute and universal injustice." This formula is from Kant, but one can of course impute it to Hobbes. "Every intermediate stage between the state of nature and the actuality of the reasonable state has still facets of injustice."[13]

So we begin: that is another formulation for the characteristic of the historical process. Beginning with absolute injustice and ending with the complete absence of injustice, called by Hegel the reasonable state. I mean, there can be acts of private injustice, of course, murder and so on all the time, but they have no legs to stand upon. There are laws forbidding them, and law courts which take care of them. Crime is not able to show its face in broad daylight. That alone is meant. I mean, Hegel does not go so far as Marx does in his notion, where there would be a notion that in the end state there will hardly be or no longer be any crimes in fact. Lenin has some great discussion about some unpleasantness which might happen in a factory.[14] There is some slacker who doesn't work like the others work in the factory, and since the state has withered away there can of course be no court to take cognizance of it. Then the other factory workers will take care of him. You can call this lynching or you can use other words. But the key point, which must be remembered, is that in the reasonable state there is no longer any injustice, i.e., there is no longer any need to recognize by the law any injustice as inevitable. As long as you have slavery, for example, or serfdom—as long as this is the case, there is objective injustice recognized, regarded as justice. The complete coincidence of law and justice, i.e., there are only just laws: this is the reasonable state and that is the end of the historical process. And the way in which Hegel talks here when he speaks of every intermediate stage between the state of nature and the actuality of the reasonable state implies that this history can come to an end, because the reasonable state, as is implied here, can become actual. As a matter of fact, in Hegel's view it has become actual. Yes?

Student: Isn't the state of nature somehow, though, outside of history, that is, in contrast to history, and therefore universal slavery?

LS: Sure, you can say that; but nevertheless, the state of nature as a state of mankind has always the fundamental human characteristic. There is some opposition between man and nature; that is clear and I think indicated by what Hegel says here about the practice of cannibalism, that people as a matter of fact do not eat human food as a matter of course as they would eat the food of other beings. And there is something apparently in man which objects to that, or which creates a problem at least which can be overcome only by special ceremonies and so on.

Student: Would all reach the reasonable state simultaneously, or would some get there before others?

LS: The state wouldn't be of any help. Say you have a perfectly wise man, let us assume for one moment, and a perfectly just man who is also substantively just—in other words, not only that he has a good will but that he knows what is just. That wouldn't make a just state. Let us assume that Socrates regarded slavery as fundamentally unjust and had more or less the just views, what would be the consequence? It would never have become the law of the land, and there would always be a conflict between justice and the law. The opinions of any individuals, however wise the opinions may be, are irrelevant if they have not been embodied in the institutions. Only by this embodiment does the reasonable state emerge. But Hegel would of course say that Socrates could not have seen that. I mean, he might have disliked the institution of slavery, but he could not have understood the deepest principle, which is possible, according to Hegel, only on the basis of the Bible, more specifically of Christianity. We come to that later. Yes?

Mr. Franke: When Hegel speaks about China and about the earliest reaches before history began, at least recorded history, though he describes how they lived in the mountains and clothed themselves with furs and so on, he never says that this was a natural state too, out of which they came by individuals giving them laws and pointing out their—

LS: You mean these tribes in the north prior to the establishment of the state, is that it?

Mr. Franke: Yes.

LS: Then Hegel would simply say that is not the natural state in the full sense, since cannibalism, for example, and other things are not of the essence of this condition.

Mr. Franke: But we don't know. Hegel must admit he doesn't know.

LS: I do not know whether Hegel had read a lot about the—

Mr. Franke: But he admits that there are no records. He proceeds into the problem presupposing—

LS: Let us assume you are right with your facts or hypothesis. This would create a minor difficulty, but what Hegel would say nevertheless is that it was there, it was possible, even if there was such a fetishistic stage also in Asia, or maybe in Europe for all we know, a million years ago.

Mr. Franke: What is the difference that it is possible in one place that the process of history begins and in another it doesn't?

LS: But the point is that in Africa there was never any indigenous progress beyond that. In China, there was also stability, to that extent it's the same as in Africa, but a stability on a much higher level. This, I think, is the only important point. And therefore Hegel regards Africa and China in different ways as typical, and the things, more or less hypothetical things to which you refer, even if true, as not typical, not fundamentally interesting.

Mr. Reinken: I think Mr. Franke is stressing the point that, especially as we get on in the book, we will come into these grinding inevitabilities of the advance—till finally it's surprising that the Counter-Reformation should succeed. Yet it just so happened, in effect, that China did raise itself after savagery and establish a central kingdom, and it also so happened that Africa did not take the steps. And he does not give a compelling account why it should have come about that—

LS: He at least gives part of the account.

Mr. Shulsky: Part of the account is in the earlier section, where he says that in the torrid zones and the frigid zones, civilizations simply can't arise. So that explains in part why Africa could never have gotten beyond where it did get. The real question, I suppose, is—

LS: Of course, if you raise the question, there are other questions concerning the time spans involved. Why are the prehistoric times—Hegel doesn't speak about the times, but they are somehow implied—so much longer than the historical times? But I think the indication is that this was an infinitely long process leading from the very beginnings of mankind, but Hegel doesn't say a word about that. I mean, we on the basis of some theory of evolution would think of some Neanderthals or what not, until these reach the state of people who possess a language. When he speaks of the origin of language, he says these very long time spans are quiet so these tribes or nations could develop.

Mr. Shulsky: We are somewhat prepared for the first civilization in China, because he has described the geography of the Asian highlands as lending itself to this type of tribal, nomadic life which would produce a patriarchy.

LS: Precisely from his point of view, these are only opportunities or conditions, not sufficient causes. I mean, some spark had to come in and it can no longer be explained except in retrospect through the fact that this stage, this particular mind or *Weltanschauung*, is intelligible as a fundamental part of the whole comprehensive system of *Weltanschauungen*, which is, you can say, history as it appears in man. Here is also another point somewhat later when he begins to speak of Asia. I think that must be around page 100 or so.

Mr. Reinken: The bottom of 99—

LS: No, where is this passage where he speaks of "Asia is the continent of the Orient." That's 99.

Mr. Reinken:

Asia is characteristically the Orient quarter of the globe, the region of origination. It is indeed the western world for America; but as Europe presents on the whole the center and end of the Old World, and is absolutely the West, so Asia is absolutely the East.[15]

LS: So in other words, from a purely geographical point of view, East and West are very relative considerations. The European continent, which is externally just one among *n* points of view, is nevertheless the absolute point of view because Europe is the center, and the end of the Old World, and absolutely the West, meaning the Occident, *das Abendland*. But Hegel of course implies that this is not an arbitrary Europe-centric point of view, but Europe is in fact the place where history has reached its culmination, where the reasonable state has come into being with all its implications. Page 103, paragraph 1.

Mr. Reinken:

> In the geographical survey, the course of the world's history has been marked out in its general features. The sun, the light, rises in the East. Light is a simply self-involved existence; but though possessing thus in itself universality, it exists at the same time as an individuality in the sun. Imagination has often pictured to itself the emotions of a blind man suddenly becoming possessed of sight, beholding the bright glimmering of the dawn, the growing light, and the flaming glory of the ascending sun. The boundless forgetfulness of his individuality in this pure splendor is his first feeling: utter astonishment.

LS: This forgetting of himself in looking at the sun, that is the first stage. The unawareness of self, and only seeing the objective, the absolute, or whatever you call it, that is Asia. No awareness, no self-knowledge strictly speaking, no self-consciousness.

Mr. Reinken:

> But when the sun is risen, this astonishment is diminished. Objects around are perceived, and from them the individual proceeds to the contemplation of his own inner being, and thereby the advance is made to the perception of the relation between the two. Then inactive contemplation is quitted for activity. By the close of day, man has erected a building constructed from his own inner sun. And when in the evening he comes—

LS: No, "which he has brought about by his labor." This is the man's product become more important than the things that he finds. His world, the man-created world, becomes more important than the given world. Also something which Marx took over.

Mr. Reinken:

> and when in the evening he contemplates this, he esteems it more highly than the original external sun. For now he stands in a conscious relation to

his spirit, and therefore a free relation. If we hold this image fast in mind, we shall find it symbolizing the course of history, the great day's work of Spirit.

LS: Yes. The beginning of the next paragraph.
Mr. Reinken:

The history of the world travels from East to West—

LS: No, it travels from the mere self-forgetting in looking at the absolute towards the awareness of man's creativity in producing his own world.
Mr. Reinken:

For Europe is absolutely the end of history, Asia the beginning.[16]

LS: There can be no doubt that, sorry as I am that I have to mention it, there is no place for America. In other words, he doesn't deny that there will be all kinds of developments in America, of which he doesn't claim to prophesy as we have seen, but there will be nothing fundamentally new, beyond that reasonable state existing in the early nineteenth century in Europe.

Now on page 104 in the second paragraph, there is this distinction which is very important between substantial freedom and subjective freedom. That is one problem which we have mentioned on an earlier occasion. Yes?

Mr. Reinken: May I ask a question about the myth?

LS: Yes. Well, it's not really a myth, but go ahead. It is an image.

Mr. Reinken: Do you feel any significance could be drawn from the fact that the first step of the sun and then the turn to the objects does remind of the peak of the story of the cave, and from there on the story is quite otherwise?

LS: Whether Hegel thought of the story of the cave when writing that I do not know. I do not see any necessity to assume that. But what astonishes us is this. We ordinarily speak of the Orient, in German *Morgenland*, the land of the morning, and Occident, *Abendland*, land of the evening; and now the sun rises, we are filled with admiration for this magnificent glow and completely inactive. We just have to wait. Let us take this as an example. And then gradually we don't look any more at the sun, but we look at the things on which the sun shines; in other words, we contemplate the terrestrial things, trees, animals, etc. However, we also work, although Hegel doesn't mention it at this stage. But then when the evening comes, we become aware of the fact that we have done a day's work, and in the simplest and clearest case, we have made something: a shoe, a table, whatever it may be. Then Hegel says this: what a man has produced himself, that of which he is fully the cause understood in the large sense—so not merely the pair of shoes and the table and so on but everything created by men, think not only of works of art but also institutions and states—this whole world is infinitely higher in dignity than the natural world. So in other words, he starts from the simple thing that we look at the sun, and then we gradually begin to work and so forth—he enlarges that. I believe there is nothing further here. But the most important implication of this passage is of course the Occident, Europe in plain English, this is the final stage.

Student: Is there no reference to man's innocence . . .

LS: No. Well, he speaks of the sun of his consciousness, which he has produced by his labor. So this sun, as he said, could not be without his production. In other words, this sun is not something coeternal with man, like conscience or something of this kind, but is something which itself comes into being through man's work. Surely there must be some germ of it, but the developed view, say, like Greek, Roman, or biblical morality, these wouldn't exist without the human production, the human development of this germ. Page 104, paragraph 2.

Mr. Reinken:

To understand this division—namely into despotism, democracy, aristocracy and monarchy—to understand this division, we must remark that as the state is the universal spiritual life to which individuals by birth sustain a relation of confidence and habit, and in which they have their existence and reality, the first question is whether their actual life is an unreflecting use and habit combining them in this unity or whether its constituent individuals are reflective and personal beings having a properly subjective and independent existence. In view of this, substantial freedom must be distinguished from subjective freedom. Substantial freedom is the abstract, undeveloped reason implicit in volition proceeding to develop itself in the state. But in this phase of reason there is still wanting personal insight and will, that is subjective freedom, which is realized only in the individual and which constitutes the reflection of the individual in his own conscience. Where there is merely substantial freedom, commands and laws are regarded as something fixed and abstract to which the subject holds himself in absolute servitude. These laws need not concur with the desire of the individual—

LS: "Desire" is too weak—"the will."
Mr. Reinken:

the will of the individual, and the subjects are consequently like children, who obey their parents without will or insight of their own. But as subjective freedom arises, and man descends from the contemplation of external reality into his own soul, the contrast suggested by reflection arises involving the negation of reality.[17]

LS: In other words, here the objective institutions, laws, customs, and so on are questioned because they are merely authoritative, and this in itself leads to their destruction, their corrosion. And only if they are truly rational, i.e., they are of such a nature that the reasonable individual legislating for himself would have established them, do they resist the corrosion and remain. Substantive, substantial freedom and subjective freedom correspond like obeying rational order blindly and obeying it knowingly, knowing that it is rational. The question of course which Hegel does not develop here is this: Can an order be rational if it is simply obeyed blindly? In other words, can the Chinese order which has this substantial freedom in a way, can it be rational because it is not transformable into subjective freedom?

There is another passage on the bottom of page 108: "The realm of subjectivity knowing itself is derived of the actual spirit. At that stage the fourth realm begins; if we look only at its natural side, it is the senility of the mind." Yes?

Mr. Reinken:

The German world appears at this point of development—the fourth phase of world history. This would answer in the comparison with the periods of human life to its old age. The old age of nature is weakness; but that of spirit is its perfect maturity and strength, in which it returns to unity with itself, but in its fully developed character.[18]

LS: "Of history." If the end of history is taken as the senile stage of the human mind, this is obviously something bad; but if we make a distinction between the old age of the body, let us say, and the old age of the mind, where it could go together with the highest wisdom, it would be different. I think these are the passages in this edition—[19]

Mr. Reinken:

—While these two realms [China and India] have remained to the present day, of the empires of the Tigris and Euphrates on the contrary nothing remains, except at most a heap of bricks; for the Persian Kingdom, as that of transition, is by nature perishable, and the kingdoms of the Caspian Sea are given up to the ancient struggle of Iran and Turan. The Empire of the solitary Nile is only present beneath the ground, in its speechless dead, ever and anon stolen away to all quarters of the globe, and in their majestic habitations; for what remains above ground is nothing else but such splendid tombs.[20]

LS: In other words, the problem which Hegel is trying to solve is that of why China and also India are the only worlds or cultures which have remained, whereas others, like Persia, Egypt, Mesopotamia, and so on have been destroyed. Hegel denies implicitly that this can be understood merely in terms of geography or location—that China, say, was so far away from the West and therefore could not be conquered by it. He tries to trace this amazing survival to the principle of China. It is clear from the context that this fact does not prove in itself that China is higher than Persia or Egypt, but the contrary. And the simple proof is that Hegel surely regarded Greece as higher than China; and Greece has not survived, as we saw a long time ago. On page 117, line 2.

Mr. Reinken:

Comparing this with the history of the Old Testament—

LS: He is speaking of the Chinese chronological dates.
Mr. Reinken:

a space of 2400 years, according to the common acceptation, intervened between the Noachian Deluge and the Christian era. But Johannes von Müller has adduced weighty objections to this number. He places the deluge in the year 3473 before Christ—thus about 1000 years earlier—

supporting this view by the Septuagint. I remark this only with the view of obviating the difficulties that may appear to arise when we meet with dates of a higher age than 2400 years before Christ, and yet find nothing about the Flood.[21]

LS: What do you say to this statement—I mean, about its character?
Student: I think he's smiling.
LS: Yes. I thought that this was the first ironical remark which I have come across at my present reading of these lectures. Yes?
Student: Would he call this a myth?
LS: No, for Hegel it is a matter of course that these chronological statements of the Old Testament are not in any way obligatory, and that was settled for people like him long before his birth. But it is obvious. No, the funny thing is that he says: I have observed this *only* with a view to the fact that someone could become doubtful of the date of the flood.

Now when he comes to speak about an . . . survey of Chinese history in chronological terms, he goes over to contemplate the spirit of China's constitution, which has always remained the same, and he says that this spirit of the constitution follows immediately from the principle of China. Do you have that?
Mr. Reinken: Page 120, paragraph 2, second sentence.

We can deduce it—that is, the constitution—from the general principle, which is the immediate unity of the substantial spirit and the individual. But this is equivalent to the spirit of the family, which is here extended over the most populous of countries. The element of subjectivity, that is to say, the reflection upon itself of the individual will in antithesis to the substantial (as the power in which it is absorbed) or the recognition of this power as one with its own essential being, in which it knows itself free, is not found on this grade of development.

LS: "Not *yet* found."
Mr. Reinken:

The universal will displays its activity immediately through that of the individual: the latter has no self-cognizance at all in antithesis to substantial positive being, which it does not yet regard as a power standing over against it—as, e.g., in Judaism, the "Jealous God" is known as the negation of the individual. In China, the universal will immediately commands what the individual is to do, and the latter complies and obeys with proportionate renunciation of reflection and personal independence.

LS: In other words, there is no consciousness of conflict, of sin as a fundamental fact. These are simple commands and they are obeyed as a matter of course. And if in a rare instance they would not be obeyed, well, then that would be taken care of, but there is no fundamental problem there.

Mr. Reinken:

If he does not obey, if he thus virtually separates himself from the substance of his being, inasmuch as this separation is not mediated by a retreat within a personality of his own, the punishment he undergoes does not affect his subjective and internal, but simply his outward existence. The element of subjectivity is therefore as much wanting to this political totality as the latter is on its side altogether destitute of a foundation in the moral disposition of the subject. For the substance is simply an individual—the emperor—whose law constitutes all the disposition. Nevertheless, this ignoring of inclination does not imply caprice, which would itself indicate inclination—that is, subjectivity and mobility. Here we have the one being of the state supremely dominant—the substance, which, still, hard and inflexible, resembles nothing but itself—includes no other element.[22]

LS: "Inclination" is a translation for the German word *Gesinnung*, which is a very bad translation, an impossible translation, but on the other hand, I wouldn't know how to translate it properly, *Gesinnung*. Mr. Mewes, do you have an idea? Mr. Franke? Well, let us say "an inner sense, a thing pointing in the right direction," not merely inclination. Yes?

Student: The other translation that he uses in most cases is "disposition," and in the etymological sense.

LS: How do they translate it when Weber speaks of the two kinds of ethics, the ethics of responsibility and the ethics of intention? What did he say?[23]

Mr. Reinken: He called it inclination.

LS: Well, "intention" would surely be better than "inclination."

Mr. Reinken: We have an American colloquialism that might come close: "I am of a mind to do something."

Student: Disposition.

LS: And also in the intellectual sense, as it were, a bit more. Yes?

Student: In this stage, custom has a very great role. But what can be the substantial basis of custom?

LS: Custom . . . you grow into custom. It is a state like that of children. All are children, and there is one father, the emperor; and this is to a considerable extent reasonable in China, but it is only substantial, substantive freedom. Substantial rationality, but not subjective. I mean, it is not understood in its reasonableness; it is handed down and accepted as if by children. Mr. Shulsky?

Mr. Shulsky: But this first passage seems to indicate that the emperor, being the one parent among all his children, somehow rises to a different level. But that would be more or less impossible, wouldn't it?

LS: No, he does, but this is exactly the point, that only he does: this is what Hegel means by despotism. Despotism is a state in which only one man is free. And this is of course then for this very reason a defective freedom, even for that one.

Mr. Shulsky: Later on he seems to give the impression that the emperor is really so much controlled by the traditions represented by *his* father that in a way he is as much of a child as all the others.

LS: Yes. Because from Hegel's point of view, one cannot be fully free if not all are. Let us see some examples that may make this a little bit clearer. On page 123, second paragraph, where he says that the paternal care of the emperor and the spirit of his subjects as children don't leave the moral circle of the family.

Mr. Reinken: Middle of the second paragraph, page 123.

> This paternal care on the part of the emperor, and the spirit of his subjects—who like children do not advance beyond the ethical principle of the family circle, and can gain for themselves no independent and civil freedom—makes the whole an empire, administration, and social code, which is at the same time moral and thoroughly prosaic—that is, a product of the understanding without free reason and imagination.[24]

LS: So Hegel explains here what he understands by "prosaic": reasonable, without free reason and fancy or imagination. In other words, calculated out plausibly. That is what he means by that: in this sense rational, but with no freedom of the imagination, no freedom of reason, not in the service of such purposes, wholly unpoetic. In the sequel he makes clear why he disapproves of the admiration for China which was very common in the seventeenth and eighteenth centuries. You know the Europeans were quite impressed by the reasonableness and the emperor who plows the field once a year. Compare this with Louis XIV, who would never have done that, and so on. And Hegel makes it quite clear why he disapproves of it. What is the reason? What is the fundamental reason why Hegel disapproves of the Chinese order, regards it as lower than the European? There is equality—this is what impressed some of them, especially Leibniz—but no freedom. In other words, everything is run by administration. People are fully, wisely administered, justly administered, but administered. And that is the fundamental defect: the paternalism. And he develops this theme by giving a considerable variety of examples, and he explains how everything depends actually on the character and the assiduity of the individual emperor. There is no life, so to speak, in the state. It all depends on the man at the top. Let us see as another example, I do not know where, it should be on page 128 or 129: that the punishment is mostly corporeal.

Mr. Reinken: Paragraph 2, page 128.

> A third point is that punishments are generally corporal chastisement. Among us this would be an insult to honor; not so in China, where the feeling of honor has not yet developed itself. A dose of cudgeling is the most easily forgotten; yet it is the severest punishment for a man of honor, who desires not to be esteemed physically assailable, but who is vulnerable in directions implying a more refined sensibility. But the Chinese do not recognize a subjectivity in honor; they are the subjects rather of corrective than retributive punishment, as are children among us; for corrective punishment aims at improvement, that which is retributive implies veritable imputation of guilt.[25]

LS: Perhaps one should translate this word by "discipline." "They are subject to discipline rather than to punishment, as the children with us." It is not strictly speaking punishment if the child is spanked, but he is simply brought back into the realm of proper conduct. No sense of honor in the Western sense of the word, which is of course something important. Honor has many meanings. But there is a story told about Themistocles before the battle of Salamis in the council of war, and the Spartan commander got very angry at a proposal of Themistocles and hit him with a whip, and then Themistocles said: *Pataxan men, akouson de,* "Whip me but listen to me."[26] And a modern officer, a modern Western officer especially of the last century would never of course be able to say: You may whip me, but only listen to me. This complete indifference to personal honor which Themistocles had—strictly objective, as Germans say, *sachlich*—forgetting about this nonsense and let us go on with our business, this concept of honor is somehow a heritage of the feudal tradition and we cannot suppose it to be present in other cultures. I mean, I have no notion of whether Hegel is entirely correct, but the fact is probably true that bodily punishment played a greater role in China, also of course applied to the highest officials in the state. You know bodily punishment was also very important in the West, but it was not applied to the nobility or the highest class of society.

Mr. Shulsky: But later on he says that the Chinese are very sensitive about insults, and he says they are very revengeful.

LS: But these are of course strictly private things.

Mr. Shulsky: Doesn't it offend one's sense of honor to be insulted?

LS: Not quite. That one regards one's body as something sacred, as it were, so that its being spanked 25 times—25 was the common number—would be an insult to the dignity of man is one thing; but to be sensitive to alleged or true humiliation is something entirely different. If people are sensitive to insults, that has nothing in itself to do with the dignity of man but with their own dignity, their own ego, whereas what Hegel has in mind is the sense that corporeal punishment is incompatible with the dignity of man. That is an entirely different proposition. Do you not see that? The mere ego—it is not I who am insulted if I am publicly spanked by some executioner, but the dignity of man is insulted. Does it not make a great difference? Because in the case of a punishment, it is understood that a court of law has found me guilty of a crime for which I am punishable with spanking. That is wholly outside of the sphere of personal sensitivity, which may come in accidentally but which is unimportant.

Mr. Shulsky: We use the term "a sense of honor" to cover both.

LS: Yes, sure. Therefore we must distinguish. In other words, is sensitivity the same as sense of honor? There is some objectivity involved. I mean this sense of humiliation people frequently have if they have been deservedly humiliated, i.e., told some unpleasant truth, this sensitivity is something fundamentally different from the sense of the dignity of man, where you do not think primarily of yourself but of some fundamental impropriety. Here on page 130, line 3 from the bottom.

Mr. Reinken:

In China, however, the distinction between slavery and freedom is necessarily not great, since all are equal before the emperor; that is, all are alike degraded, as no honor exists and no one has an individual right in respect of others. The consciousness of debasement predominates, and this easily passes into that of utter abandonment. With this abandonment—

LS: "Reprobation."
Mr. Reinken:

with this reprobation is connected the great immorality of the Chinese.[27]

LS: And here we would have to go into the background of the facts and therefore into whether Hegel's deduction of them is correct. Now next time we will continue the discussion of China, and then go over to India. Is there any point you would like to raise now? Yes?

Student: I was just wondering about the difference between obedience to substantial being, which is confined by traditions and customs, and respect for law, which is viewed as above and indifferent. What is the difference between the two?

LS: In the case of obedience, or as Hegel calls it, substantial freedom, you simply bow to the customary law and comply with it. In the case of subjective freedom, you know that if the laws are not reasonable they cannot command respect, except that you externally comply with them because you know the breach of the law is always unwise or almost always unwise, but that you know you can demand from the laws to which you are subject that they be reasonable. In other words, the principle of criticism of the law to which you are subject is admitted in the second case and not admitted in the first case. Is this clear enough?

Student: Yes, but there are so many censors in China, which has been mentioned by Hegel, who would constantly remonstrate to the emperor that such and such a law or ordinance is not good and therefore advise him to change it.

LS: Yes, but the question arises: Would this apply to the fundamental laws, or would this apply to something of the character of ordinances and so on? That would be the question, because from Hegel's point of view the mere presence of something like slavery or serfdom would already show that a large part of the population is by law excluded from having any claim to be heard. I'm sure that Hegel has done injustice to China— that was the reason why I referred to the seventeenth and eighteenth centuries—because of the repeated admiration for China. The key point is this: paternalism. In other words, a rational, wise, and just government is fundamentally wrong if there is not political freedom in the first place. Without this very powerful approach—one reads literature of the eighteenth century, Voltaire and other people—Hegel's statement is not intelligible. Aren't you Chinese, may I ask?

Student: Yes.

LS: I see. I of course have no responsibility for what Hegel says.

Student: Of course, Hegel has relied on secondary literature.

LS: Yes, surely. Naturally, entirely. It's very good you brought that up.

6   China Continued and India

Leo Strauss: I think we must take up this question, which came up . . . last time towards the end of the meeting. You spoke of the harsh judgment of Hegel on China and India.[1] Now let us first get rid of any possible sensitivities which anyone might have. I am thinking not only of our Chinese friend, but all among you who don't happen to be Protestants will be hurt sooner or later. I happen to be a Jew, and the Jews are treated not very much better than the Chinese or Hindus. Of course Catholicism, as Christianity, is treated much better but still not comparably—very unsatisfactorily. Now we must face that, and in the case of Hegel I suppose no one would assume for one moment that this was simply a prejudice of the German Lutheran of the early nineteenth century. That is a hopeless way of handling this question. But disregarding all sensitivities which any of us might have, no one today would write in this manner about China and India. Why? Let us start from there. Why is it now regarded as somehow fundamentally wrong to look at foreign cultures in this manner? Yes?

Student: I think that there are probably several reasons, one of course being the relativity of cultures, this idea that cultures ought not to be judged in harsh terms, or in especially good terms either for that matter.

LS: Yes, but is this not the consequence of a deeper view than relativism? In other words, is relativism not the consequence rather than the principle? Yes?

Student: You understand these cultures as they understand themselves.

LS: Yes, that is true. If you write a review of a book, you may have a harsh or a very favorable judgment, but first you must have understood the book. Yes, that goes without saying.

Student: But that's all you can do.

LS: In other words, the principle is that you cannot judge. This is of course not necessarily the last word of wisdom, so we cannot blame Hegel for having believed that it is possible to judge. The only question would be whether his standards of judgment are sufficient. Did you want to say something, Mr. Reinken?

Mr. Reinken: It seems to me that the only solid ground is a rather shallow ground, say, in the case of China that we have discovered that Sung[2] paintings and a few things from the Tang[3] are very good. And this corrects the error, but not much more can be said.

LS: Hegel knew that, as we shall see—knew it in a way. He knew about mountains, this beautiful landscape, he knew of that. But if we try to state Hegel's standard of judgment without any denominational indication, Hegel judges all these worlds, as we call them, with a view to two things which are highly regarded even today by many people in the West and also by many people in the East. The one let us call science, because he means something different from science by his philosophy, that goes without saying, but there is something fundamentally in common with science; and let us call the other political liberty. Now if he looks at China, India, or ancient Judea, he would say: Is there science and political liberty? No? Then they are fundamentally defective. That they are higher than, say, Africa, that of course he admits . . . but his concern with science and political freedom is paramount, and therefore he says that if people produce beautiful paintings, for example in China, that does not come into comparison with these essential things. This, I think, is what he means, and I believe that those among us who are concerned with science and political freedom cannot blame him on this ground. In other words, this is not an arbitrary standard. Now where does the blame come in, in which way? Well, I suppose if you replace Hegel's science, this all-comprehensive thing, by present-day science, which has a much narrower scope, then certain human needs are not satisfied by science, which must be satisfied elsewhere, in other ways. From this point of view, perhaps China, perhaps Zen Buddhism, perhaps India are superior. Zen Buddhism has great attractions today, as I have heard. So in other words, what has happened since Hegel is a profound change in the West by virtue of which the Western standards or values, as some people say, have lost this manifest evidence and superiority which they had in the past. And I am not speaking now of political freedom, because this, I think, has not fundamentally changed, but in the other respect. Yes?

Mr. Reinken: I was going to say that political freedom falls a little differently on our ear.

LS: You mean that what Hegel regarded as political freedom would be regarded as absence of freedom.

Mr. Reinken: I think in the vulgar ear, and our ears have been vulgarized by the change in freedom as much as the change in science. People think now that freedom is liberty to scratch the itch and to ride around in a Cadillac, whereas Hegel has a definition of freedom that makes John Knox sound like a softie: to will the law to yourself. But to will is a rather severe morality.

LS: Let me say a word about the first thing you said, which is of course very helpful. If we take the most undesirable characteristics of Western civilization—I think in French they call it Coca-Cola—then of course compared with that, I think some aspects of central African cannibalism could be considered higher. I cede that point. Now surely this is part of the story, that a certain decay of the West has taken place which not only permits us but compels us to have a much greater respect for what many peoples in the past have produced, even if that does not live up to what is highest in the Western European tradition. Surely that is one important point. But still you must not forget the survival of certain things in Hegel, in the notions of the underdeveloped countries, which means of course they are less developed. People think then chiefly of the industry and so on, but that doesn't contradict Hegel's notions at all, because industry requires science and so on. If people believe that by replacing "underdeveloped" by "emergent" they change the situation radically, I think they are mistaken, because an emerging nation is not an actual nation. There is in this sense a becoming, a defect, still defectiveness: just as a colt is not a horse proper, an emerging nation is not a nation proper. So this will not help. Let me see, you are quite right in repeating again that for Hegel the religion, and not the political things and still less the economic things, are the fundamental ones. There is no question about that. We must take this up somewhat later. Chinese history is not true history, Hegel says.

Student: He doesn't really say that.

LS: I'm sorry, you said "is not true history, we may suppose." Why are you so hesitant, only to suppose and not to say it definitely?

Student: No, I said I thought we could infer it, but maybe I was still too weak . . .

LS: You read also the preceding parts of the *Philosophy of History*? How does the work begin?

Student: It begins with a discourse on three kinds of history. The beginning of the introduction, you mean?

LS: Exactly. And does this not imply his judgment on Chinese history?

Student: Yes, it does.

LS: I mean, that would be a kind of chronicles, not on the level of Thucydides or a Caesar. So that would seem to settle that. So generally speaking, one must say that the change toward the Eastern cultures is a consequence of the self-criticism of the West. Is it not clear? To the extent to which the West had its old certainty of being on the right track, to that extent it regarded itself as superior. In order to explain at least to some extent what Hegel means by the element lacking in the East, generally speaking, Hegel uses very sophisticated and sometimes abstruse expressions. One can use a very simple expression which occurs, for example, in Aristotle and which is in a way the beginning of inner freedom in this sense. In all these old cultures, and of course also in much simpler ones, there is an equation which is not necessarily explicitly made because it is a matter of course, namely, of the good with the ancestral: the good old times, as people say today. And freedom of the mind begins the moment this equation is questioned. And I think what Hegel implies is that according to the best of his knowledge, no such questioning existed or was possible in China and India. It surely took place in Greece, we have evidence for that, and therefore from this point of view Greece plays a very great role, and Hegel tries to show how the emergence of this kind of thinking is connected with the Greek religion, with the way in which the Greeks understood their gods. So is there any other general point you wanted to discuss? Mr. Barber?

Mr. Barber: In answer to the general question of the bad taste of Hegel's judgment today—

LS: Let us put it this way: the same fairness to which China and India have claim, Hegel too has claim.[4]

Mr. Barber: I wondered if this isn't almost built into Hegel's method itself. That is, by saying that spirit is something individual and a property of the individual and that history is a development of spirit, ultimately the development of the individual, doesn't that in effect render all racial and national characteristics as characteristics of a human being as more or less accidental?

LS: In one sense, yes. We come to the question later on when he speaks of the modern state. According to Hegel's view, the modern state, the reasonable state, necessarily emerged in Protestant countries, and only Protestantism is in fundamental harmony with it; but Catholicism, to say nothing of Judaism, is not. But Hegel did not draw the inference that Catholics and Jews can therefore never be members of a reasonable state. I mean, that would be the consequence which you would seem to imply. From Hegel's point of view, precisely because Hegel was not a racialist in any sense, there is no reason whatever why Chinese or Hindus could not become members of the rational state. But they have to cease to be Chinese and Hindus in spirit, not race; as long as the Chinese believe in their emperor and the Hindus believe in their caste system, they are wholly unfit for becoming members of a reasonable state. By the way, Mao would be the first to admit that. This is where there is no difference between Marx and Hegel—but not only Marx, of course. There is never any racialism in mind. At the most what Hegel would say is that geographic conditions give a slight edge to the development of this way of thinking rather than to another. The racial conditions might do too, but this is ultimately uninteresting. There is nothing of this in Hegel. How little Hegel had to do with racialism was stated very clearly by a famous constitutional lawyer in Germany who became a Nazi himself for deplorable reasons, when he said in the moment Hitler came to power—I think it was the 31st of January, 1933: On this day Hegel died, i.e., up to this point Hegel, modified of course, was still the teacher of politics in Germany but this was something incompatible.[5] And these are simply stupid statements, based on vague notions of authoritarianism. Of course Hegel was in favor of authority, but of course quite a few people are.

Mr. Barber: What I meant to suggest was that for a nation or person who is not himself racist, in order to try to improve, let us say, some backward country, that person's culture is then regarded as more or less accidental to him. I mean, since this is no longer a relevant consideration, then any improvement of that country would have to take place along individual lines. The culture to which he belongs is no longer an object of something he's got to change, something he's got to alter. We don't improve the country X by having them get rid of their culture. There seems to be something contradictory.

LS: Yes, sure. There is a great difficulty in that and also a lot of hypocrisy. I mean, if you abolish or make the Hindus abolish the caste system, don't you interfere with their culture? You can't help that. In all these cases that takes place. If we take the simpler case, that of what the communists do, they of course also are in a way in favor of cultural pluralism, as it is called, but it means that you say and think exactly the same things in various languages. You can have all these various central African languages which they have transformed into written languages, and you can also have all kinds of pottery and folk dances as you like, but the interesting things, the important things, are of course abolished. You cannot have progress and at the same time preservation of the old culture. The old cultures become the victims of the progress, more or less. The case is somewhat different in the countries where the progress is at home originally, where the idea of progress stems from—that is somewhat different. But in the other cases, there is no doubt that these cultures are sacrificed in one way or the other. On the occasion of the baptism of Clovis, the King of the Franks, the bishop baptizing him said: "Burn what you have worshiped—your evil heathen idol—and worship what you have burned (the cross)."[6] In other words, such a radical change is not possible without discontinuities; and that people, perhaps for sound reasons of tactics, underplay that element is a purely technical question about how radical change takes place. I mean, think of such a simple thing as an old tribal organization based on slavery. You abolish slavery, you in a way destroy that culture, you modify it truly very radically. Yes?

Student: Is it possible to interpret progress in a very narrow and limited way, purely technological, and save the essential things? But apparently these are so bound up with what prevents technological advance.

LS: I believe a certain truth of Marxism comes into it: if people produce and distribute in a radically different way, this is bound to have consequences in unexpected quarters. That, I believe, is true. Now let us begin and turn to page 131 in the translation. He is speaking about the religious side of the Chinese state.

Mr. Reinken:

We come, then, to the consideration of the religious side of the Chinese polity. In the patriarchal condition the religious exaltation of man has merely a human reference—simple morality [*Sittlichkeit?*] and right-doing.

LS: No, simple *Moralität* in the German. In other words, there is no particular religious fervor in it. The sentiment going with it is limited to mere ordinary honesty and decency. Yes?

Mr. Reinken:

The Absolute itself is regarded partly as the abstract, simple rule of this right-doing—eternal rectitude—partly as the power which is its sanction. Except in these simple aspects, all the relations of the natural world, the postulates of subjectivity—of heart and soul—are entirely ignored.[7]

LS: Ja, and somewhat later in this paragraph: "In China, the individual has no aspect of this independence; he is therefore dependent also in religion, dependent namely on natural beings, of which the highest is heaven."[8] He says here in the passage we have read, first, that in the Chinese world, the relations in the natural world are ignored; and yet we find the importance of heaven. So there seems to be a flat contradiction. How is this solved? A bit later: "That heaven could in the sense of our God."

Mr. Reinken:

This heaven might be taken in the sense of our term "God," as the Lord of nature (we say, for example, "Heaven protect us!") —

LS: And not meaning heaven. But go on.
Mr. Reinken:

but such a relation is beyond the scope of Chinese thought, for here the one isolated self-consciousness is substantial being, the Emperor himself, the supreme power. Heaven has therefore no higher meaning than nature.

LS: Not "the law of nature." But this doesn't solve our question that the Chinese ignore the relations in the natural world. And yet heaven, i.e., nature, is so important to them. Read on.
Mr. Reinken:

The Jesuits indeed yielded to Chinese notions so far as to call the Christian God "Heaven" (*Tien*); but they were on that account accused to the Pope by other Christian orders. The Pope consequently sent a cardinal to China, who died there. A bishop, who was subsequently dispatched, enacted that instead of "Heaven," the term "Lord of Heaven" should be adopted. The relation to *Tien* is supposed to be such, that the good conduct of individuals and of the Emperor brings blessing; their transgressions on the other hand cause want and evil of all kinds.

LS: Now we come gradually to the point.
Mr. Reinken:

The Chinese religion involves that primitive element of magical influence over nature, inasmuch as human conduct absolutely determines the course of events. If the Emperor behaves well, prosperity cannot but ensue: Heaven must ordain prosperity.[9]

LS: And so on. And then a little bit later he says: "Hence the emperor becomes the true legislator for heaven," i.e., nature does not have that independence which it must have in order to be nature. And there is something in common with sorcery, i.e., with the African principle. So this is the solution of the difficulty. Formerly I had a student, a Westerner, who was a student of Chinese things and I pumped him at that time about matters Chinese, especially regarding the question of whether there is a Chinese word, or rather symbol, for nature. I forget entirely what I learned on that occasion. Is there a Chinese symbol which can properly be translated "nature"?

Student: It would be a modern translation, but the translation must have been in existence after the seventeenth century.

LS: I.e., after Europeans had already come to them.

Student: Yes. But this is new.

LS: I see, and not in the old texts? In other words, as a minor criticism of Hegel himself, he doesn't hesitate to ascribe to the Chinese a notion of nature—Heaven is nature—without having answered the question: Did the Chinese have any notion of nature? Or to state it still more crudely: Is there any Chinese word or symbol for nature? And one can perhaps say also that what Hegel has in mind is that this freedom, the freedom of the mind, development of subjectivity or whatever you like is connected with the emergence of a concept of nature. That would be, I think, somewhat more historically exact than Hegel's own statements, but I think in line with what he intends. Now previously I had said that the key point is the distinction between the ancestral and the good, i.e., the ancestral is not for this reason yet the good. A fantastic thought. I mean, we are so accustomed to it; but if we study older things or faraway things, we see immediately that this was the greatest change. Now how is this distinction between the ancestral and the good connected with the emergence of nature? Mr. . . .

Student: What is natural can be opposed to what is ancestral.

LS: So what is good by nature can be opposed to the ancestral, that which is good by tradition. So in other words, the two things truly belong together. At the end of the paragraph, on page 133, he gives a further example of that.

Mr. Reinken:

In the Y-King[10] certain lines are given which supply fundamental forms and categories—on account of which this book is called the Book of Fates. A certain meaning is ascribed to the combination of such lines, and prophetic announcements are deduced from this groundwork. Or a number of little sticks are thrown into the air, and the fate in question is prognosticated from the way in which they fall. What we regard as chance, as natural connection, the Chinese seek to deduce or attain by magical arts; and in this particular also, their want of spiritual religion is manifested.[11]

LS: Yes. You see, in other words, what we said before about magic, and especially in the section on Africa, is still of great importance within China, and that is the reason why he mentions it here directly. Now then he speaks on page 134 about the absence of genuine science. Now science does not mean that there is a doctrine or law available, handed down from generation to generation; science requires the development of free subjectivity, i.e., that the next generation is able to question what is handed down by the preceding generation. If this is absent, science proper is absent, although there may be a law that's a very valuable law or as he states it on page 135, bottom.

Mr. Reinken:

As to the sciences themselves, history among the Chinese comprehends the bare and definite facts, without any opinion or reasoning upon them—

LS: "Any judgment and reasoning." In other words, at most chronicles. Yes?

Mr. Reinken:

In the same way, their jurisprudence gives only fixed laws, and their ethics only determinate duties, without raising the question of a subjective foundation for them.[12]

LS: Yes, "without being concerned with an *innere Begründung*," without finding reasons say in this particular duty, why it should be a duty, of this law, why it should be a law. The absence of questioning and doubt, the absolute preponderance of tradition is crucial here. On page 137, line 10 from bottom, I believe it is.

Mr. Reinken:

The Chinese have as a general characteristic, a remarkable skill in imitation, which is exercised not merely in daily life, but also in art. They have not yet succeeded in representing the beautiful, as beautiful; for in their painting perspective and shadow are wanting. And although a Chinese painter copies European pictures (as the Chinese do everything else) *correctly*; although he observes accurately how many scales a carp has; how many indentations there are in the leaves of a tree; what is the form of various trees, and how the branches bend—the Exalted, the Ideal and Beautiful is not the domain of his art and skill. The Chinese are, on the other hand, too proud to learn anything from Europeans, although they must often recognize their superiority.[13]

LS: This sounds very strange at the end. Originally when the West emerged in Greece, one could say that the mark of the Greeks was that they are willing to learn from everyone, and the barbarians are those who refuse to learn from anyone. And Hegel seems to fall into the same defect of which he accuses the Chinese. But here, with respect to the point to which the lady referred in her paper, the great beauty of Chinese paintings, Hegel seems to be simply unfair. But he takes up this question later on, on page 158 in the center. We should read that.
Mr. Reinken:

The Hindus are depraved. In this all Englishmen agree. Our judgment of the morality of the Hindus is apt to be warped by representations of their mildness, tenderness, beautiful and sentimental fancy. But we must reflect that in nations utterly corrupt there are sides of character which may be called tender and noble. We have Chinese poems in which the tenderest relations of love are depicted; in which delineations of deep emotion, humility, modesty, propriety are to be found; and which may be compared with the best that European literature contains.

LS: In other words, he knows that.
Mr. Reinken:

The same characteristics meet us in many Hindu poems; but rectitude, morality—

LS: No, *Sittlichkeit* he says. "Rectitude" is too narrow. Read the next verse. It makes clear what he means.
Mr. Reinken:

freedom of soul, consciousness of individual right—[14]

LS: "Of one's own right," i.e., of one's own dignity as a human being, which therefore leads to the recognition of the same dignity in every other human being, are wholly separate. In other words, he doesn't deny that there are very fine and great things in China and India, but he says somehow the soul is missing, the core is missing, because his awareness of the rights of man is missing; and Hegel must be judged on this ground and on no lesser ground.

Now we come to the section on India, and we might perhaps begin at the beginning, page 139.

Mr. Reinken:

> India, like China, is a phenomenon antique as well as modern; one which has remained stationary and fixed, and has received a most perfect home-sprung development. It has always been the land of imaginative aspiration, and appears to us still as a fairy region, an enchanted world. In contrast with the Chinese state, which presents only the most prosaic understanding, India is the region of fantasy and sensibility.

LS: So in other words, Hegel starts here from the first impressions as a European would get them when confronted with them either as a traveler or as reading the literature, in translations of course. And this implies that India is higher than China, because the prosaic understanding is lower than fancy and sentiment.

Mr. Reinken:

> The point of advance in principle which it exhibits to us may be generally stated as follows: In China, the patriarchal principle rules a people in a condition of nonage, the part of whose moral resolution is occupied by the regulating law, and the moral oversight of the Emperor.

LS: Hence there is no difference in China, according to Hegel, between a breach of the moral law, as we would call it, and the breach of a rule of etiquette, because there is no inner principle of distinction; it is just the custom and you have to act with propriety. What the substance of these things is doesn't make any difference. Needless to say, this exists of course also in the West, that some people regard a false move at table as perhaps worse than a crime. But still that is not of course the considered view of the West but to be found among some snobs, however frequent or numerous they may be.

Mr. Reinken:

Now it is the interest of Spirit that external conditions should become internal ones —

LS: Not "conditions," "externally posed determinations," such as what custom prescribes regarding parents and children, guests at dinner table, and so on.
Mr. Reinken:

that the natural and the spiritual world should be recognized in the subjective aspect belonging to intelligence; by which process the unity of subjectivity and being generally — or the idealism of existence — is established.

LS: In simple language, that we understand why we act in the manner that we do and not merely because it is equally prescribed by custom or tradition; or, if it is not necessarily the case for truly irrelevant external rules of politeness — why you should take off your hat or put it on, this kind of thing — we know that is indifferent, but as a nice person one has to comply with custom in different matters, which of course means not being late, etc.
Mr. Reinken:

This idealism, then, is found in India, but only as an idealism of imagination, without distinct conceptions — one which does indeed free existence from beginning and matter, but changes everything into the merely imaginative; for although the latter appears interwoven with definite conceptions —

LS: "With concepts," in other words, not merely imaginary.
Mr. Reinken:

and thought presents itself as an occasional concomitant, this happens only through accidental combination.[15]

LS: Yes, and somewhat later, on page 140, towards the end of the paragraph he makes the point that there are wonderfully beautiful things in India, but they cease to be so beautiful in the moment we approach them from the point of view of the worthiness or dignity of man and of freedom, i.e., if we are not simply captivated by beauty but keep a cool head and think of the most important things. This is always to be understood. This he makes clear on page 141 in the first paragraph, 12 lines from the end.

Mr. Reinken:

> In this universal deification of all finite existence, and consequent degradation of the Divine, the idea of theanthropy, the incarnation of God, is not a particularly important conception. The parrot, the cow, the apes, etc. are likewise incarnations of God, yet are not therefore elevated above their nature.[16]

LS: Now in other words, this is what he calls Hindu pantheism. God is in everything, but in a fanciful manner; and therefore he as it were is incarnated in any kind of being and not particularly in man. Therefore no awareness of the dignity of man with all these consequences. On page 142, line 3 from bottom.

Mr. Reinken:

> The English, or rather the East India Company, are the lords of the land; for it is the necessary fate of Asiatic empires to be subjected to Europeans; and China will some day or other be obliged to submit to the same fate.[17]

LS: Now that's interesting, isn't it? Now doesn't Hegel do here what he loathes to do, namely, prophesy, and in addition, prophesy wrongly? How would Hegel, if he could be resuscitated, defend this statement? Mr. Shulsky?

Mr. Shulsky: Well, he would say that the only way that China avoided being taken over by a Western nation was to adopt Western principles.

LS: That is true.

Mr. Shulsky: But whether that is a sufficient argument really depends on the extent to which Chinese Marxism is just simply Marxism and the extent to which it is something Chinese. Maybe that requires a longer discussion.

LS: Yes, but I think probably Hegel would accept the first point, still.

Mr. Reinken: Not only does China exist only because she's taken on a Western character, but if it were not for the impasse between the two great European powers—because America is part of Europe, on his account—China could be put in her place very quickly.

LS: That is a question. I mean, let us assume that the situation is somewhat different: this country wouldn't have any interest in putting down China together with Soviet Russia. I mean, there is a simple axiom of foreign politics: the neighbor of your neighbor is my friend, because the neighbor is likely to be an enemy of that country. Just like de Gaulle's parleying: France, Germany, and to the east of Germany there is Russia—*n* examples from history. So let us not engage in prophecies more indefensible than Hegel's. So one could also say that Hegel admits he doesn't prophesy regarding the unessential, accidental which cannot possibly be predicted, but this could. Yes?

Student: A general question about the difference between India and China. Hegel told us that the development of the different parts of the Oriental world were roughly temporally concomitant, that they all started around 2200, and they took place roughly in the same span of years. I was just wondering how it's possible to look at various things that took place at the same time and say one represents the progress of the other and that Spirit moves from one to the other.

LS: He does not mean that the Indian spirit came into being through transformation of the Chinese spirit. He doesn't say that and doesn't mean it.

Student: Not that Indians as opposed to Chinese, but somebody—

LS: No, looking at these two spirits, the Chinese and the Hindu, Hegel finds that the Hindu spirit is superior to the Chinese spirit. I mean, whether it is chronologically later is not so terribly important, but it is characteristic of both that they are indeed very old compared with any Western figure. Mr. Shulsky?

Mr. Shulsky: In the comparison of the four Oriental civilizations, he says that India and China are in a certain sense eternal, presumably because of the natures of their spirits.

LS: In the jargon of our time: no dynamism.

Mr. Shulsky: Yes, and this was contrasted with Persia and with Egypt, which did pass away in time. Well, now he seems to be saying that the survival of India and China is just sort of accidental, but that the Chinese principle as principle can and will in fact be destroyed. And the same with the Indian principle.

LS: But they survived so long until the West was able to assert its military superiority against them, whereas the West came much too late in the case of Persia and Egypt. This is nevertheless true.

Mr. Shulsky: Well, does he mean then that these spirits were sort of by themselves eternal and that the nations passed out of existence or will pass out of existence only because of some foreign power, or does he mean that somehow—

LS: No. To begin with, one could say that it is a mere accident, but Hegel believes there is more to it than that, that in different ways and for somewhat different reasons, the Chinese order could last forever and ever, until Europe happens to change and is therefore able to conquer. But Rome couldn't because the kind of changes which took place in Rome, say, the altercation between the patricians and the plebeians, is different from the taking over of India by the Manchus[18] and many others. Hegel pointed out that because they were all absorbed by China—do you remember that?—they are absorbed, and so there was no change in the spirit of China, whereas the spirit of Rome, say, between early Rome and the Rome of the first century had changed very radically.

Mr. Shulsky: And that just raises, I think, a question, because in the beginning of the introduction he said something about the fact that a nation cannot die a violent death, you know, simply by invasion or someone taking over unless it has already died a natural death, i.e., somehow a death of the spirit, which somehow would seem to be contradicted by the tradition that China will be invaded and die a violent death.

LS: Yes, but Hegel could say that this kind of eternity is, in a way, a kind of death: the absence of any type of change. On page 144 in the second paragraph where he turns to the political life of the Hindus.

Mr. Reinken:

> With regard to the political life of the Indians, we must first consider the advance it presents in contrast with China. In China there prevailed an equality among all the individuals composing the Empire; consequently, all government was absorbed in its center, the Emperor, so that individual members could not attain to independence and subjective freedom. The next degree in advance—[19]

LS: You see this is the answer to your question about why India is more advanced than China or superior to China. Here they all are equally the children of the emperor; that is not so in India. In India there is a certain independence of the subjects, and he will explain that in the sequel. Yes?

Student: My question is then maybe we shouldn't take the idea of a super spirit, more or less, moving through various stages too literally.

LS: No, it is true only from a certain moment on, say, from when we come to Western Asia, not to say to Greece, that there is such a movement. In other words, that Rome comes after Greece, Christianity comes after Rome: this is necessary. An analysis of Christianity or an analysis of

Rome would show that somehow this is post-Greek *historically*, whereas this is not meant in the literal historical sense. Yes?

Student: I wonder if the principle leads to the fact that one true culture can exist at the same time as one superior to the other—in other words, a further development of the spirit—would not suggest in principle the possibility that spirit fully realized could present itself in an area where it did not have that kind of historical development and germination in the past. In other words, that history isn't absolutely in principle necessary to the realization of the spirit; it only happens to have happened.

LS: Then history wouldn't be rational if it only has happened to have happened. Where is the necessity? But no, Hegel would say that the co-existence of India and China implying no serious attempt on either side to conquer the other is of the essence of China and India, whereas the subjugation, say, of the Assyrian and Babylonian empires by Persia has something to do with the Persian principle, which made it possible to conquer and to integrate. The same of course was also true of Greece and Rome. Continue, please.

Mr. Reinken:

The next degree in advance of this unity is difference, maintaining its independence against the all-subduing power of unity. An organic life requires in the first place one soul, and in the second place, a divergence into differences, which become organic members and in their several offices develop themselves to a complete system; in such a way, however, that their activity reconstitutes that one soul. This freedom of separation is wanting in—

LS: "of particularization."
Mr. Reinken:

freedom of particularization is wanting in China. The deficiency is that diversities cannot attain to independent existence. In this respect, the essential advance is made in India, viz. that independent members ramify from the unity of despotic power. Yet the distinctions which these imply are referred to Nature—

LS: They "relapse into nature" would be a better, more literal translation.
Mr. Reinken:

relapse into nature. Instead of stimulating the activity of a soul as their center of union and spontaneously realizing that soul, as is the case in organic life, they petrify and become rigid, and by their stereotyped character condemn the Indian people to the most degrading spiritual serfdom. The distinctions in question are the castes. In every rational state there are distinctions which must manifest themselves. Individuals must arrive at subjective freedom, and in doing so, give an objective form to these diversities. But Indian culture has not attained to a recognition of freedom and inward morality; the distinctions which prevail are only those of occupations and civil conditions.[20]

LS: Let us leave it here for the moment. Is the point clear, the fundamental point of the difference between China and India, as Hegel sees it? Articulation is necessary. There is no articulation in the mass of subjects. The mass of subjects, even of kindly treated subjects, of children, is opposed to the single emperor. There must be an articulation within the people. Such an articulation we find in India, but it is a very imperfect articulation because articulation takes the form of castes. And what is wrong with the caste system from Hegel's point of view? Hegel makes a distinction later on between castes and estates, either in the medieval sense or in the sense in which one could still speak in the nineteenth century of estates, not merely in the political but also in the social sense of the term. What is wrong with the caste system, according to Hegel?

Student: The individual is absolutely fixed in the caste; except as an exception, there is no way one man can pass from one caste to another.

LS: Yes. And "estate" is not the best translation of the German word used, *Stände*. For example, in German you say "the estate" of a physician, of a lawyer, or of an artisan or whatever it may be, where you would say probably the "profession" in English. In German it has a somewhat broader meaning. So of course if someone is a physician or a lawyer, that depends on his choice, at least formally. Whether you belong to this or that caste does not depend on your choice, but entirely on birth. Now what about the medieval system, the feudal system, there were not castes but estates. But were these estates not also hereditary?

Student: It wasn't so much your being the son of a baron, but you had to be educated as a baron to think—you had to play the part—

LS: That is not decisive, the simple difference.

Student: The fundamental humanity of all castes in medieval times.

LS: But what is the simple empirical proof of that?

Student: Religion?

LS: Sure. A serf's son could enter a monastery and then, in other words, he could belong to the highest estates, whereas in India no one can become a Brahmin under any conditions. Hegel sees in this freedom of entering the spiritual state a foreshadowing of the modern freedom of choosing one's estate entirely. Yes?

Student: What about the objection raised in the paper about the subjective choice involved in the theory or the idea of reincarnation?

LS: We come to that later. That's a very important question. But first of all, regarding the estates, the articulation of a society, this is in a way antidemocratic because it means inequality. On page 145, line 17 from bottom, if you can count quickly.[21]

Mr. Reinken:

> Against the existence of "classes" generally, an objection has been brought—especially important in modern times—drawn from the consideration of the State in its aspect of abstract equity—

LS: —all are equal before the law, and such a distinction implies a certain inequality, and so on. How does Hegel answer that?

Mr. Reinken:

> But equality in civil life is something absolutely impossible, for individual distinctions of sex and age will always assert themselves; and even if an equal share in the government is accorded to all citizens, women and children are immediately passed by, and remain excluded.

LS: That is to say, the objection regarding women has been happily disposed of in the meantime, even in France—and the children, that is I think a matter of the future. I remember the profound remark of General Eisenhower when he was president: if the man is old enough to carry arms, he is old enough to vote,[22] which, I think, doesn't go to the root of the question. Yes?

Student: About two years ago a study was done here in the sociology department about the voting behavior of preschoolers.

LS: Of what?

Student: Of first- and second-graders.

LS: I see. In other words, why not extend the voting age to infants, and at the next stage to rats? If rats can solve problems, as we have learned, and sometimes more difficult problems than that of voting, why not? Yes, sure.

Mr. Reinken:

> The distinction between poverty and riches, the influence of skill and talent, can be as little ignored—utterly refuting those abstract assertions. But while this principle leads us to put up with variety of occupations, and distinction of the classes to which they are entrusted, we are met here in India by the peculiar circumstance that the individual belongs to such a class essentially by birth, and is bound to it for life. All the concrete vitality that makes its appearance sinks back into death.[23]

LS: Yes, and in death it becomes fossilized. The sound principle that everyone should have the occupation for which he is fitted and which he likes is replaced by a blind assignment. This leads however to a difficulty which is taken up on page 147, where Hegel says, line 4, that these differences—

Mr. Reinken:

> But that these distinctions are here attributed to nature, is a necessary result of the idea which the East embodies. For while the individual ought properly to be empowered to choose his occupation, in the East, on the contrary, internal subjectivity is not yet recognized as independent; and if distinctions obtrude themselves, their recognition is accompanied by the belief that the individual does not choose his particular position for himself, but receives it from nature.

LS: You see the connection between this defect and the absence of the notion of the rights of man. But there is another difficulty in the sequel in the sentence after the next, "Plato in his *Republic*."

Mr. Reinken:

> Plato, in his *Republic*, assigns the arrangement in different classes with a view to various occupations, to the choice of the governing body. Here, therefore, a moral, a spiritual power is the arbiter. In India, nature is this governing power.[24]

LS: Well, is there not something misleading in what Hegel says about Plato? I think this is a very characteristically misleading remark. What is the difference between Plato's system in the *Republic* and the Indian caste system?

Student: The Indian caste system has nothing to do with subjective merit.

LS: Yes, but in Plato this is also not quite so clear. Mr. . . . ?

Student: He recognized the possibility that a golden child could be born to bronze or base metal parents.

LS: So in other words, what Hegel does not say is that according to Plato the classes are distinguished according to nature, just as in India but in a different way. The individuals are picked wholly regardless of what their birth is, what their parents are. Yes?

Student: . . . fundamental distinction?

LS: No, I'm sorry, Hegel is silent about Plato's reference to nature. This is, I think, quite characteristic. Yes?

Student: He also seems to be silent about the fact that Plato is talking about the fact that a man should do what he is best suited for in this life, while the Indian is to do the best he can because in his next life he will be better off, and there's no worry about the present life.

LS: In a way, yes. That is what he means when he says the highest is destruction or death in India. He says it on page 148 in the first paragraph. Now let us read this paragraph on page 148. "Each caste —"

Mr. Reinken:

> has its special rights and duties. Duties and rights, therefore, are not recognized as pertaining to mankind generally —

LS: No, "to man as man." There are no rights and duties of man. There are none because they differ from class to class; there is nothing in common.

Mr. Reinken:

> but as those of a particular caste. While we say "Bravery is a virtue," the Hindus say, on the contrary, "Bravery is the virtue of the Kshatryas." Humanity generally, human duty and human feeling do not manifest themselves; we find only duties assigned to the several castes. Everything is petrified into these distinctions, and over this petrifaction a capricious destiny holds sway. Morality and human dignity are unknown; evil passions have

their full swing; the Spirit wanders into the dream world, and the highest state is annihilation.[25]

LS: "Destruction." What this means we will see in the sequel. Now at the beginning of the next paragraph, he says—and this was properly emphasized in the paper[26]—the key to this whole Indian system, as well as to any other system, is religion. And while Hegel knows that some of the economic factors, as we would say, are of importance, he does not regard them as the key. The key is religion and not, say, relations of production. What is behind that difference between Hegel and Marx? What is the ultimate, simple Marxian argument for why the relations of production are the key? Yes?

Mr. Shulsky: Well, man basically first has to provide for his immediate physical needs, and in doing so, certain relations grow up immediately; they develop from the most basic needs and they structure everything else.

LS: In other words, the most urgent is ultimately the key, and food is obviously more urgent for mere survival than any profound thoughts. How could one say Hegel explains that?

Mr. Shulsky: Simply the fact that man is determined by what he thinks as being the basic thing, not in the sense of the most urgent but in the sense that what one thinks about is the most important thing. And this gives you the key to the—

LS: So in the one case, the most urgent; in the other case, the highest. So one could say that Marx understands man as primarily a needy being in the sense of the bodily needs, while Hegel understands man as the deferential being. This is the issue. And I think the details where Marx or Hegel give right or wrong interpretations in given cases are much less interesting because they can more easily be corrected than this fundamental issue. This is indeed a crucial question. Now with what right could Hegel say that the highest is destruction for the Hindu? He makes this clear on page 148 in the translation, in the center of the second paragraph.

Mr. Reinken:

Abstract unity with God is realized in this abstraction from humanity.[27]

LS: What he means by this is that destruction is the disappearance as it were of everything, including men, in God: complete abnegation of oneself. Not loving God with all their heart and all their soul where the being of the individual is maintained, but the destruction. And then he gives a very vivid expression, and this is a question which was alluded to by some of you earlier regarding the justification of the caste system. On page 149, toward the end of the first paragraph, when he speaks about when Englishmen were present at such an act.

Mr. Reinken:

say that in half an hour the blood streamed forth from every part of the devotee's body; he was taken down and presently died. If this trial is also surmounted, the aspirant is finally buried alive, that is put into the ground in an upright position and quite covered over with soil; after three hours and three-quarters he is drawn out, and if he lives, he is supposed to have at last attained the spiritual power of a Brahmin.[28]

LS: Now the point here he also makes clear on page 151 when he describes the day of the Brahmin. "The business of the Brahmins consists chiefly in the reading of the Vedas." Only the Brahmins may really read them. Page 151.

Mr. Reinken:

The employment of the Brahmins consists principally in the reading of the Vedas: they only have a right to read them. Were a Sudra to read the Vedas, or to hear them read, he would be severely punished, and burning oil must be poured into his ears. The external observances binding on the Brahmins are prodigiously numerous, and the Laws of Manu treat of them as the most essential part of duty. The Brahmin must rest on one particular foot in rising, then wash in a river; his hair and nails must be cut in neat curves, his whole body purified, his garments white; in his hand must be a staff of a specified kind; in his ears a golden earring. If the Brahmin meets a man of an inferior caste, he must turn back and purify himself. He has also to read in the Vedas, in various ways: each word separately, or doubling them alternately, or backwards. He may not look to the sun when rising or setting, or when overcast by clouds or reflected in the water. He is forbidden to step over a rope to which a calf is fastened, or to go out when it rains. He may not look at his wife when she eats, sneezes, gapes, or is quietly seated.[29]

LS: And so on. Hegel describes here the innumerable burdens on the Brahmins, and he explains later that all these burdens are of course absent from the lower castes, especially the lowest caste. Hegel doesn't speak of this without reason, I mean, not only in order to show how foolish this is because there is no solid ground for them, but he also has something deeper in mind, it seems to me. Yes?

Student: This earlier passage you read about a man becoming a Brahmin is in a sense a qualification in the caste system.

LS: Yes, I read it that way. But you see, the difficulties are immense! Now what Hegel has in mind, I believe, is this: might is not right, might is never sufficient; or to use our present-day jargon, ideologies are needed because men have a sense of right. Even the Nazis' racial doctrine must ultimately be understood with a view to this fact. No rights without duties. Unreasonable rights, as in the case of the Brahmins, are of course based on unreasonable duties, but there is no possibility of any rights without duties. He indicates this later on, for example on page 152, the second paragraph somewhere, when he speaks of the interest rates.

Mr. Reinken:

> Although in the case of a Warrior, the rate of interest may be as high as three per cent, in that of a Vaisya four per cent, a Brahmin is never required to pay more than two percent.[30]

LS: So you see, in other words, it is wonderful to be a Brahmin, surely good, but again there is the price which one has to pay for being a Brahmin. If there were only advantages, if they were not deserved advantages, the caste system would break down. Of course it is sufficient that it is deserved in the view of those subject to them, and I believe this is the answer to your question regarding their former lives. Whether a man belongs to this caste or that is due to his action in a former life. That means that the caste system is just.

Student: Yes, exactly, from the Hindu point of view.

LS: No, but I mean this doctrine, this ideology is the justification of the caste system in the sense that it shows that if X is a Brahmin, he deserves to be a Brahmin, and if he belongs to the Chandala, he deserves to be a Chandala. Men need that. I mean, it is not a mere appeasement of the subject races that there be no paying. It is much more than that. It must be. On page 153, line 6 from bottom.

Mr. Reinken:

> Thus every caste has its own duties; the lower the caste, the less it has to observe.[31]

LS: In other words, the number of duties increases with the other things. Indeed that is true regarding property. Brahmins have the advantage, for they don't pay any taxes. Now it is of course very easy to separate out these economic advantages and say that that is the meaning of the whole religious system. But of course, while it appeals to a certain nastiness or cynicism, it is by no means evident. But today the inclination to do that is of course very great.

Mr. Reinken: Could one draw something from the fact that the English first tried the Sudras because they had fewer of those unreasonable duties, but the Sudras turned out not to be militarily useful, so the English were forced to use the Kshatryas, whose distinction from the Sudras is in terms of obligations of a ceremonial nature? Yet these ceremonial obligations are bound up with real military usefulness, as it so strangely happens.

LS: Yes. But if one is confronted with such a system, what we can understand immediately is of course that it is good not to pay taxes and it is good perhaps to pay the lowest interest rate. These are obvious advantages. And of course it is very good to be highly esteemed and respected, regarded as belonging to the highest caste. So why not regard these manifest advantages, high social position plus great economic advantages, as the key to the whole thing? That seems to be very plausible. And these fancy things which we do not understand, the theories—you know, regarding God and so on, and also the wholly unintelligible, the ceremonial—why not regard this as mere opiate for the people? It is very plausible. But the question is whether that is wise, whether that is true. And this cannot be settled only on the ground that this one segment, the economic segment, is immediately intelligible to us, whereas the other is not. That is obviously a merely subjective and external distinction which has no basis in the subject matter. Then he turns on page 154 to the religion. And I think we should discuss this coherently next time. Yes?

Student: On the difficulty with reincarnation, wouldn't the Indian say that his station in life is determined by merit and in that respect is similar to the European estates?

LS: Yes, but still the point is only that this is not evident. He may say that if he is now a Brahmin, he has lived very well in his preceding life, and if he is now a Chandala, he has behaved very badly in his former life. But he doesn't know that, and we do not know it. Whereas in the rational state, a man's belonging to an estate would be due to knowable facts—a man went through college and medical school and so on, and therefore he is a physician; and because he made some particularly important medical observations, he is a very famous physician. These are knowable things, but what has happened between the previous incarnation and the present one is not knowable, it is only supposed.

Student: But he seems to understand better than we that they don't understand themselves at all. I mean, when he says that they refer to these distinctions: to nature—

LS: No, sure, that is true. I mean, this would be the simplest objection on the part of the present-day historian, that Hegel doesn't take the historian's duty to understand these people as they understand themselves seriously enough. But this would not necessarily make the chief points with which he is concerned irrelevant, because a closer and more exact study could very well lead to exactly the same . . . But I agree with that, I think that's what one should do. So we'll meet again next Tuesday.

7 India Continued and Persia

Leo Strauss: Thank you, Mr. Franke, but I have not quite succeeded in understanding you.[1] You refer to a fundamental difficulty at the beginning and then you try to state it at the end, and somewhere in the middle you gave an argument which I do not remember at this moment, the argument which seemed to call into question the rationality of history.

Mr. Franke: The inevitability of history, which is the rationality.

LS: But let us first take the main point. There is no change in Asia, in China and India. And if they had been alone, there would never have come any development. But let us also think of Africa, where the same would be true to a different degree. But is this mere variety for us as beholders not an indication of the fundamental inadequacy of the non-Western development? These three entirely different ways of living—disregarding now the difference between Buddhism and Hinduism: which is the truly human way of life? By implication, the Negroes, the Chinese, and the Hindus say: This is the good life. I once talked to a Hindu about the meaning of *dharma*, which is ordinarily translated by "religion," but I learned this has a much broader meaning. *Dharma* means something like a way. There is a way of a lion and also of course a way of man. And the way of man is naturally the Hindu religion; all others are barbarians in one way or another. Therefore all these ways claim to be the true way of life, and therefore they force at least the beholder beyond that variety. It is characteristic in these societies that only the beholder is forced into that and not the Hindus, Chinese, and Negroes themselves. The reason is that there cannot be beholders there. Why can't there be beholders? Why can't there be people in China and India—of course we are speaking of premodern times—or in Africa who behold it?

Mr. Franke: Because they have the misfortune of living before the absolute moment.

LS: No.

Mr. Hewitt: Because nobody has told them about there being a different way. All they know is one way, unless a group of travelers come.

LS: Yes, it has to do with travelers, but a certain kind of traveler. Not the kind of travelers who have run away from home because they have committed murder or who want to engage in trade, but travelers who want to do what?

Mr. Franke: To reform them.

LS: No.

Student: To simply enjoy yourself.

LS: Yes. Like Herodotus. In a way Odysseus was the very beginning. And Mr. Reinken, what did you want to say?

Mr. Reinken: I was going to blame it on the Himalayas and the Red Sea.

LS: No. These are for Hegel never more than necessary but not sufficient conditions. They are co-responsible. In other words, there is no awakening of the questioning mind. In Hegel's words, "subjectivity is dormant." And Hegel's contention is that the awakened subjectivity is necessarily later than the dormant subjectivity, not only in individuals—we all know we have to be babies before we are awake and . . .—but also for the human race as a whole. Therefore there must have been a long stretch of time in which there was no possibility of such beholders. The other point is that the awakening of subjectivity is preceded first of all by a simple barbarism—that goes without saying—but also by more than that. There can be cultures as distinguished from barbarism. There must be cultures within which individuality is not yet possible.

I read to my lecture class yesterday the speech of Zarathustra in Nietzsche's *Zarathustra* "On the One Thousand and One Goals," where Nietzsche says that primarily nations only were creators of what would be called their value systems and that the individual as creator is a very late creation. This is in fundamental agreement with what Hegel says. So there had to be cultures. There had to be objectivations, religions, states, etc., political organizations of one kind or another within which individuality was as yet impossible. The Chinese or Hindus could not possibly raise the questions which Hegel raises. Therefore the question of which of the two is prior and which is the second could not arise for them. Only from a reasonable point of view which could not develop there could this question be raised.

Mr. Franke: This is not my point, though.

LS: What is your point?

Mr. Franke: When you compare the history of the peoples of the world with individual life, there is in the individual life a continuity. This continuity is lacking as between the Orient and the West. The West somehow starts out—well, there may have been culture before history, too. But what I meant to say is that the possibility that spirit can stagnate, alienate itself under less than prohibitive conditions, as in Africa or the Arctic, or in Asia, this same could have been possible in the West, unless the idea already accounted for this in that it developed that kind of nature with the Mediterranean Sea.

LS: All right. These were conditions. Europe had of course very favorable material conditions, but the more immediately important condition was that Europe came into being on the basis of western Asia, including Egypt. Only on the basis of that—say, the Persian and the Egyptian empire—was it possible as a response to it. But I think that you make a mistake in the way in which you use the word "continuity." Continuity and discontinuity do not exclude each other in the way in which you presuppose that they do. Let us start from very simple examples. Someone is sick and gets sicker and sicker, and then he dies: continuity. And yet then he is dead, and this moment: discontinuity. Whereas formerly he was defectively alive, which is the meaning of being sick, he is now something qualitatively different. That is what Hegel means when he speaks of the change from quantity into quality, which is familiar to each one of you from Marx's propaganda if not from Hegel. So continuity and discontinuity do not exclude each other. Or shall I give another example? There are continuities which are discontinuities. Think of the freezing of water: small temperature changes. One centigrade, and then you come to one centigrade more and you have ice. So this is no problem for Hegel. There is at a certain moment, by virtue of the mere quantitative additive changes, something new which can no longer be understood in terms of the old, so that you have even to reinterpret the quantitative change as a preparation of the new. And that is no longer a merely quantitative change. Yes?

Student: Does it not seem strange, though, that there should be an element of chance at the beginning of a necessary process?

LS: What is chance here?

Student: There is an element of chance that the Western spirit began this development whereas the Asian spirit didn't.

LS: But it couldn't. I tried to explain. There could not be a rational state, as Hegel calls it . . . without a preparation. Man at the beginning was wholly incapable of a rational state because he was not capable of reasoning. He could not distinguish between the good and the ancestral or whatever you might call it. Now if this is so, there must have been complete unreason at the beginning, of course unreason of a being which was potentially rational but in a state of fully dormant reason.

Furthermore, it was necessary that there be social orders incompatible with the awakening of the individual, and then the next stage was the development of orders in which the individual could imperfectly develop, let us say Greece. And then finally the order in which the individual could fully develop and be confronted by an objectively rational order, an order where awake individuals are subject to laws, etc., while knowing them to be rational in principle. I mean, there may be some minor errors, that's uninteresting. Do you see that? Only if there could be a perfect beginning would Hegel be wrong. Otherwise something of this kind must be said. Hegel's whole philosophy is based on that. In biblical terms, the creation of non-man precedes the creation of man. Therefore, there must be nature before there is man. But men at the beginning must be as close to nature as man can possibly be. That is to say, his reason must be absolutely dormant, just as reason is more than dormant in stones, trees, and animals. Mr. Shulsky?

Mr. Shulsky: But in the development, I think the question that we're confused about here is that if you look at the Western world now, you can trace it back step by step to Persia, and you can say that there could not have been a Greece if there had not been an Egypt and no Egypt if there had not been Persia. Now, the problem is that if you say that there could not have been a Persia unless there had been an India or a China before, you are faced with a problem because Persia apparently developed out of a stock of people who were in a primitive condition and had no knowledge of India or China.

LS: That is the way in which Hegel understood it. But what does Hegel mean? He says that if we go back in a strictly remembering manner, what we have in our tradition, we would still be driven back to Persia and Egypt and also to Judea. This is a minor difficulty for Hegel. But then we understand the principle of Persia and then we see this is already something very high compared with the state of nature. Does this not imply, by negating it, earlier stages? And these earlier stages, Hegel says, we find as a matter of fact in India and China. That is, I think, what he means.

Mr. Shulsky: There is a big difference, though, because India and China are there, so to speak, as a matter of fact. But a knowledge of India and

China wasn't necessary for the development of Persia, but the knowledge of Persia was necessary to the development of Greece.

LS: That has to do with a higher development. The Persians were capable of having an empire which did not absorb the conquered nations, did not Persianize them as China Sinofied the conquered. You see, this presupposes already a qualitative difference. This is the way in which Hegel argued. You say that it is a mere accident that there is China and India. But Hegel would say: I just proved to you that it is no accident because the principle of Persia is complex and implies the negation of earlier principles. This I know still from logic. I look around and see that these principles are in fact embodied in China and in India, and now you say that it is an accident after I have proven to you that it is reasonable.

Mr. Reinken: May I draw a supporting distinction for Mr. Franke? In our own tradition in the High Middle Ages we have the doctrine of the Great Chain of Being which in particular includes such things as angels between man and God, things which are logically necessary and so, in the fullness of time or whatever, come to be. Now man need not necessarily communicate with God through the angels; it is merely that there are angels as well as men. It is another possibility to be provided for. So the things which necessarily exist here are not a chain of cause and effect but just a chain of being, but everything that can happen happens.

LS: In other words, you say that Hegel's argument would be logically equivalent to a proof of the existence of angels. [Laughter] But how would Hegel reply? You cannot prove to me empirically the existence of angels, but I can prove to you empirically the existence of India and China. So that is not so simple. Yes?

Mr. Hewitt: I'm not sure that I'm clear on this, but is it that India and China are, so to speak, previous states that are so fortuitously frozen in time?

LS: Not fortuitously. That is what Hegel says. Whether he's right or wrong is another matter. These are forms of society which were, to use present-day jargon, necessarily started and could not possibly change. The only end which they could find would be subjugation by a dynamic culture of universalist claim, the West.

Mr. Hewitt: But in them we also see what the primary state in Persia would have been like before development began.

LS: That would have been an uninteresting tribal thing, in the moment in which the spirit awoke there.

Mr. Hewitt: What I am saying is: The moment before the spirit awoke, is that what China was like?

LS: No. This is something which Hegel doesn't explain very much, but it is something like a prehistoric life, the formation of tribes. Of course there is a certain difficulty about that, because he should already have said something about it. But Hegel would probably say that there is no distinctive principle there, whereas in Africa you have this distinctive principle which, however low it may be, is still a principle. The same is of course true in China and India.

Well, I am not a Hegelian, and I do not believe that one can say that history is rational. But on the other hand, one must not underestimate the immense intellectual power which was Hegel's and by virtue of which he brought to light many very interesting things.[2] The improbability that this all should be rational—that is what strikes you and Mr. Shulsky—I understand that perfectly.

Mr. Reinken: But do we then rest at the point that Zarathustra and his complex principle emerged not upon an immediate supporting, causing structure of simple principles, but that there was a jump from the tribal with no principles all the way up to level three?

LS: Yes. And only we, the beholders, can see that it marks the progress beyond India and China. The fundamental question, again, is: Why were there no beholders there? And to that Hegel has a very good answer: there couldn't be beholders because that requires the development of the individual.

Mr. Franke: How could the central principle of the Orient reappear in Persia if the absolute idea, which works itself outwards in nature and history, is not conscious of itself?

LS: Of course it is not conscious. Consciousness would presuppose the beholder, the subject, the individual. Let me use an awful word, the "emancipated"—the individual who can look in wonder. And that is of course, in the clearest case, Greece. Mr. Barber?

Mr. Barber: To say that there cannot be any beholders in these times because the spirit has not yet awakened seems to be saying that there cannot be any beholders because there are not any beholders.

LS: It means that what we take for granted is the fact that there are, to use again the simplest expression, scientific men. But man as man is not scientific man, and it required an enormous labor, as Hegel says, of the spirit until there could be scientific men. And this, as a matter of fact, took place in Greece; and Hegel must show of course how it happened, the connection between the emergence of science in Greece and this particular pantheon—Zeus, Hera, etc.—compared with the pantheon of Egypt or what you find elsewhere. What is the connection between the Olympian gods, which are as much products of the human imagination as those of Egypt—how come the people worshiping the Olympian gods nevertheless produced science and philosophy? I think that that is still a necessary question.

Mr. Barber: But couldn't an answer to that be, again, simply as Hegel indicated, that science presupposes a certain rejection of authority? He has spoken of it in terms of turning nature with tools against nature itself. The political analogy would seem to be merely that there were no successful rebels. There were no successful political rebels.

LS: But Hegel would say: Is this a mere accident? Weren't the cards stacked against any rebels unless they would do exactly the same as what the preceding prince did—slitting throats and having handwomen and then someone else comes to the throne and does exactly the same thing? Where is the interest of the spirit in such idiotic repetitions of inanities? But in Greece it was possible to get rid of tyrants, say, of the early kings, and have free conduct. Why is this? How is this connected with Zeus and Hera? Just as the emergence of science. That is the last question now.

Student: What does Hegel answer to the argument that something in potency can't move to act without something already active moving it, that the principles, the contradictions seem to have a force, a power in themselves which is greater than the whole of which they are the parts?

LS: I believe that I understand your question, and it is a very important question because one way in which Hegel presents his doctrine is exactly the actualization of a potentiality. Just as you have a germ, finally you have the oak tree. And to some extent history has this character according to Hegel, the full actualization of the potentiality. But this is also misleading. Why is that so? There is something true in that comparison. It is an unconscious process. The actors have no inkling of the end. Neither the Chinese nor the Persians nor the Greeks had any notion that what they did and produced was necessary in order to bring about the reasonable state of the nineteenth century. That is true.

Let us first see what is implied. So the actors do not know that this is what he means in saying that the ruse of reason rules individuals. I do not know whether this will be of any immediate help, but we can start from that simple schema: teleological and nonteleological. The Hegelian doctrine is both teleological—all towards the end—and nonteleological. And this is, I think, the meaning of dialectics in Hegel's sense. You do not know in any given stage, speaking now of dialectic also as used in his logic, the highest form or part of his doctrine. If you view the ends and say that you want to arrive there and ask how you go step by step, that is not dialectics. You take each stage as it is and as it presents itself, without squinting at the end, and then you are driven by looking at it and by penetrating it to go beyond that to a next stage, and so on until you arrive at a stage where the whole is completed. What was your question?

Student: In your example, the reason why the mind is driven from one stage to another is because there is also actually in our minds the realization. In other words, with regard to the dialectic of our mind, there is already a realized ideal which forces us to move through the stages. But in the historical process, the absolute spirit isn't realized, so how can it bring about anything?

LS: This potentiality of man actualizes itself under favorable circumstances and in a specific manner. It is essential that in some of these actualizations, the actualization will necessarily be a cul-de-sac, a dead end. That it should not be a dead end but a possibility should exist for going beyond it, that is already a higher stage. That is also another way of answering your question. It is necessary that there should be such dead ends, and from Hegel's point of view there are at most three of these: Africa, China, and India.

Mr. Reinken: Isn't modern Europe a dead end?

LS: No. It is a live end because it is manifestly reasonable. The Chinese or the Hindus would be wholly unable to give a reasonable account of their order. Hegel, speaking from modern Europe, can give you a perfectly reasonable account even of hereditary monarchy, and hereditary nobility, and what have you.

Now I will say a few words about Hegel's whole position which might be of some help and make my answers a bit clearer. Let us return to the simple and most obvious thing. Hegel starts of course from his alleged knowledge of the reasonable state, the modern state, which is of course understood in contradistinction to the more or less unreasonable states in the immediate past—the feudal European states and Greece and so on. But Hegel adds, naturally, that these more or less unreasonable states, including China and India, are indispensable not only for the emergence of the reasonable state but also for the emergence of the conception of the reasonable state. People could not have understood and striven for the reasonable state in former times. All this development was needed so that men could become aware of what the reasonable state truly is.

Let us contrast this with the classics. They would not speak of the reasonable state. They would speak of the city, or rather of the best polity which is according to nature. Here we see of course the opposition with Hegel very clearly. We could translate the expression "the state according to nature" literally into Latin *status naturalis*, the natural state. For Hegel, as we know, the natural state is a state of absolute barbarism. For the classics the natural state would be the state of perfection, if they would use that term. The classics also would say—and here there is an agreement with Hegel—that it is essential to realize that the good is not the ancestral. It may happen that in a given society the ancestral is good, but there is no necessity for that. The classics saw that there is a great variety of ancestral orders, but they did not make an attempt to arrange these ancestral orders in an order of a progressive kind—for example, Egypt has this rank and Persia that and so on—because they regarded these ancestral orders as infinite, as they would say. I mean, there is no principle of ordering them. To express it brutally, in an exaggerated manner, they are vagaries of the imagination: what funny and crazy things that human beings can hit on, and you want us to see here a rational order! From the classical point of view there is no possibility of a philosophy of history. Or if you want to stretch the expression "philosophy of history," you must say the philosophy of history is reduced here to one simple proposition: confusion, confusion, confusion. Always different.

There is one great man who expressed that, at least for readers who can read such books, namely, Xenophon's Greek history, the *Hellenica*. It is the only book in the world which begins with the word "thereafter." Have you ever heard such a crazy idea? I had heard once of a preacher who began his sermon with the word "but," which is much more easy to understand because it would naturally contradict the passions of his flock. But to begin a book with "thereafter"? The traditional explanation is that Xenophon's history is a continuation of Thucydides. At least that is the tradition, that Thucydides's daughter after the death of her father ... and so Xenophon at any rate wrote a continuation of that, and therefore he simply began with "thereafter," an expression which occurs hundreds of times within Thucydides naturally, say: "in this summer the people of X made this expedition and thereafter the people of Y did that." But the funny thing is that Xenophon begins not after Thucydides, but the first few pages are covered by Thucydides. This is a strange overlap. But the most strange thing is that the book ends with "thereafter." This could not be literally true. It is this. He describes the battle of Leuctra, page 362.[3] And then he says that people have looked forward to that battle because Greece was in a great confusion, and they thought that if this wicked war would be finished, there would be order and everyone would know where he stands. The Spartans were defeated, and after the battle there was as much confusion as before. In this connection the word "thereafter" is used. So the book may be said to begin with "thereafter" and end with "thereafter." And this is a defensible philosophy of history surely worth considering. That is what the classics fundamentally meant. They didn't deny that there are certain rhythms. For example, there are states which emerge, develop, have a peak, decline, and are destroyed. This happens also. But this wouldn't do away with the fundamentals. There is always something wrong. And if you do not believe Xenophon, then believe Shakespeare. I believe that it is in *Henry VI*, third part, the War of the Roses. If that were not confusion, I don't know what is.

Mr. Reinken: *The Tempest.* "A tale told by an idiot, full of sound and fury, signifying nothing."

LS: No, no, that is something else. That is said by the mad Macbeth, and you can say that has nothing to do with Shakespeare's own opinion. But here Richard at the end of *Henry VI*: the House of York has money, or the House of Lancaster. Everything is fine, the usurpation of the Lancasters; and there are some beautiful verses which I unfortunately do not remember. All is over. Those of you who have lived through a war and especially through an end of a war will know this wonderful feeling. Now there is no longer any problem. And there is only one little fly in the ointment, and that is Richard III. There is always such a Richard III around. That was the older view: there is no possibility of a final solution. And that is the fundamental difference. Therefore chance is absolute chance. Hegel also recognizes chance, of course: that this man happened to be Alexander, the son of Philip, who conquered the East, and was not a man called Philip, the son of Alexander, is of course absolute chance. That goes without saying—and quite a few other things. But for the classics chance is controlling the whole thing, whereas for Hegel chance has its place only in a subordinate manner.

Another point which I should mention. Hegel speaks of dialectics, as we know. This goes back to Plato more than to any other individual. Here the difference is quite clear. Hegel's dialectics is very potent in history and in Hegel's understanding of it. Plato's dialectics has nothing whatever to do with history. Plato's view was rather this. Men have opinions—and I am not speaking now of opinions about uninteresting things, but opinions about important matters, authoritative opinions holding together whole societies. For Plato all opinions presuppose intellect. A brute cannot have opinions. All opinions presuppose intelligence, more or less dormant intelligence, more or less awake. This is indicated by his doctrine of recollection, which is a deliberate myth. The human souls are the only souls which have seen the ideas prior to birth, and then they had to forget it. But they still are, as it were, here, and without that, men would not be men. And by virtue of that, men have opinions which are dimmed, distorted, soiled reflections of the ideas. Therefore, whenever you take up any opinion and have a reasonably good mind, then you will see that this opinion does not hold water, just as Hegel says, and that it will point beyond itself and it will point eventually to the idea. So the only way to recover this original sight or vision of the idea is dialectics, by looking at and examining opinions. But this has no direct application to history, of course. That in history, as it were, the way from lower opinion to higher opinion to full knowledge would take place, that is the peculiarity of Hegel. I thought that we should at least remind ourselves of these fundamental differences.

We have not discussed everything in last time's assignment. Let us turn to page 154, bottom.

Mr. Reinken:

> The view given of the relation of castes leads directly to the subject of religion. For the claims of caste are, as already remarked, not merely secular, but essentially religious, and the Brahmins in their exalted dignity are the very gods bodily present. In the Laws of Manu, it is said, "Let the King even in extreme necessity beware of exciting the Brahmins against him; for they can destroy him with their power, they who create fire, sun, moon, etc." They are servants neither of God nor of his people—

LS: "Of his community." He uses the Christian expression in German, *die Gemeinde*, "of his congregation."

Mr. Reinken:

> but are God himself to the other Castes—a position of things which constitutes the perverted character of the Hindu mind. The dreaming Unity

of Spirit and nature, which involves a monstrous bewilderment in regard to all phenomena and relations, we have already recognized as the principle of the Hindu Spirit. The Hindu Mythology is therefore only a wild extravagance of Fancy—[4]

LS: We can leave it at that. But did he not say: But what is wrong with that? After all, here human beings are regarded as gods. Is here the dignity of man not recognized to some extent? Hegel had said before on page 141 of your edition that they recognized also what kind of beings?

Mr. Reinken: Parrots, cats, cows, and so on.

LS: So in other words, it is not based on a sense of the dignity of man. The Brahmins are not gods *qua* the best men. This would be connected with the fact that they do not have a clear grasp of the superhuman. That is now what he is going to explain. Without some awareness of the superhuman, man cannot have dignity, as we have seen in the section on Africa. On page 155. Second half of the page.

Mr. Reinken:

> If you ask a Hindu whether he worships idols, everyone says "Yes!" but to the question, "Do you worship the Supreme Being?" everyone answers, "No."[5]

LS: That is the point. So there is a highest being that they know, that they are aware of. But this is completely separate from the objects of their worship, and that is the fundamental defect of Hindu religion. And this is what they call *Brahm*. There is some ground of everything, including of the gods, which is dimly divine, but there is no clarity regarding the relation of this ground of grounds, which is indistinguishable from nothingness because of its indeterminateness. And therefore, because of the lack of connection, there follow the fundamental defects of the Hindu religion.

There is one difficulty which I sensed again in listening to Mr. Franke's paper. Do you not have the feeling, Mr. Franke, from time to time that from some points of view China seemed to be superior to India? How did you solve this difficulty?

Mr. Franke: I didn't solve it, nor do I see that Hegel solved it. In the beginning of the section on China he refers briefly to the fact that Buddhism is a factor in China, but the section on Buddhism follows actually after India. Presumably it constitutes a higher—

LS: I think that he would say that India is characterized by both the original Hindu religion and Buddhism. This combination is higher than China itself. Yes?

Mr. Reinken: I thought that the reconciliation was that China, in its good order, is for practical purposes more like good sober Prussia than is India.

LS: You mean a strictly administrative, paternalistic state?

Mr. Reinken: Yes, good order.

LS: But paternalistic. That is important.

Mr. Reinken: From the point of view of spirit developing itself, it is undifferentiated in China, and it has made a step, albeit a faltering misstep, in India.

LS: Now let us look at page 161.

Mr. Reinken:

The proper basis of the State, the principle of freedom is altogether absent—

LS: From India.

Mr. Reinken:

there cannot therefore be any State in the true sense of the term. This is the first point to be observed: if China may be regarded as nothing else but a State, Hindu political existence presents us with a people, but no State. Secondly, while we found a moral despotism in China, whatever may be called a relic of political life in India is a despotism without a principle, without any rule of morality and religion: for morality and religion (as far as the latter has a reference to human action) have as their indispensable condition and basis the freedom of the Will. In India, therefore, the most arbitrary, wicked, degrading despotism has its full swing. China, Persia, Turkey—in fact Asia generally, is the scene of despotism, and, in a bad sense, of tyranny; but it is regarded as contrary to the due order of things, and is disapproved by religion and the moral consciousness of individuals. In those countries, tyranny rouses men to resentment; they detest it and groan under it as a burden. To them it is an accident and an irregularity, not a necessity: it ought not to exist. But in India it is normal.[6]

LS: So this seems to show a clear superiority of China to India, and also in the next paragraph the fact that the Chinese have history and that there is no history, no decent chronology and so on, in India, is also in favor of China. These were the points which you observed.

Mr. Franke: On the other hand, though, in the original account of China he says that China cannot be regarded as having a religion properly so called. That comes in only with the Buddhist principle, it seems.

LS: But I believe the point which Mr. Reinken made is more important—the articulation, however perverse, in India, the caste system as compared with the absence of articulation in China, all are equally children of the emperor. But there is more to that. Let us pursue that and see. Let us turn to page 166, second paragraph, where he has a final comparison of the two worlds.

Mr. Reinken:

> If then, in conclusion, we once more take a general view of the comparative condition of India and China, we shall see that China was characterized by a thoroughly unimaginative Understanding; a prosaic life amid firm and definite reality: while in the Indian world there is, so to speak, no object that can be regarded as real, and firmly defined—

LS: An object, in order to be an object, has to be one of a determinate and definite character; where everything flows one into the other, that is imagination, not the prosaic understanding.

Mr. Reinken:

> none that was not at its first apprehension perverted by the imagination to the very opposite of what it presents to an intelligent consciousness.

LS: "Reasonable" in the sense of prosaic reason. In other words, a pot for cooking is a pot for cooking, and if some imaginative human being sees something grand or terrible in there, that is his business, and it has nothing to do with sober, prosaic understanding of the pot as pot.

Mr. Reinken:

> In China it is the Moral which constitutes the substance of the laws, and which is embodied in external strictly determinate relations; while over all hovers the patriarchal providence of the Emperor, who like a Father cares impartially for the interest of his subjects. Among the Hindus, on the contrary—instead of this Unity—Diversity is the fundamental characteristic. Religion, War, Handicraft, Trade—

LS: Let us stop there. So that is the point: unity in China; diversity, differentiation, articulation in India. Now let us see a bit further on.
Mr. Reinken:

The Chinese, in their prosaic rationality, reverence as the Highest only the abstract supreme lord; and they exhibit a contemptibly superstitious respect for the fixed and definite.

LS: In other words, they cannot help making distinctions, but they do not make rational distinctions, but only superstitious ones.
Mr. Reinken:

Among the Hindus there is no such superstition so far as it presents an antithesis to understanding; rather their whole life and ideas are one un-broken superstition, because among them all is revery and consequent Enslavement.[7]

LS: So that we are still back where we were. Therefore, you must never forget that these are lecture notes and not a book by Hegel, and we have to do our best to liberate ourselves from the abbreviations made by surely intelligent, but very fallible listeners. Turn to page 168, line 13.
Mr. Reinken:

As the Substantial form of Spirit which characterizes China, develops itself only to a unity of secular national life which degrades individuals to a position of constant dependence, religion also remains in a state of dependence. The element of freedom is wanting to it, for its object is the principle of nature in general, heaven, universal matter.

LS: That is of course a question, whether Hegel has any right to make this identification of heaven, nature, universal matter. But we cannot go into that.
Mr. Reinken:

But the compensating truth of this alienated form of Spirit—nature occupying the place of the absolute Spirit—is ideal Unity, the elevation above the limitation of Nature and of existence at large—the return of consciousness into the soul.

LS: Go over to the next paragraph, please.
Mr. Reinken:

> The negative form of this elevation is the concentration of Spirit to the
> Infinite, and must first present itself under theological conditions. It is
> contained in the fundamental dogma that Nothingness is the principle of
> all things—that all proceeded from and returns to Nothingness.[8]

LS: That is a key progress, a superiority of India to China. I repeat only
what Hegel says without claiming to say anything about India or China,
about which I know nothing. In China the highest is a visible heaven. The
Hindus go beyond that and peer through heaven, as it were, and discover
a spiritual principle—nothingness as a ground of everything—and this
is an act of liberation. In Hegel's view, the philosophic mind has to begin
with that nothingness, with the pure ether, as he sometimes calls it. So
ultimately the Hindus are superior, transcending everything finite and
determinate. Heaven too, of course, is finite and determinate. Heaven is
not the earth. That is sufficient proof of the finiteness of heaven. Therefore the nonfinite is, to begin with, only the infinite, undefined, that which
has no distinction in itself, nothingness. And that is the beginning. This
beginning is understood somehow by the Hindus. As he says on page 169,
paragraph 2, "the abstract nothingness is the beyond of finiteness and of
what we mean by the highest being." The Hindus come closer to that.

On page 170 in the second paragraph he speaks of the spirituality of
Buddhism. But the implication always is that Buddhism, while it was
much more successful outside India than within India, nevertheless stems
from India and is a development of that. He speaks of the form in which
the spirit of the Lamaic development of Buddhism stands—
Mr. Reinken:

> is that of a living human being, while in the original Buddhism it is a de-
> ceased person. The two hold in common the relationship to a man. The
> idea of a man being worshipped as God—especially a living man—has in
> it something paradoxical and revolting; but the following considerations
> must be examined before we pronounce judgment respecting it. The con-
> ception of Spirit involves its being regarded as inherently, intrinsically,
> universal. This condition must be particularly observed, and it must be
> discovered how in the systems adopted by various peoples this universality

is kept in view. It is not the individuality of the subject that is revered, but that which is universal in him; and which among the Tibetans, Hindus, and Asiatics generally, is regarded as the essence pervading all things. This substantial unity of Spirit is realized in the Lama—[9]

LS: —in this individual, this Dalai Lama—not the mere empirical Dalai Lama, but something for which he stands, which he represents, and therefore he lacks this revolting character. And the second, he says a little bit later that what is of importance in this conception is the distinction from nature. The Chinese emperor has a power over the natural forces which he controls. But here in the case of the Dalai Lama the spiritual power is distinguished from the natural power. This is only to show that Hegel in his way tries to show the superiority of India to China.

A few more points. On page 173 in the second paragraph.

Mr. Reinken:

With the Persian Empire we first enter on continuous History. The Persians are the first Historical People; Persia was the first Empire that passed away.

LS: This "passing away" is meant quite superficially, because when we call something historical we mean that it belongs to the past. China and India are not in this sense historical because they are there, but this has a deeper meaning as we have seen before.

Mr. Reinken:

While China and India remain stationary, and perpetuate a natural vegetative existence even to the present time, this land has been subject to those developments and revolutions which alone manifest a historical condition. The Chinese and the Indian Empire assert a place in the historical series only on their own account and for us, not for neighbors and successors.[10]

LS: No, that has been misunderstood. "Not for neighbors" you may delete; that is the commentary by the translator. They are in itself, as we would say, objective things, and for us the beholders; not for them, not for the Chinese—*für sich* in German, for themselves. *An sich* and *für uns* but not *für sich*. That is what I tried to explain before. They cannot possibly see themselves. And for themselves, as far as their understanding goes, they do not belong in any context of history. The very notion is wholly unintelligible to them, but not for us.

For the Persians, they have some inkling because they view the whole historical process as a fight between Ormuzd and Ahriman. So this is a fundamentally different situation. The principle of Persia then, of the Zend people, is the light. Of course, opposed to the light is darkness, but the light is the principle of goodness. Human life is understood as taking the side of light, the good and purity against darkness. And the whole ends finally in the victory of the good and the conquest of Ahriman. In Hegel's view, this is a higher form of understanding than was reached in the nothingness of the Indians, to say nothing of the heaven of the Chinese. And the point is that this highest, the light, does not absorb the individual things or human beings but lets them be what they are; whereas for the Hindu, nothingness leads to the negation of the particulars, Nirvana. And yet it transcends nature, whereas the Chinese principle does not.

In addition, which is also interesting, it has an opposite of the same kind. Let us look at page 174, second paragraph.

Mr. Reinken:

Thus the transition we have to make is only in the sphere of the Idea, not in the external—

LS: "Is only in the concept," more literally.
Mr. Reinken:

only in the concept, not in the external historical connection.

LS: That is what we discussed. Hegel doesn't claim that there was any conscious reaction to India and China which gave rise to the Persian religion.
Mr. Reinken:

The principle of this transition is that the Universal Essence, which we recognized in *Brahm*, now becomes perceptible to consciousness—becomes an object and acquires a positive import for man. *Brahm* is not worshipped by the Hindus. He is nothing more than a condition of the individual, a religious feeling, a non-objective existence—a relation, which for concrete vitality is that of annihilation. But in becoming objective, this universal

essence acquires a positive nature. Man becomes free and thus occupies a
position face to face as it were with the highest being, the latter being made
objective for him. This form of universality we see exhibited in Persia, involving a separation of man from the universal essence, while at the same
time the individual recognizes himself as identical with that essence. In the
Chinese and Indian principle, this distinction was not made. We found
only a unity of the Spiritual and the Natural.[11]

LS: He makes clear then in the sequel that there is no principle there
for any division into castes, nor for a simple paternalism as in China,
because every man has to take part in that fight for the good against the
evil which gives him a fundamental freedom. And he develops this at
some length.

Now on page 178, when he speaks of the opposition of Ormuzd and
Ahriman: "Ormuzd is the Lord of the kingdom of Light, of Good."
Mr. Reinken:

Ahriman that of Darkness, of Evil. But there is a still higher being from
whom both proceeded, a Universal Being not affected by this antithesis—

LS: No, "not possessing itself this antithesis." Literally translated, "an
oppositionless."
Mr. Reinken:

called *Zeruane-Akerene*, the Unlimited All. The All, that is, is something
abstract; it does not exist for-itself, and Ormuzd and Ahriman have arisen
from it. This dualism is commonly brought as a reproach against Oriental
thought, and as far as the contradiction is regarded as absolute, that is
certainly an irreligious understanding which remains satisfied with it. For
the very nature of Spirit demands antithesis. The principle of dualism belongs, therefore, to the idea of Spirit, which in its concrete form essentially
involves distinction. Among the Persians, purity and impurity have both
become subjects of consciousness, and Spirit, in order to comprehend itself, must of necessity place its special and negative existence in contrast
to the universal and positive. Only by overcoming this antithesis is Spirit
twice born, regenerated. The deficiency in the Persian principle is only
that the unity of the antithesis is not completely recognized, for in that
indefinite conception of the uncreated All, whence Ormuzd and Ahriman

proceeded, the Unity is only the absolutely Primal existence, and does not reduce the contradictory elements to harmony in itself.[12]

LS: "Doesn't bring the difference back to itself." Now what do these dark sentences mean? This dualism lived on in a greatly modified manner in what came to be called Manicheanism and in a way Gnosticism in general. There are two principles, the good and the evil principle. In Western language we could say God and devil. But whereas according to the Christian or Jewish view the devil is the creature of God who has sinned and thus fallen, here these two forces are of equal status, not regarding goodness but regarding being. They are independent of each other. Still, it is very good to know that the good will vanquish the evil in the end. But still, there should be some clearer basis for that; if they have the same status, that victory seems to be an accident unless one would have to say that if most men side with the good, they will make him win and the devil lose, which is perhaps open to other objections. But the Persians were aware of the difficulty, and therefore they assumed that both proceeded from something general or universal which is oppositionless, which is beyond the opposition of good and evil. There is as it were a neutral ground of good and evil, something like the nothingness of the Hindus here [LS writes on the blackboard], and out of that emerged good and evil.

And Hegel says, without speaking of God and devil, that this dualism is not bad. Without it we cannot understand life, we cannot understand history. But what would Hegel wish? That they must come from the same root. It is necessary for Hegel. Evil must have some ground . . . But what is necessary in addition? Some bringing back, as he puts it, of the evil. Does it mean some ultimate conversion of the devil, some insight into its sin and restoration *in integrum*? It is hard to say. But it is one of these dark remarks of Hegel about evil. We have heard a bit about evil before. What was it?

Mr. Bruell: Hegel had to justify the existence of evil in the world in order to make acceptable the fact that history is reasonable.

LS: So evil is necessary. How does he stand to the traditional view? Evil is of course not necessary. And this is connected with the fact that man was created perfect and it was man's fault, his sin, which brought about evil. And for Hegel it is the opposite. The beginning is evil, absolutely evil: the state of nature. And man is not responsible for that. And out of that, and only because the beginning is evil, can perfection be decisively due to human freedom. The reasonable state is the creation of man because his starting point was the most unreasonable. And a certain vindication, justification in a certain sense, of evil is of necessity a central part of Hegel's doctrine; and there is here, I believe, an allusion to that when he speaks towards the end of this section on page 181.

Mr. Reinken:

The ritual observances of the religion of Ormuzd import that men should conduct themselves in harmony with the Kingdom of Light. The great general commandment is, therefore, as already said, spiritual and corporeal purity, consisting in many prayers to Ormuzd. It was made specially obligatory upon the Persians to maintain living existences, to plant trees, to dig wells, to fertilize deserts, in order that life, the positive, the pure might be furthered, and the dominion of Ormuzd be universally extended. External purity is contravened by touching a dead animal, and there are many directions for being purified from such pollution. Herodotus relates of Cyrus that when he went against Babylon, and the river Gyndes engulfed one of the horses of the Chariot of the Sun, he was occupied for a year in punishing it by diverting its streams into small canals to deprive it of its power. Thus Xerxes, when the sea broke in pieces his bridges, had chains laid upon it as the wicked and pernicious being, Ahriman.[13]

LS: In other words, that was not, as the Greeks thought, an act of hubris, of insolent pride, but of divine worship. This is, I think what he means by that. So I think we must now stop. And next time Mr. Barber.

8   Phoenicia, Judea, and Egypt

Leo Strauss: Thank you, Mr. Barber.[1] Your paper has shown considerable progress beyond your earlier papers in other classes. I like particularly your initial statement, which I found very good. I would like to take up only two points you made in your paper. You said that the Persian Empire in a way foreshadowed a kind of world empire embracing reasonable states, but of course it could only foreshadow it, as was clear to you. What is the most obvious difference between the Persian Empire and such a rational world state? There is a variety of states in both cases.

Mr. Barber: The Persian Empire was taken in conquest, was it not? And it would seem that a world state or rational state would be taken through mutual recognition.

LS: Yes, but we don't know enough to exclude the possibility that a world empire might be established by conquest and nevertheless be a rational order of rational states. I think the main point is that the Persian principle, the principle of the imperial state, tolerates the variety of cultures but it does not affect them, in contrast to a rational empire. Think of the British Empire according to the best interpretation which one could make: it would transform, say, India; it wouldn't permit the continuation of certain practices incompatible with what the British regard as civilization. The Persians left them alone, and corresponding to their principle, the sun, which shines on everything . . . does not transform it. Therefore I do not think that you were right in assuming that the parts of the Persian Empire were equal, according to Hegel—in other words, Babylonia especially is equal in rank to Persia, or for that matter to Phoenicia and Judea. I do not believe that he means that.

Mr. Barber: The reason I said that was in order to try to explain how these nations could conquer one another back and forth without transforming the national character of the conquered nation.

LS: But still, the Persians conquered the Babylonians, not the other way around.

Mr. Barber: I don't think that they actually conquered them in a spiritual sense.

LS: All right. But still, politically they did. Now one other point. It did not become clear from your paper what constitutes the superiority of Egypt to Persia and to all ingredients of the Persian Empire.

Mr. Barber: Well, Egypt in a sense represents a kind of progress.

LS: Why?

Mr. Barber: Because several parts of the Persian Empire taken as several parts present no opportunity for advance, whereas in Egypt there is a kind of union of these diverse elements, and a struggle results because of this peculiar combination. This now permits a kind of transition from Egypt to other states.

LS: But precisely the variety within the Persian Empire—think only of the difference between Phoenicia and Judea—does this contradiction not point beyond these two ingredients?

Mr. Barber: No, sir, because it does not seem to be a spiritual contradiction. There is no spiritual union in the empire.

LS: But still, between these two ingredients, Hegel's premise that Phoenicia and Judea can be understood simply as ingredients of the Persian Empire would perhaps have been questioned. What for Hegel is the clearest sign of the superiority of Egypt? What is the symbol of Egypt?

Mr. Barber: The Sphinx.

LS: What does that mean?

Mr. Barber: The head of a man and the body of a brute.

LS: Yes, but more primarily. What does a Sphinx do?

Mr. Barber: Asks Greeks questions?

LS: Yes. The riddle, a conscious riddle. That is the progress. There is nothing in the earlier stages which is a conscious riddle. That is my point. Thank you very much.

Now let us turn to one minor point which I happen to be able to clear up on page 182 when he speaks of this era, Ferdusi's "Shah-nameh."[2] He mentions Alexander the Great, who is called Ishkander or Skander of Roum. *Roum* is the Turkish Empire. That is very simple. *Roum* is simply Eastern Rome. Therefore the Muslims call it *Roum*, meaning by that Rome, i.e., Istanbul. That is trivial. Now let us turn to page 187, the end of the paragraph.

Mr. Reinken:

He led an expedition against the Massagetae; engaged with them in the steppes between the Oxus and the Jaxartes, but sustained a defeat and died the death of a warrior and conqueror. The death of heroes who have formed an epoch in the history of the world is stamped with the character of their mission. Cyrus thus died in his mission which was the union of anterior Asia into one sovereignty without an ulterior object.

LS: We have seen last time that there are dead-end developments in cultures, China and India. So there can be empires which have no further prospect. Persia itself points beyond itself; therefore it is historical in a way in which China and India are not historical, but its empire does not have this function. Hegel probably has in mind that if you compare the death of Cyrus with that of Alexander the Great and that of Caesar, this corresponds in each case to the . . . that Caesar was assassinated by the Republic in opposition, and Napoleon was sent to St. Helena by the British. This is all in agreement with the peculiarity of their mission. Then he speaks at the beginning of the next chapter of the peculiarity of the Persian Empire, namely, that it leaves its ingredients undisturbed, and that has to do with the principle of light.
Mr. Reinken:

As light illuminates everything, imparting to each object a peculiar vitality, so the Persian Empire extends over a multitude of nations and leaves to each one its particular character. Some have even kings of their own, each one its distinct —[3]

LS: And so on. This all persists quietly under the general light, ultimately the light of the Persian principle, of course. Let us turn to the section on Phoenicia, which is particularly interesting. Page 191, bottom. He had spoken of the Phoenicians' travels to Britain and to the Baltic. In this way a new principle emerges.
Mr. Reinken:

This opens to us an entirely new principle. Inactivity ceases, as also mere rude valor. In their place appears the activity of industry and that considerate courage which, while it bears the perils of the deep, rationally bethinks itself of the means of safety. Here everything depends on man's activity, his courage, his intelligence; while the objects aimed at are also pursued in the interest of man. Human will and activity here occupy the foreground, not

Nature and its bounty. Babylonia had its determinate share of territory, and human subsistence was there dependent on the course of the sun and the process of nature generally. But the sailor relies upon himself amid the fluctuations of the waves, and eye and heart must be always open. In like manner, the principle of industry involves the very opposite of what is received from Nature, for natural objects are worked up for use and ornament. In industry, man is an object to himself and treats Nature as something subject to him, on which he impresses the seal of his activity. Intelligence is the valor needed here, and ingenuity is better than mere natural courage. At this point we see the nations freed from the fear of Nature and its slavish bondage.[4]

LS: Yes. You see how little reactionary Hegel is, because he means of course the superiority of industry to agriculture, the intellectual superiority—a crucial point in Marxism but not only in Marxism. Human will and activity are here the first, not nature and its bounty. Agriculture depends much more on nature and its bounty, seasons and so on. This revolt against nature, that is the great principle of industry; and whether one can ascribe it to the Phoenicians is a very uninteresting question compared with the fundamental point which Hegel makes here.

One can say that this is one of the most important differences between modern political philosophy since the seventeenth century and classical—the denial of the bounty, the goodness of nature. For Aristotle or Plato that is taken for granted. You only have to read the first book of Aristotle's *Politics* when he says that nature supplies the most important things. The very simple case is that for every baby human or brute, nature provides milk. In other words, that this is not done by any human activity is the first sign of that. This difference has infinite implications.

Now, then in the sequel he speaks of the sensuality and cruelty of Babylonian, Syrian, the Phrygian Empire and how they belong together, which is quite interesting. Page 192 bottom.

Mr. Reinken:

With a merely sensuous life—this being a form of consciousness which does not attain to general conceptions—cruelty is connected; because Nature itself is the highest, so that man has no value or only the most trifling.[5]

LS: That is crucial. Cruelty comes out not directly but via the unawareness of the dignity of man. Whether this cruelty takes a so-called sadist

or so-called masochist form is fundamentally uninteresting. This is not so in Phoenicia, which is of course quite questionable, because the sacrifice of first-born children was an important institution of the Phoenician worship of Baal. But Hegel is not interested in that. He finds in Phoenicia a much higher religious principle, namely, the worship of Adonis. What is the key point in the worship of Adonis, according to Hegel? This high point which makes him forget about any Baal or Ishtar which the Phoenicians might have worshiped? What is the key point here? I do not know whether it comes out in the translation clearly enough. It must be in the second paragraph of 193 or 194. "Life regains here again its value."
Mr. Reinken:

> Life here regains its value. A universality of pain is established, for death becomes immanent in the divine and the deity dies. Among the Persians we saw light and darkness struggling with each other, but here both principles are united in one, the absolute. The negative is here too, the merely natural; but as the death of a god, it is not a limitation attaching to an individual object, but is pure negativity itself.[6]

LS: So let us leave it at this point. The death of God is the highest point of Phoenicia, and Hegel implies that there is some connection between this concept of the death of God—that the negativity belongs to the spirit itself—and what he had said about the industrial character of Phoenicia before. "Here the negative itself."
Mr. Reinken:

> But here the negative itself is a phase of deity, the natural, death, the worship appropriate to which is grief.[7]

LS: This is a key point. And the death of God: that is for Hegel, in Christianity, the death of Christ as the son of God. This is important because that implies an important superiority of Phoenicia to Judea in Hegel's eyes, because in the Old Testament there is indeed for the first time the primacy of the spirit, as he says. The light is now Jehovah, the pure one. By this very fact the break between East and West occurs. Do you have that?
Mr. Reinken:

> This forms the point of separation between the East and the West. Spirit descends into the depths of its own being and recognizes the abstract

fundamental principle as the spiritual. Nature, which in the East is the primary and fundamental existence, is now depressed to the condition of a mere creature, and spirit now occupies the first place.[8]

LS: This is the great advance made by the Jews, but what is the defect of that?

He speaks in the sequel of the exclusiveness of the Old Testament God, which is connected with the exclusiveness and intolerance of the Jewish people: no recognition of the truth in the false God. We can perhaps read that, on page 195.

Mr. Reinken:

Before him all other gods are false. Moreover, the distinction between true and false is quite abstract; for as regards the false gods, not a ray of the divine is supposed to shine into them.

LS: In other words, they are unqualifiedly rejected, and the policy of the divination of the divine in all these gods is not understood.

Mr. Reinken:

But every form of spiritual force and *a fortiori* every religion is of such a nature that, whatever be its peculiar character, an affirmative element is necessarily contained in it. However erroneous a religion may be, it possesses truth, although in a mutilated phase. In every religion there is a divine presence, a divine relation; and a philosophy of history has to seek out the spiritual element even in the most imperfect forms. But it does not follow that, because it is a religion, it is therefore good. We must not fall into the lax conception that the content is of no importance, but only the form.

LS: Meaning that it is religion. And what kind of religion is it? Go on.

Mr. Reinken:

This latitudinarian tolerance the Jewish religion does not admit, being absolutely exclusive.[9]

LS: In other words, Hegel reminds the reader in time that while he is very understanding of every form of religion, he is not of a lax tolerance of everything. That is the difference. In other words, he is perfectly willing to see the divine in the lowest form of divination without forgetting for a moment that it is very low, whereas a typical liberal of our age would say that all these things are equal because they have such a spark of the light. So it is clear that this quite extraordinary thesis is shocking to the whole tradition, that in an important respect Phoenicia should be higher than Judea. After that statement he makes clear a few other points. Let us turn to page 196, the second paragraph.

Mr. Reinken:

The spiritual speaks itself here absolutely free of the sensuous, and Nature is reduced to something merely external and undivine.

LS: Namely, it is a mere creature. It is merely created and has no divinity in itself. Yes?

Mr. Reinken:

This is the true and proper estimate of Nature at this stage; for only at a more advanced phase can the idea attain a reconciliation in this its alien form.

LS: Namely, in nature.

Mr. Reinken:

Its first utterances will be in opposition to Nature; for spirit which had been hitherto dishonored now first attains its due dignity, while Nature resumes its proper position. Nature is conceived as having the ground of its existence in another as something posited, created. And this idea—that God is the lord and creator of Nature—leads men to regard God as the exalted one, while the whole of Nature is only his robe of glory and is expended in his service. In contrast with this kind of exaltation, that which the Hindu religion—

LS: "Sublimity" is the right word.

Mr. Reinken:

sublimity, that which the Hindu religion presents is only that of indefinitude. In virtue of the prevailing spirituality, the sensuous and immoral are no longer privileged, but disparaged as ungodliness. Only the one, spirit, the nonsensuous, is the truth. Thought exists free for itself, and true morality and righteousness can now make their appearance; for God is honored by righteousness, and right-doing is walking in the way of the Lord. With this is conjoined happiness, life and temporal prosperity are its reward; for it is said, "That thou mayest live long in the land." Here too, also, we have the possibility of the historical view; for the understanding has become prosaic, putting the limited and circumscribed in its proper place and comprehending it as the form proper to finite existence: men are regarded as individuals, not as incarnations of God; sun as sun, mountains as mountains, not as possessing spirit and will.[10]

LS: In other words, this sobriety is the necessary consequence of the spirituality of the biblical God. Things are seen as they are: mountains as mountains, human beings as human beings, and so on. One can say that nature was discovered here because it was understood in its inferiority to the spirit or to the mind. But is this true? Is this true from Hegel's point of view? He speaks of it a bit later on page 197, the first paragraph, when he speaks about the Jewish history, its greatness and its defects. "Miracles disturb us too in that history." Do you have that?

Mr. Reinken:

Miracles, too, form a disturbing feature in this history, as history, for as far as concrete consciousness is not free, concrete perception is also not free. Nature is unedified—

LS: And that is the great progress, but—

Mr. Reinken:

but not yet understood.[11]

LS: That is the point. It is very strange, the way Hegel regards the belief in miracles as manifestly impossible. That was for him settled by the Enlightenment. But the historical question—in that I think that Hegel is right because, as I have said on more than one occasion, there is no Old Testament expression for nature. And therefore, when people speak of the Psalms speaking of nature, that is in a strict sense incorrect. By the way, it is also important that there is no Old Testament word for history. This is equally important. There is one old Hebrew word which could lead to the notion of nature on the one hand, and history on the other.

It means, literally translated, "generation": "these are the generations of" and so on. This expression was used in Hellenistic times for nature. But it means more immediately what happened to these generations, i.e., it means more history. But the concept itself is alien, and Hegel somehow is aware of that, as we see.

And connected with the abstractness of the Old Testament God, with the lack of articulation which Hegel finds in the Christian Trinity, is the abstractness of the service of the God—in traditional Christian language, the "carnal" character of Judaism, the seed of Abraham understood literally, not in a spiritual sense. On page 198 in the first paragraph.

Mr. Reinken:

However spiritual may be the conception of God as objective, the subjective side—the honor rendered to Him—is still very limited and unspiritual in character.[12]

LS: And by this he means both the national character and the importance of the ceremonial law. So from Hegel's point of view, the Old Testament prepares the New Testament to no higher degree than Phoenicia does, in a very different way. That is settled. Now let us turn to the section on Egypt. What is the peculiarity of that? Let us turn to page 198 in the third paragraph.

Mr. Reinken:

In Egypt we see united the elements which in the Persian monarchy appeared singly. We found among the Persians the adoration of light regarded as the essence of universal nature. This principle then develops itself in phases which hold the position of indifference towards each other.

LS: Not as equal, Mr. Barber, but as indifferent to each other.

Mr. Reinken:

The one is the immersion in the sensuous—among the Babylonians and Syrians; the other is the spiritual phase, which is twofold: first as the incipient consciousness of the concrete spirit in the worship of Adonis, and then as pure and abstract thought among the Jews. In the former, the concrete is deficient in unity; in the latter the concrete is altogether wanting.

LS: Because of the simple, unqualified transcendence of the Old Testament God.

Mr. Reinken:

> The next problem is, then, to harmonize these contradictory elements. And this problem presents itself in Egypt.

LS: To harmonize or unite these opposing elements is the task, and it is present as task in Egypt, i.e., the Egyptians are themselves aware of the task. And at the end of this paragraph he explains it a bit more, what he means by saying that it is present as a task.

Mr. Reinken:

> Thus the memorials of Egypt themselves give us a multitude of forms and images that express its character. We recognize a spirit in them which feels itself compressed, which offers itself, but only in a sensuous mode.[13]

LS: This indicates the fact that the task is present to the Egyptians. They express the problem although they cannot solve it. Let us turn to 199, bottom.

Mr. Reinken:

> In their architecture and hieroglyphics, the thoughts and conceptions of the Egyptians are expressed. A national work in the department of language is wanting, and that not only to us, but to the Egyptians themselves. They could not have any because they had not advanced to an understanding of themselves.[14]

LS: But did Hindus, Persians, and Chinese have such an understanding of themselves? And yet they had national works like the Vedas. What do you say?

Mr. Reinken: Doesn't the *Book of the Dead* which we now have go against this?

LS: Yes. But the question is whether it is a national book in the sense in which the Zend Avesta or the Vedas are national. That I do not know. Hegel would say we must see this absence of such national books in the context, and here in the context of the fact that Egypt presents a higher principle than Persia or India. All the more striking is the absence of such a book. Now let us turn to page 206, at the end of the first paragraph.

Mr. Reinken:

> Their vast edifices—such as no other nation has to exhibit and which ex-
> cel all others in solidity and size—sufficiently prove their artistic skill; to
> whose cultivation they could largely devote themselves because the inferior
> castes did not trouble themselves with political matters. Diodorus Siculus
> says that Egypt was the only country in which the citizens did not trouble
> themselves about the state, but gave their whole attention to their private
> business. Greeks and Romans must have been especially astonished at
> such a state of things.

LS: In other words, were the Babylonians more concerned with politics or the low-class Hindus? That is the question. The Egyptian people
are unpolitical, as are all other Orientals. Hegel emphasizes this fact here
because this fact is emphasized in his sources. In Greece there was a connection between the practice of the arts and citizenship, active citizenship. Not so in Egypt, and still less of course in India and other places.
Now let us continue in the next paragraph.

Mr. Reinken:

> On account of its judicious economy, Egypt was regarded by the ancients
> as the pattern of a morally regulated condition of things—as an ideal such
> as Pythagoras realized in a limited, select society, and Plato sketched on
> a larger scale.[15]

LS: This is first a statement of fact, and Hegel turns that into a value
judgment, namely, there is something anticipating Plato in the Egyptian
order. Is there any basis for this assertion that there is a connection between the Egyptian order and the order which Plato praised?

Student: . . .

LS: By the beginning of *Timaeus* it is said that the order described by
Socrates in the *Republic* reminded Timaeus, an interlocutor, of Egypt.[16]
So this is not an invention of Hegel. Hegel uses this opportunity because
it is his duty as a professor of philosophy to fight misconceptions, especially politically dangerous misconceptions, all the time, to dispose of
that. Now what does he say about it in the immediate sequel?

Mr. Reinken:

But in such ideals no account is taken of passion. A plan of society that is to be adopted and acted upon as an absolutely complete one, in which everything has been considered and especially—

LS: No. "Calculated." Everything has been figured out. Go on.
Mr. Reinken:

everything has been calculated and especially the education and habituation to it necessary to its becoming a second nature, is altogether opposed to the nature of spirit which makes contemporary life—

LS: No, "the present life."
Mr. Reinken:

the present life the object on which it acts, itself being the infinite impulsive activity to alter its forms.[17]

LS: No, "to change it," namely, the present life. It is of the essence of the nature of the mind to make the present life its object, meaning to look at it, to make it conscious and to change it. Now you see, this point here is quite remarkable. First he had spoken of passion. Such a final order established in every detail is incompatible with passion. Naturally, passion would disturb it. It is incompatible with passion. Does this remind you of something?

Mr. Reinken: "So oft as reason is against man, so oft will a man be against reason"?[18]

LS: Yes. There is this connection, the same individual. Who was that?
Mr. Reinken: Hobbes.

LS: But Hobbes says it somewhat more precisely, speaking of passion itself. He wants to revise the teaching regarding natural law and lays "such principles down for a foundation, as passion not mistrusting will not seek to displace."[19] In this respect Hegel agrees. It must be in harmony with passion. But Hegel then replaces passion by spirit, as you see in the immediate sequel in the very same sentence. What is the connection between passion and spirit, and from what point of view can they be identified?

Mr. Shulsky: The only way in which a change suggested by spiritual reflection would actually cause practical change in the political order would be through someone's passion to become a great man.

LS: Oh, I see this point. Yes. But both passion and spirit would protest against the Platonic or Egyptian order using the same word: no freedom. Passion claims freedom, the mind claims freedom, and there is a certain connection between them according to Hegel. This freedom both of passion and of the mind is provided for in the reasonable state as Hegel understands it. How is the freedom of passion provided for in the reasonable state? These are things which are very familiar to all of us from daily life, but we have only to see how they appear in the theoretical formulation. Yes?

Student: Through self-legislation?

LS: Passion is not self-legislating. That is the trouble with it. Yes?

Student: Through wealth? Through property?

LS: Yes. But that is too general. You come closer. Well, the reasonable state in Hegel's understanding includes the relative freedom of what he calls *bürgerliche Gesellschaft*, which is the translation both of civil society and of bourgeois society. He means the economic sphere in the sense of Adam Smith. Here you have it. I mean, the businessmen who are concerned with enriching themselves are not necessarily reasonable, self-legislating men, but they are surely prompted by the passion of self-enrichment. Private vices are public benefits. This is accepted by Hegel. But not only the free economy and free choice of professions — free choice of professions also belong to a higher realm. You know, there is no free choice of professions in Plato's *Republic*; you have to take the job which the wise man assigns to you because they believe that they know better what is good for you than you do. Yes?

Mr. Bruell: Could a question be raised by the fact that the passion for wealth or property that is exercised in the economic sphere is relatively a low passion compared with—

LS: That was settled for Hegel somehow, that this kind of paternalistic regulation, which is the alternative, is degrading to the dignity of man. That was already settled before Hegel, at least by Kant. Let us call this kind of thing going on in daily life and especially in economic life "the pursuit of happiness." That is the key point in Kant's teaching. To dictate to another man what kind of happiness he should pursue means to assert the role of his tutor, and this is incompatible with freedom.[20] Everyone must be able to pursue happiness as he sees it, provided that he doesn't understand happiness in a way that is wholly incompatible with living together. Then he must be stopped. But in matters which are compatible with living together and even with a wealthy and prosperous society, by all means. Mr. Glenn?

Mr. Glenn: Do I understand Hegel correctly to say that passions are made compatible with the rational state by allowing the existence of something within the rational state which is not rational? Maybe the unregulated market, for example.

LS: Well, there are of course limits. That is clear. But yes, in this respect he accepts the whole Locke-Smithean view. He makes it a part of the rational state. That is settled.

Mr. Glenn: It is very difficult for me to—

LS: Well, are you a socialist by any chance?

Mr. Glenn: Hardly.

LS: So then you should not have any difficulty understanding it.

Mr. Glenn: What I meant was it is hard to believe that the rational state—

LS: Perhaps you are a victim of those people who call Hegel a deifier of the state and a precursor of totalitarianism, which is simply not true. Hegel accepted the constitutional monarchy of the nineteenth century, which was quite authoritarian but the opposite of totalitarian. The freedom of the economic sphere was taken for granted. It had to be protected, of course, by prohibitions against fraud, the protection of property, and so on. That was clear. In this sense, Hegel is a liberal.[21]

Student: I was wondering why in the introduction in the long paragraph with reference to passion and reason he did not bring it up then. I don't want to make a long point out of this. It may not be worth it, but on page 23 he gives this long paragraph on the idea of . . . universal history.

LS: There he is thinking primarily of the passion of the world-historical heroes, which is not meant here. But there is of course a connection between, say, Adam Smith and the world-historical hero, namely, in both cases man brings about an order which he does not intend. Let me state it more precisely. In the economic sphere, the man is concerned with his profit and only with his profit, and yet this anarchy, this disorder, leads to the best order. Is this clear? Something similar happens in history. Men are not concerned—what did the Persians or Phoenicians think about the reasonable state? They did not have any inkling of that, but they pursued their goals as they understood them, and yet through that passionate pursuit of their goals the rational state came into being. So you know what happens in the economic sphere. At any given time, whenever there is freedom of enterprise, it happens historically in the whole stage of history that the best order is brought about by people who do not think of that order. The traditional view was of course that this is altogether impossible: someone has to think of the order in order to bring it about, be it the government in the case of society or be it God in the case of religion. Yes?

Mr. Shulsky: Does this assume then that once the rational state is realized, in fact the passions of the respective world-historical figures will be able to be turned somehow into simply economic passions, the simple pursuit of happiness within the established order?

LS: No. In the first place, the economic passions must retain their freedom, of course, within the reasonable state. Otherwise it wouldn't be a reasonable state. Now as for the world-historical individuals, they are no longer necessary.

Mr. Shulsky: So what happens to these people who have a passion which in other times might have made them world-historical?

LS: They cannot be strictly speaking world-historical anymore, i.e., in an epoch of a new and higher level. But what they can do is—think of a man like Churchill. He protects the reasonable state against insanity. This, of course, is always possible. Churchill did not introduce a new principle as, in a way, Napoleon or Alexander the Great did. In other words, this is still possible, naturally. For example, say some Englishman who would civilize India beyond what Hastings[22] and other people had done, that is a good example from Hegel's point of view. He thought very highly of Hastings. He would do the same thing, pardon me, to China. We have seen that it is necessary that Europe conquers and Europeanizes China. That would be a great deed, but still no new principle, only expansion. Mr. Barber?

Mr. Barber: This principle, this replacing of passions with spirit, does it have any connection with a metaphysical or theoretical primacy of practice over theory?

LS: Yes, there is some, but that is complicated. Let us leave it for the time being only at this fact, that today we use the word "passion" very frequently in a favorable sense, very far removed from the sense which it had, say, in Stoicism but not only in Stoicism. The traditional view was that the passions must be controlled by reason. But sometimes in speaking of a man as a "passionate soul" we praise him, not thinking of any control of passion by his reason. And I would say that a great change has taken place in this respect, a kind of emancipation and glorification of passion. That is never an ingredient of Hegel.

Mr. Barber: Without explaining it, then, you are saying that behind

Hegel's thought there is a notion of a superiority, let us say, of practice as we might understand it over theory.

LS: No. Ultimately, Hegel retains the supremacy of theory. But it comes out rather in this way. What is the object of theory? In Aristotle, the highest object of theory is the cosmos and the mind governing the cosmos. But for Hegel, the highest object of theory is, one can say, what man has done in the whole course of history. So that practice and its products are the state. From Aristotle's point of view it would be absurd to say that the state has a higher philosophic status as an object than the cosmos. For Hegel it is elemental that all are art. For Aristotle these are subordinate subjects; for Hegel these are the highest subjects of theory. So we can say that theory for Hegel deals with the products of practice, the products of human actions much more than with the natural. This is entirely contrary to the original Aristotelian scheme.

Student: Why then, if this is so, that theory is higher than practice, would a leading Hegelian decide to work with the Common Market than to study theory?

LS: You are speaking of Kojève now.[23]

Student: Yes. Presumably for Hegel it would be a higher thing to write, because by writing other people would come to see the rational order. But if theory were higher in itself, then wouldn't the person who understood Hegel merely sit back and contemplate the state rather than trying to . . .

LS: I see. I do not know what Kojève would say, but I guess he would say that since the truth has been fully discovered and laid bare by Hegel, and he has learned it from Hegel, sitting at his feet, the best that he can do—after he has presented it to the world in a book—is to act according to it.

Student: Then there is nothing intrinsically high about contemplating the truth. It is hard to try to bring it into effect. That is the point.

LS: I do not know whether Kojève would honestly say that. But I think that he would say that he is free to do it and he is in a much better position than any other practitioner because he has the best theoretical vantage. Or let us say out of simple human decency, because if people like him would not go into politics, what would happen? He must do his duty.

Mr. Reinken: Another point. You mentioned a thread of Spinoza coming into Hegel, that the highest form of contemplation was of the universal in the concrete particular. And if Hegel and Kojève have worked out the rational state, what better way of contemplating it than making it the Common Market so that at the various functions . . .

LS: But for Hegel it is clear that the absolute mind, the highest form is philosophy, and that is meant as purely theoretical philosophy, whereas the state belongs to the objective mind, lower than the absolute mind. Yes?

Student: Wouldn't you say that the changed status of passions has as much to do with the coming of Christianity as with modern political thought?

LS: You mean because of the passion in the sense of the passion of Christ?

Student: Well, I don't mean necessarily just in the strictly etymological sense, but in the fact that this passion is in a certain sense the summit of human affairs . . . not even an act, but a suffering.

LS: But there is a certain great difficulty, and difference among Christians exists—between Catholics and Protestants—whether the perfect happiness of man does not consist in the beatific vision which is a form of contemplation. But surely we are exposed to much better knowers of these things than I am, but as far as I understand, it was understood that there is an ingredient of the practical necessarily in beatific vision because of the element of law. Is this not so? You wouldn't say so?

Student: No.

LS: What about you?

Student: I don't know.

LS: Well, you are obliged to know it, and not with a view to your prelims in the political science department. I think so, as far as I remember. Now let us continue where we left off because there is something else which is important. In other words, the opposition of the mind to this kind of systems, such as the Platonic republic or the Egyptian order.

Mr. Reinken:

This impulse also expressed itself in Egypt in a peculiar way. It would appear at first as if the condition of things so regular, so determinate in every particular contained nothing that had a peculiarity entirely its own. The introduction of a religious element would seem to be an affair of no critical moment, provided the higher necessities of men were satisfied. We should, in fact, rather expect that it would be introduced in a peaceful way—

LS: Let us stop here for one moment. So this is a crucial argument against Egypt, what we have seen before, this finality of the order. Yet the highest requirement is that of religion. And religion seems to go well with a determined, detailed order of life, for example in Judaism. What about the Egyptian religion? And now we get the answer.

Mr. Reinken:

> But in contemplating the religion of the Egyptians, we are surprised by the strangest and most wonderful phenomena, and perceive that this calm order of things, bound fast by legislative enactment, is not like that of the Chinese, but that we have here to do with a spirit entirely different, one full of stirring and urgent impulses.

LS: In other words, the Egyptian religion is in no way static. And that shows the great superiority of Egypt. Then, in the sequel he speaks of the Egyptian religion. Let us read the beginning of the next paragraph.

Mr. Reinken:

> The fundamental conception of that which the Egyptians regard as the essence of being rests on the determinate character of the natural world in which they live; and more particularly on the determinate physical circle which the Nile and the sun mark out.[24]

LS: He explains this more fully in the next paragraph on page 208. The Egyptian myth.

Mr. Reinken:

> This basis of the life of the Egyptians determines, moreover, the particular tenor of their religious views. The controversy has long been waged respecting the sense of meaning of the Egyptian religion. As early as the reign of Tiberius—

LS: We do not have to go on. But at any rate, he tries to explain how these two ingredients, the sun and the Nile, are understood by the Egyptian myth and ingredients of it, and then he brings in the story of Osiris in the second half of that paragraph. What is the peculiarity? "Here again, pain or suffering is seen as something divine."

Mr. Reinken:

> Here, again, pain is regarded as something divine, and the same honor is assigned to it here as among the Phoenicians.

LS: In other words, this highest element, apart from Judea, which existed. Phoenicia is preserved in the Egyptian order. Yes?
Mr. Reinken:

Hermes then embalmed Osiris, and his grave is shown in various places. Osiris is now judge of the dead and lord of the kingdom of the shades. These are the leading ideas: Osiris, the sun, the Nile; this triplicity of being is united in one knot. The sun is the symbol in which Osiris and the history of that god are recognized, and the Nile is likewise such a symbol. The concrete Egyptian imagination also ascribes to Osiris and Isis the introduction of agriculture, the invention of the plow, the hoe, etc.; for Osiris gives not only the useful itself—the fertility of the earth—but, moreover, the means of making use of it. He also gives men laws, a civil order, and a religious ritual. He thus places in men's hands the means of labor and secures its result. Osiris is also the symbol of the seed which is placed in the earth and then springs up, as also of the course of life. Thus we find this heterogeneous duality—the phenomena of nature and of the spiritual—woven together into one knot.[25]

LS: And this means something higher than anything that has gone before. And in the next paragraph he makes clear that Egypt is characterized by a radical symbolism much more than any earlier or later nation. Everything is meaning. Everything is symbol. This has to do with the fact that Egypt is the riddle, knowing itself as riddle and unable to solve itself. This is symbolized by the Sphinx. He develops it more fully in the sequel. We cannot go into that. Let us turn to another point which is interesting for its own sake on page 211 in the second paragraph.
Mr. Reinken:

Egyptian worship is chiefly zoolatry.

LS: Animal worship.
Mr. Reinken:

We have observed the union here presented between the spiritual and the natural. The more advanced and elevated side of this conception is the fact that the Egyptians, while they observed the spiritual as manifested in the Nile, the sun and the sowing of seed, took the same view of the life of animals. To us, animal worship is repulsive. We may reconcile ourselves to the adoration of the material heaven —

LS: Why "material heaven"? "Material" is an addition of the translator.
Mr. Reinken:

but the worship of brutes is alien to us; for the abstract natural element seems —

LS: He means the heavens or the sun.
Mr. Reinken:

seems to us more generic and, therefore, more worthy of veneration. Yet it is certain that the nations who worshipped the sun and the stars by no means occupy a higher grade than those who adore brutes, but contrariwise.

LS: Because otherwise Egypt would be much lower than those who worshiped only heaven.
Mr. Reinken:

For in the brute world the Egyptians contemplate a hidden and incomprehensible principle. We also, when we contemplate the life and action of brutes, are astonished at their instinct, the adaptation of their movements to the object intended, their restlessness, excitability and liveliness; for they are exceedingly quick and discerning in pursuing the ends of their existence, while they are at the same time silent and shut up within themselves.

LS: "Mute."
Mr. Reinken:

We cannot make out what it is that possesses these creatures —

LS: "These beasts."
Mr. Reinken:

these beasts, and cannot rely on them. A black tomcat, with its glowing eyes and its now gliding, now quick and darting movement, has been deemed the presence of a malignant being, a mysterious, reserved spectre.

The dog, the canary bird, on the contrary, appear friendly and sympathizing. The lower animals are the truly incomprehensible. A man cannot by imagination or conception enter into the nature of the dog, whatever resemblance he himself might have to it.

LS: "Might wish to have." Apparently there were some dog worshipers already in Hegel's Germany.
Mr. Reinken:

It remains something altogether alien to him. It is in two departments that the so-called incomprehensible meets us—in living nature and in spirit. But in very deed, it is only in nature that we have to encounter the incomprehensible; for the being manifest to itself is the essence of spirit. Spirit understands and comprehends spirit.[26]

LS: And therefore it is quite consistent, if we wish to land eventually in the incomprehensible, in the mere mystery, that we should worship brutes. The purpose of the statement is here clear, namely, to defend the Egyptians against criticism that their animal worship might show a lower level. On the contrary, Hegel says. In Herodotus, who is Hegel's chief source for what he says about Egypt and also Persia, the Egyptians are presented as exaggeratedly pious, worshiping everything. And Socrates swears by the dog, the god of the Egyptians, which is another sign of this universality. And now the final formulation of that, on page 213 in the second paragraph in the center.
Mr. Reinken:

The hidden meaning, the spiritual, emerges as a human face from the brute. The multiform Sphinxes, with lions' bodies and virgins' heads, or as male Sphinxes (*androsphynges*) with beards, are evidence supporting the view that the meaning of the spiritual is the problem which the Egyptians proposed to themselves, and the enigma generally is not the utterance of something unknown, but is the challenge to discover it, implying a wish to be revealed. But, conversely, the human form is also disfigured by a brute face, with a view of giving it a specific and definite expression. The refined art of Greece is able to attain a specific expression through the spiritual character given to an image in the form of beauty and does not need to deform the human face in order to be understood. The Egyptians appended an explanation to the human forms, even of the gods, by means of heads and masks of brutes; Anubis e.g. has a dog's head, Isis a lion's head with bull's horns, and so forth.[27]

LS: Now let us see page 214, paragraph 2. That is the summary of this point.

Mr. Reinken:

We thus see Egypt intellectually confined by a narrow, involved, close view of nature, but breaking through this; impelling it to self-contradiction, and proposing to itself the problem which that contradiction implies.[28]

LS: The abandonment of that contradiction. The *Aufgabe*, which is in German ambiguous but I think it means "abandonment." So in other words, the contradiction is not sufficient. You can live in a contradiction without being bothered by it. Most of us most of the time do exactly that. But to become aware of that is a higher stage, and then still another stage is to try to overcome that. That is, the Sphinx—the riddle, the enigma—is the formula for Egypt; and therefore it points to the overcoming of the enigma and that is then Greece. In other words, the pre-Egyptian cultures have not reached that stage where they see an enigma *as* enigma, as something which must be solved. They see mysteries, they do not see them as enigmas which must be solved. That is the peculiarity.[29]

9   The Greek World

Leo Strauss: Thank you very much. That was a very fine paper.[1] Can I see your last page, because I didn't quite hear something that you said.

Let me try to state your criticism more generally, and then we may come to the particulars you mention. Hegel had said earlier when speaking about his philosophy of history that it presupposes philosophy, that is, Hegel's philosophy. But it is not entirely dependent on that. In a certain way Hegel's philosophy of history is empirical, and you raised the question: How empirical is it? Now if you say that Hegel disregards certain features which are manifest, Hegel could of course answer immediately that these are not essential. The point which he made is that pure *empeiria* which is not selective and doesn't make the distinction between the essential and the unessential is sheer stupidity. That is clear. That is, I believe, even generally admitted today in various forms in positivistic epistemology.

But how does Hegel proceed in a general way? We have now read half of his work and we should be able to say something about this. We must be liberal in the good sense of the word, of course, giving the individual the opportunity to have his say without as it were preventing him from finishing his sentence when he says something which we do not like or do not understand. You can take the example of Egypt, Persia, India, or Greece in all cases. What does he do? There is an infinite variety of facts—of course, more facts were accessible to him in the case of Greece than in the other cases. How does he proceed? You gave the example of his silence on Hades, on the Netherworld, and he speaks only of the Olympian gods. You are correct. This is an incomplete picture of Greek religion if you disregard the Netherworld. Many, many things have been written after Hegel about the worship of the Netherworld, which Hegel knew. *Antigone* was one of his favorite plays. How would Hegel argue?

Student: Well, he has been looking throughout at what each particular person sees as highest.

LS: Even more superficially. What is peculiar to that? Now belief in a kind of Hades, or in the Old Testament *Sheol*, that kind of thing we find elsewhere too. But where do we find gods of human shape and beautiful gods who are the chief gods? However important Hades may be, Zeus is much more important. He would say that the specifically Greek gods are the beautiful gods, and that is what he says. How do we know that they were beautiful? What is our chief source, our most direct source?

Student: First we have the statues.

LS: The plastic art. So Greek divinity is inseparable from art. So he calls it the religion of art. This is one point. Now let us take another example regarding Egypt, where he also selects arbitrarily. Why does he select the pyramids in the first place?

Student: My argument is that he had two reasons for doing it. They were the first to consider the soul immortal; they considered the dead very important. And further, I think that there was a symbolic reason.

LS: But I think that the first superficial and very powerful reason that is most striking is: Where else do you have pyramids? This peculiar kind of fantastic building proves to be a tomb of kings. Therefore, this peculiar concern with death which shows itself in the embalming of bodies is the peculiarity of Egypt. Similar considerations apply to the Sphinx, especially since in this case the link between Greece and Egypt is so clear. A Greek hero well known to us through still present tragedies was the one who solved the riddle of the Sphinx. And Hegel believes that this was a direct presentation of the Greek self-consciousness. The Greeks knew themselves as people who *had* solved the riddle which the Egyptians had not solved and which the other Oriental nations had not even raised. So here that is solid evidence. And if someone says that there never was an Oedipus, it was a mere myth and so forth, Hegel would say: Are not such myths much more revealing about human beings than chronicles about income, the revenues of kings, or maybe victories and defeats? That is not a bad point. Now Hegel takes the story of Oedipus very literally. What was the riddle which he sought?

Student: He was asked the question about what animal has this nature. And the answer is "Man."

LS: . . . as Aristotle would say. So in other words, the Egyptians still did not know that the solution to the riddle was man. And now Hegel reminds himself of another notorious fact known to every schoolboy, surely, at that time, namely, that one of the most famous Greek gods, Apollo, had an oracle in Delphi and from there one of the great advices or counsels is given. In a way the most famous of all was "Know thyself." And "Know thyself" does not mean to know thyself as Mr. Smith with such and such grades, such and such banking account, and so many brothers and sisters, but it means to know thyself as a human being. For example, one symbolization is a skeleton: no immortality. So the Greeks were concerned with self-knowledge, i.e., knowledge of man, of what man is. And this is only the other side of the Oedipus story.

Now what did you say, on the basis of Hegel of course, about Oedipus's crimes or sins?

Student: Hegel uses the idea that Oedipus's knowledge of man was connected with the crimes.

LS: Yes.

Student: What I took that to mean was that his particular sort of understanding of man was such that it was merely an ideal or abstract—I don't know how Hegel would describe it—understanding of the universal form and it was connected with knowing that the species of universal man had a spirit, but not that the particular man in the civil society or that particular people were free; and similarly, Oedipus's crime was connected with the fact that he didn't know the particular facts about himself and about his own relationship to his own civil society.

LS: In any case, the knowledge remained in one way or another abstract. Hegel does not suggest that this might be an essential part of the Greek story, that to have solved the riddle of the Sphinx is in itself to have committed the most terrible crime. That he does not suggest. In other words, the most terrible fundamental crimes are parricide and incest with one's mother. And to know the truth about man, which in a way includes all truth, is only possible for a man who has committed crimes. In other words, he doesn't suggest that Oedipus is not fully self-conscious, that he doesn't know what it means to solve the riddle of the Sphinx.

Student: If he does suggest it, I missed it.

LS: No. Because last time we spoke of it briefly, and one of you said that he does suggest it. But after having reread it, I see again that he does not suggest it. The thought would not be completely alien to Hegel, although he does not use it, as is shown by something that we will discuss next time. But perhaps the gentleman who reads the paper next time can help us in that matter. Mr. . . . . , is there some awareness in Hegel that seeking the most important truth is in a way the greatest crime? Socrates was justly condemned. Of course the atrocities of Oedipus are not mentioned in the case of Socrates, but this is only a matter of a more massive or less massive presentation of the same fundamental problem.

Now which of the particular difficulties or objections to Hegel did I not discuss which you think should be discussed?

Mr. Reinken: At the end there was something about the question: How conscious were the Greeks of poetry being imitation?

LS: Yes, that's a wonderful question. It was indeed implied. How would you reply to Mr. Reinken's question?

Student: I think he's directly repeating the question I raised.

LS: But how did I answer that question implicitly? [Laughter] No, it's not far-fetched. Now you shouldn't laugh about that. Sometimes I make jokes voluntary or involuntary, but that was neither one nor the other. The point is this. Hegel demands two things. On the one hand, empirical procedure: let's look at the Greeks intelligently, not forgetting the wood for the trees. But on the other hand, we must bring with us philosophy, Hegel's philosophy. Now therefore he interprets the empirical data from a shamelessly Hegelian point of view, and therefore he doesn't take seriously for one moment the Greek notion of art as imitation.

Student: Why is it that he doesn't take that seriously but does take the Egyptian awareness of death and not the Hindu awareness of death seriously?

LS: First let us see the main point. Hegel takes the massive facts, say, the Homeric documents, and especially as presented to us most visibly in Greek plastic art. And he says: Look around; where else did you find that? That is one thing. And of course he will also add immediately the *polis*, of which he speaks later: free small states with this high development of public speech, etc. The things which are truly known to every one of you who has taken any course in general civilization—I believe that is the name of the course—I mean, the massive facts that everyone knows. Then Hegel says: Of course that must be interpreted. And the categories underlying the interpretation are supplied by Hegel's philosophy, naturally. I am aware that there are certain problems here which concern both the soundness of Hegel's historical interpretation and the truth of his philosophy. Now we come to the specific point. In the case of the Hindus, you said he did not consider the concern with immortality.

Student: And the reason that I thought that he didn't was that the Hindus were not aware that their own theory might apply to mortality, whereas the Egyptians were explicitly aware of that.

LS: Does anyone know how Hegel would defend himself regarding India? What is the most peculiar thing of Hindu or Indian religion as Hegel saw it? The highest?

Mr. Reinken: Indefinite nothingness.

LS: Nirvana, the complete absorption of the individual into the one absolute. Now compared with that, the things which play around, as it were, and come from a less high inspiration are dismissed. The Greeks had no Nirvana, but instead of that they had Olympus. Similar considerations would apply to Egypt. Yes?

Mr. Reinken: Narrowly on the point of whether Greek thinking is concrete and looking at things which are or fanciful: the last sentence that he has about *manteia* is on the bottom of page 236. "*Manteia*, in fact, is poesy. Not a capricious indulgence of fancy, but an imagination which introduces the spiritual into the natural. In short, a richly intelligent perception." Now I think that this is Hegel's formula for that mean that the Greek spirit has between the merely submitting to nature of the Oriental and the consciously fictitious nature of—

LS: No. What he has in mind is that in mantic, *mantike*, you have the two elements. First, the things which are to you or me wholly unintelligible, the sounds and noises or whatever it may be. And then there is someone else's . . . called the interpreter. And it is this to which he refers here. An oracle is meaningless without the clearly distinguished interpretation. The natural noises which the Pythia produces when sitting on the tripod, on the one hand: in themselves, they are merely natural; you can even say that they are nonsensical. Or take the intestines of some animal. And then there is some interpreter, who clearly distinguished here the natural and the spiritual that he has in mind.

Mr. Reinken: And this is the character of Greek poesy.

LS: No, on the contrary. Greek religion is poetry. You cannot turn it around and say that Greek poetry is always Greek religion. You know that there was some poetry which was not religious. I wanted to speak about that anyway. The Greek gods—everyone has seen some of these statues or copies of them. But we know something else from literary sources and from great authorities. One, who Hegel quotes more than once, is Herodotus's statement. Who gave the Greeks their gods? For the ordinary Greek understands only that the gods are there, that goes without saying. But Herodotus, reflecting, raises the question: Where do they come from? And what did he say?

Student: Homer and Hesiod.

LS: Yes. And everyone would call Homer and Hesiod poets. The Greeks already called them poets, although Homer himself didn't call himself a poet.

Mr. Shulsky: My point was, didn't that mean that Hegel's understanding of the Greeks was not really so far different from at least some of the Greeks' understanding of themselves? In other words, Herodotus implies to a certain extent that the recognition of the gods was as much an act of creation as an act of perceiving what was already there, although the average Greek might not have thought that.

LS: Well, of course Hegel knew Greek philosophy quite well, but what he is concerned with, at least in the part that we discussed today—and in a way in the whole presentation—is the prephilosophic understanding of Greekness by the Greeks. About the philosophers he wrote in his history of philosophy, but this he wanted to understand, and therefore he took the naive, philosophically unreflective utterances as the most important.

Mr. Shulsky: But my question would be: Is his final understanding of Greek poetry so different from the understanding of the Greeks? Is there a common ground between the two understandings, that it was as much creation as it was simple possession? It was an activity of the individual; it wasn't simply passive, perceptive.

LS: I would say that the understanding must be profoundly different, although there are important points of agreement, for this reason: Which part of philosophy, according to the now prevailing view and the view of Hegel, deals with poetry and culture and this kind of thing?

Mr. Shulsky: Well, at present it would be aesthetics.

LS: Yes. There is a very large and very beautiful aesthetics lecture available. What is the theme of aesthetics? The term was coined only in the eighteenth century, but what was the theme of aesthetics in a general way?

Mr. Shulsky: The way in which works of art affect us.

LS: No.

Mr. Reinken: The beautiful.

LS: The beautiful. And Hegel is perhaps more responsible than anyone else for this change, that aesthetics is concerned with the beautiful in art and not with the beautiful simply. Hegel does discuss in his aesthetics what he calls the natural beautiful, say, a beautiful human body. And primarily for the Greeks the beautiful is the human body, or even that of a horse—a living horse is more beautiful than a beautifully sculptured horse which has no life. And in this respect, for Hegel it is opposite. The sculptured horse is higher in rank than the living horse. We will come to that later. So this is a radical difference. It has to do with the posture towards nature: the Greeks on the one hand, and Hegel on the other. When Hegel speaks about these matters he uses the term "nature" from his point of view, i.e., in connection with matters in which the Greeks would not have spoken of nature. We will come across some of these passages.

Student: Aristotle's doctrine of nature doesn't mean a slavish copying of sensations. It has to do with the development of the potencies already found in nature, so it becomes an idealizing act for Aristotle. Wouldn't this go along with Hegel's view of art? The idealizing is a spiritual activity, and putting the ideal form into concrete matter to produce a beautiful work of art.

LS: Up to this point, yes. But would there not still be a difference concerning the question of nature? For Aristotle the beautiful *par excellence* — of which he speaks also in his *Metaphysics,* perhaps more than in his *Poetics* — is not the work of art, it is the beautiful order of the cosmos, a living being, the order of numbers and such things. Yes?

Student: The truly . . . but Hegel would agree with that too.

LS: No, not more beautiful.

Student: . . .

LS: No, you cannot possibly use some pigeonholes and administrative arrangements. For Hegel, the true is radically distinguished from the beautiful and higher than it. And for Plato and Aristotle, somehow the true and beautiful coincide on the highest level, the ideas. Whether we can immediately understand it or not is another matter.

Student: But they wouldn't disagree that the beautiful is somehow an anticipation of the true? Hegel doesn't say that they are unrelated.

LS: No, I would agree with that. I believe that this will become clearer once we turn to specific questions. Now let us begin, or is there anyone with an urgent question about what we just discussed? Then we turn to page 215 in the first paragraph, when he says with other peoples, history consists of a series of events.

Mr. Reinken:

While among other nations history consists of a series of events — as, for example, that of the Romans, who century after century lived only with a view to conquest and accomplished the subjugation of the world — the Egyptians raised an empire equally mighty, of achievement in works of art whose ruins prove their indestructibility and which are greater and more worthy of astonishment than all other works of ancient or modern time.[2]

LS: So the deeds of the Egyptians are works of art, not political deeds. This is one of the observations, the empirical facts, out of which Hegel weaves his construction. Now let us turn to the third paragraph on the same page. There are a few passages which I will read to you as they are translated literally. "As a nation views the essential man, so is that nation itself, so is its character." And then, speaking a bit later of the immortality of the soul: "This, that the soul is immortal, should mean that the soul is something else than nature. Mind is independent for itself." The thought that the mind is immortal, that is in paragraph 4, page 215. Perhaps you can read this.
Mr. Reinken:

But this proposition—that the soul is immortal—

LS: "The mind is immortal," he says here.
Mr. Reinken:

that the mind is immortal is intended to mean that it is something other than nature, that spirit is inherently independent. The *ne plus ultra* of blessedness among the Hindus was the passing over into abstract unity, into nothingness. On the other hand, subjectivity—when free—is inherently infinite. The kingdom of free spirit is, therefore, the kingdom of the invisible, such as Hades was conceived by the Greeks. This presents itself to men first as the empire of death—to the Egyptians as the realm of the dead.[3]

LS: A nation is what it is by virtue of what it looks up to, what it regards as the highest, as the divine. The highest is this mind. Therefore, the rank of a culture depends upon the extent to which it has understood mind in its peculiarity. There is here a difficulty. The German word *Geist*, which I translated here as "mind," also means "spirit." "Mind" points to the philosophic tradition and "spirit" points to the theological tradition. This is indistinguishable in the German word. You have "the Holy Ghost" in English. So you could, in other words, translate the same word both by "mind" and "ghost," which would be very awkward in a translation, but you must keep this in mind.
The Egyptians discovered the immortality of the soul. The Jews did not know of it—we have seen that in the chapter on Judaism. That is axiomatic for Hegel, that there is no immortality of the soul in the Old Tes-

tament. Most so-called critical scholars today agree with Hegel, but it is by no means universally admitted. Hegel later explains that the embalming of the dead and the doctrine of metempsychosis is below the level of the belief in the immortality of the soul. Yet this habit of embalming bespeaks a respect of the human body, and as such it is something noble, regarding the body as the abode of the mind. On page 218, paragraph 1.

Mr. Reinken:

> If death thus haunted the minds of the Egyptians during life, it might be supposed that their disposition was melancholy. But the thought of death by no means occasioned depression. At banquets they had representations of the dead (as Herodotus relates) with the admonition, "Eat, drink for such a one wilt Thou become when thou art dead." Death was thus to them rather a call to enjoy life.[4]

LS: The respect of the body which we find in their practice of embalming is connected with their enjoyment of life. A certain union of the mortal or human and the immortal or divine has been achieved in Egypt. In the sequel Hegel speaks of the relation of Egypt to the Orient in general and to Greece in particular, where he uses the Oedipus story. We have spoken of that before. But there are a few more points. On page 221 at the beginning of the second paragraph.

Mr. Reinken:

> The inward or ideal transition from Egypt to Greece is as just exhibited. But Egypt became a province of the great Persian kingdom, and the historical transition takes place when the Persian world comes in contact with the Greek.[5]

LS: Do you see the use of the word "historical" here? What does this mean?

Mr. Reinken: Empirical in contradistinction to —

LS: Well — yes?

Mr. Shulsky: Doesn't it simply mean outward?

LS: Yes, but I think that it means more clearly the political. And it wouldn't be surprising because, after all, even today if someone tells you that he is a historian, you take it for granted that he is a political historian. Otherwise he would say that he was an art historian, an economic historian, or some other kind, e.g., a historian of science — in other words, historian qualified. But a historian simply is a political historian. I note this only as an interesting reminder of this state of things. By the way, in the sequel it becomes perfectly clear. Read on, Mr. Reinken.

Mr. Reinken:

> Here, for the first time, an historical transition meets us, viz. in the fall of an empire. China and India, as already mentioned, have remained; Persia has not. The transition to Greece is, indeed, internal, but here it shows itself also externally as a transmission of sovereignty —

LS: "Empire."
Mr. Reinken:

> an occurrence which from this time forward is ever and anon repeated.

LS: In the sequel he makes clear that, as we know already, permanence as we find it in India and China is not in itself a sign of superiority. We have discussed this at great length. Here he gives an example.

Mr. Reinken:

> Unperishable mountains are not superior to the quickly dismantled rose exhaling its life and fragrance.[6]

LS: In other words, permanence is not as such superior to the internal thought, which has very crucial implications and is, in a way, underlying the more recent development where the notion of sempiternity or eternity has been abandoned. Page 222, at the bottom . . . I have here a more recent edition of Hegel's *Philosophy of History* which contains quite a few passages which are not available in the older edition or in the English translation. Let me see what he says here about the peculiarities of the Greeks. "In the Oriental world the moral substance and the subject are opposed to each other. The moral substance is known as natural or abstract. The moral is despot for the subject and shows itself done by the will of a single one who is opposed by the unfree subjects."[7] This is changed radically in Greece. You must not forget that here Hegel speaks of the Orientals in general, and therefore of the Old Testament in particular too. How is this intelligible? He says that Greece is the realm of the Occident, of the human mind, of the self-awareness of the human mind. How is this possible? How can he say this about the Bible? Oriental despotism, that is the famous formula: all are subjects except one whom all fear and who according to Hegel cannot himself be truly free because of the unfreedom of everyone else. How could this possibly be applied to the Old Testament? How can we understand that?

Student: Would he mean the despotism, as it were, of God?

LS: Yes, exactly. Therefore he uses the phrase "of the unique"; the only one, *einzig*. So what you find in the Orient is a fear of the lord with a small *l* or with a capital, and this is fundamentally changed in the Occident and especially in Greece. That is his point. Now on page 223, in the second paragraph, you find one of these statements of Hegel's where one can perhaps blame him.

Mr. Reinken:

> The highest form that floated before Greek imagination was Achilles, the son of the poet, the Homeric youth of the Trojan War.

LS: By the way, that is a very fine reproduction of Hegel. I do not know whether he did it consciously. Somewhere Plato says "the Achilles of Homer" in the Greek phrase where you say, for example, "Solomon of David," meaning "the son of David." That is "the son of the poet."

Mr. Reinken:

> Homer is the element in which the Greek world lives, as man does in the air. The Greek life is a truly youthful achievement. Achilles, the ideal youth of poetry, commenced it; Alexander the Great, the ideal youth of reality, concluded it. Both appear in contest with Asia.[8]

LS: That is enough. So in other words, the youthfulness of Greece is symbolized in the fact of Achilles at the beginning and Alexander the Great at the end. Here of course what would we say about these assertions?

Student: Alexander's character . . . his individuality would be praised throughout history.

LS: No. Something very simple. In the case of Alexander the historical figure, the necessity of Alexander having died young. You know, the Homeric gods and these things, they are obviously essential to Greece, but that Alexander should have died young cannot possibly have this essential character. This is the difficulty which I find when he makes such remarks.[9]

Mr. Reinken: Perhaps it was appropriate that a juvenile delinquent should knock over the Persian Empire.

LS: That's not what he means. Now the Greeks are the first who did not begin their formation of culture only with nature, starting from scratch as we would say, but by presupposing and transforming a foreign culture. This is higher than to be simply autochthonous from Hegel's point of view. Let us turn to page 226, line 3.

Mr. Reinken:

At the origin of their national unity, separation as a generic feature, inherent distinctness of character, is the chief point that has to be considered. The first phase in the subjugation of this constitutes the primary period of Greek culture. And only through such distinctness of character and such a subjugation of it was the beautiful, free Greek spirit produced. Of this principle we must have a clear conception. It is a superficial and absurd idea that such a beautiful and truly free life can be produced by a process so incomplex as the development of a race keeping within the limits of blood relationship and friendship. Even the plant, which supplies the nearest analogy to such a calm, homogeneous unfolding, lives and grows only by means of the antithetic activities of light, air and water. The only real antithesis that spirit can have is itself spiritual, viz. its inherent heterogeneity through which alone it acquires the power of realizing itself as spirit. The history of Greece exhibits at its commencement this interchange and mixture of partly homesprung, partly quite foreign stocks.[10]

LS: And so on. So this passage shows clearly that Hegel had nothing to do with any racialism. I mean the nonautochthony, the heterogeneity is essential for the higher levels, and the defect of the Orientals would be, from this point of view, that they have not been sufficiently mixed with one another. But this I say only in passing, against an absurd, stupid misunderstanding of Hegel altogether.[11] The questioning of the value of autochthony goes together with the questioning of the supremacy of agriculture compared with industry, of which we have spoken before. The sea and living on the sea is in a way superior to a merely landlocked life. You remember that. But those of you who know the classics of Greek political philosophy must be quite impressed here by this Hegelian remark.

Mr. Reinken: The best city that the Athenian stranger suggests, you build it way back from the sea, of course.

LS: That is clear. But this point regards the heterogeneity of the population.

Mr. Shulsky: He mentions that Attica was especially mixed racially, but that they were the people who could claim to be autochthonous.

LS: In other words, here he appeals from a less informed Athens to a better informed Athens. But in the philosophic texts, do they not speak about the homogeneity and heterogeneity of the population? Mr. Bruell?

Mr. Bruell: I thought he might be referring to Greeks and barbarians.

LS: Pardon?

M. Bruell: The Greeks are considered in a certain sense homogeneous, as opposed to barbarians.

LS: But in more specific terms.

Mr. Reinken: The city is preferred to the diverse empire because there is the homogeneity. Aristotle speaks of *homonoia*, and Plato tells us that the great unifying myth of the society is that the men are all brothers.

LS: But the mere fact that it is a myth of course means that it must not be literally true. That is not the point. There is a discussion in Plato's *Laws*. I only looked up my reference to it in my discussion of Plato in *The History of Political Philosophy*, on page 56.[12] You might look that up. Plato suggests that a certain heterogeneity of the settlers of the new city is good for it, but only a certain amount. This only in passing. But the more important and more obvious remark on this subject you find right at the beginning of the *Politics*. How is the *polis* presented there?

Student: Is that the discussion of unity and diversity, the degree of unity that is good for the *polis*?

LS: No. That is in the second book.

Student: It is the natural expansion of the family.

LS: Exactly. The family, the village. So in other words, the great land farmer who has ten or fifteen sons and each has his own household. A small village. And that goes on, and they unite with other villages, and then there is the *polis*. Now what does this difference between Aristotle and Hegel mean? What Aristotle says there is not necessarily crucial for this question. Yes?

Mr. Shulsky: Isn't this really a part of Aristotle's question of the natural development of the *polis* as opposed to the totally created nature of the *polis*?

LS: Exactly. In other words, what Aristotle wants to show here at least is that the city is natural. He wants to show therefore that it could have come into being: even this coming into being could have been perfectly natural via the village as he describes it. That is indeed true. He wants to counteract the view that the city is altogether conventional, i.e., has come into being necessarily by nothing but contract. That's not necessary. Yes?

Mr. Shulsky: Well, that wouldn't be Aristotle's final view, would it? That it was just a natural expansion of the family.

LS: Surely not. The coming into being is one thing and the being or essence is another thing, sure. But the difference truly is this: for Aristotle, the fundamental distinction which is underlying this discussion is that between nature and convention, and for Hegel it is that between nature and mind. And this affects everything, including the question of art.

Now here is another point, a remark which occurs also in the translation when he speaks of what the tools which man makes mean. He says that it is a rule of reason by which nature is turned against nature. In other words, certain natural qualities, say, of a hammer, are turned against other natural qualities, say, of wood. But both qualities are natural. But that one has become a tool that can be used is no longer merely natural, is a work of the mind. And Hegel goes on to say that these human inventions belong to the mind, and such a tool which a man invents is a higher thing than a natural thing, for it is a mental, spiritual thing. So the artifacts have a higher status than the natural facts. None of the Greek philosophers would have said that. That is the key difference, and it affects also the relation of the works of art to natural beauty.

Now there are many more passages. Page 227, bottom. Hegel says here in passing that the natural nationality is a very obscure matter. In German . . . But the spiritual, intellectual difference between nations has nothing to do, or is not identical, with the natural nationality, with the merely ethnic one. Yes, on page 227, bottom.

Mr. Reinken:

We have just spoken of heterogeneity as an element of the Greek spirit, and it is well known that the rudiments of Greek civilization are connected with the advent of foreigners. This origin of their moral life—

LS: No, here he says that one can compare Greece in this respect with North America. Do you have that? Also a land of immigrants of heterogeneous origins.

Mr. Reinken: Page 228.

We thus observe a colonization by civilized peoples, who were in advance of the Greeks in point of culture, though we cannot compare this colonization with that of the English in North America, for the latter have not been blended with the aborigines, but have dispossessed them.

LS: So this is very interesting. Yes, read this passage again. "Therefore one cannot compare."
Mr. Reinken:

We cannot compare this colonization with that of the English in North America, for the latter have not been blended with the aborigines, but have dispossessed them.[13]

LS: This is not altogether irrelevant. Hegel doesn't mean this in the sense of a moral judgment. We know that Hegel was not an anticolonialist. You have to admit that. But it is interesting for the question regarding America. Remember we discussed the question of an American principle which might emerge in the future, and I believe that it is implied that America is an offspring of Europe, whereas the Greeks, by creating a synthesis as it were of their own and something foreign, created something new, and the same cannot be said of America as Hegel saw it.

Mr. Reinken: On Hegel's principles, would not our . . . the melting pot . . . We would now claim that America is not England all over again.

LS: Hegel does not say that, considering the preponderance of the European element in America—unless you were to say that the Negro element has such a profound effect, something which James Baldwin[14] wishes to suggest. But whether that is a defensible thesis is controversial, as far as I know.

Mr. Reinken: But merely within the European, mixtures have taken place that never took place on the continent of Europe. One never found English and Hungarians in such proximity, and that makes a difference.

LS: Yes, but I know some Hungarians living in England and making a very good go of it. [Laughter] Now on page 231, end of the first paragraph. He compares the Crusades to the Trojan war.
Mr. Reinken:

So, likewise in the Middle Ages we see the whole of Christendom united to attain one object—the conquest of the Holy Sepulchre. But in spite of all the victories achieved, with just as little permanent result. The Crusades are the Trojan War of newly awakened Christendom waged against the simple, homogeneous clarity of Mohammedanism.[15]

LS: Some of you will have read Spengler. What struck me here is that this is the kind of thing which Spengler does all the time. These parallels in different cultures, especially of course in the medieval and modern worlds on the one hand, and in the Greek world on the other hand. This is very striking, to say that the Trojan war is the Crusades of Greece or that the Crusades are the Trojan war of Western Europe.[16]

Let us go on to a bit later when he speaks about the *Iliad*.[17] Yes? Mr. Reinken:

When Ulysses, among the Phaeacians, has thrown his discus further than the rest, and one of the Phaeacians shows a friendly disposition towards him, the poet recognizes in him Pallas-Athena. Such an explanation denotes the perception of the inner meaning, the sense, the underlying truth; and the poets were in this way the teachers of the Greeks—especially Homer. *Manteia* in fact is Poesy—not a capricious indulgence of fancy, but an imagination which introduces the Spiritual into the Natural—in short, a richly intelligent perception. The Greek Spirit, on the whole, therefore, is free from superstition, since it changes the sensuous into the sensible.[18]

LS: That is the key point: Greek religion is poetry, not superstition. That is its peculiar greatness and freedom. Now he comes gradually to the core of the problem. And one point which Hegel constantly makes—and defensibly—is that there were all kinds of superstitions in Greece, but that these are simply archaic and foreign relics. This is not the essence of the Greek religion, although it is there. What justifies Hegel in making this distinction? In other words, why is this distinction justified by Greek religion itself? Hegel has a reason. I do not know whether it came out in your assignment for today, Mr. . . . What is the reason why Hegel is entitled to make such a distinction between the Greek proper and the archaic and/or foreign?

Student: I think that I know what you are referring to. I think that it is in the next section, particularly the spirit of the Greek gods.

LS: The simple distinction the Greeks themselves make in their stories. There were the old gods who ruled originally, Chronos and Ouranos and so on, and then the rule of Zeus and the new generation of gods. Therefore the Greeks had an awareness that there was an older stratum of gods and subjectively of beliefs which played a role until the end, but which was no longer ruling and predominant. That is, I think, his justification.

On page 238, in the second paragraph.

Mr. Reinken:

> In summing up the constituents of the Greek Spirit, we find its fundamental characteristic to be, that the freedom of Spirit is conditioned by and has an essential relation to some stimulus supplied by Nature. Greek freedom of thought is excited by an alien existence; but it is free because it transforms and virtually reproduces the stimulus by its own operation.

LS: In other words, for Hegel it does not make a great difference whether this external thing which stimulates the creative action comes from nature or from other nations. It is not their own. And to that extent its freedom has its origin in something alien. And therefore, that is the limited character of Greek freedom compared with modern freedom. Yes?

Mr. Reinken:

> This phase of Spirit is the medium between the loss of individuality on the part of man (such as we observe in the Asiatic principle, in which Spiritual and Divine exist only under a Natural form), and Infinite Subjectivity as pure certainty of itself—the position that the Ego is the ground of all that can lay claim to substantial existence.

LS: In other words, the infinite subjectivity as the pure certainty of itself is alien to the Greek mind, the thought that the ego is the soil for everything which claims to be valid. Therefore we find dependence on things alien to the ego, nature. But nevertheless, the freedom of the mind is recognized within these limits, and therefore Greece is higher than the Orient.

Mr. Shulsky: This second principle which he takes to be the principle of modern . . .

LS: Yes, and of Christianity altogether. Only modern philosophy, as well as Hegel, gives the adequate interpretation of what Christianity means.

Mr. Reinken:

The Greek Spirit as the medium between these two—

LS: "As the mean."

Mr. Reinken:

as the mean between these two, begins with Nature, but transforms it into a mere objective form of its (Spirit's) own existence; Spirituality is therefore not yet absolutely free; not yet absolutely self-produced—is not self-stimulation. Setting out from surmise and wonder, the Greek Spirit advances to definite conceptions of the hidden meanings of Nature. In the subject itself too, the same harmony is produced. In Man, the side of his subjective existence which he owes to Nature is the Heart, the Disposition, Passion, and Variety of Temperament: this side is then developed in a spiritual direction to free individuality; so that the character is not placed in a relation to universally valid moral authorities, assuming the form of duties, but the Moral appears as a nature peculiar to the individual—an exertion of will, the result of disposition and individual constitution. This stamps the Greek character as that of Individuality conditioned by Beauty—

LS: Why not "beautiful individuality"? And we will see that while it is the beautiful individuality as shown in the Greek gods, it is nevertheless fundamentally deficient. But this is the great progress made by the Greeks beyond the Orient, according to Hegel. Yes?

Mr. Reinken:

the Greek character, as that of beautiful individuality, which is produced by Spirit, transforming the merely Natural into an expression of its own being.

LS: In other words, it still needs the natural as means of expression. Now let us continue.

Mr. Reinken:

The activity of Spirit does not yet possess in itself the material and organ of expression, but needs the excitement of Nature and the matter which

Nature supplies: it is not free, self-determining Spirituality, but mere naturalness formed to Spirituality—Spiritual Individuality. The Greek Spirit
is the plastic artist, forming the stone into a work of art.[19]

LS: Let us stop here. And that is also the limit of it. It is beautiful individuality, but not yet spiritual individuality. Mr. Shulsky?

Mr. Shulsky: Does he mean this simply as the character of the Greek
gods and the Greek poetry, or does he mean it to apply to the philosophy
as well?

LS: He speaks about that later. What Socrates and Plato did, he speaks
of that later. But even there it did not lead to an understanding of spiritual
individuality. That will become clear.

Mr. Shulsky: But it wasn't simply a question guided by considerations
of beauty?

LS: No. Socrates was ugly, as we know. Hegel knows that. Nevertheless, the Greeks, even the philosophers, did not yet understand spirituality in the radical way. They don't know anything of the *Cogito ergo sum*,
to put it very simply, which is for Hegel the fundamental principle. Or,
as Hegel also put it, the conscience did not exist for the Greeks. We will
come to that later. Who will read the paper next time? Mr. . . . ? You
will have to give us a lot of enlightenment. Then of course the question is whether Socrates's *daimonion*, that demonic thing in which he
trusted, is not the conscience. That we will have to see. But here he does
not speak yet of the philosophers. Now let us turn to page 239, second
paragraph.

Mr. Reinken:

It must be added, that while the Greek Spirit is a transforming artist of
this kind, it knows itself free in its productions; for it is their creator, and
they are what is called the "work of man."

LS: Yes, the "work of man," using the biblical expression in the German
term *Menschenwerk*. They are only idols, of Zeus and Hera and so on.
Now he goes on correcting the ordinary religious views.

Mr. Reinken:

They are, however, not merely this, but Eternal Truth, the energizing
of Spirit in its innate essence, and quite as really not created as created
by man.

LS: That is the point which I believe you had in mind. In a way, they merely reproduce. When Phidias presents Zeus and he is guided in that by his having seen and heard Pericles speaking, so that even some peculiarities of Pericles's head are ascribed to Zeus—even that is nevertheless a sincere attempt to present Zeus visibly. That he used the help supplied by this Zeus-like man, Pericles, is perfectly legitimate . . . Yes?

Mr. Reinken:

> He has a respect and veneration for these conceptions and images—this Olympian Zeus—this Pallas of the Acropolis—and in the same way for the laws, political and ethical, that guide his actions. But he, the human being, is the womb that conceived them, he the breast that suckled them, he the Spiritual to which their grandeur and purity are owing. Thus he feels himself calm in contemplating them, and not only free in himself, but possessing the consciousness of his freedom; thus the honor of the Human is swallowed up in the worship of the Divine. Men honor the Divine in and for itself, but at the same time as their deed, their production, their phenomenal existence; thus the Divine receives its honor through the respect paid to the Human, and the Human in virtue of the honor paid to the Divine.[20]

LS: So in other words, what more do you want? The complete reconciliation of the human and the divine. And what is wrong with that? Speaking again quite simply in terms of facts which anyone knows from the general civilization course.

Mr. Shulsky: Well, first of all, they weren't aware that this applied to every individual.

LS: But in terms of this point, the complete reconciliation of the human and the divine. How did the Greeks call the gods or, for that matter, men?

Student: They were afraid of the gods.

LS: No, as Hegel understood them, not so much.

Student: They asked the gods' help in battles and so on. It wasn't a complete reconciliation, but there was some thought that gods had control over natural things.

Student: Gods were called the immortals.

LS: Exactly. Men were the mortals, gods the immortals or rather the deathless ones, so there was no full reconciliation between the divine and the human because there was no awareness of the god who died. That is the peculiarity of Christianity, and out of this the true reconciliation between the divine and the human comes. And the Crucifixion is not beautiful in the same way in which the Homeric Zeus, the . . . Zeus or Hera is beautiful, the reason being that there is a fundamental difference between truth and beauty, and truth is higher than beauty. We may therefore say that the ugly belongs, in a way, to the truth. The ugly: pain, suffering, death. The almighty gods are living easily . . . They have also their kinds of worries about rather ridiculous things, but fundamentally they live in ease, watching what their favorites do, like people who have set [wagers] on horses. They are not truly involved, and therefore there is no true reconciliation. But it is a beautiful reconciliation, and if beauty were the highest consideration, the Greeks would be right.

How much of the so-called aestheticism of the nineteenth century is implied in this sentence, that from the point of view of beauty Greekness is unsurpassable? Much of the bad classicism of the nineteenth century of course also belongs to that. So the Greeks have indeed understood this. That is the reason why Hegel prefers Greekness to the Old Testament: the human gods. But the higher thought according to Hegel is that the one God has become man and died as man, truly God and truly man. Whether Hegel understands that in the Christian orthodox manner is very doubtful. Hegel sees it at least as an expression of the speculative truth. In the sequel he gives a clear plan of what he wants to discuss at the end.

Mr. Reinken:

> Such are the qualities of that Beautiful Individuality, which constitutes the centre of the Greek character. We must now consider the several radiations which this idea throws out in realizing itself. All issue in works of art, and we may arrange under three heads: the subjective work of art, that is, the culture of the man himself; the objective work of art, that is, the shaping of the world of divinities; lastly, the political work of art—the form of the Constitution, and the relations of the Individuals who compose it.[21]

LS: Philosophy does not occur here, as you see. That comes in only in the discussion of the third, the political work of art, the *polis*, in its decay. And that is the place of Greek philosophy in Hegel's philosophy of history as distinguished from his history of philosophy. And there we will see whether and to what extent he will bring it out properly; and there is an unintentional but not unconscious criticism of Greek philosophy noticeable throughout, as we will see while we go.[22]

LS: We will be particularly interested next time in his analysis of the Greek *polis* as he understands it. It is explicitly based on Montesquieu's famous saying that virtue is the principle of democracy. And of course, democracy is a *polis*; a modern representative democracy would not be a *polis* and would not need virtue to that extent. Those of you who would like to understand this better might very well read this in Montesquieu's *Spirit of Laws*. It is near the beginning of the book, which deals with democracy, where you will find the matrix out of which Hegel's . . . grew.[23] If you do that you will be confronted with many surprises. In other words, Hegel's somewhat strange notion of democracy is already Montesquieu's.

10 The Greek World Continued

Leo Strauss: You did not make clear one point.[1] I remind you of what we discussed last time, the empirical character of Hegel's procedure. He starts from very massive facts, the beautiful gods in human shape and the *polis*, some sort of political freedom also peculiar to Greece, and public deliberation. And then there is also Socrates and all that he implies. Now how does Hegel understand the connection between original Greekness and Socrates? This did not become clear.

Student: I see. I think that he believes the freedom which exists in Greece is the germ of the Socratic questioning of the customary.

LS: Is any historical, empirical evidence used by Hegel to show the connection between original Greekness and Socrates?

Student: I didn't see how he spelled out that point.

LS: Does anyone? Mr. Bruell?

Mr. Bruell: Through the sophists . . .

LS: No. That was already corruption. Prior to the corruption? The democratic *polis*, as he calls it, using democracy in a very large sense. What is the connection between Greek democracy as understood by Hegel—I mean the healthy democracy, prior to the Peloponnesian war—and Socrates? How does a democracy proceed? Debate. There was debate, and you could even make something technical out of the debates. That is an art.

Student: Well, that accounts for the sophistry.

LS: But still, originally there was a kind of native oratory: public speeches, public debate. And there is a connection between public debate about public matters and Socratic debate.

Student: I had the impression, though, from the text that when the sophists taught that sophistry originated from some independent source, the sophists came along and saw the debates and then taught the people how to debate.

LS: Yes, but what does this mean? It is sophistry, and more radically, Socrates is the opposite of original Greekness, as Hegel says. But since it is the negation, the antithesis of original Greekness, it must be understood as stemming *from* Greekness. In other words, original Greekness is the necessary matrix of Socrates. Also, if we look at the Greek gods, what is the connection between the Greek gods and Socrates—taking Socrates now for a general term designating this novel and unheard-of thing? What is the peculiar character of the Greek gods?

Mr. Shulsky: Well, they weren't there originally. They were there by overthrowing the original order of things. They established a certain possibility by questioning the order.

LS: In other words, they were emphatically not the oldest gods. Is this what you mean?

Mr. Shulsky: Yes.

LS: Yes, that is also true. So the simple equation of the good and the ancient could not well be maintained because then Chronos and Ouranos would be the highest god and not Zeus. That is true. But also the other point. How does he call the Greek religion?

Student: The religion of art.

LS: Yes. So the artists, the artisans, whether sculptors or poets, make the Greek gods. They make them and at the same time they did not make them, as he said somewhere. But they also made them, and therewith there is the element of human spontaneity and creativity implied which can then lead to a more radical assertion of human . . . You remind us of the fact that, according to Hegel, there is no conscience in the Greek religion, which means of course . . . We must never forget that.

Student: Also there is no conscience in their constitution generally.

LS: Yes, sure. No conscience. Does this make sense?

Student: One thing that I thought of when I read that statement is the conflict between the democratic notion of justice and the oligarchic notion of justice that Aristotle talks about in the *Politics*. This indicates a different opinion in the *polis* about the nature of political right, and I think Hegel would have a hard time—

LS: But what should Hegel say to this objection?

Student: I think he would have to admit that it existed in the Athenian *polis* from very early times.

LS: You base your critique of Hegel on Aristotle. Hegel generally says the Greek commonwealth is a democracy, which is flatly contradicted by Aristotle because there were nondemocratic commonwealths, and also by Thucydides and so on. This is an untenable thesis at first glance. Therefore Hegel must understand the word "democracy" in a very different sense than that in which Aristotle and Thucydides or the ordinary Greeks understood it.

Student: He understands it, as he says, as a regime where there is a kind of equity and moral basis.

LS: An equality.

Student: Yes, an equality is recognized and this requires in Hegel's view a very basic equality of the citizens.

LS: One can of course say—which is a very poor answer, but which is to begin with an answer—that Hegel simply accepted this description of the classical city from Montesquieu. Montesquieu spoke of that in a general way. The most fantastic statement of Montesquieu is when he tries to describe what democracy meant and means. One of the most powerful documents, according to Montesquieu, is—of all things—Plato's *Republic*. So he must have meant something very different from what everybody else understood by democracy. But this is a very long question in Montesquieu himself. We must see later on what the precise reasons of Hegel himself really are. But what about the conscience? Do Plato and Aristotle speak of the conscience?

Student: As I said, the only reason I can see that Hegel collapses the Platonic, Aristotelian, and Greek distinction between nature and convention is that he sees morality as not grounded upon nature. Therefore the Greek standard of natural justice appears to him to be just a custom, and there is no fundamental distinction between that and a particular law.

LS: But the simple question: Do Plato and Aristotle ever mention the conscience? Never. The term comes up later, but not with our meaning, in some Stoic texts. But it does not exist in Plato and Aristotle. But to this there is an obvious objection. Someone can say that it is very pedantic to stick to the word "conscience" or its Greek equivalents. Do we not have a very clear case of the conscience in classical Greek literature, in Plato, as a matter of fact?

Student: The *Apology*.

LS: Yes. But what thing?

Mr. Reinken: The *daimonion* of Socrates.

LS: And Hegel would say that that is already the disintegration. In addition, this is the question: whether Hegel believes the *daimonion* is something like the conscience or not; whether Socrates himself understood the *daimonion* as something which can be called with some propriety the conscience. You were quite right in also pointing out that Hegel is silent about the heterogeneity within the Greek city, namely, the rich and the poor and this kind of thing. He is not entirely silent about it, but he seems to present the Greek *polis* as consisting only of virtuous men, at least in the good times, which cannot literally be true. You must see that later. Yes?

Student: Isn't there a clear case in Plato . . . of a man passing a dead body—I think that it is in your article?

LS: Well, it is, as a matter of fact, in Plato's *Republic*, when he tries to make clear that there is a difference between spiritedness and desire. The man had the desire to look at these corpses—a very morbid desire—and then he got angry at himself on account of this low desire.[2] Here you see anger is noble and desire is base. That is the context. But the same man of course eventually succumbs and says: You cursed eyes—I forget the exact wording—have you taken your fill? But what is there of conscience? There is a conflict within man between desire and reason, but also between desire and anger, desire and spiritedness. Spiritedness is not conscience. Reason as reason is not conscience. The expression "I am conscious of something" occurs—*conscientia* in Latin, *sunoida moi* in Greek, literally translated, "I know together with myself." There is a certain dualism within me. You can know something together with somebody else. For example, surely not you but somebody else can be conscious of a fellow knower of a criminal; and you can be a fellow knower of your own criminal inclinations. That is, I think, the most simple rule. But the development of that into a concept of a conscience is a long step. Is there any other point you want to bring up? Well, then, let us turn to our text. On page 241 in the first paragraph.

Mr. Reinken:

> Man with his necessities sustains a practical relation to external Nature, and in making it satisfy his desires and thus using it up, has recourse to a system of *means*. For natural objects are powerful and offer resistance in various ways. In order to subdue them man introduces other natural agents; thus turns Nature against itself—

LS: All right. Literally, "uses natural things against natural things." For example, uses iron against wood. Yes?

Mr. Reinken:

natural things against natural things, and invents instruments for this purpose. These human inventions belong to Spirit, and such an instrument is
to be respected more than a mere natural object.[3]

LS: Yes. That is the point. I think we have mentioned this before.
The artifacts are of a higher rank than natural things because they are of
spiritual-mental origin. In the next paragraph he speaks of "ornament,"
which is a common desire for adorning oneself, which is a common human trait but which was changed in Greece, and therefore this throws
light on Greekness. Page 241, second paragraph. We cannot read everything. The key point is this: the barbarians adorned themselves with
things outside of themselves, gold, silver, ivory, and so on. The Greeks
too did that, but for the Greeks the most important way of adorning
themselves was the perfection of their bodies. I believe it is the center of
page 242 in your edition.
Mr. Reinken:

> But while on the one side they have too much independent personality to
> be subjugated by superstition, that sentiment has not gone to the extent of
> making them vain; on the contrary, essential conditions must be first satis-
> fied before this can become a matter of vanity with them. The exhilarating
> sense of personality, in contrast with sensuous subjection to nature, and
> the need, not of mere pleasure, but of the display of individual powers, in
> order thereby to gain special distinction and consequent enjoyment, con-
> stitute therefore the chief characteristic and principal occupation of the
> Greeks. Free as the bird singing in the sky, the individual only expresses
> what lies in his untrammeled human nature—to have his importance
> recognized. This is the subjective beginning of Greek Art—in which the
> human being elaborates his physical being, in free, beautiful movement
> and agile vigor, to a work of art.[4]

LS: And later on page 242, center, where he says the dependence of
nature is put aside, but something natural which man can use in order to
show himself, in order to exhibit himself, is close to him and is fit to be
made to serve as a sign of his aptitude, willpower, energy. And this natural
thing is his body. This he has immediately, i.e., by nature. And he finds
himself in it in a natural manner, without having done anything to bring
this about. And therefore, this is more directly human if the adornment

consists in improving the body and in making it as beautiful as possible without cosmetics. Yes?

Mr. Shulsky: In the paragraph which we just read, he says that in developing his body, the individual only expresses what lies in his untrammeled human nature. This would seem to imply that there is, so to speak, a natural, developed, healthy state of the body, and the spiritual force is only what leads man to develop his body to this state. But it would seem more consistent with Hegel's whole philosophy to say that the spiritual element is just a transforming of the body without guidance from nature, so to speak. As he goes on he says it becomes a spiritual thing.

LS: Still, Hegel says the dependence on nature is less if the adornment is this improvement of the body than if the adornments are taken from outside, gold and so on.

Mr. Shulsky: The improvements themselves, what the good state of the body is, couldn't be, according to Hegel, simply a natural conception. There couldn't be a naturally good body which men would strive to—

LS: Well, in a limited sense. The difference between health and sickness is of course accepted by Hegel. But we will come to that question you have in mind very soon on the basis of Hegel's own utterances.

Mr. Reinken: Mustn't we say that for the Greeks in contradistinction to the barbarians, nature—the natural—restricts them much more severely as an end? Barbaric display can have an almost Hindu variety and indefinitude, but the notion of the Apollo Belvedere[5] is just about one sort of notion of the healthy actual Greek, and they haven't the barbarous freedom.

LS: The Greeks do not have—?

Mr. Reinken: In contradistinction to the Hindus.

LS: Yes, but I think that this will be cleared up later. Hegel would put the emphasis on this—whether you depend on externals or whether you transform something which is in a way external to the soul, but on the other hand is not simply external, one's own body.

Student: Is it important that the instrument is a means, but the work of art is not a means, that it is an end in itself? He begins by talking about instruments as enformed objects. Then he gets to a work of art which is also an enformed object, but not as a means.

LS: Yes. It is not ultimately in the service of satisfying the bodily needs; therefore, art is higher than craft.

Student: Perhaps that would have some bearing on the question about these different factions within the state, because the state as a work of art is not a means of the satisfaction of any end, but it is an end in itself. Although there would be these factions, they have to be seen in the context of the state as an end.

LS: Yes. Let us wait until we come to that, whether Hegel does not misconstrue, misinterpret the Greek democracy. Now let us turn to page 244. I believe that that is the beginning of the section on Greek religion.

Mr. Reinken:

> If the subject of Song as thus developed among the Greeks is made a question, we should say that its essential and absolute purport is religious. We have examined the idea embodied in the Greek spirit; and religion is nothing else than this idea made objective as the essence of Being. According to that idea, we shall observe also that the divine involves the *vis naturae* only as an element suffering a process of transformation to spiritual power. Of this natural element, as its origin, nothing more remains than the accord of analogy involved in the representation they formed of spiritual power; for the Greeks worshipped gods as spiritual. We cannot, therefore, regard the Greek divinity as similar to the Indian—some Power of Nature for which the human shape supplies only an outward form.[6]

LS: And in other forms, we may add, as well. Not merely the human form.

Mr. Reinken:

> The essence is the Spiritual itself, and the Natural is only the point of departure. But on the other hand, it must be observed that the divinity of the Greeks is not yet the absolute, free Spirit, but Spirit in a particular mode, fettered by the limitations of humanity—still dependent as a determinate individuality on external conditions.

LS: He doesn't bring out in the translation the following sentence: "This essential thing the Greeks have no longer found in the natural, the external, but in the internal."[7] And that means that the spiritual is not natural but freedom, and hence human. Therefore Greek religion is the religion of art, of beauty. Now there is a section here which unfortunately is not in the translation because it is not in the earlier edition. I would like to state this as follows. The Greek gods, these beautiful figures, are of more than human perfection but still of human shape. This means that for the Greeks, only the perfected man is divine, or, to use a biblical expression, only the perfected man is in the image of God, not man *as* man. And this is decisive for the later development. In other words, what we would call the nondemocratic character of the Greeks, even of Greek democracy, that is implied in that. Only men of a certain perfection are truly human beings, not man as such; and therefore this leads to the fact, which Hegel points out, that the famous anthropomorphism of Greek religion is imperfect because it abstracts from the ugly, the imperfect, suffering, pain, death. And this is according to Hegel the superiority of Christianity, because God has become a suffering man and has died. God appears in products of the human imagination and not in the flesh. That is the limitation of Greek anthropomorphism.[8]

On page 249 of your translation in the second half. Here is another passage which we should briefly discuss. This is only one side, that the mind is that into which it makes itself. To use a Greek term, the human is virtue, and this means, of course, politically, that the *polis* should consist of virtuous men only, if possible. That is the starting point of Montesquieu and therewith of Hegel. And this is what Hegel objects to. The other side is that the mind is that which is originally free, not merely by our making ourselves into free men. That freedom is its nature. Here you have the word "nature" in a very crucial context. Freedom is the nature of the mind. Therefore, all men are by nature free. In more practical terms, they are potentially free and cannot be treated as slaves. And this side the Greeks have not yet understood, precisely because they have not understood themselves, meaning as human beings. In still more simple terms, the Greeks had no inkling whatsoever of the rights of man. The Greeks knew of the rights of the virtuous man, and this was very important compared with Oriental despotism, but it was also a severe limitation.

Now let us turn to page 249. The Greeks have not deified nature, but they have transformed the natural into something spiritual. It is a defect of the Greek gods that they are not anthropomorphistic enough. They are idealized, fleshless human beings. In the Christian religion it is said that God has appeared in the flesh, and this is the fundamental defect of Greekness. Now let us turn to page 249, second half. "If God is to appear."

Mr. Reinken:

If God himself is to be manifested in a corresponding expression, that can only be the human form: for from this the spiritual beams forth. But if it were asked, does God necessarily manifest himself?, the question must be answered in the affirmative, for there is no essential existence that does not manifest itself. The real defect of the Greek religion as compared with the Christian is, therefore, that in the former, the manifestation constitutes the highest mode in which the divine being is conceived to exist, the sum and substance of divinity, while in the Christian religion, the manifestation is regarded only as a temporary phase of the divine. Here the manifested God dies and elevates himself to glory. Only after death is Christ represented as sitting at the right hand of God. The Greek god, on the contrary, exists for his worshippers perennially in the manifestation, only in marble, in metal or wood, or as figured by the imagination. But why did gods not appear to the Greeks in the flesh? Because man was not duly estimated, did not obtain honor and dignity, till he had more fully elaborated and developed in the attainment of the freedom implicit in the aesthetic manifestation in question. The form and shaping of the divinity, therefore, continued to be the product of individual views. One element in Spirit is, that it produces itself, makes itself what it is; and the other is, that it is originally free, that freedom is its nature and its idea. But the Greeks, since they had not attained an intellectual conception of themselves, did not yet realize Spirit in its Universality—had not the idea of man and the essential unity of the divine and human nature according to the Christian view.[9]

LS: This is the translation of the passage which I read before. The Greeks did not know, as he put it, that freedom is the nature of the mind. They knew only that kind of freedom which is man's work. Man makes himself free, say, by controlling his passions. And this side of man is all very well: virtue, in Greek language. The more fundamental freedom by virtue of which every man is by nature free—and therefore also the vicious man responsible for his vice but fundamentally free and therefore an object of respect, of human respect—this, according to Hegel, they did not see.

Now what is the theological equivalent of that? The gods, the beautiful gods, idealized human beings, are absolutized. They are not seen to be a "phase," as he translates it—a *Moment* in German—among many phases. He thinks of course of the Trinity, God the Father and God as having become man, the Son. That is the theological equivalent, according to Hegel, of the Greeks' unawareness of that fundamental freedom which he calls the freedom of his nature, which antedates any possible liberating virtue. Hegel also puts it this way, more or less in that neighborhood but I think it is lost in the translation: the Greek gods are too subjective because they are too objective, and vice versa. They are too subjective, they are too much the work of the human imagination, because they are too objective, they are not seen as part of the whole, God. Let us turn to the second paragraph on page 244.

Mr. Reinken:

> In the idea of the Greek spirit, we found the two elements, Nature and Spirit, in such a relation to each other that Nature forms merely the point of departure.

LS: In other words, they do not remain completely with the natural, as the Orientals do.

Mr. Reinken:

> This degradation of Nature is in the Greek mythology the turning-point of the whole, expressed as the war of the gods, the overthrow of the Titans by the race of Zeus.[10]

LS: In other words, this is the empirical basis for Hegel's assertion: the notion that the younger gods are the ruling gods and there was originally another kind of god who has been overthrown. And Hegel interprets it as the victory of the mind or the spirit over nature. Now he develops then in the sequel the point which is very important that the Greek gods are not symbols. There are attempts made so frequently in late antiquity to say that Zeus stands for, say, kingly power. They are impossible, because the gods are true individuals. And while one may see the preponderance of one spiritual element in god number 1, and of another in god number 2, it is impossible to reduce them to any such formula. This has to do with the fact that the natural element, while being overcome by the spiritual element, is still present, which cannot be reduced to any purely spiritual meaning. On page 247, line 15 from bottom.

Mr. Reinken:

> Preservation of the original myth brings us to the famous chapter of the mysteries already mentioned. These mysteries of the Greeks present something which, as unknown, has attracted the curiosity of all times, under the supposition of profound wisdom. It must first be remarked that their antique and primary character, in virtue of its very antiquity, shows their destitution of excellence, their inferiority.[11]

LS: The oldest is not the most venerable, but the lowest. In Hegel's time there were still quite a few people who believed that the oldest strata of Greek religion—and some people thought that the mystery religions were the oldest—were for this very reason the most profound. Clearly contradicted by Hegel.

We have to turn to a number of other passages which are also not in our translation. When he comes to speak of the Greek *polis*—the Greek state, as he says—he mentions a number of points which I will read to you. "For Oriental despotism there was no place in Greece. Here the individuals as mixed [meaning of mixed origin—LS] are strangers to each other, not connected with each other by nature."[12] In the Orient, he implies, there was always this natural bond which was decisive. In China the whole land understood as a single family, and of course in Judaism the seed of Abraham, the house of Jacob. Here in Greece, according to Hegel, it was just as in Rome according to the old description of Rome, which was a kind of asylum for all kinds of criminals in the neighborhood. But this made the glory of Rome. They were not of one stock. Therefore, according to Hegel, there could not be despotism, the natural root of despotism as it were being the paternal power indefinitely enlarged.

The thought which Hegel develops here, of which he speaks all the time, is the democratic character of the Greek *polis*. With the Greeks the dignity of man depends on the good use of his freedom or, to use the Greek term, on his virtue, his virtuous activity, not on his quasi-innate freedom—this plays no role whatsoever. In the Orient there is no awareness of the dignity of man, nothing but fear of the lord with a small or a capital *l*.

In Christianity and modernity, we find the freedom of man as a subject who calls everything before the tribunal of his conscience or reason. That does not exist in Greece. Therefore, in Greece we have only the dignity of the citizen, not the dignity of man. And who is and who is not a citizen is determined practically by the *nomos*, by the law, but the law is here custom, something which is not known to be the work of reason. That is the decisive point: age-old, sacred custom, but not known to be the work of reason. This is the limitation of Greek rationality. There is not yet awareness of the right of subjectivity. Right means here simply the common good, and even the possibility of a conflict with the private good is not visualized. To be truly a human being means to be dedicated absolutely to the *polis*, to be a good citizen. That is virtue. On page 252 at the top there is something which we may need.

Mr. Reinken:

> The Greeks occupy the middle ground of *Beauty* and have not yet attained the higher standpoint of Truth.[13]

LS: In other words, this position which the Greeks take, the intermediate position between Oriental unawareness of freedom and Christian-modern full awareness of freedom, is the standpoint of beauty as distinguished from the point of view of truth, which we may take to mean that truth includes ugliness and the recognition of the rights of the morally ugly men. He comes to speak of Montesquieu a little bit later. "The chief moment of democracy is."

Mr. Reinken:

> The main point in Democracy is moral disposition. *Virtue* is the basis of Democracy, remarks Montesquieu; and this sentiment is as important as it is true in reference to the idea of Democracy commonly entertained. The Substance of Justice, the common weal, the general interest, is the main consideration —

LS: Here you understand why Montesquieu can call Plato's *Republic* a democratic book, because here everything is sacrificed to the common good.

Mr. Reinken:

> but it is so only as custom, in the form of Objective Will, so that morality properly so-called — subjective conviction and intention — has not yet manifested itself. Law exists, and is, in point of substance, the Law of Freedom — rational and valid because it is Law, that is, without ulterior sanction. As in Beauty the Natural element — its sensuous coefficient — remains, so also in this customary morality, laws assume the form of a necessity of Nature. The Greeks occupy the middle ground of Beauty and have not yet attained the highest standpoint of Truth.[14]

LS: In other words, the subjective basis of the laws has not yet been seen, and there is therefore something reminding of nature, the sub-spiritual, the sub-mental, and this is what we mean by beauty; where the spiritual/

mental appears in sensuous appearance, in sensuous shape, and therefore not as itself.

The principle of democracy is virtue. Hegel simply accepts this famous statement of Montesquieu. We cannot possibly go into how Montesquieu meant it in the first place, it would be a long story. But let us leave it here simply so: democracy's principle is virtue, i.e., only among virtuous men. Virtuous means here that their humanity is identical with their citizenship. There is no higher consideration than the fatherland. To use a modern phrase: "my country right or wrong." There is nothing to which you can possibly appeal or in the light of which you can judge your country. This is what is here meant.

But we must also take this in a broader sense, and this was partly intended, at least by Montesquieu if not by Hegel. But for Hegel too it is understood that the principle of the reasonable state is not virtue, because then only virtuous persons could be citizens or at least have full citizen rights, and imagine how difficult that is. You can limit citizen rights from the point of view of property qualifications or educational qualifications or race or what have you, I mean visible, manifest features. But you cannot limit citizenship on the basis of virtue in any serious sense of the word. Why?

Mr. Reinken: Who will judge?

LS: Yes. If there are very great rewards connected with virtue, actions in agreement with virtue will be forthcoming. No one can make himself richer than he is because there are easy ways of checking banking accounts and so on. The same applies to size or any other visible things. But virtue cannot be the basis. Hegel's point, and we will speak of that later, is that when you make the attempt to base democracy on virtue, you arrive at Robespierre's Terror, because merely external actions do not make a man virtuous. You have to look into his heart. He must have the right *Gesinnung*, the right moral intention; and therefore, here there is only one possibility: you trust or do not trust. And if you do not trust, the guillotine is the only way of getting rid of the citizens lacking virtue.

But is there not something more immediately relevant for us today in this assertion that the principle of democracy is virtue? What about Marxism? Marxism claims to be fundamentally democratic, as you know, although not in the transitional stage but eventually, I mean in the endstate. But must not Marxism in one way or another assert that the principle of democracy is virtue—I mean, that in this final democracy all men will be virtuous? Rousseau, who has a lot to say about democracy, especially in the modern meaning of the term, made this distinction. What is vice? There is one source of vice in man, the fundamental source, which is self-love—which Hobbes calls self-preservation, including even comfortable self-preservation, *amour de soi*. This is based on the natural needs of men. Now what happens to the natural needs of men in the final Marxist society? They are satisfied through the economy of plenty, as they say. Rousseau, however, did not believe that a perfectly virtuous society is possible, because he held that society is coeval with a kind of vice rooted in what he called *amour-propre*, which means the desire for superiority and recognition of one's superiority. This grows up as soon as we have society and lasts as long as there is society. Therefore, this *amour-propre* would from Rousseau's point of view also prevail in a Marxist society. There is administration of things, but it makes a great difference whether you are at the top of the administration of things or in a lower echelon. That is inevitable. Also the wives of these outstanding administrators will be affected, and as wise men of old said, they will be more affected even than their husbands. What is the Marxist view of the desire for distinction, meaning for surpassing others, of the future of *amour-propre* in the final society? Regarding *amour de soi*, self-love, we have seen no one has to commit any crimes because he is hungry or starving or so on.

Mr. Shulsky: In the more modern interpretations, this is more or less done away with by psychological methods.

LS: But that is very un-Marxist. That is the famous combination of Marx and Freud which is so popular in this country but is not Marxist.

Mr. Reinken: I take it that the Marxists hold that the desire for distinction is a distinction of men of one class against men of another class, that pride is not the competing arrogance of nobility but of the noble riding peasants down in his coach. Since in the future society there will be only one class, strange to say there won't be any emulation among the equals.

LS: Yes. They will be all brothers. Equality, fraternity takes away this point. This I thought that we should mention in passing.

Now let us go on with Hegel. The Greeks did not know the conscience or the good will, i.e., bowing only to the law which one has given to oneself and only on that basis bowing to the law of the land. Differently stated, the *polis* for its own consciousness did not rest on any notion of the natural law. There was immediate identity of the particular will, the will of the individual, with the general will. That is virtue. If I will without any effort what is good for the community, and my private interest is stifled by this very fact, then I am a one hundred percent patriotic and public-spirited citizen. Hegel comes to speak somewhat later, on page 252, line 11 following, on the radical difference between ancient and modern democracy. He must of course speak to that because his contemporaries after all had gotten an inkling of democracy through the French Revolution, and some of them through what they had heard about America, and so he must explain that.

Mr. Reinken:

> The democratic constitution is here the only possible one: the citizens are still unconscious of particular interests, and therefore of a corrupting element: the objective will is in their case not disintegrated. Athene the goddess is Athens itself—i.e., the real and concrete spirit of the citizens. The divinity ceases to inspire their life and conduct, only when will has retreated within itself—into the *adytum* of cognition and conscience—and has posited the infinite schism between the subjective and the objective. The above is the true position of the democratic polity, its justification and absolute necessity rest on this still immanent objective morality. For the modern conceptions of democracy this justification cannot be pleaded.

LS: I.e., virtue as a dependable principle cannot possibly be the basis of democracy in modern times. Yes?

Mr. Reinken:

> These provide that the interests of the community, the affairs of state, shall be discussed and decided by the people; that the individual members of the community shall deliberate, urge their respective opinions and give their votes; and this on the ground that the interests of the State and its concerns are the interests of such individual members. All this is very well; but the essential condition and distinction in regard to various phases of Democracy is, What is the character of these individual members?

LS: More literally, "who are these individuals?" meaning what *kind* of people?

Mr. Reinken:

> They are absolutely authorized to assume their position, only in as far as their will is still objective will—not one that wishes this or that, not mere "good" will.

LS: In other words, two people can have equally good wills and very different notions of what the common good is. So the mere good will doesn't help. They must also have the same objective will, they must will the same things virtuously.

Mr. Reinken:

> For good will is something particular—rests on the morality of individuals, on their conviction and subjective feeling. That very subjective Freedom which constitutes the principle and determines the peculiar form of Freedom in our world—which forms the absolute basis of our political and religious life, could not manifest itself in Greece otherwise than as a destructive element.[15]

LS: "As corruption." The radical difference between ancient and modern democracy—modern democracy is based on the error that the multitude of emancipated individuals can govern. The Greek individuals in a Greek democracy are not emancipated. They were citizens and nothing but citizens, and therefore there was fundamental harmony. There was not merely consensus in the sense in which the word is now used, but fundamental unanimity. What Hegel has in mind here is the distinction to which Rousseau had referred and which he takes up between the *citoyen*, the citizen, and the bourgeois, the man chiefly concerned with his private interest. In the sense in which Rousseau and Hegel use the word, all citizens of a modern democracy are bourgeoisie. They all have a clearly defined private interest with which they are primarily concerned. They are not one hundred percent patriots. Or to state it in a language with which you are more familiar, perhaps: the modern democracy is based on the distinction between state and society. And there is no such distinction in the *polis*. So society means variety of interest—conflict, competition, heterogeneity—and these people of conflicting interests cannot be virtuous in the classical sense. In the moment the emancipation of every individual has in principle been achieved—and this emancipation has its good and its bad side as we shall see—in that moment, virtue can no longer be the principle. Mr. Shulsky?

Mr. Shulsky: This would be an argument against Rousseau's notion of the general will. The fact that each individual is required to think in terms of the general will isn't sufficient. They would have to come themselves to the same conclusion as well.

LS: You must not forget that in *The Social Contract* he states the ideal conditions of just order. There would be this fundamental homogeneity, i.e., in the most important respects there is unanimity. The difference of opinion can concern only particular measures which cannot be so important. But very complicated other things are needed, as appears more and more in Rousseau. That is a very long question. But Hegel of course thinks not only of Montesquieu but also of Rousseau. That is quite true.

Mr. Shulsky: In other words, Hegel is saying that Rousseau's idea of the state governed by the general will would meet the requirements of classical antiquity, but couldn't actually exist in the modern world.

LS: Yes, absolutely. To that extent, Rousseau's *Social Contract* was an impossible proposal. You cannot have small states anymore, to state it in more practical terms, as the *polis* was.

Now here is a passage which I didn't find in the translation: "In the Greek city there is not yet a right of the abstract universal, i.e., not yet a government as a particular organization under which the particular interest is both restrained and also satisfied."[16] In other words, the distinction between government and the *demos*, the people, does not exist there. In modern times the independence of the government as a particular organization is essential. Every citizen as such is a part of the government. If you take government in the narrowest sense, in the sense of only the executive, then of course not everyone is a member of the government. You have to be elected for an office. But the fundamental governmental activity is not what he calls executive, but the legislature—the deliberative, according to Hegel and Aristotle—and this is the work of the whole citizen body. There is therefore not yet a distinction between the people and the government. In modern times this distinction is essential.

There are other things which are not in the translation and which I must try to translate to you. "The constitution itself cannot be an object for the Greek democracy. There cannot be deliberations and decisions about the constitution. But the constitution is exactly this: that the citizens deliberate and make decisions."[17] Do you understand that? Particular laws referring to the constitution can of course be made, but the constitution proper is presupposed in any deliberation, in any legislative act, and therefore the constitution itself cannot be an object for the Greek democracy, because democracy means that the citizens deliberate and make decisions. Can we still understand that?

Mr. Shulsky: In Athens there were many important changes of the constitution or what we would call the constitution.

LS: To what extent were they an act of deliberation?

Mr. Shulsky: They did away with the powers of the Areopagus. That was a deliberative decision.

LS: There is something to what you say, but let us take the simplest example. The American Constitution is a product of deliberation, as everybody knows. But Hegel thinks of something more profound than the detailed provisions of the Constitution, namely, the very beginning. What is the very beginning of the Constitution? The people. This simple thing was not the subject of deliberation. The people or their representatives deliberated about the peculiar structure of the legislative, executive, and judiciary, but that the people had to decide was the most fundamental thing upon which everything else depends, not a king ruling by divine grace or a society divided into a hereditary nobility and something else. This is what Hegel means. The fundamental thing underlying all these points—to some extent even the nonviolent changes taking place—were based on the premise that the last word is with the *demos*. And this therefore could not be the subject of deliberation.

In other words, what Hegel has in mind is this. Whereas according to the modern doctrines, especially of French origin, the fundamental act was the constituent assembly where the people established the constitution and therewith became truly members of the civil society, there is no such thing in Greece. And the constituent assembly presupposes, of course, if you take the doctrine literally, that these individuals assemble and then deliberate. As Hobbes and others present it: Shall we have a kingship, an aristocracy, a democracy, or some mixture of the two? These people are not yet citizens. These are the emancipated individuals of which the Greeks did not know and of which we know. In this respect, this freedom of the individual, Hegel goes fully with the moderns.

Hegel is very critical of many of the theories of the eighteenth century, that goes without saying, but he has this point in mind. You must assert a fundamental sovereignty of the individual, i.e., of every individual, if there are to be politically relevant rights of man. That is the point, because if the *polis* is first, then the rights of man cannot be the first thing. They may come in, but in a secondary manner. Yes?

Mr. Shulsky: Why isn't this fundamental assumption not a constitution that can't be deliberated upon? Or is it considered as a result of philosophy rather than as the starting point of a constitution—I mean the fact that the constituent assembly is elected and represents individuals.

LS: How did Hegel speak of this before when he spoke of the same thing? This peculiar position in between nature and man, which he also means by the point of view of beauty which the Greeks had. Therefore, there is no absolute beginning with the free individual, be it the passionate individual or the conscientious individual. And that is the essential defect, according to Hegel.

Student: You explained the change taking place in the Areopagus in this way, but what about the change when the royal houses were overthrown? You would say that this isn't an act of deliberation, that this is a violent overthrow that somehow just happened?

LS: Hegel speaks about this only in a very general way. He says they had ceased to have any function and they disappeared partly by self-destruction. I think he puts the emphasis on the self-destruction.

Student: It seems that there was a change whereby people who were not citizens overthrew royal houses and became citizens by choosing tyrants.

LS: That was later. The tyranny was separated from the republican period, from the original royalty, as Hegel says. Do you mean Pisistratus[18] in Athens after Solon? Or do you mean the old kingly house?

Student: . . .

LS: This belongs to the prehistory, the period in which Greece formed itself and was not yet Greece.

Student: The period of the kings, you say, was not yet—

LS: That was "not yet," it was only potentially.

Mr. Shulsky: The main point would simply be that there was never a deliberate forming of a *polis* with an *ekklesia* that then somehow got the power to establish rules. This was never deliberately done. It just sort of happened.

LS: Yes. Even that would not be of interest to Hegel because the key point is the way in which the existing and formed *polis* understood itself, and there it did not look back. There were some memories of founding acts, and in these founding acts the kings played a role—in Athens, for example, Theseus, who settled together a variety of villages. But this is obviously not a constituent assembly according to the strict revolutionary doctrine.

Mr. Bruell: How does Hegel take it that Aristotle simply says that the city is first in the most important sense?

LS: In the sense in which Aristotle means that—first not in time, but in rank—Hegel accepts that. This will become clearer later on. He discusses in the immediate sequel the conditions of the Greek *polis*, and this is very empirical and not very difficult. For example, the smallness of the

Greek *polis*, the institution of slavery, and lastly the oracles. On page 254 bottom.

Mr. Reinken:

> Another circumstance that demands special attention here is the element of Slavery. This was a necessary condition of an aesthetic democracy, where it was the right and duty of every citizen to deliver or to listen to orations respecting the management of the State in the place of public assembly, to take part in the exercises of the Gymnasia, and to join in the celebration of festivals. It was a necessary condition of such occupations, that the citizens should be freed from handicraft occupations; consequently, that what among us is performed by free citizens—the work of daily life—should be done by slaves. Slavery does not cease until the Will has been infinitely self-reflected—until right is conceived as appertaining to every freeman, and the term freeman is regarded as a synonym for man in his generic nature as endowed with Reason. But here we still occupy the standpoint of Morality as mere Wont and Custom, and therefore known only as a peculiarity attaching to a certain kind of existence.[19]

LS: The consciousness, that is the abstract man. Man in general as free has not been possessed by Socrates, Plato, or Aristotle. This emerges with Christianity, according to Hegel. Of course it is surely an exaggeration that there were no artisan citizens in the Greek cities, especially in Athens. But the key point in Hegel is simply the radical distinction between man and citizen. We of course also make the distinction: not every living man is an American citizen. But for the Greeks there is, so to speak, no possibility of becoming a citizen unless you are the son of a citizen father and a citizen mother. There are other crucial implications of that as discussed by Aristotle when he speaks of the relation of the virtue of man to the virtue of the citizen.

When in the sequel he speaks—and this is particularly important—of Athens and of Sparta, the peaks of Greek political life, Hegel has on the whole the judgment which I think most of us would have today: that altogether, Athens was infinitely superior to Sparta. This creates a minor difficulty—not exactly a difficulty—for Hegel because Plato and Aristotle seem to prefer Sparta to Athens. We might perhaps look at page 261, line 9.

Mr. Reinken:

The blame with which we find them—the Athenians—visited in Xeno-phon and Plato, attaches rather to that later period when misfortune and the corruption of the democracy had already supervened. But if we would have the verdict of the Ancients on the political life of Athens, we must turn, not to Xenophon, nor even to Plato but to those who had a thorough acquaintance with the state in its full vigor—who managed its affairs and have been esteemed its greatest leaders—that is, to its Statesmen. Among these, Pericles is the Zeus of the human Pantheon of Athens.[20]

LS: Pericles, the greatest of all statesmen that have ever been. Whether Hegel said it only once after a good breakfast or whether this is his fi-nal opinion, I do not know. At any rate, he makes clear that the funeral speech in Thucydides, not Socrates, is the key to Athens. And that is very important, and one could draw from this a conclusion which is not suffi-cient, but I think that one would have to argue it out: that Hegel was more democratic in a way than Socrates, Xenophon, Plato, and Aristotle—in other words, because of their Spartan leanings—which wouldn't be too surprising. Later on—and it is not in your translation—he says: Pericles, "the greatest statesman of ancient and modern times."[21] So there is no doubt that Hegel meant it. He says this on the basis of the old stories, not only in Thucydides but also in Plutarch and other places. He mentions the signs of his absolute, full dedication to his fatherland. He mentions one thing here which he probably found in Plutarch—I have not looked it up—that Pericles never laughed. In other words, he was so deadly se-rious in his dedication to the city that he never laughed. And he went to no banquet after he had become a statesman.

The question is: From Hegel's point of view, can there be a statesman like Pericles in any later age? And I think not. This perfect harmony of the citizen and man belongs to the standpoint of beauty, which has been destroyed by the opening up of the abyss of individuality, for good or for ill. In this connection, when he speaks of Athens, he says—and this is no surprise, but we must mention it: "Art and science are the ideal manners in which the spirit of a nation becomes conscious of itself. And the highest which a state can achieve is that art and science are developed within it and reach a height which corresponds to the spirit of the nation."[22] This is the highest purpose of the state, not power or something else. But it must not try to produce this as its own work; it must generate itself by itself. In other words, no state-organized science and art. The state must give science and art the possibility to develop—and to some extent of course stimulated by proper recognition.

The key point which he develops in the sequel is this. The corruption of the Greekness means the emancipation of the individual, and this takes place on two levels. On the low level, the selfish desires and the passions. Alcibiades is the greatest specimen. And then the other is thinking, the conscience. That is represented by Socrates. The limitation of the Greeks was the immediacy of the validity of the gods and the law. They were simply there. No question arises. Just think of Plato's *Crito*. The laws appear to Socrates. They are there and no one asks where they come from. They have not gone through the universal doubt of modern times and the deepening of that by Kant, one might say. On page 268, second paragraph, line 11 following.

Mr. Reinken:

> With the Sophists began the process of reflection on the existing state of things, and of ratiocination.

LS: In German, *Raisonieren*, which has a very negative meaning, almost of griping.

Mr. Reinken:

> That very diligence and activity which we observed among the Greeks in their practical life, and in the achievement of works of art, showed itself also in the turns and windings which these ideas took; so that, as material things are changed, worked up and used for other than their original purposes, similarly the essential being of Spirit—what is thought and known—is variously handled; it is made an object about which the mind can employ itself, and this occupation becomes an interest in and for itself. The movement of Thought—that which goes on within its sphere—a process which had formerly no interest—acquires attractiveness on its own account. The cultivated Sophists, who were not erudite or scientific men, but masters of subtle turns of thought, excited the admiration of the Greeks—

LS: "Amazed the Greeks."

Mr. Reinken:

> For all questions they had an answer; for all interests of a political or religious order they had general points of view; and in the ultimate develop-

ment of their art they claimed the ability to prove everything, to discover a justifiable side in every position.[23]

LS: In other words, what they did, we can say, was this. The immediacy, the unquestioned acceptance of the gods and the law, was replaced by the demand for proof: How do you know? And we find Socrates, who opposes the sophists but accepts the principle that you cannot leave it at the immediacy and have to find a basis for that. Somewhat later on page 281 Hegel goes so far as to call Socrates "the inventor of morality," not merely the discoverer of morality but the inventor, which doesn't mean that Hegel doesn't regard morality as self-subsisting in a sense; but nevertheless, without being known, morality is not proof. To that extent, one can speak of an invention. Then he develops the thought that the fate of Socrates is a true tragedy because both the city of Athens and Socrates were right. This collision, perfectly justified on both sides, made it highly tragic. We have to leave it at that.

11 The Greek World Continued and the Roman World

Leo Strauss: Thank you very much. I was very glad that you raised this question towards the end of your paper,[1] that because Rome is so unpleasant and unsavory compared with Greece, it must constitute a progress beyond Greece. What you said points in the right direction, although your use of the terms "objectivity" and "subjectivity" is probably in need of some revision. I limit myself to a term which you used before which is more easily intelligible. Rome is emphatically prosaic contrasted with the poetry of Greece. The question, then, would be this: In what sense does prosaification, if we may say so, constitute a progress?

Student: The poetry which had marked the previous period was a consequence of the immersion in and closeness to nature that the spirit was involved in. So the spirit abstracts or withdraws from nature, becomes more prosaic.

LS: Yes. Perhaps one can say it more simply. Which is the element of truth? Which is the language of truth? Poetry or prose?

Student: Prose.

LS: Definitely, according to Hegel. He quotes poets from time to time, sometimes from memory and therefore involuntarily changing the text, but he says definitely that the language of philosophy is prose, and to that extent that is at least a sign. Another question must be raised, although I am unable answer it. We have already found an example of prosaicness in Hegel's philosophy of history before. Do you remember that?

Student: China.

LS: Yes. Now it is necessary to understand precisely the difference between Chinese and Roman prose. What are the most striking differences?

Mr. Reinken: Perhaps the Roman emperors are much more prosaic. That Rome culminates in a very prosaic notion of the law which has little reference to the son of heaven.

LS: It is in a way even independent of the emperor. In addition, Rome is of course, in spite of the deplorable character, the heir to Greece. All that the Greeks brought forth was transported bodily to Rome and became an ingredient of Rome. I think that we can leave it at that. I thank you again for your paper, which was very good.

I have to say a word about the paper of Mr. . . . which I have read in the meantime and which I also liked very much. I would like to say a word about your epilogue, where you rise to great heights, and therefore it's the most exciting part of your paper, which doesn't mean the best. [Laughter] "At the stage of Greek history which we have just considered, the dissolution of the beautiful was essentially complete. And although in the next section Hegel will call upon Alexander to justify philosophy, and though its dissolution was necessary for the emergence of pure spirit, I think that it is clear that Hegel looks back upon the political work of art and customary morality—meaning Greekness—with a sigh, a sigh which, perhaps, gave rise to this quotation from Nietzsche: 'All of morality is a continuous forgery without which the sight of man's soul would be impossible. From this point of view the concept 'art' may be much more comprehensive than one commonly believes.'[2] Could it be, then, that Hegel's demand for an absolutely rational world order has something in common with Nietzsche's extreme antirationalistic reaction?" What is the thing in common according to you between Hegel and Nietzsche?

Student: . . .

LS: In other words, you hesitated to write it down or what? If you had known that I would read it to the class you would have refrained from writing it down?

Student: Had I known what I thought the connection was, it wouldn't have been so dramatic when I wrote it down. What I had in mind was Hegel's idea that he was going to rescue Western civilization from the Enlightenment. The restoration of religion and morality in a new unity . . .

LS: All right. Let us leave it at that. And?

Student: In doing that, he is rejecting the notion of reason or the amount of certainty that was created during his lifetime.

LS: Hegel? Oh, no. According to Hegel's claim, he is much more rigorous than the Enlightenment was.[3]

Student: Sure. But in a different way.

LS: But what is the position of art in Hegel's system? Let us never forget what we have read: the distinction between beauty and truth; beauty is lower than truth. And Nietzsche says, one can say, just the opposite. Nietzsche says that he looks at science, the quest for truth, in the perspective of art, and at art in the perspective of life. But this turning around of the order of art and science is the crucial difference between Hegel and Nietzsche.

Student: Yeah, that's the crucial difference. But the fact that Hegel seizes upon beauty as the characteristic of the Greeks which he clearly admires . . .

LS: But here the difference in this point regarding the pure spirit related to the impure spirit which underlies art, Nietzsche again takes the opposite view of Hegel. There is no pure spirit from Nietzsche's point of view.

Student: . . .

LS: No. They are radically different. Nietzsche learned quite a few things from Hegel, but in the decisive respect they are radically opposed. Even this remark—with this enlargement of the term art, which Nietzsche here presupposes—that all morality is the product of art in the widest sense, the product of human creativity and of the creativity which does not obey any rational order, this is the opposite of Hegel. Hegel could also speak of such creativity, but he would say that these creative acts form in hindsight a rational order. From Nietzsche's point of view there is no such rational order.

Student: Yeah, in hindsight, but he wouldn't say that the Greeks saw the work of art as an essentially rational thing. Hegel's hindsight . . .

LS: But the order—the sequence Greece, Rome, and then Christianity—is for Hegel a rational order, i.e., a progressive order. Nietzsche denies that. From Nietzsche's point of view, Greece is the peak of things, and it goes down then towards modernity. He hopes then for a new peak beyond modernity, what he calls the superman. It is an entirely different notion. This was misleading, what you said earlier. Yes?

Student: In Hegel's criticism of Greece, doesn't he imply that with the full development of the rational spirit all of our concepts, including presumably—though it's not stated—those of truth and falsity, will essentially be created by man? And if that is so—

LS: Not created by man. Created perhaps *in* man by a superhuman logical necessity. Never forget that Hegel has to do with the mind or spirit which is to some extent at home in man, but it is not mere man. For Nietzsche it is apparently different. It is man and not pure spirit.

Student: The creations of spirit do not have an outside standard to look to see whether or not they are true creations.

LS: In Hegel? No. After all, Hegel wrote his *Logic*. This is meant to be as universally and objectively valid as any other system ever could be, perhaps even more. If you have understood the *Logic*, you will see that the Greeks were simply wrong in the decisive points. There can be no doubt, I think, about that.

But I would like to take up a point which occurs at the end of last time's assignment, which we simply did not have time to discuss. And this is a question of very great bearing for the whole of Hegel's teaching. I remind you of the fact that Hegel asserts more than once what we can call the primacy of religion. In other words, the core of a culture is religion. Now we have seen that something which has never happened before happened in Greece. In Greece, too, religion is primary, but in Greece for the first time religion is questioned. The corruption of Greece consists precisely in this questioning of religion. This corruption has however a different side, as we have seen last time — or at least those of us have seen who have read that passage in Hegel; I don't think we have been able to discuss it in class. What is this questioning of religion positively speaking in Greece? What is the corruption of Greekness in the positive sense? The corruption of Greekness has also a positive side. Who corrupted the Greeks?

Student: The sophists?

LS: The sophists were only a prelude. The true corruption was?

Student: Socrates.

LS: So in other words, the corruption of Greekness means the transformation of Greek religion into Greek philosophy. On page 270 or thereabouts in the translation, this remarkable sentence occurs: "Now the question was raised whether gods are and what they are." This is the fundamental change. In other words, a thing that we have never seen before, that the corruption of a nation or a culture has at the same time a positive meaning.

Now let us put this on a somewhat broader basis in Hegel's interpretation of Greekness altogether. Man awakens from his subjection to nature in which he is by nature. He awakens or becomes aware of his tutelage to nature as something to be overcome. He becomes aware of his unawareness of himself as a free and spiritual being. I do not have to repeat that Hegel's interpretation of Greekness is of course not identical with the Greeks' interpretation of Greekness, by which I mean the philosophic interpretation. According to that interpretation, natural man is a part. One can say this, with a slight reservation: the Greek is, from the point of view of Aristotle, the natural man as part of the natural world because he is aware of his situation, where the other men are more or less enthralled by *nomoi*, by conventions. And this is connected with the fact that Hegel replaces the distinction between *physis* and *nomos* by that between nature and mind.

Now let us come back to the Socrates question. Here is the awakening of subjectivity, which contradicts Greekness and Greek religion. Now what does it mean? The subjectivity is awake if it can question all objectivity, even the most venerable one, and raise the question, Is it? and What is its cause? or as he stated here: Now the question is raised whether gods are and what they are. In this question of course the question of morality is implied. To see that this is not without foundation, I will read to you a passage from a Platonic dialogue called *Timaeus*. Here we have this point. He has given an account of what we can call the cosmic gods, the gods connected with the stars.

> Concerning the other divinities, to discover and declare their origins is too great a task for us, and we must trust to those who have declared it aforetime, they being, as they affirm, descendants of gods and knowing well, no doubt, their own ancestors. It is, as I say, impossible to disbelieve the children of gods [men like Homer or Hesiod—LS], even though their statements lack either probable or necessary demonstration; and inasmuch as they profess to speak of family matters, we must follow custom and believe them. Therefore let the generation of these gods [the noncosmic gods, the Olympian gods—LS] be stated by us following their account in this way. Of Gaia and Ouranos were born the children Oceanos and Tethys; and of these, Phorkys, Cronos, Rhea, and all that go with them; and of Cronos and Rhea, were born Zeus and Hera and all those who are, as we know, called their brethren; and of those again, other descendants. Now when all the gods, both those who revolve manifestly [the stars—LS] and those who manifest themselves as far as they choose [there arbitrary will comes in—LS] had come to birth [and so on and so forth—LS].[4]

Here you have a distinction which we can say between the cosmic gods and the Olympian gods, and only the cosmic gods are taken seriously. I believe that you see the obvious irony of the remark about the other gods that their children, meaning the poets, are the only ones who would know about them. Accepted on trust, no proof there is possible because of the arbitrariness of their manifesting themselves. To repeat this point, in Greece religion is for the first time questioned, and not merely by criminals who do not accept anything but their lowest advantage, but by men of a very high order. And this meant the transformation of Greek religion into philosophy. This had to do with the awakening of subjectivity for the first time in Greece. But this was only a provisional and insufficient awareness of subjectivity. The final one is that which we find in modern times and which reveals itself in the possibility of the reasonable state in contradistinction to the beautiful *polis*. The *polis* is not reasonable, it is beautiful. The modern state is not beautiful. No one will say that it is, however much he may be enamored of it. Think only of bureaucracy: who could possibly call that beautiful? But it may very well be reasonable. This reasonable state in its turn has also a religious foundation. It has been rendered possible and demanded by the Christian religion in contradistinction to Greek, to say nothing of Roman religion. Thus the question arises: Is then the reasonable state, built as it is on Christianity, essentially Christian?

What Hegel means by this is something which you have heard *n* times in German civilization courses. From this point of view, it is nothing far-fetched. The modern state is based on the recognition of the rights of man. The rights of man have been recognized for the first time in Christianity, according to Hegel. Today this is the usual view, for example, that the American ideal goes back to the Judeo-Christian heritage. The question then is whether the reasonable state is essentially Christian, or do we find here also an equivalent to what we have seen in Greece, namely, a transformation of Christian religion into philosophy? This is the question.

In a passage which I believe does not occur in your translation but which I have here in Hegel's *Philosophy of History*, Socrates has not died innocently. This reminds me of the sole joke which Socrates made with a laugh. Ordinarily he joked with a poker face. When he was condemned to death, one of his most touching disciples said to him: How terrible, Socrates, that you have been condemned to death unjustly, whereupon Socrates said: Would you prefer me to have been condemned to death justly? And he laughed.[5]

So Socrates did not die innocently. This would not be tragic, but only touching. His fate however is tragic in the true sense. Our commonwealth, our state, is entirely different from that of the Athenian people, since our state can be altogether indifferent toward the inner lives of individuals, even towards religion.[6]

The Athenian state had to be concerned with the faith, belief, opinions of the individuals. Therefore, Socrates was justly accused and condemned. But the modern state is, or can be, altogether indifferent to the religion of its members. That is very strange.

I will read to you a few more passages, one from Hegel's *Philosophy of Right*, paragraph 270. This paragraph is *the* paragraph dealing with religion and church.

> The state can demand from all its members [here he is speaking of the reasonable state—LS] that they belong to an ecclesiastical community, to a religious congregation, but to any of them, for the content of religion is no concern of the state. It only can demand that every citizen belong to a religious association. [That is one remark—LS] People say that the individuals must have religion, but if they mean by it that their minds should be pressed down in the state, this would be a very bad meaning of the proposition. But if the people mean that men should have respect of the state, of this whole of which they are branches, then this takes place in the best way. They respect the state through the philosophic insight into the essence of the state. But, failing that insight, religious feeling can also lead to that. In this sense the state may need religion and faith [i.e., it does not necessarily need it—LS].[7]

This is the fundamental view of Hegel; and if there is any contradiction between the one, where he says that everyone must be a member of a religious community, and the other, that the state is indifferent to it, it would be our task—Hegel doesn't do it for us—to resolve that contradiction.[8]

Hegel takes up this question also in a number of passages in his *Lectures on the Philosophy of Religion*. I haven't seen an English translation of it. If anyone would like to have the references from the German I will gladly give it to him or her. Yes? *The Philosophy of Religion*, volume 15 of his collected works, pages 256, 263–64, 266–67, volume 16, page 344, 354–56.[9] He speaks of the way in which people know the religious truth, the truth of Christianity in the final stage. There are three stages in this respect. The first stage is that of the immediate, naive religion and faith; the second that of the so-called educated class, the enlightened part; and, finally, the third stage, the stage of philosophy. Then he tries to make clear that the more religion is understood in its philosophic school, the less it is powerful as mere naive religion and faith. To that extent, one can speak of a going-down, a decay, a decline of religion. And this is, as Hegel calls it, a disharmony, and he doesn't wish to end his lectures in a disharmonious manner. But what is the use of it? This disharmony is actual in reality, just as in the time of the Roman Empire, since the universal unity of religion had disappeared and the divine was profaned, and furthermore the whole political life was chaotic and without trust, and reason fled into the form of private law. The particular good and evil of the individual became the purpose. So even now, since a similar change has occurred in the naive conscience, i.e., in the actuality, the unity of the inner and outer no longer exists and is not justified in faith. This disharmony has been dissolved for us in philosophic knowledge. But this reconciliation of mind, thought, with religion is only a partial one since there are only a few philosophers. What becomes of the nonphilosophers in this final stage? This is more or less the end of the *Lectures on the Philosophy of Religion*.

For the time being we can say the people at large are still religious. Hegel does not raise the question, but he forces us to raise it: How long will this last? We don't need Hegel to become aware of this problem, but Hegel was aware of it, and this is of crucial importance to understand Hegel's notion of the end of history, the end in the old sense of the word: the peak of history, the completion of history has been achieved in Hegel's time. But isn't this, as we have heard him say before, that the owl of Minerva begins its flight in the dusk — isn't this the status of religion, namely, that the philosophers transform the religious truths into philosophic truths? But this means of course that the religious truths are considerably changed. But what becomes of the mass of the people?[10] In simple practical terms, in one of the most advanced parts of Germany, Sachsen-Weimar, where Goethe was a minister, the man in charge of the Protestant clergy was Herder, who was also a philosopher and a poet of sorts. There were all kinds of things, which kinds of questions, or rather which kinds of answers were expected of the young clergymen there. They were surely no longer orthodox Lutherans, and all kinds of difficulties showed themselves there on the practical level.

Now how can we understand this transformation of prephilosophic religion into philosophy? Hegel has developed this at great length, especially in his *Phenomenology of the Mind* in the section dealing with the Enlightenment. One can roughly state it as follows. The traditional view was that there is a difference between faith and reason. Faith is supernatural and has suprarational insights. Faith needs, since it is not rational in itself and in its object, external credentials: tradition and miracles. At any rate, its content is suprarational, but its suprarationality is of course not evident to reason. From the point of view of reason, it is unable to distinguish as reason between the suprarational and the intrarational. The suprarational cannot be evident to reason. Now what Hegel claims to have done is to have shown that the substance of the faith of Christianity is rationality. This required considerable sacrifices. For example, the belief in miracles and in the sacredness or quasi-sacredness of the biblical text, the biblical stories: this was of course sacrificed. But we will see later what Hegel means by the Christianity which he believes to have been transformed into philosophic insight and in this way to have saved.

Student: Was Hegel aware of the Averroist tendencies?

LS: I doubt that. Of course, in a general way he knew of that. You know, there are always various kinds of antiquarian knowledge around and there were some historians of philosophy, at least Brucker[11] in Germany and Thomas Stanley[12] in England in the seventeenth century. But much more importantly, of course, Pierre Bayle,[13] his *Dictionnaire Philosophique*, in which, if I remember well, there is an article on Averroes.[14] But it doesn't play any role. You know, a man may know of something without its playing any role for him. Hegel knew in a general way that the Greek philosophers, for example Proclus[15] and some of his predecessors, tried to interpret the Greek pagan religion in philosophic terms. That he knew, of course, and he speaks of it in his philosophy of history. But the true character of Averroes I believe he did not know. No. There is even some indirect evidence of that: he rejects the whole notion—at least in his *History of Philosophy*—of a distinction between exoteric and esoteric teaching.

Student: . . . Rousseau in the *Social Contract* . . . the flight of the owl of Minerva and the question of the mass of people.

LS: No. That philosophy, science, is destructive of society, that is what Rousseau clearly said in the *First Discourse* and also in some other things. Hegel repeats this, as we have seen. But the difficulty is whether Hegel means that this was very clear in Greece, or whether it is an eternal necessity so that it would apply to the modern world as well. I believe that Hegel meant it also with regard to the modern world, and that is exactly part of the prose. The fundamental problems of men are solved. We know what the reasonable state is. Well, there are all kinds of little troubles, you have here and there an old-fashioned dictator like Salazar[16] or Franco. The other thing which we have witnessed in the meantime and he did not in any way anticipate: he thought that there are no longer any important tasks for man. All fundamental questions, theoretical and practical, are solved. Enjoy that. But the trouble is that when you are at such a peak there is also at least the possibility of a going down, intimated by Hegel more than once and broadcast by Spengler in our age and some other people. So let us turn then to page 271 in the third paragraph.

Mr. Reinken:

> After the fall of Athens, Sparta took unto herself the Hegemony: but misused it—as already mentioned—so selfishly, that she was universally hated. Thebes could not long sustain the part of humiliating Sparta and was at last exhausted in the war with the Phocians. The Spartans and the Phocians—the former because they had surprised the citadel of Thebes, the latter because they had tilled a piece of land belonging to the Delphin Apollo—had been sentenced to pay considerable sums of money. Both states, however, refused payment; for the Amphictyonic Council had not much more authority than the old German Diet—

LS: Or than the new United Nations.

Mr. Reinken:

> which the German princes obeyed only so far as suited their inclination. The Phocians were then to be punished by the Thebans; but by an egregious piece of violence—by desecrating and plundering the temple at Delphi—the former attained momentary superiority. This deed completes the ruin of Greece; the sanctuary was desecrated, the god, so to speak, killed.

LS: Let us turn a little bit later. The further consequence is a quite naïve one, as he says.

Mr. Reinken:

> The next step in advance is then that quite simple one, that the place of the dethroned oracle should be taken by another deciding will—a real authoritative royalty.

LS: Yes. A *real* royalty, not the royalty of the god of Delphi. So in other words, ultimately you need recourse to a will. The highest will ruling the Greeks was in fact the Delphian oracle, the will of Apollo. But the powerlessness of Apollo was revealed by the act of the Phocians. And now an actual, earthly human will, namely, that of Philip of Macedon, took the place. Read on here, because the sequel is also quite interesting.

Mr. Reinken:

> The foreign Macedonian King—Philip—undertook to avenge the violation of the oracle, and forthwith took its place, by making himself lord of Greece. Philip reduced under his dominion the Hellenic States, and convinced them that it was all over with their independence, and that they could no longer maintain their own footing. The charge of littleness, harshness, violence, and political treachery—all those hateful characteristics with which Philip has so often been reproached—did not extend to the young Alexander, when he placed himself at the head of the Greeks. He had no need to incur such reproaches.[17]

LS: What does this difference between Philip and Alexander mean? Could Alexander have made himself the master of Greece without these hateful things? It seems that he was lucky. His father had done the dirty jobs so that he did not have to do them. So the evil is a necessary ingredient of world history, and Alexander could afford to be noble because his father had done it.

He speaks here immediately afterwards about Aristotle, who was, after all, Alexander's teacher. And he calls Aristotle "the deepest and most comprehensive thinker of antiquity" and "the deepest thinker, perhaps, also in comparison with the modern times." So not Plato. It is hard to say who he regards as possibly competing in modern times with Aristotle. Possibly himself. And he has frequently been compared with Aristotle. Here he says at the end of this paragraph, which is not in your translation: "Plato has not educated a statesman; Aristotle, however, a true king."[18] This is a sign—not a proof, but a sign—of the superiority of Aristotle.

When he speaks, on page 272 bottom, of Alexander's greatness—let us read that.

Mr. Reinken:

> Thus accomplished, Alexander placed himself at the head of the Hellenes in order to lead Greece over into Asia.

LS: No, you don't have to read that. A bit later. "The greatness and the interesting character of this work."

Mr. Reinken:

The grandeur and the interest of this work were proportioned to his genius—to his peculiar youthful individuality—the like of which in so beautiful a form we have not seen a second time at the head of such an undertaking. For not only were the genius of a commander, the greatest spirit, and consummate bravery united in him, but all these qualities were dignified by the beauty of his character as a man and an individual.[19]

LS: This reminds of his judgment on Pericles, whom he had however praised more highly. On page 273, the third paragraph.
Mr. Reinken:

Alexander had the good fortune to die at the proper time, that is, it may be called good fortune, but it is rather a necessity. That he may stand before the eyes of posterity as a youth, an early death must hurry him away. Achilles, as remarked above, begins the Greek World, and his antitype Alexander concludes it: and these youths not only supply a picture of the fairest kind in their own persons, but at the same time afford a complete and perfect type of Hellenic existence.[20]

LS: So in other words, that we shall have a beautiful picture of beautiful Greekness, Alexander had to die so early. This is a strange implication of Hegel's rationalism, that everything has to be reasonable.[21] He defends here Alexander against the modern philistines who judge historical heroes in moral terms. Here he says, among other things, one must not blame him for having brought blood and war into the world. One must be finished with blood and war when one begins to study world history. In other words, one must be through with this kind of weak nerves, shuddering at war and blood. This, I think, is a quite characteristic remark.

In the sequel he mentions Plato's *Republic* again and says that, rightly understood, Plato's *Republic* is not something which Plato figured out for himself but the true nature of Greek morality, namely, the complete subordination of the individual to the *polis*. If this is the principle of Greekness, then of course Plato drew all his conclusions from that.

Now we turn to the Roman section. Let us see, on page 278. Let us read the first paragraph.
Mr. Reinken:

Napoleon, in a conversation which he once had with Goethe on the nature of Tragedy, expressed the opinion that its modern phase differed from the ancient through our no longer recognizing a destiny to which men are absolutely subject, and that policy occupies the place of the ancient fate (politics is fatality). This, therefore, he thought must be used as the modern form of destiny in tragedy—the irresistible power of circumstances to which individuality must bend. Such a power is the Roman world, chosen for the very purpose of casting the moral units into bonds, as also of collecting deities and all spirits into the pantheon of universal dominion, in order to make out of them an abstract universality of power. The distinction between the Roman and the Persian principle is exactly this, that the former stifles all vitality while the latter allows its existence in the fullest measure. Through its being the aim of the state, that the social units in their moral right should be sacrificed to it, the world is sunk in melancholy: its heart is broken, and it is all over with the natural side of Spirit, which has sunk into a feeling of unhappiness. Yet only from this feeling could arise the supersensuous, the free Spirit in Christianity.[22]

LS: In other words, the natural had to be not only overcome but transcended, as it was to some extent in Greece. But the natural had to be completely depreciated, to be deprived of all intrinsic charm, so that the complete break with naturalness in Christianity, the complete otherworldliness would become possible.

There is another point which we have to consider. There is one term which he uses, this must be on page 279 top: "Here in Rome now we find this abstract, this free universality, this abstract freedom, which on the one hand posits the abstract state."

Mr. Reinken:

Here in Rome, then, we find that free universality, that abstract freedom which, on the one hand, sets an abstract state, a political constitution and power, over concrete individuality; on the other side, creates a personality in opposition to that universality—the inherent freedom of the abstract Ego, which must be distinguished from individual idiosyncrasy.[23]

LS: "From the individuality." Personality is not individuality. That's the key point. And the Romans are the discoverers of personality. What Hegel has in mind is the concept of the person as a legal concept and the recognition of man, first of some man but eventually of all men as legal persons, which is something very narrow compared with the full individuality but which is of great importance because of its potential universality. Out of the legal person of formal law there will grow the fuller individuality later on.

Hegel makes clear that Rome was from the outset not natural in any way, nor did it have the originality going together with naturalness. From the very beginning it was something arbitrary and violently fabricated. He develops this at considerable length. For example, the story of the Sabine women, which shows an all-male society of robbers and other rabble. There is no true human unity, no affection of any kind. And what do you say regarding this argument? Hegel alludes to that in the context. Hegel gives also another example, the foundation of Rome. What is the foundation of Rome? I mean, which act . . .

Student: The unnatural fratricide, Romulus and Remus.

LS: Yes. The foundation of Rome was not only in crime but in fratricide, in the killing of the nearest. Now ordinarily when we read that story, it reminds us of course of the biblical story: Cain murdering his brother Abel, and being the first founder of a city. It is to that extent of the same sort. But Hegel sees something which I at least did not so easily see at the first point, namely, that the story of Romulus and Remus is told by the Romans about their own city. Therefore it is true historical evidence. I mean, whether these fables are true stories is of no interest to Hegel, but a nation which can tell this story about its own origin thereby reveals its soul. That is Hegel's argument against all historical critics as they had arisen especially in the nineteenth century. He mentions Niebuhr,[24] the most famous of them and . . . But the key point for Hegel is not whether this is a historical fact. Hegel's great objection to the historical critics is of course that many things which they think are the true facts are merely plausible hypotheses. They are not more demonstrable than the old stories, but the old stories have this great advantage: they reveal the thinking of the people themselves. If you look at this, where in the world do you find a nation which has given such a terrible account of its own origins? Hegel says to us, and I think here rightly, that this is most important for understanding them. And of course also the story of the Sabine women. These were originally outcasts and only outcasts, the people around Romulus. From this point of view it's quite important. Did you want to say something?

Mr. Reinken: To expatiate on the difference, which was that Romulus killed Remus for the sake of the city because a dog jumped over the walls, but Cain founded his city after he had been turned away by God.

LS: But still, the story of Cain is not told by the citizens of the city founded by him. That is the crucial point. And the other point, so that we see how Hegel proceeds, he does not proceed like a modern historian. He refuses to recognize this approach. But he says: Look at this kind of account which reveals the character of Rome. Or take another thing for which Rome was quite famous, to which he refers or alludes all the time: the *patria potestas*, the immense legal power of the father and husband in Rome which went much beyond what you found in any other nation at least at that time known. Hegel could have added other evidence in order to show the superiority of the Greeks to the Romans. And he was, I take it, aware of that. And that is what some of the greatest Romans thought about Rome in comparison to Greece. This would only confirm it. They expressed themselves with some reticence. There was no perfect freedom of expression in Rome.

For example, Plutarch of course was a Greek and he had no inner obligation to think more highly of the Romans, but when you read his *Parallel Lives*, in each case he compares a great Greek to a great Roman. The apparent emphasis is on how similar these Greeks and these Romans were, especially at the end where he gives an explicit comparison: he married his aunt, and *he* married his aunt, or whatever it might be—usually something more relevant. But what he never brings out in the explicit comparison, but what comes out when you read the book, is the very great differences between these Greeks and the Romans, differences as a rule speaking in favor of the Greeks. But of course, even Romans like Lucretius and Cicero make it quite clear that in the most important respects the Greeks are their true teachers. So in other words, the general assertion of Hegel has very good foundations.[25]

LS: — You refer to what Cicero says about the origin of the word *religio* in Rome, and Hegel says: This is very characteristic of the Romans, this narrow, ritualistic, ceremonial understanding of religion. Rome lacks religious freedom, both the freedom of beauty of the Greeks and the freedom of spirit of the Christians. Roman religion is found limited, serving particular purposes—used as an instrument for government, for example. Yet this has an important implication, according to Hegel. This means that it recognizes the worldly particular in its nonreligious secular character. Let us turn to page 292, line 4, when he speaks about the Roman gods.

Mr. Reinken:

The divinities peculiar to them are entirely prosaic.

LS: That is sufficient also for showing Hegel's method. Hegel knew and speaks of the fact that the Greek Olympian pantheon is, in a way, also the Roman pantheon. Zeus is Jupiter, Hera is Juno, and so on and so on. But he asks: What are the gods peculiar to the Romans, the gods which do not have a parallel in the Greek pantheon? They reveal to us the peculiarity of the Romans.

Mr. Reinken:

> The divinities peculiar to them are entirely prosaic; they are conditions, sensations, or useful arts, to which their dry fancy, having elevated them to independent power, gave objectivity; they are partly abstractions, which could only become frigid allegories—partly conditions of being which appear as bringing advantage or injury, and which were presented as objects of worship in their original bare and limited form. We can but briefly notice a few examples. The Romans worshipped Peace, Tranquility, Repose, Sorrow, as divinities; they consecrated altars to the Plague, to Hunger, to Mildew, Fever.[26]

LS: And he would simply say: Show me the parallels of that in Greece. He develops that in the sequel. The Roman gods are not the works of love of the beautiful as the Greek gods at their highest were.

A further point which I believe he does not make in this edition but which is here: the Greek and Roman games, the contests. The greatest form of the Greek contest is the contest of the tragedies. What is the place of these contests in Rome? What has the same popularity as tragedy has in Athens? The gladiators. Lions, Negroes, and gladiators took the place of the tragedies for the Romans.[27] If this doesn't show it, what should? Let us turn to page 294 in the center of the first paragraph.

Mr. Reinken:

> In place of human sufferings in the depths of the soul and spirit, occasioned by the contradictions of life, and which find their solution in Destiny, the Romans instituted a cruel reality of corporeal sufferings: blood in streams, the rattle in the throat which signals death, and the expiring gasp were the scenes that delighted them. This cold negativity of naked murder exhibits at the same time that murder of all spiritual objective aim which had taken place in the soul.

LS: Yes, and can you read the next paragraph?
Mr. Reinken:

> The distinct elements of Roman religion are, according to what has been
> said, subjective religiosity and a ritualism having for its object purely su-
> perficial external aims.

LS: The subjective inner religiosity, meaning a religiosity which remains only within as feeling and does not come to fulfillment and expression in actions, gestures, and so on.
Mr. Reinken:

> Secular aims are left entirely free, instead of being limited by religion—in
> fact they are rather justified by it. The Romans are invariably pious, what-
> ever may be the substantial character of their actions. But as the sacred
> principle here is nothing but an empty form, it is exactly of such a kind that
> it can be an instrument in the power of the devotee; it is taken possession
> of by the individual, who seeks his private objects and interests; whereas
> the truly Divine possesses on the contrary a concrete power in itself. But
> where there is only a powerless form, the individual—the Will, possessing
> an independent concreteness able to make that form its own, and render it
> subservient to its views—stands above it.[28]

LS: One can say that the mere prose of life, without any reference to
the nonprosaic, is the discovery of the Romans. This is not the same as
the discovery of *techne*, of the productive arts, which also are emphatically
prosaic—shoemaker, carpenter, and so on. What is the difference? In the
arts, the emphasis is on the knowledge, ability, and skill of the producer;
and here the concern is not with any skills, but with the mere ends, say,
property or the power of the state. What Hegel tries to convey here is
that Rome was manifestly superior to Greece. There cannot be any doubt
about it. Yet in the decisive respect, Rome constitutes a progress beyond
Greece. There is no longer the tutelage of nature which was in Greece,
but there is also no longer the charming union of nature and mind which
is charming and therefore also deceptive and untrue. Instead, we find an
external union, which cannot fool anyone, of religious formalism, mere
ceremonialism, and finite prosaic content, the finite ends of the property
owner. Implied in this is that the Roman is not simply citizen in the way

in which the Spartan was citizen and to some extent also the Athenians. A sphere of privacy is recognized, according to Hegel, for the first time, and that is crucial. Hegel would say that whereas it was in fact recognized in Greek cities, in principle it was not, and therefore Plato's *Republic* is the true story of the Greek *polis*. Let us see one more passage. On page 281, in the second paragraph.

Mr. Reinken:

> We observed subjective inwardness as the general principle of the Roman World. The course of Roman History, therefore, involves the expansion of undeveloped subjectivity—inward conviction of existence—to the visibility of the real world. The principle of subjective inwardness receives positive application in the first place only from without—through the particular volition of the sovereignty, the government. The development consists in the purification of inwardness to abstract personality, which gives itself reality in the existence of private property; the mutually repellent social units can then be held together only by despotic power.

LS: The mutually repellent persons, he says, and this is used advisedly. There is no bond between these property owners as property owners, each having the right to use and misuse his property. Therefore the only bond which can eventually hold them together is despotic power. Yes?

Mr. Reinken:

> The general course of the Roman World may be defined as this: the transition from the inner sanctum of subjectivity to its direct opposite. The development is here not of the same kind as that in Greece—the unfolding and expanding of its own substance on the part of the principle; but it is the transition to its opposite, which latter does not appear as an element of corruption, but is demanded and posited by the principle itself.[29]

LS: What does he mean by that? In Rome, in contradistinction to Greece, the final state is not corruption but fulfillment. This terrible condition under the Roman emperors is in a way that which Rome always was, the complete unholiness of this the present life. This is the truth of Rome which comes out, and this unholiness was there from the very beginning because the religion was an instrument of government, an instrument of any narrow, finite purposes. This points to the opposite in modern times, the reconciliation of this life and the other life in modernity. One more point on page 296.

Mr. Reinken:

In the first period, several successive stages displayed their characteristic variety. The Roman state here exhibits its first phase of growth under kings.

LS: When he speaks a bit later about the information concerning the first Roman kings.

Mr. Reinken:

As regards the accounts of the first Roman kings, every datum has met with flat contradiction as the result of criticism; but it is going too far to deny them all credibility. Seven kings in all are mentioned by tradition; and even the "Higher Criticism" is obliged to recognize the last links in the series as perfectly historical. Romulus is called the founder of this union of freebooters; he organized it into a military state. Although the traditions respecting him appear fabulous, they only contain what is in accordance with the Roman Spirit as above described. To the second king, Numa, is ascribed the introduction of the religious ceremonies. This trait is very remarkable from its implying that religion was introduced later than political union, while among other peoples religious traditions make their appearance in the remotest periods and before all civil institutions.[30]

LS: Yes, this is indeed very remarkable. But I wonder whether that is literally true, because there were all kinds of oracles and things going with Romulus. This statement occurs somewhere in Livy. This is rather the interpretation of Rome given by Machiavelli, and one has to wonder to what extent Hegel has hardly seen Rome. He had of course access to the ancient sources, but he had also read Machiavelli. To what extent had he seen Rome through the eyes of Machiavelli? Machiavelli's is a very tough interpretation of Rome. But the principle which he states is, I think, a sensible one. The fables of a nation and especially the fables about its own origin are as important in order to understand that nation as the most massive facts demonstrated by excavations and documents, etc. We will stop here and continue next Wednesday.

12 The Roman World Continued and the Advent of Christianity

Leo Strauss: You had a particularly difficult task, I am aware of that.[1] Perhaps you can restate to us briefly the crucial point? Since history is rational, the fact that Christianity emerged within the Roman Empire must be understood in the light of the fundamental agreement and, also, antithesis of the Roman and the Christian principle. What is that which they have in common?

Student: The idea of spirit, the universal discovery of the particular with the universal . . . the universal is found in the embryo . . . the particular, the individual subjectivity . . . In Rome, there's no mediation between the two; Christianity introduces the principle of the unity of the universal with the particular, the relationship characterizes—

LS: Yes. But what is the situation of the individual under the Roman emperor?

Student: It is a condition of absolute slavery.

LS: Yes, in one sense, but not quite, because otherwise it would simply be Oriental despotism.

Student: He is recognized through his legal rights.

LS: This may be precarious, but still it is there. That is very important. So the individual is recognized, although not all individuals are recognized. But still, since the difference between free men and slaves becomes more irrelevant, one can even speak of the recognition of all men in the late Roman Empire. But what is the situation of the individual under the Roman emperors?

Student: He gives himself up to fate. He has no spiritual self.

LS: An empty life. It is a life of misery. But how does Christianity transform that? I mean in the first step. How does Christianity interpret that emptiness or misery?

Student: It transfers the separation into the individual man, it takes the role of subjectivity.

LS: How is this emptiness or misery called by Christianity?

Student: Sin.

LS: Sin. And this gives the emptiness a totally different meaning. Therewith it points to the possibility of forgiveness or reconciliation. Or, differently stated, what is the peculiarity of pagan Rome compared with everything we found before, either in the Orient or in Greece?

Student: The development of some subjectivity.

LS: Yes. But it can be stated negatively. Rome was the first culture, the first society, which was not natural, according to Hegel. In Greece already we found the overcoming of nature by mind or spirit, but there is at the same time the harmonious union of the two in Greek beauty. In Rome there is no longer such a union. There is mere non-nature, if in its most . . . forms. The mere assertion of will or force, especially what he says about the foundation of Rome. He doesn't even mention explicitly that Romulus was suckled by a she-wolf, which would of course confirm only what we have discussed last time. This transcending of nature in the Roman principle links it up with Christianity, where it is done in a much more radical way.

Now I would like to return these papers. Mr. Glenn, there is only one point which I would like to make. You say that the Roman state was founded on military art, not on nature. "In Rome the spirit first became independent of nature for its stimulation. Nature is no longer the matter of spirit. Spirit, and therefore reason, is its own matter. But Rome was also founded before"—this is I think correct what you say there—"But Rome was also founded before its religion. Apparently religion supplies in Rome a connection between nature and spirit. Spirit is not yet completely independent of nature." This is in a way true, but I don't believe Hegel emphasizes it. "In view of the difference between Roman religion and the previous religions we have seen, it seems questionable to me whether Hegel any longer views religion as the most fundamental manifestation of the people's spirit." Here I am somewhat doubtful, but it is surely a consideration worthy of being made. Thank you.

Here is another paper. Mr. . . . . "The real difficulty in Hegel's treatment of Alexander is not his abstraction from Alexander's life, meaning from certain unsavory aspects of that life, but the actual character of the advance he seems to represent. The subjugation of Asia is not an advance of the idea but as such merely the working out of the Greek destiny. But the Hellenization of Asia is an advance, for the higher Greek spirit was impressed on the East. Still this was not an advance of the idea, but a diffusion of one stage of it, the Greek stage." But still is this not a very important change which made possible the Roman?

Student: . . .

LS: Surely. Alexander still belongs to Greece, but this is a changed Greece, the Alexandrian Greece. And this particular change makes intelligible to some extent the next stage, namely, Rome. Then you say: "The emancipation from nature begun by the Greeks is completed by the Romans." I believe that one can say that. Completed of course only in the sense of the emancipation, not in the sense that it is fulfilled. Let us turn to page 298.

Mr. Reinken:

> The Kings were expelled by the patricians, not by the plebeians; if therefore the patricians are to be regarded as possessed of "divine right" as being a sacred race, it is worthy of note that we find them here contravening such legitimation; for the King was their High Priest.

LS: Literally, they acted against legitimacy.

Mr. Reinken:

> We observe on this occasion with what dignity the sanctity of marriage was invested in the eyes of the Romans. The principle of subjectivity and piety (*pudor*) was with them the religious and guarded element; and its violation becomes the occasion of the expulsion of the Kings, and later on of the Decemvirs too.[2]

LS: Hegel adds the Latin word *pudor* to make quite clear the point he has in mind. *Pudor*—or in Greek *aidos*, sense of shame—this existed and was especially powerful in Rome within certain limits. The implication is that this is not the conscience. When we read the passages in Greek or Latin texts, they speak of *aidos*, of sense of shame. The nearest modern equivalent would be the conscience, but it is not the conscience. And the most simple proof of that is the most elaborate statement about sense of shame which we have in the Greek literature towards the end of the fourth book of Aristotle's *Ethics*. Do you remember Aristotle's teaching about *aidos*, or sense of shame?

Student: It is good for the young, but not for mature men.

LS: It is not a virtue, because a gentleman, a perfectly . . . man would never do anything of which he is ashamed, and therefore he doesn't have it. Young people should have it because they can't help still making mistakes. And this shows clearly how different it is from what we understand by the conscience.

Student: Doesn't Aristotle say in the *Rhetoric* that it is this passion which generates the virtue of courage?

LS: Yes. But you must not forget that when he discusses subjects in the *Rhetoric*—the various passions—in the first place it is the passions. We must never forget that. To that extent there is no contradiction, of course, with the *Ethics*. But apart from that or implied in that, the level at which Aristotle discusses in his *Rhetoric* is definitely lower, a much more popular view than he takes in the *Ethics*. True courage would not be based on a sense of shame. But in a cruder way, especially if you think of younger people, young soldiers, there it would be based on a sense of shame, what the others would think if he ran away and so on.

There is a passage which is not in your edition.

> The plebeians haven't gained anything by the expulsion of the kings. The kings had protected the plebs against the patricians, and prevented them from oppressing the plebs. In this way, the people owe everywhere also in modern times to the king their liberation from the suppression by the aristocracy. [He draws this general conclusion—LS] There is aristocracy in England [that was more or less before the Reform Bill[3]—LS] because the royal power is insignificant. This is the eternal relation—that ordinarily the lower class people are protected by the kings, but the people are fooled and unite themselves against their advantage with the middle class by which they are suppressed.[4]

The Reform Bill situation more or less, and this is of some interest with a view to Hegel's political views in this time. He says somewhat later:

> In considering this Roman constitution one cannot help feeling that aristocracy is the worst constitution, although Aristotle thinks that the *aristoi* should rule. The Roman aristocracy in itself was not as dead as that of Venice, for example. They had their laws and their inner vitality, and thus in Rome two extremes were united which established somehow an equilibrium among themselves [meaning the patricians and the plebs—LS]. But this is the worst, for even this third, the equilibrium itself, would have to be as a definite power, as a mean and point of support, and would have to be as such actual. But this was not the case in Rome [meaning this

would have to be supplied by a third element, the monarchy as Hegel thought would be the case in the constitutional monarchy of the nineteenth century—LS].[5]

This criticism of Aristotle is something which we must keep in mind. Let us turn to page 304, second paragraph.
Mr. Reinken:

> It would be a wearisome task to pursue the wars of the Romans in Italy; partly because they are in themselves unimportant—even the often empty rhetoric of the generals in Livy cannot very much increase the interest— partly on account of the unintelligent character of the Roman annalists in whose pages we see the Romans carrying on war only with "enemies" without learning anything further of their individuality—e.g. the Etruscans, the Samnites, the Ligurians, with whom they carried on wars during many hundred years.

LS: In other words, in contrast to Thucydides where the individuality of Athens and Sparta is clear, or in Herodotus where the individuality of the Persians and the Egyptians and so on comes out so vividly. And indeed, when one reads in Livy the old story about the Volsci or Aequi or whoever they were, it cannot possibly be of any interest whether it is these or those. I believe that when Machiavelli makes some of these changes in the reports of early Roman history, replacing the Volsci by the Aequi, he does this with the intention to bring this out. It doesn't make the slightest difference. Go on.
Mr. Reinken:

> It is singular in regard to these transactions that the Romans, who have the justification conceded by World History on their side, should also claim for themselves the minor justification—

LS: He speaks first of the "great right, the grand right of world history," and that they are also concerned with the "little right."
Mr. Reinken:

> in respect to manifestos and treaties on occasion of minor infringements of them, and maintain it as it were after the fashion of advocates. But in political complications of this kind, either party may take offence

at the conduct of the other, if it pleases, and deems it expedient to be offended.[6]

LS: In other words, the only right which is truly respectable is the world-historical right and not the little right—positive international law, treaties, and so on where interpretation always has a great possibility of showing its virtues and vices. Now page 308, center.
Mr. Reinken:

> The relation to other nations was purely that of force. The national individuality of peoples did not, as early as the time of the Romans, excite respect, as is the case in modern times. The various peoples were not yet recognized as legitimated. The various states had not yet acknowledged each other as real, essential existences. Equal right to existence entails the union of states, such as exists in modern Europe, or a condition like that of Greece in which the states had an equal right to existence under the protection of the Delphic god. The Romans do not enter into such a relation to the other nations, for their god is only the Jupiter Capitolinus; neither do they respect the sacra of the other nations (any more than the plebeians those of the patricians); but, as conquerors in the strict sense of the term, they plunder the Palladia of the nations.[7]

LS: The key point: the Romans do not respect the national individuality of nations, as is habitually the case today, as he says. He means, of course, in modern Europe. The Romans are in a sense monotheists, although they are for all practical purposes polytheists. Their god is only the Jupiter Capitolinus, and therefore they do not respect the other nations. The Roman state is a universal state, therefore, in principle but nevertheless a universal state of which only Romans can be citizens. I think that what he implies is that just as in Greece the recognition by all cities of the Delphic god led to a recognition of one city by the other, the Christian character of the modern states makes it possible and necessary for the individual Christian state to recognize the other ones. Page 309, line 5.
Mr. Reinken:

> From Asia, luxury and debauchery were brought to Rome. Riches flowed in after the fashion of spoils in war, and were not the fruit of industry and honest activity; in the same way as the marine had arisen, not from the necessities of commerce, but with a warlike object.[8]

LS: Yes. "For the purpose of war." In other words, industry and commerce are morally superior to war. In this respect, Hegel is in entire agreement with English development represented especially by Locke. Now page 310, paragraph 3.
Mr. Reinken:

We thus see the most terrible and dangerous powers arising against Rome; yet the military force of this state is victorious over all. Great individuals now appear on the stage as during the times of the fall of Greece.

LS: The development, the emancipation of the individual belongs to a time of decay. Pericles already, and Alcibiades of course, the great philosophers and so on. The same is true of Rome, he says. Prior to the decay there is a prevalence of types, as represented by families and so on. The individuals as individuals were not important.
Mr. Reinken:

The biographies of Plutarch are here also of the deepest interest. It was from the disruption of the state, which had no longer any consistency or firmness in itself, that these colossal individualities arose, instinctively impelled to restore that political unity which was no longer to be found in men's dispositions. It is their misfortune that they cannot maintain a pure morality, for their course of action contravenes things as they are, and is a series of transgressions.

LS: "Crimes." Let us be quite clear.
Mr. Reinken:

Even the Gracchi, the noblest, were not merely the victims of injustice and violence from without, but were themselves involved in the corruption and wrong that universally prevailed. But that which these individuals propose and accomplish has on its side the higher sanction of the World-Spirit, and must eventually triumph.[9]

LS: In other words, world history has a tragic character to the extent that crimes are necessary, noble crimes. Yet of course ultimately world history is not tragic because there is a final reconciliation, a final victory of right. Let us turn to page 311, second paragraph.
Mr. Reinken:

In this way, the world-wide sovereignty of Rome became the property of a single possessor. This important change must not be regarded as a thing of chance. It was necessary, postulated by the circumstances. The democratic constitution could no longer be really maintained in Rome, but only kept up in appearance. Cicero, who had procured himself great respect through his high oratorical talent, and whose learning acquired him considerable influence, always attributes the corrupt state of the republic to individuals and their passions. Plato, whom Cicero professedly followed, had the full consciousness that the Athenian state as it presented itself to him could not maintain its existence and therefore sketched the plan of the perfect constitution accordant with his views. Cicero, on the contrary, does not consider it impossible to preserve the Roman republic, and only desiderates some temporary assistance for it in its adversity. The nature of the state, and of the Roman State in particular, transcends his comprehension.[10]

LS: This is a very interesting criticism and very characteristic of Hegel. What do you say of this criticism, which of course later on in the nineteenth century was presented in a much more radical form by the famous German historian of Rome, Mommsen?[11] Cicero is presented as a man without any understanding of what was going on.

Student: I would say that that was probably based on unfamiliarity with the *Republic*. Is that correct?

LS: No. Cicero's *Republic* was discovered in 1825 or 1822,[12] I don't know the exact date. Hegel may not have known it.

Student: Because I think that there Cicero takes a much more pessimistic view.

LS: But I don't think that this goes to the root of the matter. Cicero surely took the side of the Senate, of the old order against Caesar's revolutionary action. There is no doubt about that.

Mr. Reinken: The difference between Cicero and Plato is that Cicero was in the active business of saving the state, which he did at least twice.

LS: Yes. That is a good point. Of course, that is quite true. Plato knew—he says so somewhere in the Seventh Letter—that he has come late in Athens, so that there was no longer any possibility of a restoration. But there is of course a difference, because what was in Athens in Plato's time and what he regarded as a decay was democracy, but Plato knew that this democracy, however low it might seem to him, was nevertheless a golden age, as he almost put it, compared with the attempt at restoring the old which had been attempted by his kinsmen Critias, Charmides, and other people—what now would be called a brutal fascist reaction. And after all, Plato was twenty when this happened and was for a moment attracted by the fine words of justice. Then, after he had seen how they acted, the old despised democracy appeared to be like the golden age in retrospect. But Plato knew that certain things were no longer possible in his own times. But in Cicero's case, the case was of course somewhat different. Plato accepts the democracy. Cicero tries to preserve some freedom which he was sure would be endangered by the rule of a single man. That is the very great difference.

But Hegel, looking at the thing in hindsight, sees what wonderful things came out of this terrible Caesarism, namely, the emergence of Christianity and the modern world. Therefore, Cicero did not understand and see the wave of the future.

Student: I would say that Hegel's views are clouded by his views of necessity in history, whereas Cicero wouldn't have that view.

LS: Yes, but is this not connected with the fact that in the situation you cannot tell what will happen?

Student: That is probably true, but I could never have imagined Cicero having a notion of necessary causes in history. He would say that there is a chance to preserve this order, and let's try.

LS: In practice, everyone must do this no matter what theory he may have because he does not truly know the future. But what is the difference here? Knowledge? First of all, if we take Marxism, for example, the assumed knowledge of the future. You know that the stronger force is the wave of the future; therefore it is foolish to resist. This was indeed absent from Cicero, of course. It was clear for him that the preservation of the republican institutions is the best that you can have under the circumstances. And he stuck to that, sacrificing his life. Mr. . . . ?

Student: This is about the earlier quote about the difference between Roman universalism and the modern state. I don't understand why the modern state would be more tolerant of other national principles than Rome was, and why the modern states shouldn't try to work somehow towards a universal world state based on the rational order of a monarchy, according to Hegel.

LS: There was a time when Hegel sympathized very much with Napoleon's attempt to unify Europe, at least continental Europe. This would be something like the closest approach to a universal state possible in the circumstances then. At this time he had abandoned that, obviously, and he saw that the recognition of what de Gaulle now calls "the Europe of the fatherlands," a number of free and equal independent states, is characteristic of Europe and should be preserved.

Student: He mentions something like China couldn't take over the West, but the West might take over China through her ideas. Wouldn't the same sort of thing happen? Consider that if history was just the working-out of every state adopting the essentially German or essentially European idea of freedom, then supposedly all the national characteristics and differences would be worked out and there would be no reason for national differences then, although there might be in Hegel's time, according to his view.

LS: If we limit ourselves to what he says in the passage, he indicates a reason. None of these European states claims that its gods, the gods which it respects, is as such the universal God. The Germans don't say, at least they didn't say in Hegel's time, that God is a German God and the God of the Germans more than of any other nation, whereas the Romans said that their god, Jupiter Capitolinus, is as the Roman god destined to rule over the whole globe, according to Hegel's statement there.

That is a great question: To what extent Hegel can oppose, say, at least the unification of Europe? That is true. But in fact I think that he took it for granted later on. The maximum that I find in his later writings is his statement that a war among the European nations is now senseless. That he said in his *Aesthetics* somewhere.[13] In other words, that all the wars that came later, especially those by which Germany was unified under Bismarck, are not provided for by Hegel. I don't believe there is anything one can say beyond that. Or one must rewrite Hegel completely, as was done in our time by Kojève, who, synthesizing Hegel and Marx, speaks of the homogeneous and universal state, not merely society, which is that towards which all present-day modern movements are concurring. But this is clearly no longer Hegel himself, but Hegel corrected in the light of Marx, or Marx corrected in the light of Hegel.[14] The correction of Marx is obvious. Not a stateless society but a state, a government, will also be at the end of days. Let us turn to page 315, second paragraph, the second half.

Mr. Reinken:

In the person of the Emperor isolated subjectivity has gained a perfectly unlimited realization. Spirit has renounced its proper nature, inasmuch as limitation of being and of volition has been constituted in unlimited, absolute existence. This arbitrary choice, moreover, has only one limit, the limit of all that is human—*death*; and even death became a theatrical display. Nero, for example, died a death which may furnish an example for the noblest hero, as for the most resigned of sufferers. Individual subjectivity thus entirely emancipated from control, has no inward life, no prospective nor retrospective emotions, no repentance, nor hope, nor fear—not even thought; for all these involve fixed conditions and aims, while here every condition is purely contingent. The springs of action are none other than desire, lust, passion, fancy—in short, caprice absolutely unfettered.[15]

LS: Which includes the possibility that an individual emperor might be virtuous, but seen in the light of the principle of government, it is a mere accident. It is a mere caprice of Marcus Aurelius that he wants to be virtuous, as it is a caprice of Domitian to be appeased.

Mr. Shulsky: Is he saying that, in general, whenever there is no spiritual struggle there wouldn't be any spiritual life? That the emperor, in a sense, has it too easy. He gets everything . . .

LS: No. I think that it is more than that. There is the loss of every moral substance. This is essential to the Roman order as freed from nature, so that the simple natural affections—for example, in the family relation—which play a role in all other previous nations, are from the very beginning weakened, not to say in principle destroyed, and therefore nothing remains but arbitrary will and force. The natural . . . after all external restraint was taken away by the universal conquest had to come this way. Yes?

Mr. Shulsky: Isn't this a somewhat similar situation to what would happen in the modern world? There would be no further development. There would be a spirit entirely wrapped up in itself with no contact with nature. You get the same type of degeneration.

LS: You mean at the end.

Mr. Shulsky: Well, at this time.

LS: No, for a very simple reason: because the modern state based on the recognition of the rights of man and everything that entails is necessarily characterized by what we can call the rule of law in contradistinction to any arbitrary will. In Hegel's notion of monarchy, the monarch is only the individual who signs on the dotted line. The decisions are prepared by the high officials, supposedly men of high education and properly trained for their job. I think the difficulty to which Hegel's notion of the final state is concerned has nothing to do with his concept of the state itself, except in this way: he believed that it is possible to preserve the hereditary monarchy and hereditary nobility which is a part of his scheme against this enormous power of the democratic movement of which he was somehow aware but before which he somehow closed his eyes. This is of course a very great change. But apart from that, the reasonable state—the state based on the rights of man and issued in reasonable laws, assuming that the laws are framed by competent people, and not merely under popular pressure—that was the meaning of his concern with government ruling in its own right and not merely by popular delegation.

Mr. Shulsky: I wasn't thinking so much of the modern monarch but of the private citizen in the modern state.

LS: This is a different story. You are thinking of the passage from the *Philosophy of Religion* which I read last time about this discord, that the state has fundamentally a religious basis, but it also has not.

Mr. Shulsky: Yes. But also from here where for the individual citizen, when the only real connection with any sort of spiritual struggle is done away with, the connection with any material struggle is done away with as well, and that the only legitimate principle is a spirit entirely wrapped up in itself.

LS: Let us assume that such a thing is possible: a new kind of emptiness, a thought with which Max Weber more than played, but this emptiness would be of a radically different kind from the emptiness which you find, according to Hegel, in the Roman Empire, would it not?

Mr. Shulsky: Well, it wouldn't be this complete playing-out of the desires. It would be different in that sense. But it would result in the same complete lack of contact with anything substantial, wouldn't it? Because the only legitimate principle which a person could look up to would be his freedom. He knows that he is free and independent, but there's nothing to do, there's no activity that is a goal or that's important in any sense.

LS: Do you mean something like what Nietzsche spoke of in the section on the last man?

Mr. Shulsky: In a sense.

LS: Yes. This would indeed be something very different from the Roman Empire. This is precisely not misery but apparent happiness. People have forgotten; "we have invented happiness," he says.[16] Here these Roman citizens, constantly hearing another outrage of the government, are not in this position.

Mr. Shulsky: I was comparing more the modern citizen with the Roman emperor, who was apparently happy too because of his complete power.

LS: Yes. But he is of course very much in danger all the time.

Mr. Reinken: If you are looking for parallels, perhaps our juvenile delinquents and our unhappy college students are a little like this.

LS: Yes. I thought of this. I believe that there is nevertheless a fundamental difference. I say this not because I am very sanguine but because we must not overlook fundamental differences, and the mere awareness of these dangers is something which we have to be grateful for.

Now in the sequel he develops a further point that this organism of the state is dissolved into the atoms of private persons. What he means by private persons could also be called, as it has been called by Kojève in his interpretation of these things, the bourgeois: the bourgeois in contradistinction to the citizen. Rousseau's distinction was taken up by Hegel and then transformed by Marx. The man who does not fight for his country, who is not a citizen and has no participation in government, is a mere property-owning subject and devoid of all public spirit. That is what Rousseau meant by the bourgeois, and Hegel accepted that to some extent. But here of course, in the Roman world, that would be as true of the rich as of the poor, because the poor would be merely the actually propertyless but eager to own property. The same would even be true of the slaves, because they can be emancipated any day and can be given a legacy, and then they would already be free property holders. On page 317, line 12 from bottom.

Mr. Reinken:

> That, therefore, which was abidingly present to the minds of men was not their country or such a moral unity as that supplies. The whole state of things urged them to yield themselves to fate and to strive for a perfect indifference to life—

LS: This resignation was necessary because of the radically immoral character, not bound by any law, of the government.

Mr. Reinken:

> an indifference which they sought either in freedom of thought or in directly sensuous enjoyment. Thus man was either at war with existence or entirely given up to mere sensuous existence. He either recognized his destiny in the task of acquiring the means of enjoyment through the favor of the Emperor, or through violence, testamentary frauds, and cunning; or he sought repose in philosophy, which alone was still able to supply something firm and independent: for the systems of that time—

LS: It is important that he is not speaking of philosophy in general, but of such a philosophy as belongs to a period of public misery.

Mr. Reinken:

Stoicism, Epicureanism, and Scepticism—although within their common sphere opposed to each other, had the same general purport, viz. rendering the soul absolutely indifferent to everything which the real world had to offer.

LS: In other words, escapism, as we would say today. Yes?

Mr. Reinken:

These philosophies were therefore widely extended among the cultivated: they produced in man a self-reliant immobility as the result of Thought, i.e. of the activity which produces the Universal. But the inward reconciliation by means of philosophy was itself only an abstract one—in the pure principle of personality; for Thought, which, as perfectly refined—

LS: No, "which as pure."

Mr. Reinken:

which as pure, made itself its own object, and thus harmonized itself, was entirely destitute of a real object, and the immobility of Scepticism made aimlessness itself the object of the Will. This philosophy knew nothing but the negativity of all that assumed to be real, and was the counsel of despair to a world which no longer possessed anything stable—

LS: "Anything stable objectively." He doesn't say "objectively."

Mr. Reinken:

It could not satisfy the living Spirit, which longed after a higher reconciliation.[17]

LS: So this was then in a way the peak of the Roman Empire, these philosophies which supply abstract reconciliation. The individual philosopher finds a refuge entirely within. He does not find a reconciliation with the object, with life, because life is sheer misery from which you have to escape. This reflection here, which we find also in other writings of Hegel, is in a way the starting point of the Marxist critique of Hegel.

In his doctoral dissertation, which is devoted to Epicureanism, this is not merely meant as a historical study but as a philosophic critique of Hegel. Is the reconciliation with reality which Hegel claimed to have achieved in his philosophy not also such an abstract reconciliation and therefore in need of a supplement? Now this supplement could of course no longer be philosophy. The supplementation to Hegel could not be given in a philosophic manner because this would still be an abstract reconciliation. Therefore political action, ultimately revolution, will bring about reconciliation.

Here we come to the section on Christianity, which is in a way the most important part of the whole work. Perhaps we read first the beginning of that section.

Mr. Reinken:

> It has been remarked that Caesar inaugurated the Modern World on the side of reality, while its spiritual and inward existence was unfolded under Augustus.

LS: What does he mean by "Caesar's opening of the New World"? Well, the conquest of Transalpine Gaul and to some extent of Germany and Britain, i.e., these nations which were the bearers of the further development. The Germanic nations, as Hegel usually calls them.

Mr. Reinken:

> At the beginning of that empire, whose principle we have recognized as finiteness and particular subjectivity exaggerated to infinitude, the salvation of the World had its birth in the same principle of subjectivity—

LS: This is a fundamental agreement between Romanism and Christianity.

Mr. Reinken:

> viz. as a particular person, in abstract subjectivity; but in such a way that, conversely, finiteness is only the form of his appearance, while infinity and absolutely independent existence constitute the essence and substantial being which it embodies. The Roman World, as it has been described—in its desperate condition and the pain of abandonment by God—came to an open rupture with reality, and made prominent the general desire for a satisfaction such as can only be attained in "the inner man," the Soul—thus

preparing the ground for a higher Spiritual World. Rome was the Fate that crushed down the gods and all genial life in its hard service, while it was the power that purified the human heart from all specialty. Its entire condition is therefore analogous to a place of birth, and its pain is like the travail throes of another entire spirit, which manifested itself in connection with the Christian religion. This higher spirit involves the reconciliation and emancipation of spirit; while man attains the consciousness of spirit in its universality and infinity. The absolute object, truth, is spirit, and as man himself is spirit, he is present to himself in that object, and thus in his absolute object, has found essential being and his own essential being. But in order that the objectivity of essential being may be done away with, and spirit be no longer alien to itself—may be with itself—the naturalness of spirit—that in virtue of which man is a special, empirical existence—must be removed, so that the alien element may be destroyed and the reconciliation of Spirit be accomplished.[18]

LS: Here Hegel alludes to his general assertion that nature is in itself spirit, but spirit in an alienated form which is not aware of itself. And this destruction of this . . . is the true reconciliation. The Roman world has purified the human mind and heart from all particularity because it recognized only the individual as an abstract legal person. All men are actually or potentially persons. The slaves, for example, can be emancipated by any arbitrary action of their master. All are equally subject to a particular subjectivity, that of the emperor, and with no genuine bond uniting subjects and ruler, rulers and ruled. And this is so since the ruler is only a particular subjectivity: this individual. There is no satisfaction in the subjection to him; hence purification from all particularity. Page 319, line 7 from bottom.

Mr. Reinken:

The element of subjectivity that was wanting to the Greeks we found among the Romans; but as it was merely formal and in itself indefinite it took its material form from passion and caprice—even the most shameful degradations could be here connected with a divine dread.[19]

LS: So in spite of this very low form in which this principle was found in Rome, the principle itself implies an advance, a progress beyond Greekness. This is in accordance with what we have seen before.

In the sequel on page 320 following, Hegel takes up the issue of Judaism again. You know, he had spoken of it before when he spoke of the Oriental nations. But here he brings out what was not proper for him to bring out in speaking of the Orientals, and that is the story of the God of sin, the radicalization of that dissatisfaction characteristic of the Roman Empire—an essential dissatisfaction, an essential misery characteristic of the Roman Empire. Page 320, line 10 from bottom.

Mr. Reinken:

> That contradiction which afflicts the Roman world is the very state of things which constitutes such a discipline—the discipline of that culture which compels personality to display its nothingness. But it is reserved for us of a later period to regard this as a training; to those who are thus trained, it seems a blind destiny, to which they submit in the stupor of suffering. The higher condition, in which the soul itself feels pain and longing—in which man is not only "drawn," but feels that the drawing is into himself—is still absent. What has been reflection on our part—

LS: "What has been *only* reflection on our part." In other words, we, looking at this subject of the Roman Empire, see that, but they did not see it. "What was only our reflection." Yes?

Mr. Reinken:

> What has been only reflection on our part must arise in the mind of the subject of this discipline in the form of the consciousness that in himself he is miserable and null. Outward suffering must, as already said, be merged in the sorrow of the inner man. He must feel himself as the negation of himself. He must see that his misery is the misery of his nature, that he is in himself a divided and discordant being.

LS: And later he says of this spirit that we find the mythical presentation right at the beginning of the Jewish books, in the history of the Fall.

Mr. Reinken:

> Of this Spirit we have the mythical representation at the very beginning of the Jewish canonical books, in the account of the Fall. Man, created in the image of God, lost, it is said, his state of absolute contentment, by eating of the Tree of Knowledge of Good and Evil. Sin consists here only

in Knowledge: this is the sinful element, and by it man is stated to have trifled away his Natural happiness.

LS: Hegel cannot of course accept that literally; therefore he calls it "mythical." Because there cannot have been a perfect beginning, that we know. Now let us see how he interprets it.
Mr. Reinken:

This is a deep truth, that evil lies in consciousness: for the brutes are neither evil nor good; the merely Natural Man quite as little. Consciousness occasions the separation of the Ego, in its boundless freedom as arbitrary choice, from the pure essence of the Will—that is, from the Good. Knowledge, as the disannulling of the unity of mere Nature, is the "Fall," which is no casual conception, but the eternal history—

LS: No. "Which is not a contingent fact, but the eternal history of the spirit." So in other words, he doesn't take the story literally. Now he comes to the point, he makes it quite clear.
Mr. Reinken:

For the state of innocence, the paradisaical condition, is that of the brute. Paradise is a park, where only brutes, not men, can remain.

LS: Going back to the original meaning of the word . . . in Greek, which means a kind of zoo.
Mr. Reinken:

For the brute is one with God only implicitly. Only Man's Spirit (that is) has a self-cognizant existence. This existence for self—this consciousness—is at the same time separation from the Universal and Divine Spirit. If I hold to my abstract Freedom, in contraposition to the Good, I adopt the standpoint of Evil. The Fall is therefore the eternal *mythos* of Man—in fact, the very transition by which he becomes man.

LS: So in other words, it is not simply bad. Very far from it. That is already the interpretation of the Fall taken by Kant and accepted by Hegel.[20] So man becomes man only by virtue of this separation, by this knowledge of his subjectivity.
Mr. Reinken:

Persistence in this standpoint is, however, Evil, and the feeling of pain at such a condition, and of longing to transcend it, we find in David, when he says: "Lord, create for me a pure heart, a new steadfast spirit."

LS: The word "create" must be taken very literally here. It is truly a creation in the sense of the first sentence of the Bible, which comes out in the English translation clearer than in the German.
Mr. Reinken:

This feeling we observe even in the account of the Fall; though an announcement of Reconciliation is not made there, but rather one of continuance in misery. Yet we have in this narrative the prediction of reconciliation in the sentence, "The serpent's head shall be bruised"; but still more profoundly expressed where it is stated that when God saw that Adam had eaten of that tree, he said, "Behold Adam is become as one of us, knowing Good and Evil." God confirms the words of the Serpent.

LS: In other words, by the Fall man has become divine.
Mr. Reinken:

Implicitly and explicitly, then, we have the truth, that man through Spirit—through cognition of the Universal and the Particular—comprehends—

LS: "By this split." Man is not God, and yet in a way man is divine.
Student: That quotation, "Behold man has become *as* one of us." The fact that the quotation is "*as* one of us" implies really that God is saying not that man becomes divine, he has become like divinity only in this respect.
LS: Hegel would say that this is the decisive respect—knowledge.
Student: . . .
LS: But, still, the question is whether knowledge is not more important than immortality. Hegel will take up the question of immortality later.
Mr. Reinken:

Implicitly and explicitly, then, we have the truth, that man through Spirit—through cognition of the Universal and the Particular—comprehends God himself. But it is only God that declares this—not man: the latter remains, on the contrary, in a state of internal discord.

LS: In other words, man, Adam, does not know that he has become like God by knowledge.

Mr. Reinken:

> The joy of reconciliation is still distant from humanity; the absolute and final repose of his whole being is not yet discovered to man. It exists, in the first instance, only for God.[21]

LS: In other words, this points to Christianity, according to Hegel, because what was not so in the Old Testament becomes so in Christianity, in the first place in Jesus as the Christ—who is divine, who is God—and then eventually in all human beings insofar as they are Christians. Judaism has seen, and this is a great step, that man as man is a sinner, wholly alienated from God and yet to be redeemed by God. The carrying through of this is not to be found in Judaism, according to Hegel, but in Christianity. Hegel develops this more fully in the sequel. There is the truth of Christianity as a speculative truth which is the identity of the subject—i.e., of man—and God. The awareness of this identity is the knowledge of God in his truth. The content of truth is the mind or spirit itself, the living movement within itself. The nature of God, to be pure spirit, becomes manifest to man in the Christian religion. But this speculative truth is not sufficient. The speculative truth must also become visible, sensual certainty. So the second person of God, God's son, must become incarnated as man.

And what happens later is just the opposite: the liberation from the acceptance of the visible Jesus Christ as merely carnal, and the spiritual understanding of Jesus as the Christ which leads eventually to what Hegel regards as the speculative truth fully understood in his doctrine. That is the key point which he makes in the immediate sequel. The spiritual understanding of Christ is opposed to the carnal understanding, which implies the disregard of the miracles and of the sacredness of the mere text of the Gospels as a matter of course. Particularly important is one passage which we should surely consider on page 326, third paragraph.

Mr. Reinken:

> We have next to consider how the Christian view resulted in the formation of the Church. To pursue the rationale of its development from the Idea of Christianity would lead us too far, and we have here to indicate only the general phases which the process assumed. The first phase is the

founding of the Christian religion, in which its principle is expressed with unrestrained energy, but in the first instance abstractly. This we find in the Gospels, where the infinity of Spirit—its elevation into the spiritual world—is the main theme. With transcendent boldness does Christ stand forth among the Jewish people. "Blessed are the pure in heart, for they shall see God," he proclaims in the Sermon on the Mount—a dictum of the noblest simplicity, and pregnant with an elastic energy of rebound against all the adventitious appliances with which the human soul can be burdened.[22]

LS: Let us look at the other page, "Further on."
Mr. Reinken:

Further on, this doctrine, as the natural consequence of its appearing in an abstract form, assumes a polemical direction.

LS: More literally, "it becomes polemical."
Mr. Reinken:

"If thy right eye offend thee, pluck it out and cast it from thee; if thy right hand offend thee, cut it off and cast it from thee. It is better that one of thy members should perish and not that thy whole body should be cast into hell." Whatever might disturb the purity of the soul should be destroyed.

LS: There are similar remarks about property and acquisition. He quotes him again and says, "work for subsistence is rejected."
Mr. Reinken:

Labor for subsistence is thus reprobated: "Wilt thou be perfect, go and sell what thou hast, and give it to the poor, so shalt thou have a treasure in heaven, and come, follow me." Were this precept directly complied with, a social revolution must take place; the poor would become the rich. Of such supreme moment, it is implied, is the doctrine of Christ, that all duties and moral bonds are unimportant as compared with it.

LS: Now read the end of this paragraph. "Herein lies an abstraction."
Mr. Reinken:

Here then is an abstraction from all that belongs to reality, even from moral ties. We may say that nowhere are to be found such revolutionary utterances as in the Gospels; for everything that had been respected is treated as a matter of indifference—as worthy of no regard.[23]

LS: So the break with nature is with everything, really, even with all natural morality. It is unqualified. And on this basis a new understanding of morality in particular becomes possible, but this takes the whole course of the history of Christianity until Hegel's time. We cannot read this all. The main points will become clearer. Only one passage in the second half of page 335.

Mr. Reinken:

From time immemorial it has been customary to assume an opposition between Reason and Religion, as also between Religion and the World; but on investigation this turns out to be only a distinction.

LS: Not an opposition.
Mr. Reinken:

Reason in general is the Positive Existence of spirit, divine as well as human. The distinction between Religion and the World is only this—that Religion, as such, is Reason in the soul and heart—that it is a temple in which Truth and Freedom in God are presented to the conceptive faculty.

LS: Meaning, not to reason. In German, *Vorstellung*—"representation" would be the literal translation. That is something subrational.
Mr. Reinken:

The State, on the other hand, regulated by the self-same Reason, is a temple of Human Freedom concerned with the perception and volition of a reality—

LS: No, "is a temple of human freedom in the element of knowledge and the willing of reality."
Mr. Reinken:

whose purport may itself be called divine. Thus Freedom in the State is preserved and established by Religion, since moral rectitude in the State is only the carrying out of that which constitutes the fundamental principle of Religion.

LS: But that is of course not merely "only." As Hegel calls, it is a higher stage.

Mr. Reinken:

The process displayed in History is only the manifestation of Religion as Human Reason — the production of the religious principle which dwells in the heart of man, under the form of Secular Freedom.[24]

LS: You see the passage we discussed last time or the time before last, which is not in your edition: "Our form of state is something radically different from that of the Athenian people since our form of state can be altogether indifferent towards the inner lives, even towards religion."[25] The actualization, the fulfillment, of religion — in this case, of the Christian religion — is that religion becomes visible as human reason. That is to say that what was traditionally thought to be suprarational becomes fully evident to the fully developed human reason. Correspondingly, that the religious principle which dwells in the heart of man is produced also as worldly freedom. That this inner freedom of the mind, of the soul, becomes externalized and therewith comes into its own as worldly freedom, that is, political freedom.

Mr. Shulsky: What does it mean to say that the state is indifferent towards the inner life? Because it seems as if there isn't any more inner life that is specifically inner, because it is, so to speak, incorporated into the state.

LS: The modern state as Hegel sees it demands, according to him, that everyone be a member of a religious association, but the state is not interested in which. Take the most famous case, Prussia, for example. There were Catholic subjects as well as Protestants, although according to Hegel Protestantism, as opposed to Catholicism, comes closer to the full truth of Christianity. But Hegel also included the Jews. In other words, the modern state is tolerant. That is absolutely essential. And therefore in this sense the state is indifferent to the inner life. Whether a man is a philosopher and his peculiar religious philosophy is the philosophy of religion which Hegel presents, or whether he is a nonphilosophic Protestant, Catholic, or Jew, or whatever it may be, this doesn't make any difference to the state. That is what he means. The recognition of the rights of man, the recognition of the infinite value of the individual, this is much more important than the other things because, according to Hegel, this is the full realization of Christianity.

Mr. Shulsky: In the sense that this is the full realization, any inner life is in a sense irrelevant because there is no possible inner truth that couldn't be externalized, that already is a part of the state.

LS: This externalization, this recognition in deed of the humanity of every other human being is the full truth of Christianity as Hegel sees it, but which cannot be theoretically stated except in the form in which Hegel states it in his speculative philosophy.

Mr. Shulsky: According to this philosophy, then, which is somehow at the basis of the state, there isn't any inner life at all. It's not the same tolerance towards religion as we would think of as in this country where the state doesn't claim to . . .

LS: Hegel knew this, although he didn't know it in its special American form: the view that God cannot be known rationally; the maximum we can say is that God is, but nothing else. And Hegel rejects this. If this is so, then necessarily the emphasis would be concentrated on revealed religion in contradistinction to human reason, because the full truth about God is not accessible to reason. It is only available through revelation. Hegel wishes to make reason sovereign, and therefore the full knowledge of God, the perfect knowledge of God, must be accessible to reason.

There is a sentence in Spinoza's *Ethics*; I will speak it from recollection: "We know the essence of God."[26] Simply that. That is Hegel's view. I mean, at least Hegel knows it, and Hegel believes that everyone who takes the necessary troubles and is not particularly ill-fitted for this kind of study will also know the essence of God after having studied Hegel's *Phenomenology of the Mind* or *Logic*, and therefore there is no longer any claim of revealed religion to be the support or the guide for the highest form of the state. Reason can and must do it because it is seeing what faith only hopes for; and seeing is admittedly superior, other things being equal, to merely seeing through a glass darkly.

Mr. Shulsky: This tolerance of his is just a tolerance of whatever might be necessary for these nonphilosophers to have some glimpse of the truth and to fulfill themselves in some way. In other words, it allows people to be religious because essentially their religion can't do any harm.

LS: I think it is more. Hegel surely rejects this view. But the difficulty which exists from Hegel's point of view is that the alleged philosophic insight cannot but affect more and more also the mass of people. And this is a discord of which he speaks also at the end of his *Philosophy of Religion*. Hegel would never be as cynical as Voltaire: *Après nous, le déluge*—afterwards, the deluge. But in a way, he closed his eyes. Kant before him did not believe that irreligion would ever become socially powerful. Hegel apparently had some feelings that this was too sanguine.[27] Yes?

Student: Didn't Kant think that the essential points of moral philosophy, which had to do with action, were easy to understand for the common man? Did Hegel have the same view that everybody could really become a philosopher . . . essential aspect?

LS: No. Hegel was sure that much more is needed to know one's duties properly—I mean, not externally, because then you only have to ask someone versed in the laws of the land what you may or may not do. But to see the rationality of these laws—maybe the irrationality—that is truly knowledge of law, and this is not open to everybody but requires study and sometimes deep study.

Student: Do you think that the *Philosophy of History* is Hegel's attempt to give a philosophy to the masses? A substitute for the *Logic?*

LS: No. There is a difference between all lectures of Hegel, whether they are on the philosophy of history, on aesthetics, on religion, or on whichever subject, from the books which he published. They are not elaborated to the same extent. What we in fact read is always a composite made from the lecture notes of different hearers. That is of course a difference of some importance. I would assume that Hegel had some reticence, but much less than earlier philosophers, and he in a way rejects the principle of reticence. When he discusses the question of the traditional distinction which was still well known in his time between an esoteric and exoteric teaching—he does this in his lectures on the history of philosophy—he simply rejects that. He doesn't wish to have anything to do with it. And I think Hegel and his contemporary Schleiermacher[28] were more responsible than any other individuals for the fact that the distinction between esoteric and exoteric has ceased to be of any importance. I mean, also for the historians, not only for practice.

13 Interlude

The Concept of the Philosophy of History

Leo Strauss: Thank you very much. You had, as in a way everyone before you, a difficult assignment.[1] In your particular subject there was one difficulty due to the translation. The translator always speaks of "German" things, whereas Hegel mostly speaks of Germanic, which is not the same as German, especially in German itself. *Germanisch und deutsch* are clearly distinguishable things. Any impression which anyone might have gotten that Hegel is a kind of Germanic, Teutonic nationalist would be wholly wrong. Nothing is further from Hegel's mind. He means the old German . . . when he speaks of the original stratum. And for this he refers, as you have said, to Tacitus. And he accepts to some extent Tacitus's very flattering description, but this description of Tacitus was of course made for intra-Roman purposes, to remind these corrupt Romans of a people which were not corrupt.

There is one word which Hegel uses to describe the thing which he believes is peculiar to the Germanic people, and therefore also to the Germans proper, and that is also not translatable. In one case which you quoted, the English translation was "heart." The German word is *Gemüt*. Absolutely untranslatable. Mr. Mewes knows that. This is something of which many Germans are very proud, especially Germans who came to other countries where they did not find that *Gemüt*. Now what is it? It is very hard. I cannot translate it, but I will give you perhaps one illustration at the lowest level. A *gemütlicher Abend*, a *gemütlich* evening, or a *gemütlich* beer club. Something where you are perfectly at your ease and everyone is friendly and outspoken. That is very important. That is another part of the German understanding, that the Germans are honest people. Goethe has said the harshest word about *Gemütlichkeit*; he said that it is the indulgence of one's own and other people's weaknesses. A very easygoing posture, so Goethe did not have much use for it. Hegel tries to interpret in this way in a language which is translatable. It has to do with the inner man as distinguished from any external things, including of course also manners on all levels. I have often heard from people who came from Germany especially to this country and Great Britain that they couldn't understand why people were very friendly and courteous, i.e., they behaved in a way in which in Germany friends would behave towards each other. And then they saw of course that this courtesy was, as they put it, very superficial and deceptive because there was no indication of friendship. This is another simple illustration of the negative side of this kind of thing. We will perhaps say something more when we come to the passage.

In this whole assignment Hegel contrasts two radically different forms of Christianity: the one which seemed to be much more promising because it emerged within the Roman Empire itself, Byzantium; and the other which seemed to be much less promising, that of the northern barbarians. And yet Hegel's view is that the latter was in fact pregnant with a great future, whereas Byzantium was a kind of dead end. How can you restate this point? What was the reason that nothing came out of Byzantium and the whole development came out of Europe?

Miss Heldt: It seems to me that part of it has to do with the idea of the development of the Christian principle. You put it into Byzantium—he answers that they had a very good system of government. He mentions the Justinian Code.

LS: But what kind of government was it?

Miss Heldt: It was an absolute and arbitrary government.

LS: In the coincidence of power spiritual and power temporal, and this was the root. In the West, among these barbarians, there was a possibility of a development towards freedom, although this was not genuine freedom as long as they remained at the tribal stage for many centuries to come. Or, as Hegel puts it more precisely, in the old culture of the East, Byzantium, Christianity was superimposed on an old culture of a wholly non-Christian character. Therefore this higher stratum could not permeate, enliven, and restore the lower, whereas among the Germanic tribes there was nothing of any high character; there was simple barbarism. There was nothing to oppose the acceptance. The old German tribes had no culture whatsoever, and they were therefore open to this possibility of accepting Christianity, of course originally in a very crude manner. But they had no heritage of their own, no specifically Germanic inheritance which hampered the possible development of Christian thought. I believe that that is one of the crucial points.

What about the other alternative which Hegel discusses here, Islam?

Of course Islam is not Christianity, that goes without saying. But if we state it in very general terms today as ordinary historians, why was this Islamic world in a way much more civilized than Christianity in the early Middle Ages? One has said, and I think quite rightly, that in Islam the Renaissance antedated the Middle Ages. The acceptance of Greek science and philosophy took place in the ninth and tenth centuries, and later on came the Dark Ages in Islam. This is an undeniable fact. How come? Without speculating, why did Islam lose its great power, not only of expansion, relatively soon, whereas it took a longer time in the Christian world and it lasted there much longer? After all, what is happening now is the Westernization of the whole world taking place in spite of communism, a work of the West, i.e., of an originally Christian world and surely not the work of an Islamic world. The Islamic nations are as much emerging nations as the other emerging nations. How come? I mean, quite externally and superficially—after all, that's a question which one must raise.

Miss Heldt: First, I think that you have to look at the country in which they live. On the deserts it is a roaming life, primarily.

LS: Yes. But they conquered the Fertile Crescent very soon, and Egypt and northern Africa, which is also rather fertile, and they went very deep into Europe—into Spain, even into France, and into Sicily, and so on. It was touch and go. Gibbon plays with the notion that they might have conquered Europe, and then today, as he puts it in the eighteenth century, in Oxford the Koran might be expounded instead of the New Testament.[2] Why did the opposite take place?

Miss Heldt: The Islamic religion provides a basis for political organization that Christianity didn't in the German world.

LS: Yes, but that leads us into very subtle things. But if we start from the external things—for example, you said something about location. The core of Islamic power was in Asia, i.e., close to these devastators, the Turks and their kin, who were not permitted to enter Europe. They were also very close, and it was also sometimes touch and go, but in the main they were defeated, whereas the Turks defeated the Arab nations. That is one point which one must not forget. But beyond that, speaking first of the entirely external things without going into the principles of religion, the tremendous achievements of modern Europe were made possible through such things as astronomy, seafaring, and the invention of the compass, and in all these matters the Arabs were much more advanced, say, around 900. Baghdad was the place to go if you wanted to study these things, and there was nowhere in Western Europe. For some time the Arabs were the leading discoverers. That was completely changed by the fifteenth century, and surely beyond that. How come? How come the development of these sciences which are so important for human power, the natural sciences in the widest sense, collapsed there more or less and developed in the West? What were the centers of study in Christian Europe?

Miss Heldt: The monasteries . . .

LS: And universities. Yes. The corresponding things in Islam did not give the same leeway to the secular sciences. That was one very important point. And Hegel would of course say that there is a necessary connection between Islam not making use of science to the degree to which Christianity made use of it. He quotes a famous leader of the Muslims—what was his name?—Omar the conqueror of Alexandria.[3] Yes?

Student: These books either say what the Koran says or they say what Augustine is saying; in either case, you don't need them.

LS: If they say what the Koran says, they are superfluous; if they say anything different they are detrimental; *ergo* let us burn libraries. I do not know whether that is a true story or not. At any rate, in Christianity the worldly sciences were accepted and integrated into the teaching. But there is something else which is not directly connected with it but is also a brute fact. This is the development of free cities in the West, first in Italy, and then also in Germany and France. The cities in the East were residences, they were not an affair of the citizen body. Max Weber has discussed this question quite well and put all the evidence together about the difference between the Western cities, which in a way continue the old city tradition of Greece and Rome, and the Eastern cities—I mean, not only of the Islamic world, but also in India and China, which were primary residences where the ruler and his court were the core of the city.[4] Cities became the centers of civic freedom and to some extent also intellectual freedom. Hegel mentions all these things and tries to link them up with the fundamental radical difference between Christianity on the one hand and Islam on the other.

We have to interrupt this course in order to remind ourselves of the whole context, going beyond Hegel: the very notion of a philosophy of history. (May I suggest that someone close that door? For reasons that only Sigmund Freud could explain, it disturbs me.) If we go back to the very notion of political philosophy, it was based from the very beginning on the difference between the good and the ancestral: the *agathon* and *patrium*. You will find this in the second book of Aristotle's *Politics*. We can say with some justice that the good means the rational. That is surely the way in which Hegel understands it. But what about the ancestral or, rather, since the ancestral is necessarily many, the various forms of the ancestral? One could say they are divinations or fragments of *the* good and even soiled fragments of it. There is an infinite variety in this respect, at least possibly. No rhyme and reason. One can say this was the Platonic view of this problem. Hegel says: No, there is an order among these ancestrals. I hope that you have no difficulty in understanding the word. It is meant to be a literal translation of the Greek *patrium*, the ancestral institutions, thoughts, etc. There is an order among them and an ascending order. Not only is the end towards which they point—whether they are African or Chinese—rational, the way towards the end is itself rational. It could not have been different. Therefore one can also say, turning it around, that the rational is the final ancestral. So there is always some harmony between the rational and the ancestral. At the end there is complete reconciliation of reason and tradition. The proof of this is allegedly given in Hegel's philosophy of history.

Now philosophy of history, to remind you of that again and again, is a characteristically modern thing: there is nothing which one can properly call philosophy of history in premodern times. But even in modern times we do not yet find it in the founding stage, the stage of Machiavelli, Hobbes, Locke, or Descartes. The term was coined in 1750, that is to say almost yesterday as these things go, by Voltaire. I do not go into the question of what Voltaire meant by it, but we are of course not concerned merely with the term. But as for the matter, one can say it emerged—and that has often been said—in Vico's *New Science*, earlier than Voltaire. Vico tries to present an ideal, eternal history. It is interesting that it is an ideal history and therefore not history pure and simple. In Rousseau's *Second Discourse*, he explicitly gives a history of man which is truly philosophic in inspiration. No proper names occur. Now what leads to this development of which Vico and Rousseau are perhaps the first outstanding writers? In the case of Vico, it is the question of natural law in the sense of the moral law. Here a question arises. Natural law cannot exist and have obligatory power—a law which has no obligatory power is no law—if it is not duly promulgated. And the natural law is not duly promulgated among all the peoples in the world which are not sufficiently developed, as people would say today. In other words, the basis of this development is the connection between the notion of natural law and the origins of mankind.

The Christian natural law teaching in particular was of course based on the biblical notion of the origin of mankind: divine creation. A first couple. When this was questioned and a very imperfect beginning was assumed, then the question arose how these very imperfect beings could have had any inkling of any rational provisions or commands. The natural law, which is a law of reason, cannot have been known and hence been obligatory at the beginning but only after a long development. This means that the root of the development leading to history is not historical discoveries of some kind, as it is presented sometimes in popular presentations. People suddenly heard of the Indians in America or other people who were in no way provided for by the biblical account as it was always understood. These historical discoveries came in only in a subsidiary fashion. The fundamental question concerns the beginnings of mankind, a question which could have been raised and was in fact raised prior to the discovery of America, and surely wholly independently of it. I do not deny that these arguments taken from fact—say, from the American Indians, and also the peoples hitherto unknown, the Chinese, for example—did play a certain role. You can see that when you read Locke's *Essay concerning Human Understanding*, the first part and the reference to this fact. There is even an older tradition of this kind connected with the Socinians. They are those people who now are called Unitarians. They were called after an Italian, [Fausto] Sozzino, who founded this group.

The view that men's beginnings were imperfect, barbaric, savage, cannibalistic, whatever you call it, was of course not new. It was the view of the ancient philosophers, as you can see most clearly from Plato's *Laws* if you read it carefully, and from Lucretius's poem, book 5.[5] But very strangely, this view did not lead in antiquity to anything like a philosophy of history. Lucretius's fifth book is particularly interesting in this respect. Lucretius gives what now would be called a history of man from the cannibalistic beginnings up to the foundations of cities, etc. But what is the difference between Lucretius's account and the apparently similar account which Rousseau gave of it in the *Second Discourse*? Rousseau's *Second Discourse* is based on Lucretius; therefore the question is particularly pertinent. Very simply, for Lucretius this process takes place infinitely often. The earth comes into being, later on man, and then there are these various stages from simpleminded idiots at the beginning, and then on and on, and then also an end of the earth, of course, an end of mankind. Whereas in the modern view—in all these writers, whether Hegel, Rousseau, or whoever you take—there is only one historical process. Of course, the Marxists naturally are included; this is crucial. Even in Vico one can find some traces, though not very important ones, of this infinite repetition. The reason is this: classical philosophy, whether Platonic or Epicurean, was, we can say, cosmological. It was concerned with the cosmos and saw men within the cosmos and saw therefore something like the changes in human thoughts and in human societies within the cosmic context.

In modern philosophy this is no longer the case; therefore in order to understand the genesis of this modern notion of history one would have to understand what it means that this preponderantly cosmological approach was replaced by another approach. One would also, in the first place, have to find a good word for that other approach, because without some designation we are still worse off than with it. For the classics, the cosmos is, we can say, in itself, and it is to be discovered by man. This is somehow changed now. Of course every physicist today would naturally also say, provided he does not follow a special epistemological school but says what he is actually doing, that he will discover what is in itself. But nevertheless, in modern times this became doubtful. A simple expression of this change is Hobbes's remark that we understand only what we make,[6] i.e., if we merely discover something, it is essentially unintelligible. We understand only what we make. By the way, this sentence of Hobbes's was taken over by Vico, who used it for his purposes, because if we discover only what we make, then, since we obviously didn't make the cosmos, the cosmos can no longer be the guiding theme. For Descartes, the beginning is the thinking ego, not the cosmos.

Now one can, as some people have done, make the distinction in the following way: that premodern philosophy—these terms are not the best by any means, but they are perhaps useful as a way towards understanding—that premodern philosophy was "objectivistic"; modern philosophy is fundamentally "subjectivistic." Now subjectivistic not in the sense of relativism, of course, but that the thinking, understanding subject is the origin of all meaning. This distinction is reflected within a distinction closer to our immediate interest, the distinction between the natural law, say in the Thomistic sense, and the rights of man. The emphasis shifts in modern times from the natural law in the older sense to the rights of man. And the rights are called in continental European terminology— not Anglo-Saxon—"subjective rights," which is an indication of the connection. Now these points to which I alluded and which need a very long discussion are however only the necessary but not the sufficient condition of the discovery of history, as is simply proved by the fact that such people as Hobbes and Descartes had the same and even a greater indifference to history proper than the traditional philosophers had.

I will not try to develop this any further. But I would like to mention only one other point we have to consider if we would like to answer the question: What is at the bottom of the fact that in the last 150 years people speak of history as philosophically relevant? That history is relevant in other respects was always understood and is wholly uninteresting. For example, if you are engaged in a war which is not going too well, then it is a matter of ordinary common sense known at all times that you have to find out why you started that war, what were the previous events, were there other wars in that region and how did they go, etc. These are all historical studies without any philosophic interest . . .

To mention another point of philosophic interest, we have mentioned before that within political philosophy itself, the key change at first sight is that from the concern with the best regime—with *ariste politeia*, which must be possible but is not necessarily actual at any time, its actualization depending on chance—to Machiavelli's opposition to these imagined commonwealths, the best regimes sketched more or less in detail by the ancients. Taking one's bearings by how men do live in contradistinction to how they ought to live still led to ideals, but to a new kind of ideal, closer to earth, whose actualization is probable. And the probability of the actualization is due to enlightenment. Say Hobbes or Locke discovers what the best regime is, and of course that best regime is not actual—and surely in most parts of the earth it is not actual, even if there should be an approximation to it in blessed England. Still, Locke publishes his book, people read it and become convinced of it. The readers are naturally the emphatically literate people, ordinarily at that time people belonging to the higher classes—not only professors but also parsons, for example, and other opinion leaders, as they are now called, who influence the nonliterate and half-literate people. In other words, if enlightenment is necessary, if the spreading of knowledge is a necessary consequence of the acquisition of knowledge, then the actualization of the best regime is necessary. Is that not so? Chance is controlled. Is this point clear?

Mr. Reinken: It is a necessary consequence.

LS: Aristotle has discovered the best regime, let us say; and of course he doesn't have a ghost of a chance to put it into practice because he doesn't have the power. Assuming that Aristotle did discover the best regime, what about the readers of Aristotle or his students in the widest sense? Is the truth not compelling? Must they not admit that he is right? Of course their interest may be against it, and we know what Hobbes said: "As often as reason is against man, man is against reason."[7] But this doesn't last forever. You know, this may still happen in the case of the old fogies, but their sons, younger and more generous, would say: No, it is indeed not in my interest to keep this tremendous estate and have these people all as serfs. It is unjust and I can't stand it. Maybe one, maybe two. Gradually this leads further, this will spread. This is one crucial point.

This is connected with another point. The necessity of enlightenment is based on another necessity, namely, on the necessity of intellectual progress. Man has reached a certain stage of understanding, but only a certain stage. That is to say, there are many obscure spots on the intellectual globe, but they solicit interest. The next generation already has the acquisitions of the preceding generations within them, acquired while they study. They stand on the shoulders of the preceding generation, and that is where the saying, made famous by Pascal, comes from: that dwarfs standing on the shoulders of giants see farther ahead than the giants.[8] In other words, there is no unbecoming immodesty if we say that we are wiser than these great men of the past. We are dwarfs, but standing on their shoulders somehow, without their merit, we know better. All these kinds of things came together and made it compelling for man in the eighteenth century to say that the human mind necessarily progresses and its results necessarily spread. And then by the spread of knowledge the people become enlightened and opinion is changed; and if opinion is changed, power is changed, because power will now move in a different direction than it moved before it was enlightened.

These very simple things—which we have forgotten because they have become entirely a matter of course—were certain "acquisitions" of the seventeenth and eighteenth centuries which altered the nature not only of political philosophy but of political life very profoundly. Add this to what I said before, the Machiavellian thing, starting from the low ground. The older philosophy, appealing to the highest demands of virtue, didn't find many takers for the very simple reason that you were promised a perfect society, but at the price of severe self-sacrifice. But now you were told that by indulging your desire for wealth, for example—judiciously, of course, investing properly and wisely—you would not only become a rich man but a greater benefactor of mankind than anyone else. Because if you are a rich man and give alms, what kind of help is that? That drunkard will go to his establishment as he went before. But if you make it possible and necessary for him to be a hardworking, honest, sober, austere worker, you benefit him and his family and so forth. This is a fantastic picture, but it is not a fairy tale. It is a very important part of what happened in the last centuries.

This is a crucial element of the conception of history as it emerged in modern times. All of this is presupposed by Hegel, integrated into his philosophy. He fully accepted the modern economic teaching of Adam Smith. He integrated it. Naturally, by integrating it into this whole, he also modified it. That is surely true. The consequence is the teaching which Hegel pronounced with particular authority, that the actual and the rational necessarily coincide, whereas the traditional view was the commonsensical view that they don't necessarily coincide; it is chance if they coincide. The most specific construction is this, that there is an absolute epoch in which the full coincidence of both takes place, the fulfillment, the epoch in which all fundamental theoretical problems—who cares about the cat and the mole and such trivial questions—all fundamental problems, theoretical and practical, are solved. The practical problems, not only on paper, in blueprints, but in fact. The modern state exists. This is the situation in Hegel. Now there is here this difficulty which we have mentioned more than once. This full knowledge has been called since time immemorial "wisdom," but one also distinguished between theoretical and practical wisdom. What Hegel has primarily in mind is the theoretical wisdom, because the knowledge of the best polity, the best regime, however we might call that, is in Hegel not a matter of a practical philosophy in the Aristotelian sense; but the philosophy of right, as Hegel calls it, is as theoretical as his *Logic*, for example. This theoretical wisdom has the unfortunate characteristic that it belongs to a period of decay, the point which Rousseau made to the disgust of many people in his *Discourse on the Arts and Sciences*, but which is accepted by Hegel, as we have seen, in his philosophy of history. In Hegel's very telling formula, the owl of Minerva—the goddess of wisdom—begins its flight in the dusk. So when we have reached wisdom, the dusk begins.

Now where do we find traces of that dusk according to Hegel? For Hegel, the fundamental—that does not mean the highest—but the fundamental phenomenon of what we now call culture is religion. A nation gives to itself the definition of its being in its religion, as he puts it. Now what happened to religion? We know that there is a variety of religions leading up to the absolute religion, Christianity, culminating in the reconciliation of the absolute religion, Christianity, with the world. Originally Christianity was simply unworldly; obviously it did not permeate the world in its first stage because the world was pagan, but even in the early Christian stage, including the Middle Ages, there was a separation of the worldly and the unworldly, and that is Hegel's chief objection to the Middle Ages. Eventually, Christianity permeates the world, or to put it another way, Christianity becomes worldly and not in a negative sense: Christianity becomes worldly, i.e., it completely transforms the world. Christianity becomes completely secularized.

As a consequence, as Hegel puts it—we have seen the passage—the modern state, the rational state, is indifferent to religion. It is secular also in this sense. Especially striking are the passages in Hegel's *Lectures on the Philosophy of Religion,*[9] towards the end and also in other passages, where it ends with a discord, as he himself calls it. Christianity has become fully understood, i.e., religion has been transformed into philosophy taught by Hegel at the University of Berlin. The true theology is Hegel's philosophy, i.e., it is no longer theology proper. This of course affects the students and in a wider sense all the educated classes or, as they said in the nineteenth century, the classes of culture and property. But there are also the common people. What about them? They surely do not have the comfort of Hegelian philosophy. Hegel cannot do more than shrug his shoulders. He knows that sooner or later the circles of property and culture-think will affect the simple people. The circles of culture and property cannot always stop conversation when a maid enters at a dinner. That is the practical way in which these things happen. Or they cannot always speak a foreign language, say, French instead of German, which was also a simple device. So the common people will gradually be affected by what is going on among their betters, but they don't become philosophers or anything like philosophers. They are in a difficult situation, a discord. Hegel has no comfort for us at this point.[10]

But there is something else which today is regarded as a sufficient substitute. According to a very crude and vulgar saying of Goethe, who was once asked to write something in his diary, and he wrote down: "He who possesses science and art, possesses religion. He who does not possess science and art ought to possess religion."[11] It is not a very good . . . What about art, of which we hear so much? Hegel makes it quite clear: art cannot have the position with us which it had with the Greeks. We have seen that the Greek world was a world of sensible beauty, of art. That is no longer possible afterwards. As Hegel puts it in his *Aesthetics* somewhere:"Art in respect of its highest destiny is for us a matter of the past,"[12] i.e., there may be people who still produce sculptures, paintings, poems, dramas, but they can no longer be matters of the first rank. That is absolutely impossible. Art can no longer be what it was in its highest times, say, in Greece and in the Middle Ages: a bond of the whole society. In these worlds, the greatest works of art were intelligible and appealing to every member of the society. The depth of understanding would differ, naturally, from individual to individual, but everyone could understand the Madonna. They knew what the Madonna was and what this meant. The same is of course true of Zeus or Athena. Art can no longer be something in which the whole society recognizes itself and its best. The time for art has gone. In other words, the later art, as we have it today, appeals to certain small circles. But as we have seen from the reaction of General Eisenhower and Khrushchev to abstract painting[13]—I believe there are some other examples nearer to home—this is no longer intelligible for the whole community. You have to be a kind of specialist, just as you have to be a specialist in theoretical physics, to understand it. Art can no longer have this function.

What takes the place? Hegel would say that there are two things. At the top, naturally, philosophy, including science. And I think the authority of science, at least, is unquestionable in our age. The other is the rational state, revealing itself in reasonable laws. This is a bit more complicated, but still there is no question that law still has in principle this authority in our age, however poor enforcement of law and so on might be.

This is the phenomenon which Hegel has seen clearly. What came later on was what Max Weber called "the disenchantment."[14] But Hegel understood it, I think, more precisely. Religion and art have ceased to be forces keeping society together. That they still exist within society does not contradict what Hegel says. The meaning of "disenchantment" in Weber is not quite the same as in Hegel. I mention it only in passing. The man who popularized Hegel's view is Spengler, the decline of the West understood as the decline of the last culture. No further culture is possible.

Now if this is so, if the absolute epoch is the end stage with this ambiguity, it is at the same time the fulfillment and the beginning of the way down. How can this be reconciled with the belief in providence to which Hegel refers and which is at least a clear enough popular expression of what Hegel surely thought? Five thousand years up to the peak in around 1800. Let us be generous. One thousand or two thousand years for the spread of it, so that all the loose ends which still exist might be taken care of, one of the loose ends being that China and India have to be completely Westernized, this kind of thing. Then what Spengler called the "universal fellahinism." You know what *fellahin* are? The Arabic expression for the poor peasant populations, especially in the Nile Valley. Heirs of the oldest culture in the world and completely deprived of any meaning. Just mere relics, leftovers. Until, of course, human life becomes impossible on earth after—the estimates change, two billion years now? And all this takes place only on the earth. The infinite universe is a desert: nothing of any interest to the mind, nothing spiritual happens there, at least as far as we know. Is this not a terribly depressing picture of the whole, and not one which would correspond to any notions of a world governed by divine providence?

What would Hegel say? I believe he would say that we must not be impressed by sheer bulk, by immense numbers regarding space or time, billions of years or the same regarding space. These infinite deserts of space or time are the very condition for the relatively small space and time where reason is actual on earth. And this is the peak. The justification of everything else is the peak. All these masses of uninhabited and uninhabitable stars, or seeming stars, or whatever it may be, all these deserts— even on earth there are lots of deserts—all of this is necessary for the sake of the mind understanding itself. Did Hegel give us that analysis of nature as we know it or believe to know it, showing that nature had to have this character, these peculiar infinities or immensities at any rate, in order to make history possible? This leads to quite a few other questions. I see the time has so advanced, it is of very little use now to begin then.

May I add one point? The question of time especially comes up. Between six billion years and a split second there is only a quantitative difference, as is indicated by the use of numbers. The real difficulty arises when we speak of infinite time, a time which can no longer be numbered—we cannot strictly call it eternity, but it is surely in no way numerable. Therefore the question is: What is time? According to the Aristotelian notion, time is necessarily related to motion; and if there is a time at which there is no motion whatsoever, there was no time. According to what I have read about these present-day speculations of physicists, we come back eventually to a hydrogen atom, which was there; in the moment it became decomposed, then motion started. But up to this point, there was no motion, no time. So time is finite. That is one part of this argument. One can also show the problem of infinite time is a fundamental difficulty on other grounds.

Student: Would you say—[15]

LS: —Rousseau regarded it as necessary, but Rousseau attached a much greater importance than Hegel to the purely mechanical causation—the climate, population pressures, etc.—as distinguished from the intrinsic needs of the mind towards its own actualization.

Student: Then philosophy of history must ultimately rest on a dualistic kind of system.

LS: It is hard to say to what extent Hegel's doctrine is dualistic, if nature is only the alienated form of the mind. That is what Hegel says. Mind which has so externalized to itself that it is no longer recognizable as such; and only by deeper study can one see that even in this mindless form it is still mind which has made itself, as it were, mindless. But what do you have in mind? Because then you would turn around and say: What about Marx?

Student: Well, Kant would be the first, because there is nothing other than mind.

LS: The case of Kant is different because there is no doubt that Kant speaks of philosophy of history. But the philosophy of history is not, if one may say so, a part of his system. That is one of the most obvious difficulties in Kant. In Kant's system there is the critique of pure reason, the critique of practical reason, and the critique of judgment. Philosophy of history doesn't play any role there. The problem comes up nevertheless and is treated by him in some more occasional writings. To give only one reason why Kant is not immediately relevant here, the problem of the philosophy of history arises in the context of the question: Will the just order be actualized? Will it be actually established on earth? Will virtue become fully actual? But is there not an alternative to philosophy of history in the answer to this question? Assuming we are tolerably decent people, we try to be tolerably virtuous, but we don't quite succeed. Our virtue is more or less always imperfect. This is very unsatisfactory and we want to have a fully virtuous humanity. To some extent that depends on the political organization. It is possible to be compelled by the political order to be nasty and mean to your fellow man. It's possible; then the laws may make it a punishable offense not to be nasty; then it's not possible. So one thing of great importance is to have the right political order. But assuming that the order is right, so we are not compelled by law to act immorally, we will still not be moral fully. What hope is there for morality? The hope cannot be fulfilled by the establishment of the best political order, because this does not solve all difficulties.

You see how corrupt you are—if I may say so, I do not mean you in particular. In former times people thought—some people, that is—that we have a chance beyond our earthly life. There is a life after death, the immortality of the soul. And so while we cannot become fully virtuous in our finite life on earth, we have a chance after death. This is a part of Kant's system. The immortality of the soul is a postulate of pure reason. I would say that because the immortality of the soul is a postulate of pure reason, the philosophy of history is very uninteresting for Kant. It is not wholly unimportant, but the solution is in life after death.

Now let us draw a general conclusion. The emphasis on historical redemption increases in proportion as the concern with redemption in eternity decreases. Does this not make sense?—[16]

LS: I think the whole difficulty of Kant's moral-political teaching is really concentrated in the fact that Kant sees the importance of the political. There is no question that for Kant the just political order, the rights of man and so on, is of crucial importance. But they were only a part of a larger whole, and therefore the philosophy of history could only be an almost marginal part of Kant's teaching. Differently stated, the problem of the individual which is not solvable by any social or politic improvement of any kind retains its full force for Kant; therefore he has a relatively small interest in the philosophy of history. That is the point where Kierkegaard, criticizing Hegel, rejoins Kant. The indifference or quasi-indifference of Kierkegaard to world history is in a way a return to Kant on the part of a moralist who does not expect as much from politics as Hegel does.

For Hegel it is understood that if you have the right social order there will of course be crimes, naturally. That is easy; that is not a fundamental problem because we have our policemen, district attorneys, gallows, etc. So the actualization of morality means you have a reasonably decent state in which there will always be a certain amount of crime and vice—that goes without saying and we take it in our stride; that cannot be helped. And don't make too much fuss about the true virtue, purity of intention; that only leads to hypocrisy. A man who behaves decently on the whole is a virtuous man, and the worms which he might find by analysis in his heart or bosom, they are of no interest. In this respect Hegel reminds me a bit of Aristotle but goes much beyond him because Hegel never wrote an *Ethics*; and when he speaks about the virtues he assumes we all know what these virtues are, that we are supposed to have them and that we are more or less decent people. There is no hard searching. This leads to all kinds of bad things, and this is of course what Kierkegaard opposes, this social-political solution that the concern for purity of the heart has lost its meaning almost completely. And that meant a return to Kant.

But to come back to the great interest of Kant, it is truly that he was confronted by an already existing philosophy of history: there was Herder, whose name you are familiar with. And Kant had somehow to face it, but he faced it in this way: by not permitting its entrance into the system proper. And that which blocked the entrance directly was the immortality of the soul. This makes perfect sense, doesn't it?

This was more of a lecture than a seminar, if we disregard your paper, but we will take up the subject of your paper the next time.

14 The Middle Ages

Leo Strauss: That was a very satisfactory paper.[1] You selected your quotation wisely because it makes perfectly clear where Hegel stands. You pointed out that Hegel's view of the Middle Ages is not peculiar to him. How would you call this view of the Middle Ages, if it is not Hegelian in particular, if it is simply a negative judgment of the Middle Ages?

Student: What I meant was that his objections to the content of the Catholic Church at that time were fairly common.

LS: Where? Be specific.

Student: I was just referring to the Protestant Reformation.

LS: I see, so the Protestant Reformation. And what about feudalism, which he also includes in his condemning statement?

Student: He must stand with the Enlightenment philosophy.

LS: Yes, the bad Gothic. That is clear. The final judgments of Hegel are not so different from what quite a few Protestants and men of the Enlightenment had said. What is the difference? What is the peculiarity of Hegel's view?

Student: His basis for the Reformation can be understood as almost purely secular.

LS: Yes. This is not immediately clear from our previous readings because we have not yet read what Hegel says about the Reformation, and in addition, I believe it is not simply true. What are the most obvious differences between Hegel and Voltaire in these matters? For Voltaire it was a terrible barbarism but it is not justifiable; Hegel says that he sees a necessity. That is a great difference, as appears from your very quotation. He uses unusually strong language, as is clear from your paper: "The infinite lie." What does he mean by that? The simplest thing: here you have the Holy Roman Empire, a state which is sanctified by being holy, and what is it in fact? Lawlessness. And the only glimmers you will find of some emerging political order which is not lawless are the cities. But what is much more important for Hegel is the fact that higher than the power temporal is the power spiritual, the holy Church; and according to Hegel, it was not only in fact most unholy, but it was necessarily most unholy. If you take the extreme case, say, what he says about Africa, there he doesn't use such strong language because there is no high claim. These merely natural men, savages, don't claim to be civilized, higher, and so on. But here the contrast between the claim and the reality is shocking, but Hegel does not leave it at indignation and condemnation. He is very much concerned with condemning. In other words, there could not have been modernity but for the horrors of the Middle Ages. We must never forget it.

Now let us turn to a discussion of the passages. We have to proceed at a rather fast pace because we have so little time. We begin at page 336 where he speaks about Byzantium. At the beginning there is a remark where he says that "the Roman Empire comprised the whole civilized earth," which means India and China do not belong to it because they were never part of the Roman Empire. And not because they are simply uncivilized, that would be true only of Africa, but they are dead-end streets; there is no future. Then he speaks of how the late pagans, after Christianity was victorious, looked at the situation. Page 336 paragraph 2, towards the end, after the quotation.

Mr. Reinken:

All that was contemned is exalted; all that was formerly revered is trodden in the dust. The last of the pagans express this enormous contrast with profound lamentation.[2]

LS: Hegel of course does not look at it from the pagan point of view, because for Hegel the contemptible and the condemned are in a fundamental sense higher than the glorified. In Hegel's *Phenomenology of the Mind*, the fundamental discussion deals with master and slave, the great theme. For Hegel there are no natural slaves. The slave is the one who just gives in, who rather switches than fights; and the master is the one who rather fights than switches. [Laughter] That doesn't depend on anything in their natures, but on an act of will. So slavery and mastery are neither conventional nor natural but due to acts of will. The whole construction of the philosophy of history in the *Phenomenology of the Mind* starts from this fact: that the master who has this contempt for violent ends uses the slave, exploits him, and enjoys himself. This is the dead-end street,

whereas the slave who works, who transforms nature, who thus understands the matter which he has to transform—this is the starting point of
all true civilization. That is directly opposite to the Aristotelian scheme.
You see that however far Hegel is from democracy in the narrow political
sense, this fundamental democracy is a part of Hegel.

In the sequel he speaks of the superiority of Western Latin Christianity from the Christian point of view. In the West, the root of all culture
or civilization is Christianity, on which the ancient heritage is grafted
secondarily. These Germanic tribes became familiar with classical culture
only via Christianity, whereas in Byzantium the opposite was the case:
the classical pagan culture antedated the Christianization. And therefore
the modern world which arose from Latin Christianity and not from
Greek Christianity is radically Christian. The same would not be true of
Byzantium.

Let us turn to page 338 when he speaks of Byzantium. Here we can
see how the Christian religion can be abstract and as such weak, precisely
because it is so pure in itself spiritually. This is peculiar of Byzantium
rather than of the West. The otherworldliness of Christianity implies
the possibility that it leaves the world absolutely as it is, and since this
world as it is exerts some power, it will corrupt the purity, whereas in the
West the opposite was at least attempted. There occurs a passage which
in my edition is underlined. "The Byzantine Empire is the great example
of how the Christian religion can remain abstract in a civilized or cultured
people, if the whole organization of the state and of the laws is not recon-
structed according to Christian principles."[3] The implication is that in the
West the opposite happened, not to begin with but over many centuries.
But only the Western world is truly Christian.

Let us turn to page 341, first paragraph. The beginning of the section
on the Germanic world.

Mr. Reinken:

The German Spirit—

LS: "The *Germanic* Spirit."
Mr. Reinken:

The Germanic Spirit is the Spirit of the new World. Its aim is the realization of absolute Truth as the unlimited self-determination of Freedom—
that Freedom which has its own absolute form itself as its purport. The

destiny of the Germanic peoples is to be the bearers of the Christian principle. The principle of Spiritual Freedom, of reconciliation, was introduced into the still simple, unformed minds of those peoples; and the part assigned them in the service of the World-Spirit was that of not merely possessing the Idea of Freedom as the substratum of their religious conceptions, but of producing it in free and spontaneous developments from their subjective self-consciousness.[4]

LS: This of course must be properly understood. The key point is that the Germanic nations had, so to speak, nothing of their own. Christianity, however poorly understood, was their deepest substance; therefore a truly nonpagan culture arose in the West and only in the West. When he says that true freedom developed there because of the subjective self-consciousness—the conscience, we can say—Hegel means of course not the undetermined conscience, so that anything which a man says my conscience dictates, but that the conscience must determine itself. This self-determination must take place in a universally valid manner. It cannot be a mere idiosyncrasy of one kind or another, but rather freedom which is not merely formal but has its absolute form for its content. The true freedom is not merely possible as religious substance within the conscience, but it must produce in the literal sense, bring forth into a world. And this is the work of Europe.

Mr. Reinken: Page 342, line 12.

For the Christian world is the world of completion; the grand principle of being is realized, consequently the end of days is fully come. The idea can discover in Christianity no point in the aspirations of Spirit that is not satisfied.

LS: The idea meaning the philosophic reason, understanding. Christianity is the complete satisfaction.

Mr. Reinken:

For its individual members, the Church is, it is true, a preparation for an eternal state as something future; since the units who compose it, in their isolated and several capacity, occupy a position of particularity.

LS: In other words, it is still this Mr. X, Mr. Y, etc.

Mr. Reinken:

But the Church has also the Spirit of God actually present in it, it forgives the sinner and is a present kingdom of heaven. Thus the Christian World has no absolute existence outside its sphere—

LS: In other words, it has no longer any absolute without.
Mr. Reinken:

outside its sphere, but only a relative one which is already implicitly vanquished, and in respect to which its only concern is to make it apparent that this conquest has taken place.[5]

LS: This could refer also to the future conquest of India and China, of which we have heard something before. But it could also refer to the fact that there are still quite a few ingredients of the Christian world that are not yet Christianized, but they no longer have any substance, any intellectual or spiritual power in themselves. The Christian world has no "without." There is no longer any "without" in any sense. It is radically meant: there is nothing. What about heaven and the heavenly bodies? Are they not without the Christian world? What about Newton? Didn't he and Newtonian physics conquer them and make them man's properties by understanding them fully? . . . The Germanic nations, by becoming Christianized, acquired *the* absolute principle, and therefore they need no longer any other principle to be taken over from any foreign nation or culture. They could develop the absolute culture entirely by themselves by developing the seed laid in them, but their principle is not Germanic— that is crucially important—i.e., not particular, but universal. God has become man and not a German.

The deeper meaning of this question of the "no without" I cannot possibly go into. The most important specimen of a "without" for Hegel probably would be what Kant taught about the thing in itself, which is something without not only man's actual knowledge, but without any possibility of man's knowing it. In other words, "no without" as Hegel understands it excludes the suprarational revelation or any of the absolute mysteries which would of course also be without man. Everything has become rational, has been understood. In other words, "without" means, first, what transcends the human world; and second, what transcends the human understanding. There is nothing which transcends the human understanding, reason; and there is nothing which transcends the human world. Nature is integrated into culture, not only due to the fact that nature has been cultivated, animals have been tamed, etc., but also because we have purely theoretical knowledge like Newtonian physics. This is also an integration into a human whole. There is in no sense a "without." The true doctrine is in a way "without"; it is beyond history in that it is located at the end of history. But being the end of history, it still also belongs to history. This, I believe, we should keep in mind. Let us read the continuation.

Mr. Reinken:

We have therefore to look for another principle of division. The Germanic World took up the Roman culture and religion in their completed form.

LS: "As ready-made" would be a better translation. Yes. Then he speaks about the Germanic religion and this is very unimportant. "The Christian religion, which they accepted."

Mr. Reinken:

had received from Councils and Fathers of the Church, who possessed the whole culture, and in particular, the philosophy of the Greek and Roman world, a perfected dogmatic system.

LS: Again, I would translate that as "a ready-made, dogmatic system." He wants to emphasize how little the Germanic nations were creative.

Mr. Reinken:

The Church, too, had a ready-made hierarchy. To the native tongue of the Germans, the Church likewise opposed one ready-made—the Latin. In art and philosophy a similar alien influence predominated—

LS: Really, that's much too weak. "The same alienness came completely from without." Let us drop the next sentence. So the Germanic world seems to be externally only a continuation of the Roman world. After all, Rome itself had become Christian.

Mr. Reinken:

but there lived in it an entirely new Spirit, through which the World was to be regenerated—the free Spirit, viz. which reposes on itself—the absolute self-determination of subjectivity.

LS: Obstinacy, almost. Literally translated it is "obstinacy." The obstinate subject, accepting it and remaining obstinate, opposes it.

Mr. Reinken:

To this self-involved subjectivity, the corresponding objectivity stands opposed as absolutely alien. The distinction and antithesis which is evolved from these principles is that of Church and State. On the one side the Church develops itself as the embodiment of absolute Truth; for it is the consciousness of this truth, and at the same time the agency for rendering the Individual harmonious with it. On the other side stands secular consciousness, which, with its aims, occupies the world of Limitation—the State based on Heart—

LS: *Gemüt*.

Mr. Reinken:

or mutual confidence and subjectivity generally.

LS: He says *Treue*. Fidelity, not in the religious sense, but in the sense of loyalty.

Mr. Reinken: Trust?

LS: No, it is the feudal principle. Fidelity not in the religious sense, but in the sense of the loyalty which the vassal owes his lord and vice versa. Go on.

Mr. Reinken:

European history is the exhibition of the growth of each of these principles severally, in Church and State; then of an antithesis on the part of both—not only of the one to the other, but appearing within the sphere of each of these bodies themselves, since each of them is itself a totality—

LS: "*The* totality."

Mr. Reinken:

the totality; lastly of the harmonizing of the antithesis.[6]

LS: This is the overall formula for European history, as you see. The Germans accepted something ready-made, alien to them, but what they accepted was something new which had never informed a world before. The basis is now, for the first time, Christianity. And here we have a characteristic conflict between the absolute truth, the objective truth, represented by the Church, and the individual who bows to it but at the same time also has his peculiar obstinacy. The latter leads to the state. A conflict between the two is necessary because each of the two opponents—Church and state, ultimately the absolute truth and the subject—is the totality. Each raises an absolute claim. For this reason, there is a conflict within each—within the Church and within the state. The claim to totality on the part of the Church is easily understood. It is *the* truth. But how can the individual claim to be the totality? The truth must become evident to the individual. It must ultimately justify itself before the tribunal of the individual, and to that extent the whole objective truth becomes the subject. He develops this a bit further on page 344, first paragraph.

Mr. Reinken:

The second period develops the two sides of the antithesis to a logically consequential independence and opposition—the Church for itself as a Theocracy, and the State for itself as a Feudal Monarchy. Charlemagne had formed an alliance with the Holy See against the Lombards and the factions of the nobles in Rome. A union thus arose between the spiritual and the secular power, and the kingdom of heaven on earth promised to follow in the wake of this conciliation. But just at this time, instead of the spiritual kingdom of heaven, the inwardness of the Christian principle wears the appearance of being altogether directed outwards and leaving its proper sphere. Christian freedom is perverted to its very opposite, both in a religious and secular respect. On the one hand, to the severest bondage; on the other hand, to the most immoral excess of barbarous intensity of every passion. In this period, two aspects of society are to be especially noted. The first is the formation of states, superior and inferior suzerainties exhibiting a regulated subordination so that every relation becomes a firmly fixed private right, excluding a sense of universality. This regulated subordination appears in the feudal system. The second aspect presents the antithesis of Church and State. This antithesis exists solely because the Church, to whose management the Spiritual was committed, itself sinks down into every kind of worldliness—a worldliness which appears only the more detestable, because all passions assume the sanction of religion.

LS: What is the necessity in that? The Church is the truth. This is wholly unself-contradictory. Where does the antithesis come in? Well, some points will be developed later, but the Holy Church requires, in the medieval understanding, the distinction between the clergy and the laity. The state is as such an affair of the layman, with a character of its own which is not wholly determined by the Church. We cannot now go into the various medieval doctrines, but in a general way, a certain independence of the secular government is admitted even by the strictest papalists. So this has a principle of its own, and this principle is not the ecclesiastical principle, not the true principle, the absolute truth; therefore it must be one of nontruth. And the nontruth is the mere individual, the mere subject and the relations among the mere individuals. No universal proper, only private rights.

The contradiction comes out, furthermore, in this way. The Church, in order to be within this world of lawlessness, must acquire power and wealth, and therefore it becomes involved in all the terrible things going with power and property. And as he makes clear in the immediate sequel, the Reformation changes this because the Reformation recognizes the right of worldliness much more fundamentally than the medieval church did. And according to Hegel the Enlightenment, as you will see next time, simply continues the Reformation and therefore leads to the final solution in the modern state. On page 345, second paragraph.

Mr. Reinken:

We may distinguish these periods as Kingdoms of the Father, the Son, and the Spirit. The Kingdom of the Father is the consolidated, undistinguished mass, presenting a self-repeating cycle, mere change—like that sovereignty of Chronos engulfing his offspring. The kingdom of the Son—

LS: This is pre-Christian. It could also be Islam, for that matter.
Mr. Reinken:

is the manifestation of God merely in a relation to secular existence— shining upon it as upon an alien object.

LS: "As something alien." Therefore the world is not integrated.
Mr. Reinken:

The Kingdom of the Spirit is the harmonizing of the antithesis.[7]

LS: In other words, the modern development is the Kingdom of the Spirit. It is not an accident, I believe, that Hegel omits "holy." On page 346, in the second paragraph.

Mr. Reinken:

> The third epoch may be compared with the Roman World. The unity of a universal principle is here quite as decidedly present, yet not as the unity of abstract universal sovereignty, but as the Hegemony of self-cognizant Thought. The authority of Rational Aim is acknowledged, and privileges and particularities melt away before the common object of the State.

LS: "Common purpose of the state." In other words, as long as you have a rule of privileges, of private rights. More precisely, according to Hegel there is no public right in the Middle Ages. There are only private rights, because there is no general will.

Mr. Reinken:

> Peoples will the Right in and for itself; regard is not had exclusively to particular conventions between nations, but principles enter into the considerations with which diplomacy is occupied. As little can Religion maintain itself apart from Thought, but either advances to the comprehension of the Idea, or, compelled by thought itself becomes intensive belief—or lastly, from despair of finding itself at home in thought, flees back from it in pious horror, and becomes Superstition.[8]

LS: In the case of right or law you have a definite progress from private right to public right, from a merely positive international law based only on treaties to principles of international law. But what about the case of religion? In the case of religion, the progress is not so clear because religion proceeds or progresses to the concept, i.e., to the true philosophy. Or else it decays into lower forms of religion: a merely internal, pietistic faith, if not superstition. That is important; it confirms what we said in an earlier discussion about the dubious state of religion in the end of the world. Let us then turn to page 350, first paragraph. This section deals with the migration theme. "These tribes have created kingdoms."

Mr. Reinken:

> These people did, indeed, found kingdoms—

LS: He means here the Slavonic peoples especially, and the Hungarians and so on.

Mr. Reinken:

> and sustain spirited conflicts with the various nations that came across their path. Sometimes, as an advanced guard—an intermediate nationality—they took part in the struggle between Christian Europe and unchristian Asia. The Poles even liberated beleaguered Vienna from the Turks; and the Slavs have to some extent been drawn within the sphere of Occidental Reason. Yet this entire body of peoples remains excluded from our consideration, because hitherto it has not appeared as an independent element in the series of phases that Reason has assumed in the World. Whether it will do so hereafter is a question that does not concern us here; for in History we have to do with the Past.[9]

LS: That is a most important passage. Those who say that Hegel did not admit an end of history base themselves on this passage. You find this interpretation very simply stated, for example, in Collingwood's *Idea of History* in the section on Hegel, but also elsewhere.[10] And this seems clearly to confirm this view. The future is unknowable, and therefore knowledge, reason cannot possibly deal with the future. History can only deal with the past. Hitherto the Slavonic nations did not play any role in the history of the mind. Is this argument conclusive?

Mr. Reinken: Just because history has to do with the past, you might on a higher ground know that there isn't going to be any more history.

LS: Yes. Something of this kind, I would say; we must only try perhaps to state it somewhat more precisely. The fact that there may be all kinds of interesting developments in the European East does not necessarily mean that there can be an entirely new principle there. For example, for Hegel the peak is constituted by the developments in the Protestant countries, especially Germany and England. There are very great differences between Germany and England of which Hegel was aware. In some respects Germany was better in history, in other respects England. But the fundamental principle is the same. Therefore, whether the Slavonic nations develop something different from how Germany or England are actually constituted or something closer to the Catholic countries, this no one can possibly know, but there cannot be a new principle. This is not contradicted by what Hegel says here. This is, I believe, what you meant, Mr. Reinken. In the immediate sequel Hegel speaks of the peculiarity of the Germanic nation.

Student: The fact that he uses the phraseology "the Slavs appear as independent elements in the series of phases that reason has assumed," doesn't that imply something more than the Slav might be a really good phase of reason?

LS: I see your point and it is well taken. An independent moment, as he puts it, an independent phase. That is true, but the question nevertheless would be how deep this could possibly go in the face of what Hegel says generally about what happened in modern times—the secularization of Christianity culminating in a way in the French Revolution or rather in the post–French Revolutionary state. It is impossible to see how there could be any fundamental change, although perhaps an interesting variation. This of course became crucial for the rational thinkers of the nineteenth century who were under the spell of the German philosophy of Hegel and Schelling and who were looking for the mission of Russia—something which fundamentally had gone wrong in Western Europe and which only Mother Russia, because of her Byzantine past, could give to the world: the true Christianity. That was their claim: the true Christianity would reassert itself in Russia. In the writings of Dostoyevsky, both the novels and the political writings, you find quite a few references. That is at least my chief source of knowledge about these matters. In a very strangely modified manner, that lives on in communism. One simple formula used by these emphatically Slavonic writers—by the way, Tolstoy himself too—is the two capitals of Russia, the one founded by *the* man of the Enlightenment, the enlightened despot Peter: Petrograd. It even had a German name until the First World War: Petersburg. Only in 1914 did they call it Petrograd. The other one, the truly Russian capital, is Moscow. Both in Tolstoy and in Dostoyevsky the emphasis is on Moscow, and in Dostoyevsky there is even the demand that Moscow must again be made *the* capital of the true Russia. And this was doubtless done by the people who then renamed Petrograd into Leningrad.

In the immediate sequel Hegel speaks of this peculiarity of the Germans, which he calls with the German word *Gemüt*. Hegel is not as enthusiastic about it as many Germans are. He makes clear that *Gemüt* is surely not the same as character. That is Hegel's way of criticizing it, as a kind of depth which is a murky depth. That is a Hegelian expression used sometimes. Hegel has no great use for that. Let us turn to page 353 in the second paragraph.

Mr. Reinken:

The union of the two relations—of individual freedom in the community and of—

LS: By the "community" he means the local community. One could almost say the city.
Mr. Reinken:

and of the bond implied in association—

LS: "Association" meaning the guilds and such things.
Mr. Reinken:

is the main point in the formation of the State. In this duties and rights are no longer left to arbitrary choice, but are determined as fixed relations—

LS: That is, legally fixed relations.
Mr. Reinken:

legally fixed relations, involving, moreover, the condition that the State be the soul of the entire body, and remain its sovereign—that from it should be derived particular aims and the authorization both of political acts and political agents—the generic character and interests of the community constituting the permanent basis of the whole. But here we have the peculiarity of the Germanic states, that contrary to the view thus presented, social relations do not assume the character of general definitions and laws but are entirely split up into private rights and private obligations. They perhaps exhibit a social or communal mold or stamp, but nothing universal; the laws are absolutely particular, and the Rights are Privileges. Thus the state was a patchwork of private rights, and a rational political life was the tardy issue of wearisome struggles and convulsions.[11]

LS: This is a clear statement of the difference between the feudal order at its best, including what it became in the cities, and the reasonable state. We turn to the chapter on Islam. There is a certain superiority of Islam to medieval Christianity, as you find on page 355 bottom.
Mr. Reinken:

In short, while the West began to shelter itself in a political edifice of chance, entanglement and particularity, the very opposite direction necessarily made its appearance in the world, to produce the balance of the totality of spiritual manifestation. This took place in the Revolution of the East, which destroyed all particularity and dependence, and perfectly cleared up and purified the soul and disposition; making the abstract One the absolute object of attention and devotion, and to the same extent, pure subjective consciousness—the Knowledge of this One alone—the only aim of reality—making the Unconditioned the condition of existence.[12]

LS: Literally "the relationness," the relation of existence. The Christian medieval world leads in the feudal order to the complete disappearance of the general or universal in the particular rights and privileges. At this moment Islam emerged or, more, at this moment it became a threat to Europe. And here you have according to Hegel's presentation the most radical assertion of the denial of particularity. *The* one God and before God all men equal, and this was of decisive importance for social life. In this respect, as appears in the sequel, Islam is superior to Judaism, because Judaism belongs to one particular nation, whereas Islam claims to be universal. Mohammed is said to have been sent to the white and the black. Islam attempts to subjugate the world to the Spirit, the universal, as he says on page 357. He who converted to Islam received completely equal rights with all other Muslims, the very opposite of feudalism in every respect. But Islam is not exactly the solution from Hegel's point of view. He compares this abstract universalism and egalitarianism to that of the French Revolution.

Mr. Reinken:

La religion et la terreur was the principle in this case—

LS: The fact that Islam converted by conquest, by the sword: holy war. In other words, there is a fundamental contradiction between the spirituality which Islam in one sense serves and the means by which it spread, because the sword is not an instrument of conviction. It may be an instrument of persuasion, though.

Mr. Reinken:

as with Robespierre, liberty and terror. But real life is nevertheless concrete, and introduces particular aims; conquest leads to sovereignty and wealth, to the conferring of prerogatives on a dynastic family, and to the union of individuals.[13]

LS: In other words, it cannot remain at that primary equality of all Muslims, because there are concrete purposes, as Hegel puts it, which cannot be disposed of by reference to the single end of man. And then on page 359, bottom.

Mr. Reinken:

> The meanest Saracen, the most insignificant old woman approached the Caliph as his equals. Unreflecting naiveté does not stand in need of culture; and in virtue of the freedom of his Spirit, each one sustains a relation of equality to the ruler.[14]

LS: That is another expression of the same thought. This equality of all Muslims means also indifference to the inequalities coming from culture. And without culture, there is no reasonable state, culture necessarily introducing inequality. So medieval Christianity offers indeed the articulation of society without which society cannot be good. But this is an unreasonable articulation. Islam is free from the unreasonable articulation but does not offer a basis for any articulation; therefore medieval Christianity and Islam are strictly opposites, so their secular fight was more than a political phenomenon. But Islam proved unable to undergo the changes towards a higher stage, whereas Christianity proved to be able.

Then he speaks of the empire of Charlemagne and the development of medieval societies there. Page 363, bottom.

Mr. Reinken:

> In Charlemagne's time the ecclesiastical body had already acquired great weight. The bishops presided over great cathedral establishments with which were also connected seminaries and scholastic institutions. For Charlemagne endeavored to restore science, then almost extinct, by promoting the foundation of schools in towns and villages. Pious souls believed that they were doing a good work and earning salvation by making presents to the church; in this way the most savage and barbarous monarchs sought to atone for their crimes—

LS: He gives other examples, but the key point is that religion did not at that time have the power over the minds to restrain the avarice of the powerful.

Mr. Reinken:

for religion had not yet such an authority over men's minds as to be able to bridle the rapacity of the powerful. The clergy were obliged to appoint stewards and bailiffs to manage their estates. Besides this, guardians had charge of all their secular concerns, led their men-at-arms into the field, and gradually obtained from the king territorial jurisdiction, when the ecclesiastics had secured the privilege of being amenable only to their own tribunals and enjoyed immunity from the authority of the royal officers of justice. This involved an important step in the change of political relations, inasmuch as the ecclesiastical domains assumed more and more the aspect of independent provinces enjoying a freedom surpassing anything to which those of secular princes had yet made pretentions. Moreover, the clergy contrived subsequently to free themselves from the burdens of the state and opened the churches and monasteries as asylums—that is, inviolable sanctuaries for all offenders.

LS: For criminals.
Mr. Reinken:

This institution was on the one hand very beneficial as a protection in cases of violence and oppression; but it was perverted on the other hand into a means of impunity for the grossest crimes.[15]

LS: So what Hegel tries to show here is the dialectic of the medieval church. The point is that not by accident but by an essential necessity the Church became corrupted. Pious men left their property to the Church with a view to the salvation of their dead. The Church was not eager to acquire property, but it couldn't help acquiring property. But once you have property, property is bound to have its effects. People who would not have been interested in becoming churchmen if the Church had been poor now became interested in becoming churchmen, naturally, as it would always happen. And this is not something which depended on anybody's ill will, but on an inner necessity.

What he says here, that the side by side of religion and immorality—a theme that is well-known in Germany by a famous formula, an expression occurring in Goethe's *Faust* when he speaks of the medieval Church as punishing the heretics but gracious to the sinners—this has its two sides, because the graciousness to the sinners can lead to a neglect of the necessary severity of criminal justice, a greater concern with purity of faith, with obedience to the Church, than with merely moral or legal defects. An important point.

Then in the immediate sequel he develops the point which was made by Mr. . . . . The life and spirit of the medieval church is an infinite life, and the infinity consists in the fact that it is the unholiness of the holy. Let us turn to page 368, line 6 from bottom.

Mr. Reinken:

> We might be inclined to regard the picture of the noble and rational constitution of the Frank monarchy under Charlemagne—exhibiting itself as strong, comprehensive, and well-ordered, internally and externally—as a baseless figment. Yet it actually existed; the entire political system being held together only by the power, the greatness, the regal soul of this one man—not based on the spirit of the people—not having become a vital element in it. It was superficially induced—an a priori constitution like that which Napoleon gave to Spain, and which disappeared with the physical power that sustained it. That, on the contrary, which renders a constitution real, is that it exists as Objective Freedom—the Substantial form of volition—as duty and obligation acknowledged by the subjects themselves. But obligation was not yet recognized by the Germanic Spirit, which hitherto showed itself only as 'Heart' and subjective choice; for it there was as yet no subjectivity involving unity, but only a subjectivity conditioned by a careless superficial self-seeking. Thus that constitution was destitute of any firm bond; it had no objective support in subjectivity.[16]

LS: A seemingly paradoxical expression . . . : "Without the objective support in subjectivity." The reasonable state is not always possible, as we know from Aristotle. But Hegel gives a somewhat different reason. And this is paradoxical, of course, because man is the rational animal. Why should a rational constitution not always be possible? Aristotle had said that there are tribes which are by nature incapable of the best regime, and there are many situations in which people who would be susceptible to a good regime are by accident not capable of it. All kinds of accidents could make it impossible. For Hegel the key point is that the spirit of the people must be prepared for it, as people would say today. An *a priori* constitution, meaning a constitution which is not in harmony with the spirit of the people, is condemned to failure. This subject is now in a way at the forefront of discussion and is not always honestly faced because of the embarrassing implications for some nations, but the problem nevertheless exists, as is easy to see. The constitution must have an objective support in subjectivity, meaning in the spirit of the people, in their subjectivity.

He develops this at greater length. There was no rule of law—of the general will, we could say—in the Middle Ages, although Hegel doesn't use here the expression. He says only no rule of the general. But why is this rule of law necessary? What is the root of it? Fundamentally, if we go down to brass tacks: the need for protection. In the Middle Ages the protection was supplied by powerful individuals, not by the state, not by a general will, not by the union of all individuals who need protection. Hence the rule of general injustice, because even if the individual lord is an honest and pious man, the whole thing is unjust because of the lack of principles, the general lawlessness. Page 370, bottom.

Mr. Reinken:

> The valor that now manifested itself was displayed not on behalf of the State, but of private interests. In every district arose castles; fortresses were erected, and that for the defense of private property, and with a view to plunder the tyranny. In the way just mentioned, the political totality was ignored at those points where individual authority was established, among which the seats of bishops and archbishops deserve a special mention. The bishoprics had been freed from the jurisdiction of the judicial tribunals and from the operations of the executive generally. The bishops had stewards on whom at their request the Emperors conferred the jurisdiction which the Counts had formerly exercised. Thus there were detached ecclesiastical domains—ecclesiastical districts which belonged to a saint. Similar suzerainties of a secular kind were subsequently constituted. Both occupied the position of the previous Provinces or Counties. Only in a few towns where communities of freemen were independently strong enough to secure protection and safety did relics of the ancient free constitution remain.[17]

LS: The general lawlessness is due to the absence of freedom. No freedom, because no freedom for all. For such freedom for all requires subjection of all to law, and this is the fundamental defect, according to Hegel, of the feudal order, although in an external sense the Middle Ages were very legalistic. But Hegel would raise the question: What kind of laws were they? Were they reasonable laws, or were they particular laws given on the basis of accidental situations by an emperor or king to this or that duke or count and so on? Hegel developed this in a very legible way in his critique of the British Reform Bill of 1832, one of his last writings, where the point of his criticism is that no conclusions can be drawn from the British Reform Bill as to what should be done on the European continent, because British law is still so shot through with things of feudal origin — i.e., with essentially irrational, arbitrary, accidental things — that it cannot possibly be the model for continental Europe.[18]

In spite of all this splitting up of all general things through the feudal order, there was something general, and that was of course the Church. Hegel then describes how its supremacy was in fact established, especially by Pope Gregory VII. But precisely by this solitary action by which the independence of the Church was guaranteed, the Church became involved in worldly power and in worldly purposes, which led to a worldly understanding of the spiritual. The mediation between God and man in Christ is not spiritually understood, but carnally, namely, that this mediation takes place through the Church and its practices, including, among other things, the worship of relics and so on. The Catholic understanding leads to spiritual, absolute servitude in the midst of the religion of freedom, i.e., of Christianity.

According to Hegel, this is connected with the absolute separation of the spiritual and temporal principles, for that separation leads to the subjugation of the laity to the clergy. Consequently the separation of the spiritual and the temporal leads to a gross misuse. Page 379, bottom. Mr. Reinken:

With this perversion is connected the absolute separation of the spiritual from the secular principle generally. There are Two Divine Kingdoms — the intellectual in the heart and cognitive faculty, and the socially ethical whose element and sphere is secular existence. It is science alone that can comprehend the kingdom of God and the socially Moral world as one Idea, and that recognizes the fact that the course of Time has witnessed a process ever tending to the realization of this unity. But Piety as such, has nothing to do with the Secular: it may make its appearance in that sphere on a mission of mercy, but this stops short of a strict socially ethical connection with it — does not come up to the Idea of Freedom. Religious feeling is extraneous to History, and has no History —

LS: "Piety," he says. Piety is outside of history and without history. Mr. Reinken:

for History is rather the Empire of Spirit recognizing itself in its Subjective Freedom, as the economy of social morality in the State. In the Middle Ages that embodying of the Divine in actual life was wanting; the antithesis was not harmonized. Social morality is represented as worthless, and that in its three most essential particulars.[19]

LS: Which he develops in the sequel. What is the key point? In the Middle Ages, piety has not yet been subjected to science. Now science, of course, is meant not in the positivistic sense but in the sense of Hegel's true philosophy. Without the subjection of piety to science, there is no freedom, and, which is more immediately grave, the supremacy of piety is incompatible with true *Sittlichkeit*, which he translates as social morality.

Then Hegel shows this in three cases, taking the three vows of chastity, poverty, and obedience as example. Social morality, *Sittlichkeit*, requires the sanctity of matrimony, labor, and obedience to rational laws. And, according to Hegel, the three vows which give the clergy its character—and the clergy is higher than the laity—cast aspersion on matrimony, work, and obedience to rational laws. One can say in passing—although this will become clear, perhaps, from the rest of the book—that Hegel sees in the asceticism of the Catholic Church the root of immorality. Differently stated, the true morality is not ascetic. This is a long, long story in modern times going up to the present time.

The three contradictions of the medieval Church—which are not clearly connected, as far as I could figure out, with his critique of the three vows—are these. The first point is that the truth is here only something given, something positive. Hegel refers to the suprarational character of the teaching of faith. The second point is that the priest owes his dignity to the indelible character of the priest, i.e., not to his qualities of the mind and heart. For example, he doesn't cease to be a priest because of his unchastity. And lastly, the vow of poverty is contradicted by the immense wealth of the Church. By rejecting this asceticism, this fundamental immorality is done away with. And here you see the great importance of the adoption by Hegel of Adam Smith's political economy, which was a frank embracing of the fact that the fundamentally unlimited acquisition of wealth is not only good but indispensable for any morality. The accusations which Hegel gives are of course the ones we know from the Protestant criticism of the Middle Ages.

Hegel emphasizes that according to the Catholic teaching, marriage is a sacrament, but he says that since the higher stage is that of celibacy, an aspersion is cast on marriage. Hegel himself was a married man, and there was a kind of revenge on Hegel with respect to this point, and therefore indirectly in favor of the Catholic Church, from a very unexpected quarter: from Nietzsche, in his *Genealogy of Morals*. In the most exciting part, the third part, which is entitled "What Is the Significance of Ascetic Ideals?" he enumerates many great philosophers, especially of classical antiquity but also some from modern times, like Descartes, Spinoza, and Leibniz, who were also not married. And Nietzsche raises the question: Can there be a married philosopher? [Laughter] There is of course a very famous married philosopher whom everyone knows: Socrates. But Nietzsche has a simple answer: he is the subject of a comedy. So this is not merely a jocular matter. This simple rejection of the ascetic ideal which Hegel here implies has its other side too, as shown by the fact that the three vows, as Nietzsche develops at great length, are the vows of the philosophers too, on entirely non-Christian grounds. But there is a remarkable agreement there.

Next time we will have Mr. Reinken and Mr. . . . .

15   The Middle Ages Continued

Leo Strauss: Thank you very much, Mr. Reinken, for your paper, which was not only very good, but also—and I believe I speak for the class—very delightful.[1] You were the first one, I believe, whose paper was accompanied by enjoyment. That is not meant as a criticism. When reading Hegel himself, one is not induced to smile. So it is from a non-Hegelian point of view that the smiling comes in.

Now I would like to use this opportunity to say something about Mr. Reinken. He is a very unusual man. He is by training a mathematician, and I believe he is the only member of the student body here who came into this department via coming to my courses, and not so much for courses in political science but for some strictly idiosyncratic reasons. And then he attracted the attention of one of my colleagues—who has nothing whatsoever to do with political philosophy in any manner, shape, or form—whom he impressed not only by his native intelligence but also by his very broad reading. So he knows much more about political history, in particular diplomatic history, than some full professors do. So he became eventually a normal member of this department, and I am very happy about this development. I hope you don't mind these personal remarks. I never had an opportunity to make this remark to anyone.

You make many good points and important ones. Some will be repeated when we go over the text. I will only mention a few things. When we read Hegel's analysis of the Middle Ages prior to what we read today, we observed that the overall judgment of the Middle Ages is the ordinary Protestant judgment, only Hegel deepens it very much. But the broad judgment is the same. Now what about Hegel's view of the Reformation and what the Reformation means in the long run? Is this a peculiarity of Hegel, or does it have a broader matrix?

Mr. Reinken: The secular view of Protestantism is a step in the right direction, but only a step.

LS: Is this a peculiarity of Hegel?

Mr. Reinken: I think not. It is characteristic of the Enlightenment generally.

LS: Exactly. The understanding of the Enlightenment as an outgrowth of the Reformation, in a way more consistent than the Reformation, was very common. Do you know the key word which allegedly connects the Reformation and the Enlightenment?

Mr. Reinken: "Liberty of conscience"?

LS: You can put it this way. I believe the more common expression is "the right of private judgment," the notion being that in the Catholic system the authority of the Church tells you what to believe or not to believe, whereas according to the Reformation every Christian reads the Bible in his mother tongue and forms his judgment on the basis of his own reading. Now this was of course not quite so simple, as no one knew better than Hegel, because the Reformation, especially the Lutheran confirmation, culminated in certain official formulations of the dogma and in a certain radical scripturalism. But this minor excrescence of the old-fashioned views were then disposed of by the Enlightenment. A large part of the Lutheran dogma does not have direct New Testament backing. That was the first . . . reaction. Then the radical people like the Socinians and the Unitarians later on dropped the whole Trinitarianism, and of course naturally also original sin and everything that goes with that.

But the notion that the Reformation is fundamentally the same as the Enlightenment was very popular. In Rousseau, for example, it is presented in this way, and it is still very common in our time. Only in our age, in the last thirty or forty years, was there a rather passionate reaction to it connected especially with Karl Barth,[2] who brought out the fact that the Reformation is not in any way the Enlightenment. Barth was a Calvinist, but this difference is not decisive. So this is one point which is not peculiar to Hegel. What is of course peculiar to Hegel is the precision of the analysis of the peculiarity of the Reformation and how this turns into the Enlightenment.

What you said about Hegel's notion of morality is, I think, quite sound. In this respect he has something in common with Aristotle, but in a modern way. For Hegel there is no question that there can be decent men, and any self-searching that shows there are all kinds of worms effective in the best of men is unimportant if their actions are decent. If the man as a whole has led a decent life, then he is a decent man, and it is morbid to go beyond that. That is what you meant, didn't you?

Mr. Reinken: I don't know where I brought that in.

LS: No. I think that you said this. Hegel goes much beyond Aristotle in his treatment of the virtues, especially in the *Philosophy of Right*, where there is no longer a doctrine of the virtues necessary for Hegel. The good man is the good citizen in the good society, and the good society is the reasonable society. In other words, by being a loyal member of it, living according to its laws and being a patriotic citizen according to his station—a simple citizen, or high official, or whatever it may be—that is all which is reasonably required of man. The whole problem of sin and evil is overcome. That was a necessary stage of human development where the evil of man, the sinfulness of man had to be the primary preoccupation. This tornness of man—Hegel speaks of the "unhappy consciousness," that's the Christian consciousness—is overcome by a more advanced order. I think that you understood that even if, as you say, you did not know that you understood it. One may speak truth without knowing it. You referred frequently to the categorical imperative. What do you mean by that? Is Hegel a Kantian?

Mr. Reinken: Reason has no rule coming from outside itself. Reason is both the matter and the intelligent form. Reason provides the content.

LS: Hegel starts from the categorical imperative. In other words, right intention is decisive. But he absolutely denies that you can deduce from that directly any substantive duties. He says a lot about the hypocrisy to which that leads. If you are clever enough, you can give the formal character of rationality to any content. So there is something else. What is necessary is a union of the right subjective principle, the good will as Kant calls it, and the substantive objectivity which is indeed rational but which cannot simply be deduced from that form. The criticism of Kant's morality plays a crucial rule in Hegel's whole thought, most visibly in the *Phenomenology of the Mind*, but also in his *Philosophy of Right*. Part of it will come out in our readings today.

One more point only. You noticed an agreement between Hegel and Machiavelli, which is slightly disguised, but you discerned it. But what is the difference from Machiavelli? This is one point, the tough side of political life.

Mr. Reinken: Machiavelli's prince, Cesare Borgia, brings about the order knowing full well what he is working for. But Alexander did not know that he was bringing about the free West.

LS: In more general terms, without going into these particular historical things, the truth discovered by Machiavelli or stated by him with particular force is one thing. The rule of reasonable laws is of course ultimately decisive for him. Only when Hegel thinks of the rule of reasonable laws does he know this element of power is implied. And if there were any doubt about it, it would be supplied by this remark on Machiavelli.

I would like to say a few words about the paper which I wrongly attributed to Miss Abbott but is a paper by Miss Perkins. There are a few passages which I will read.

> For Hegel, religion is the focus of the knowledge of the identity of the individual and the divine. Because there is in this identity a connection to the political principle, the state rests on religion and has its roots in it. But religion is the relation of the absolute in the form of sentiment, imagination and faith, that is, in the form of piety. We have seen in the Middle Ages that piety can exist in the presence of and can even foster that which is most irrational, coarse and vile. Piety, according to Hegel, does not recognize the notion of duty towards the state. This duty is recognized only through reason, meaning in contradistinction to sentiment, imagination, and faith.

I think that that is a fair statement. "Religion is the deepest builder of convictional loyalty, but its content is a matter of indifference to the state." We have read passages to this effect. Hegel says that, but he has a kind of preference for Protestant Christianity. But this cannot be made a legal obligation. This will come out in our discussion next time. "Thus the separation of the Church and the State, and the decline of the former, is a matter of necessity and fortuitousness." Why did you say fortuitous?

Miss Perkins: Because some of the necessities which brought about the reasonable state were to be deplored by Hegel, but I think this one is applauded by Hegel.

LS: But under no circumstances was it fortuitous. It was necessary, a blessing in disguise and well-disguised, but it was necessary. To the extent to which it was fortuitous it would be uninteresting to him. "In those religions which recognize the true only in its separate, abstract—in its untrue form—Hegel says God is represented in the abstract form as the highest being Lord of heaven and earth, living in a remote region far from human actualities. Perhaps this God's world is the cosmos." I didn't follow the last sentence.

Miss Perkins: The cosmos is the realm of nature which, I think, according to Hegel, man cannot understand and is not really connected with reason.

LS: That is not quite true. It is reason, but reason in an alienated form. I may speak of it at the end of today's meeting. Thank you very much.

Now let us turn to the beginning because—if I may make a criticism of Mr. Reinken's paper which does not alter my overall view which I stated—you did not make sufficiently clear the dialectic, the inner necessity of this alleged perversion of Christianity which is the Middle Ages. Let us turn to page 389, second paragraph, which is the beginning of today's assignment.

Mr. Reinken:

> The Church gained the victory in the struggle referred to in the previous chapter, and in this way secured as decided a supremacy in Germany as she did in the other states of Europe by a calmer process. She made herself mistress of all the relations of life, and of science and art; and she was the permanent repository of spiritual treasures.

LS: He speaks here, by the way, of the present. "She has made herself" and "she is" the permanent exhibition of the spiritual treasures. That is not uninteresting, because Hegel looks at the epoch from the epoch's point of view. He must do that in order not to use hindsight. He wants to show the Middle Ages as they were and how they understood themselves, how they had to transform themselves into something else.

Mr. Reinken:

> and she is the permanent repository of spiritual treasures. Yet notwithstanding this full and complete development of ecclesiastical life, we find a deficiency and consequent craving manifesting itself in Christendom, and which drove it out of itself. To understand this want, we must revert to the nature of the Christian religion itself and particularly to that aspect of it by which it has a footing in the present in the consciousness of its votaries.

LS: "In the presence of the self-consciousness." So Hegel says: Look at the Middle Ages as they came to be after the Church has won its decisive victory over the German emperors, the fight over the investiture and so on. Everything was perfect, and yet something drove the Church beyond, and what was that? A part of this perfect solution was the presence of self-consciousness. But this presence of self-consciousness was not fully satisfied, and the Church had therefore to go beyond this stage. Now what does "presence" mean here? It is underlined in the German edition. What does "presence" mean? Well, in the first place, one could say it is the opposite of the past, of tradition. Whether this is true or not will appear from the sequel. Go on.

Mr. Reinken:

> The objective doctrines of Christianity have been already so firmly settled by the councils of the Church that neither the medieval nor any other philosophy could develop them further, except in the way of exalting them intellectually so that they might be satisfactory as presenting the form of thought.

LS: In other words, this was always perfectly all right, and no Christian living in the Middle Ages could find any fault with that.

Mr. Reinken:

> And one essential point in this doctrine was the recognition of the divine nature as not in any sense an otherworld existence, but as a unity with human nature in the present and actual—

LS: "In the present," underlined again. No "actual."

Mr. Reinken:

> But this presence is at the same time exclusively spiritual presence. Christ as a particular human personality—

LS: "As this human being."

Mr. Reinken:

> has left the world. His temporal existence is only a past one. That is, it exists only in mental conception.[3]

LS: A literal translation would be "only represented"; in German, *vorgestellt*. But if you translate it into English or, for that matter, into Latin, as Hegel knew as a matter of course, then what you see represented is of course not "present"; it is "re-presented." Now what does "presence" mean there? Presence is opposed not so much to the past, but to the beyond. "Presence" is presence in this world. And it must be, in Christianity, spiritual presence. It is also opposed to the past, namely, to what is only represented and not directly present. In other words, the difficulty with the medieval Catholic position is concerned with the status of the presence of Christ in this world. How is he present?

Mr. Reinken:

And since the divine existence on earth is essentially of a spiritual character, it cannot appear in the form of a Dalai Lama.

LS: You remember that. In case you don't read the papers about Tibet,[4] you know it from Hegel himself.

Mr. Reinken:

The Pope, however high his position as the head of Christendom and the vicar of Christ, calls himself only the servant of servants. How, then, did the Church realize Christ as *a definite and present existence?*

LS: How, then, did the [Church] possess within itself Christ as "this one," unexchangeable with any other "this one"?

Mr. Reinken:

The principal form of this realization was, as remarked above, the Holy Supper, in the form it presented as the Mass: in this the Life, Suffering, and Death of the actual Christ were verily present, as an eternal and daily repeated sacrifice. Christ appears as a definite and present existence—

LS: Christ appears as "this one." It is Christ himself as "this one."

Mr. Reinken:

in a sensuous form as the Host, consecrated by the Priest; so far all is satisfactory: that is to say, it is the Church, the Spirit of Christ, that attains in this ordinance direct and full assurance. But the most prominent feature in this sacrament is, that the process by which Deity is manifested, is conditioned by the limitations—

LS: No. "Fastened," "fixed," as "this one."

Mr. Reinken:

that the Host, this thing, is set up to be adored as God.

LS: Whether that is the correct interpretation of the Catholic teaching of transubstantiation is a matter which we must leave open. But here—and that is the point—Christ is present, but he is present in the Host, meaning in each particular congregation in this Host.

Mr. Reinken:

The Church then might have been able to content itself with this sensuous presence of Deity; but when it is once granted that God exists in external phenomenal presence, this external manifestation immediately becomes infinitely varied; for the need of this presence is infinite. Thus innumerable instances will occur in the experience of the Church, in which Christ has appeared to one and another, in various places; and still more frequently his divine Mother, who as standing nearer to humanity, is a second mediator between the Mediator and man (the miracle-working images of the Virgin are in their way Hosts, since they supply a benign and gracious presence of God).

LS: You see again the word "presence." The concern with presence is a legitimate concern, according to Hegel, but is misunderstood by Catholic Christianity.

Mr. Reinken:

In all places, therefore, there will occur manifestations of the Heavenly, in specially gracious appearances, the stigmata of Christ's Passion, etc.; and the Divine will be realized in miracles as detached and isolated phenomena.

LS: Again, as "this one" or "that one" in a particular way.

Mr. Reinken:

In the period in question the Church presents the aspect of a world of miracle; to the community of devout and pious persons natural existence has utterly lost its stability and certainty.

LS: Why has it utterly lost its ultimate stability?

Mr. Reinken: Miracles popping up all over the place?

LS: Or could. This alone deprives natural existence of its ultimate certainty.

Mr. Reinken:

Rather, absolute certainty has turned against it, and the Divine is not conceived of by Christendom under conditions of universality as the law and nature of Spirit, but reveals itself in isolated and detached phenomena, in which the rational form of existence is utterly perverted.[5]

LS: So the Church is concerned with a sensible, carnal Christ, and this leads to the belief in miracles. The divine is within the world, that is true. But in Catholic Christianity, the divine is within the world not as law and nature of the spirit, but as interruption of the lawfulness. Hegel has sketched first the power and beauty of the Church in this way. But it is also understood that there is need for evidence of its truth. The Church must be present in this world, must be a visible Church as it is in Catholicism. But visible *as* Church, Hegel says, visible to the mind's eye. Yet in fact the visibility of the Church is dependent on miracles, traditions, and so on. Now the next paragraph.
Mr. Reinken:

In this complete development of the Church, we may find a deficiency: but what can be felt as a want by it?

LS: In other words, what we feel as a deficiency has no historical significance because it did not affect medieval man. Only an effect felt by the medieval Church could induce it to undergo any changes. Is this clear?
Mr. Reinken:

What compels it, in this state of perfect satisfaction and enjoyment, to wish for something else within the limits of its own principles—without apostatizing from itself? Those miraculous images, places, and times, are only isolated points, momentary appearances—are not an embodiment of Deity, not of the highest and absolute kind. The Host, the supreme manifestation, is to be found indeed in innumerable churches; Christ is therein transubstantiated to a present and particular existence: but this itself is of a vague and general character; it is not his actual and very presence as particularized in Space.

LS: In other words, the multiplicity of hosts deprives this Host of the absoluteness. It cannot be *the* absolutely sacred because there are many of them. Yes?
Mr. Reinken:

That presence has passed away, as regards time; but as spatial and as concrete in space it has a mundane permanence in this particular spot, this particular village, etc. It is then this mundane existence in Palestine which Christendom desiderates, which it is resolved on attaining. Pilgrims in crowds had indeed been able to enjoy it; but the approach to the hallowed localities is in the hands of the Infidels, and it is a reproach to Christendom that the Holy Places and the Sepulchre of Christ in particular are not in possession of the Church. In this feeling Christendom was united; consequently the Crusades were undertaken, whose object was not the furtherance of any special interests on the part of the several states that engaged in them, but simply and solely the conquest of the Holy Land.[6]

LS: Because of the Sepulchre, the uniqueness. What then is the link? The carnal understanding of Christianity. A carnal presence as an absolute presence which the Host as being many hosts could not have. Only a single carnal thing, this one in this world. And this condition was fulfilled only by the Holy Sepulchre.

As for the beginning of this section, not the need or defect which we feel in studying a historical phenomenon, but the need or defect which the historical subject itself feels can explain this history, the concrete development. Let us take an extreme example. If we study some early Greek doctrine or work of art and find it very defective, this cannot possibly explain the development of Greek art. Our feeling wasn't there. We have to find out what defects felt by the Greeks of the time led, say, from archaic art to classic art, and the same applies here. In order to show how necessary that is, let us say that we find the Middle Ages defective. This would not explain that something else came out of it. We also find China and India defective. We saw they were dead-end streets and nothing came out of them. Only a defect felt by medieval men—whereas no defect was felt by the Indians and Chinese according to Hegel's hypothesis—can explain why mankind went from the Middle Ages to modernity.

Again, regarding this construction which Hegel makes of the Crusades, we must also see the empirical basis. You will remember that Hegel's philosophy of history is in one sense empirical. And he raises the question: What is that visible act of Christendom as a whole most characteristic of the Middle Ages? And then, of course, not 1066 and all that—this was a limited thing in Britain—but the Crusades. Hence it is necessary to understand the Crusades from the very principle of medieval Christianity. Up to this point, Hegel's thought is clear. Let us read the next paragraph.

Mr. Reinken:

> The West once more sallied forth in hostile array against the East. As in the expedition of the Greeks against Troy, so here the invading hosts were entirely composed of independent feudal lords and knights; though they were not united under a real individuality, as were the Greeks under Agamemnon or Alexander. Christendom, on the contrary, was engaged in an undertaking whose object was the securing of the definite and present existence—

LS: Of the "this one" again. The true peak of individuality.

Mr. Reinken:

> This object impelled the West against the East, and this is the essential interest of the Crusades.

LS: I believe the comparison of the Trojan war and the Crusades was repeated by Spengler—I couldn't swear to that—but from a very different point of view: you know, that all the cultures go through the same kind of development. But Hegel is much more interested in the radical difference. There could not be a single leader like Agamemnon, or for that matter Alexander the Great, because the peak, the "this one," was Christ. But Christ is understood carnally here—Christ's sepulchre. Go on.

Mr. Reinken:

> The first and immediate commencement of the Crusades was made in the West itself. Many thousands of Jews were massacred, and their property seized; and after this terrible prelude, Christendom began its march. The monk, Peter the hermit of Amiens, led the way with an immense troop of rabble. This host passed in the greatest disorder through Hungary, and robbed and plundered as they went, but their numbers dwindled away, and only a few reached Constantinople. For rational considerations were out of the question. The mass of them believed that God would be their immediate guide and protector. The most striking proof that enthusiasm almost robbed the nations of Europe of their senses is supplied by the fact

that at a later time, troops of children ran away from their parents and went to Marseilles, there to take ship to the Holy Land. Few reached it; the rest were sold by the merchants to the Saracens as slaves.[7]

LS: The Crusades thus were much more irrational than the Trojan war. The Trojan war was declared to be irrational by some Greeks because it was immensely foolish for a single woman of doubtful manners to bring this enormous sacrifice. This one must remember. But Hegel says the Crusades were still much more irrational. And this is of course in connection with his whole judgment of the Middle Ages.

Let us turn to page 393, line 10. The result of the Crusades.

Mr. Reinken:

You must not look for the principle of your religion in the Sensuous, in the grave among the dead, but in the living Spirit in yourselves. We have seen how the vast idea of the union of the Finite with the Infinite was perverted to such a degree as that men looked for a definite embodiment of the Infinite in a mere isolated outward object. Christendom found the empty Sepulchre, but not the union of the Secular and the Eternal; and so it lost the Holy Land.

LS: In other words, the external failure of the Crusades was a necessary consequence of the irrationality of the fundamental conception.

Mr. Reinken:

It was practically undeceived; and the result which it brought back with it was of a negative kind, viz., that the definite embodiment which it was seeking—

LS: Again, the "this one."

Mr. Reinken:

the *this* embodiment which it was seeking was to be looked for in Subjective Consciousness alone, and in no external object; that the definite form in question—

LS: Again, the "this one."

Mr. Reinken:

the *this* one in question presenting the union of the Secular with the Eternal, is the Spiritual self-cognizant independence of the individual.

LS: "Of the person," he says here.
Mr. Reinken:

Thus the world attains the conviction that man must look within himself for —

LS: "for the this one which is of a divine character."
Mr. Reinken:

Subjectivity thereby receives absolute authorization and claims to determine for itself the relation to the Divine. This then was the absolute result of the Crusades, and from them we may date the commencement of self-reliance and spontaneous activity. The West bade an eternal farewell to the East at the Holy Sepulchre, and gained a comprehension of its own principle of subjective infinite Freedom. Christendom never appeared again on the scene of history as one body.[8]

LS: So this was the absolutely decisive event. The bond between the worldly and the eternal must indeed be found in this one which is the Aristotelian *tode ti* — *this* one as distinguished from any general or universal. *This* table, *this* man, *this* dog, *this* house as that which is truly in Aristotle's scheme in contradistinction to the form or to the concept, as you can say. So the bond between the worldly and the eternal must be found in a *this* one, but not in any *thing*, only in the subjective consciousness, in the ego. I, *this* one. Because the ego, too, is a *this* one. Another man is not I. Therefore the Crusades is the turning point.

Now on page 394, line 3 following, when he speaks of some particular crusades. The Spanish crusades against the Saracens in southern Spain. "The Spaniards allied with Frankish knights."
Mr. Reinken:

undertook frequent expeditions against the Saracens; and in this collision of the Christians with the chivalry of the East — with its freedom and perfect independence of soul — the former became also partakers in this freedom.

LS: In one respect, Islam is superior to medieval Christianity: freedom and complete independence of the soul. This, in spite of all the defects of Islam of which Hegel has spoken before, made Islam superior to medieval Christianity. One could perhaps say there is no Islamic clergy comparable to the Catholic clergy. This is a sign of that. Page 395, line 3.

Mr. Reinken:

> The fall of the Church was not to be effected by open violence, it was from within—by the power of Spirit and by an influence that wrought its way upwards—that ruin threatened it.

LS: In other words, this is a quite teleological statement, as you see here. Theoretically, it would be thinkable that the political powers of the Middle Ages might have reduced the power of the Church and in a way subordinated the Church to worldly power. But this would not have been good, for open violence would have been understood then as merely this-worldly, as merely sinful. Therefore the undermining of the power of the Church had to come from an entirely spiritual ground. Now on the same page, line 18.

Mr. Reinken:

> A rupture, the first of its kind and profound as it was novel, took place. From this time forward we witness religious and intellectual movements in which Spirit—transcending the repulsive and irrational existence by which it is surrounded—either finds its sphere of exercise within itself, and draws upon its own resources for satisfaction or throws its energies into an actual world of general and morally justified aims, which are therefore aims consonant with Freedom.[9]

LS: So in other words, no merely political subjugation of the Church, but the development was in two ways: either the spirit goes within itself or else it turns towards the actuality of universal and justified purposes which, because they are universal and justified, are purposes of freedom. The first phenomenon is the order of monks and of knights—Franciscans, Dominicans, Templars and so on—of which he speaks in the immediate sequel. And the other thing is the development of scholastic theology which took place in the High Middle Ages after the first Crusades. He speaks of it on page 397, second paragraph, where he compares scholastic disputations to the tournaments of the knights. These are tournaments of thought. It is a kind of knightly philosophy from Hegel's point of view, by which he implies that scholastic disputation, originally called dialectic if we go back to Aristotle, is not dialectic in Hegel's sense. This only in passing. Now the second phenomenon is the turning towards universal, justified purposes of which he speaks on page 398 following, and that is the transition of feudalism into the state. The Church was absolutely superior morally, in spite of all its defects, to sheer feudalism because feudalism did not have a spiritual rational principle. But in the moment the state emerged, the situation was fundamentally altered. Let us read page 398, second paragraph.

Mr. Reinken:

> The moral phenomena above mentioned, tending in the direction of a general principle, were partly of a subjective, partly of a speculative order. But we must now give particular attention to the practical political movements of the period. The advance which that period witnessed presents a negative aspect in so far as it involves the termination of the sway of individual caprice—

LS: "Subjective" caprice. Let us keep this word in mind.

Mr. Reinken:

> and of the isolation of power. Its affirmative aspect is the rise of a supreme authority whose dominion embraces all—a political power properly so called, whose subjects enjoy an equality of rights, and in which the will of the individual is subordinated to that common interest which underlies the whole.

LS: "The substantial purpose." Yes. "And this is the progress."

Mr. Reinken:

> This is the progress from feudalism to monarchy. The principle of feudal sovereignty is the outward force of individuals—princes, liege lords; it is a force destitute of intrinsic right. The subjects of such a constitution are vassals of the superior prince or *seigneur* to whom they have stipulated duties to perform, but whether they perform these duties or not depends upon the *seigneur's* being able to induce them so to do by force of character or grant of favors. Conversely, the recognition of those feudal claims themselves was extorted by violence in the first instance; and the fulfill-

ment of the corresponding duties could be secured only by the constant exercise of the power which was the sole basis of the claims in question. The monarchical principle also implies a supreme authority, but it is an authority over persons possessing no independent power to support their subjective caprice; here we have no longer caprice opposed to caprice; for the supremacy implied in monarchy is essentially a power emanating from the political body, and is pledged to the furtherance of that equitable purpose on which the constitution of a state is based. Feudal sovereignty is a polyarchy—

LS: "Feudal rule," let us say.
Mr. Reinken:

We see nothing but lords and serfs. In monarchy, on the contrary, there is one Lord and no Serf, for servitude is abrogated by it, and in it Right and Law are recognized; it is the source of real freedom.

LS: And then, a little bit later. "But through the arbitrary."
Mr. Reinken:

will of an individual exerting itself—

LS: Which is a characteristic of monarchy.
Mr. Reinken:

so as to subjugate a whole body of men, a community is formed; and comparing this state of things with that in which every point is a centre of capricious violence, we find a much smaller number of points exposed to such violence. The great extent of such a sovereignty necessitates general arrangements for the purposes of organization, and those who govern in accordance with those arrangements are at the same time, in virtue of their office itself, obedient to the state.[10]

LS: What is the state, then, as far as we can gather from this passage? We have seen that the feudal arrangement is based on sheer superiority of force: violence. What do we find in the monarchy? Here monarchy is the state. One is reminded of a very famous definition of the state. What is the definition of the state which is most popular in present-day political sociology? Let us never forget our brother disciplines.

Mr. Reinken: Monopoly of violence.

LS: Monopoly of violence. Who made this definition? Max Weber. So Hegel says in a way that the difference between the monarch, the state, and feudalism is that the state has the monopoly of violence. But Hegel, being a broader man than Max Weber, doesn't leave it at that. Something else is as important. And what is that?

Mr. Shulsky: The fact that a large state has to be administered by set rules and that these aren't changed on a simply arbitrary basis.

LS: In other words, the monopoly of violence is only the condition of the rule of law, and therefore the state is characterized by rule of law in the first place and monopoly of violence in the second place. Monopoly of violence means the abolition of private violence. "Monopoly" is a very silly word. Only one seller of violence—that is the literal meaning. We have seen this in the case just settled by Judge Leighton, who denied that these policemen had bought the violence in a legal manner, i.e., that it was a mere buying and not a mere taking without right.[11]

In the sequel, Hegel makes quite interesting remarks about the various forms taken by the transformation of feudalism into the modern state. He emphasizes the importance of nations. In the most obvious and important cases, these states were nation-states—France, Spain, England. Germany and Italy are the difficult cases; they got their national unity very late. It would be an interesting question, which Hegel does not take up here, whether there is a necessary connection between the modern state and the nation. In order to answer that question one would of course have to know in the first place what a nation is. If one takes the commonsensical definition, a nation is a group of men who use the same language and are or believe themselves to be—it doesn't make the slightest difference—of the same descent. Then you get into trouble in the case of, e.g., Switzerland, where they use three different languages, or whether the Dutch language is a different language from German. That is a long question. The northwestern Germans understand the Dutch better than they would understand southern Bavarians. Great difficulties arise here. But in a crude way of course it is true that the modern states are nation-states.

Needless to say, this concept of nation had infinite practical consequences, as you all know, for the self-determination of nations. And especially in the case of the underdeveloped, alias emergent, nations, where you don't know who makes them nations; whether some so-called intellectuals who simply transform a former colony, a unity which existed only by virtue of that deplorable fact of colonialism, justify the fact that this, what was formerly French Togo, is now[12]—I forget what it is, but any of you who are studying these things could tell us.

Then there follows in the sequel a remark on Switzerland, and especially on the origin of Switzerland and the three primary cantons of Switzerland; and here he makes a remark about gunpowder to which you referred. That is on page 402. He remarks that the peasants defeated the knights in Switzerland.

Mr. Reinken:

The peasants, with club and iron-studded mace, returned victorious from a contest with haughty steel-clad nobles, armed with spear and sword, and practiced in the chivalric encounters of the tournament. Another invention also tended to deprive the nobility of the ascendancy which they owed to their accoutrements—that of gunpowder. Humanity needed it, and it made its appearance forthwith. It was one of the chief instruments in freeing the world from the dominion of physical force, and placing the various orders of society on a level.

LS: Freed man from the undesirable kind of wars.

Mr. Reinken:

With the distinction between the weapons they used, vanished also that between lords and serfs. And before gunpowder fortified places were no longer impregnable, so that strongholds and castles now lose their importance. We may indeed be led to lament the decay or the depreciation of the practical value of personal valor—the bravest, the noblest may be shot down by a cowardly wretch at safe distance in an obscure lurking place; but, on the other hand, gunpowder has made a rational, considerate bravery—Spiritual valor—the essential to martial success. Only through this instrumentality could that superior order of valor be called forth—that valor in which the heat of personal feeling has no share; for the discharge of firearms is directed against a body of men—an abstract enemy, not individual combatants. The warrior goes to meet deadly peril calmly, sacrificing himself for the common weal; and the valor of cultivated nations is characterized by the very fact that it does not rely on the strong arm alone, but places its confidence essentially in the intelligence, the generalship, the character of its commanders; and, as was the case among the ancients, in a firm combination and unity of spirit on the part of the forces they command.[13]

LS: But the interest is that they have gunpowder. That is something which would have been considered. And also the following question. Hegel, in the sanguine nineteenth century, could believe—which we no longer believe—that this abstractness of fighting, brought about by gunpowder, does away with hatreds. And that, I think, has not proved to be true. But this only in passing.

It is very terrible. We will not be able to finish this discussion, but one more thing. In the next paragraph, he quotes a passage from Machiavelli. Let us limit ourselves to the barest necessity. When he speaks of the papal territory in Italy there were innumerable dynasts, and yet they were all subjugated to the rule of the pope. Do you have that?

Mr. Reinken:

How thoroughly equitable in the view of social morality such a subjugation was, is evident from Machiavelli's celebrated work *The Prince*. This book has often been thrown aside in disgust as replete with the maxims of the most revolting tyranny, but nothing worse can be urged against it than that the writer, having the profound consciousness of the necessity for the formation of a state, has here exhibited the principles on which alone states could be founded in the circumstances of the times. The chiefs who asserted an isolated independence, and the power they arrogated, must be entirely subdued; and though we cannot reconcile with our idea of freedom the means which he proposes as the only efficient ones and regards as perfectly justifiable—in as much as they involve the most reckless violence, all kinds of deception, assassination and so forth—we must nevertheless confess that the feudal nobility, whose power was to be subdued, were assailable in no other way, since an indomitable contempt for principle, and an utter depravity of morals, were thoroughly ingrained in them.[14]

LS: In other words, Machiavelli was perfectly right, as you rightly understood him. He doesn't suit our notions. That reminds me of a remark which Churchill made in his *The Gathering Storm* when he spoke of Mussolini's attempt to subjugate Ethiopia, knowing very well that Britain had conquered these territories before and so they didn't have a great right to protest against this effort themselves. He said it simply wasn't suitable to the temper of the twentieth century.[15] If in the nineteenth century, you know, the Italians had tried to conquer Ethiopia but failed dismally, that would have been entirely different. And Hegel says that if, *per impossibile*, there would be a similar mess in the nineteenth century, you couldn't do anything. What can you do against people who are one hundred percent criminals other than to subjugate them? Cesare Borgia sets a beautiful example of the use of deception in inviting these people to a negotiation table and then, while they are sitting there, having them massacred.[16] Is this more inhuman than formally declaring war against these people and having much greater bloodshed on both sides? Hegel takes a very tough line here.

A very grand passage occurs on page 406, paragraph 2, where he tries to summarize the medieval development. Read only the last sentence which is on page 407. "Mankind has not been liberated so much from servitude as through servitude." That is a great sentence and surely in need of profound consideration, that men owe many blessings to servitude. In a way, that is the whole lesson of Hegel's *Phenomenology of the Mind*: the serf, the slave, subjugated by the master, succumbing to the master because of a failure of nerve in the life-and-death struggle, this man has to work and does not enjoy the fruits of his work—the fruits of his work are enjoyed by the master—but is the origin of a higher culture because he is compelled to actualize all the powers of his mind and of his heart in order to acquire self-respect. This is a very profound thought with deep present-day implications into which I do not wish to go for reasons of simple propriety.

Then he speaks about the importance of art. A certain overcoming of the medieval Church took place in the development of high art. Hegel contends that the beautiful art, let us say leading up especially to the Renaissance art, and pious art are two very different things. The French speak of a certain kind of pious art which they call *l'art de Saint Sulpice*, the kind of simple religious art which they sell in the neighborhood of the Church Saint-Sulpice in Paris. Hegel has something like this in mind. I think that it is inevitable from any religious point of view, not only Christian, that art has something which is not entirely in agreement with the spirit of piety. In one of Gide's novels—*The Narrow Gate*, I believe, is the English title—this is very beautifully developed by Alissa, the heroine.[17] I only draw your attention here to that. And he speaks of course of humanism, let us read what it means.

Mr. Reinken:

> For Art received a further support and experienced an elevating influence as the result of the study of antiquity (the name *Humanioria* is very expressive, for in those works of antiquity honor is done to the Human and to the development of Humanity).[18]

LS: In other words, you see here the connection between the discovery of the "this one" in the human subjectivity and humanism. And Hegel would have to explain to us why humanism of the sixteenth century is claiming to be a restoration of classical ways of thinking, not simply a restoration but a modification.

On page 410 at the end of paragraph 2, Hegel makes a point which is very characteristic when he speaks of the age of discovery and the discovery of the magnet and the compass.

Mr. Reinken:

The recognition of the spherical figure of the earth led man to perceive that it offered him a definite and limited object, and navigation had been benefited by the new-found instrumentality of the magnet enabling it to be something better than mere coasting: thus technical appliances make their appearance when a need for them is experienced.[19]

LS: In other words, the mere history of technology would never explain anything. How many discoveries and observations have been made which were forgotten in the moment they were made because there was no felt need for them? Therefore, we have to go back to the center of the human mind in order to understand the history of that.

We will have to discuss quite a bit in the sequel, but the time is up. The next time will be the last meeting, so this will be a rather incomplete discussion of Hegel's *Philosophy of History*. But as you all are aware, even if we had—as I could have ordered for my times—two-and-a-half-hour, then three-hour seminars, the discussion would still be very insufficient for exhausting the wealth of what we find in Hegel.

16   The Reformation, Enlightenment, and French Revolution

Leo Strauss: Now I turn to Mr. Schaefer's paper. You had to take up the most difficult and grave questions.[1] If I start from the last, what is the precise difference, stated simply, between Hegel and the Enlightenment?

Mr. Schaefer: The Enlightenment believed that it had established what should be the proper role for all men's thought, not only for the majority of men. Secondly, the Enlightenment believed that it could deduce the principles of morality from social instincts discovered in man rather than from a metaphysical principle.

LS: I wonder whether this goes to the root of the matter. But there is something which you said that Hegel shares with the Enlightenment.

Mr. Schaefer: He shares with the Enlightenment the belief, first of all, that men have increased their freedom in a sense through science by being able to enjoy the fruits and . . . nature to a set of laws, and also because I think that he believes that for most men it is good that philosophy can be popularized and make people think that they have attained the status of philosophers.

LS: Well, that is a bit vague. Could one not say that Hegel shares with the Enlightenment its this-worldliness with all its implications? But where does he deviate from the Enlightenment?

Mr. Schaefer: The way he describes the Enlightenment, it cut off a realm of thought for man, metaphysics and religion. This is most brought out by the fact that in one paragraph he says: "The Enlightenment banished all of the speculative," and two paragraphs later he describes the principle of the freedom of the will as speculative.

LS: Because it did not know the freedom of the will as Hegel understands it. That is the point.

Mr. Schaefer: But Hegel, I think in the introduction to the *Philosophy of History*, implies that the principle can be known without looking to history, and he is only trying to provide some demonstration of it for people in general like tracing it through history.

LS: I don't think that this will do. One could say that the Enlightenment as Hegel understands it—he thinks of course chiefly of the radical French Enlightenment—was fundamentally natural science and a model of political science based on natural science. In other words, a precursor of what we have now. This he regards as radically defective. The key point is for him that the natural in the fullest sense cannot make intelligible freedom. And therefore he agrees there with Kant at this point, although he has also certain differences with Kant.

Let me turn to two other points. You began by making some remarks about the difference between Hegel and Hobbes. One can perhaps state the difference as follows. In the first place, Hobbes does not simply teach that monarchy is the best order. That is a kind of recommendation. It doesn't have, according to his own statement, the same certainty as the general teaching about the character of the sovereign, that he must have these and these powers. But that the sovereign should be one man is not a necessity from Hobbes's point of view. But that doesn't go to the root of the matter because there are various kinds of monarchy, the kind which he calls institutional and the kind which he calls patrimonial—if this is the term which he uses, patrimonial; I am speaking from memory. At any rate, this is crucial. Hegel would never accept the patrimonial, patriarchal monarchy as a possible form of monarchy, only the institutional, constitutional monarchy.

The greatest difficulty which your assignment poses concerns of course the question of Catholicism. There are these statements to which you refer which deny that a reasonable state is compatible with Catholicism, and the consequence would seem to be that only Protestants can be full members of the reasonable state. Hegel clearly did not mean this. He did not draw this conclusion. The reasonable state is not in this sense a Protestant establishment state. How is this possible if Hegel's judgments on the Catholic Church, which occur again here with very great force, are his last word about Catholicism?

Mr. Schaefer: I think that Hegel would say that it would be possible for Catholics as well as Protestants to be members of a rational state if they took their religion less seriously than the men of the Inquisition and of the Crusades, that is, if they were willing to say that they didn't want to accept anything incompatible with the state.

LS: Who is the great political hero of Protestantism according to Hegel?

Mr. Schaefer: Frederick II of Prussia.[2]

LS: And he was a Lutheran. Still, what was his persuasion? What kind of company did he keep? French philosophers: Voltaire and so on. So Frederick the Great was an enlightened despot who accepted the principle that everyone should become blessed according to his fashion. According to his private view, perfect tolerance . . .

Then what about the Enlightenment? Hegel presents the Enlightenment as a kind of necessary continuation of Lutheranism, of the Reformation, freedom of judgment of each still bound by the Bible and Luther and Calvin, but in the Enlightenment the Bible itself loses this authoritative character. But is it true from Hegel's point of view that the Enlightenment necessarily proceeds from Protestantism? Who is the archrationalist according to Hegel?

Mr. Schaefer: Descartes.

LS: Yes, and Descartes was a Catholic. So in other words, Hegel emphasizes more than once that in certain respects Catholicism was superior to Protestantism.

Mr. Schaefer: I think that the difference is this. He says that religion is the form in which truth exists for nonabstract consciousness. So I think he would say that whereas it is possible for a philosopher, a man of deep insight, to become enlightened without changing his religion, for the people at large for whom their religious disposition is more important and who can never fully understand the truth, they must first have a reformation before they can accept the political teachings of the Enlightenment.

LS: At any rate, for Hegel the enlightened view out of which, through Kant, his own view came is not simply a product of the Reformation. We can go into this later. This is our last meeting, and we must discuss the most important points. Let us begin on page 451, line 5 from bottom. Hegel had given a brief account of what had happened up to his time. Hegel died in 1831, that is to say after the July Revolution in France.[3]

Mr. Reinken:

At length, after forty years of war and confusion indescribable, a weary heart might fain congratulate itself on seeing a termination and tranquillization of all these disturbances.

LS: He says, "an old heart," literally translated. He was sixty years old and died a year later.
Mr. Reinken:

> But although one main point is set at rest, there remains on the one hand that rupture which the Catholic principle inevitably occasions, on the other hand that which has to do with men's subjective will.

LS: The Catholics—that is one great difficulty. And the other is the one caused by the non-Catholics, especially by the "completely enlightened people."
Mr. Reinken:

> In regard to the latter, the main feature of incompatibility still presents itself—

LS: "Of one-sidedness," the main one-sidedness.
Mr. Reinken:

> one-sidedness still presents itself in the requirement that the ideal general will—

LS: No, "that the general will should be also the empirically general."
Mr. Reinken:

> that is, that the units of the state, in their individual capacity, should rule, or at any rate take part in the government.

LS: "That the individuals as such should rule or participate in the government." In other words, a simplistic solution of Rousseau's problem. The general will is the will of the preponderant majority.
Mr. Reinken:

> Not satisfied with the establishment of rational rights, with freedom of person and property, with the existence of a political organization in which are to be found various circles of civil life each having its own functions to perform, and with that influence over the people which is exercised by the intelligent members of the community and the confidence that is felt

in them, "Liberalism" sets up in opposition to all this the atomistic principle, that which insists upon the sway of individual wills; maintaining that
all government should emanate from their express power, and have their
express sanction.

LS: "Consent." "The explicit consent."
Mr. Reinken:

Asserting this formal side of Freedom—this abstraction—the party in
question allows no political organization to be firmly established. The
particular arrangements of the government are forthwith opposed by the
advocates of Liberty as the mandates of a particular will, and branded as
displays of arbitrary power. The will of the Many expels the Ministry from
power, and those who had formed the Opposition fill the vacant places,
but the latter having now become the Government, meet with hostility
from the Many, and share the same fate. Thus agitation and unrest are
perpetuated. This collision, this *nodus*, this problem is that with which
history is now occupied, and whose solution it has to work out in the
future.[4]

LS: This is probably the strongest statement in favor of the view that
Hegel still sees unsolved fundamental problems.[5] That is the general importance which this passage has for our overall problem. What precisely
is the problem? The rights of man, let us use this simple expression. This
principle is recognized now; and if it is not recognized, this will come. But
what is lacking in the liberal doctrine, liberal as it was understood in the
early nineteenth century?

Mr. Shulsky: What we could call democratic government.

LS: In other words, this liberalism tended to be democratic. There
were still property qualifications and this kind of thing, but it tended to
be democratic.

Student: There has to be a disposition in the whole people to accept
reasonable principles.

LS: But this is too general. That doesn't help us. How do we get a
government? That is the question. In other words, Hegel denies that the
rights of man include political rights strictly speaking, a right to participation in government. And what is the reasoning behind that?

Student: The individual will may not be rational. The individual majority wills may not will what's right.

LS: To repeat again, one must recognize the freedom of each. No abridgement of these rights on account of race or creed. That goes without saying for Hegel. But this does not include the right of each to participation in government via voting since government rests on a principle different from freedom, and this principle is competence and excellence, which not every man has.[6] Hegel had spoken of monarchy, but he also makes clear that the monarch is not the truly governing man. He has to formalize and finalize the decision by signing on the dotted line, but who frames the decision?

Mr. Shulsky: He seems to favor a civil service.

LS: The ministers or high officials, and they are supposed to be competent and honorable men. A high-class civil service, including of course a military service, which guarantees its continuity by cooptation, naturally. You know, who will be minister next time will be a same member of the same governing group, not governing class. The question is whether this is not much more unreal than constitutional democracy, if it is a democracy which has a written or unwritten constitution guaranteeing stability of government. What Hegel regards here as an absolutely terrible thing — that as soon as the opposition comes into power there will be another opposition — is not necessarily such a terrible thing, as we have come to see in some of the more stable countries.

But the main point for the overall judgment is that here Hegel does not see a clear way of how the West . . . will find its way between the acceptance of the rights of man with its political implications — in other words, the democratic solution — or what he regards as better, the rights of man without the political implications, i.e., without democratic consequences. All kinds of things are possible there. Something like the so-called constitutional monarchy of Prussia in his time, which was not very constitutional — it did not have a written constitution at all, but had a certain orderliness and regularity of procedure and was surely not an arbitrary despotic regime. And in another way, one could find it perhaps in the Napoleonic Caesarism which came to France after the failure of liberalism in 1848. But Hegel doesn't seem to have thought of democracy at all.

Now let us go to some other passage — and as much as we can cover in the short time. We have not finished the section on the Reformation which we discussed last time. We have seen what Hegel says in praise of the Reformation, but what was the defect? Let us turn to page 424, the third paragraph.

Mr. Reinken:

In the first instance this reconciliation must take place in the individual soul, must be realized by feeling; the individual must gain the assurance that the Spirit dwells in him—that, in the language of the Church, a brokenness of heart has been experienced, and that Divine grace has entered into the heart thus broken. By Nature man is not what he ought to be; only through a transforming process does he arrive at Truth. The general and speculative aspect of the matter is just this—that the human heart is not what it should be. It was then required of the individual that he should know what he is in himself; that is, the teaching of the Church insisted upon—

LS: He means here the Protestant Church.
Mr. Reinken:

man's becoming conscious that he is evil. But the individual is evil only when the Natural manifests itself in mere sensual desire—when an unrighteous will presents itself in its untamed, untrained, violent shape; and yet it is required that such a person should know that he is depraved, and that the good Spirit dwells in him. In fact, he is required to have a direct consciousness of and to experience that which was presented to him as the speculative and implicit truth. The reconciliation having, then, assumed this abstract form, men tormented themselves with a view to force upon their souls the consciousness of their sinfulness and to know themselves as evil. The most simple souls, the most innocent natures, were accustomed in painful introspection to observe the most secret workings of the heart with the view to a rigid examination of them. With this duty was conjoined that of an entirely opposite description; it was required that man should attain the consciousness that the good Spirit dwells in him, that divine grace has found an entrance into his soul. In fact, the important distinction between the knowledge of abstract truth and the knowledge of what has actual existence was left out of sight. Men became the victims of a tormenting uncertainty as to whether the good Spirit has an abode in them, and it was deemed indispensable that the entire process of spiritual transformation should become perceptible to the individual himself. An echo of this self-tormenting process may still be traced in much of the religious poetry of that time. The psalms of David, which exhibit a similar character, were then introduced as hymns into the rituals of Protestant churches. Protestantism took this turn of minute and painful introspection, possessed with the conviction of the importance of the exercise, and was for a long time characterized by a self-tormenting disposition and an aspect of spiritual wretchedness; which in the present day has induced many persons to enter the Catholic pale, that they might exchange this inward uncertainty for a formal, broad certainty based on the imposing totality of the Church.[7]

LS: This is a point which we must not forget. This is the essential defect of Protestantism, according to Hegel. He speaks of it somewhat earlier, of having something pedantic about it, something sad, pettily moralistic. That is the same point which he means here. There is no objective certainty. The certainty of salvation must be found within the individual. And then how can he find it? He must observe himself and see with his own eyes the sinfulness in himself as well as the breakthrough of divine grace as well. And this is the meaning which the subjectivism of the Reformation takes on in practice and which leads to a dead-end street. Hegel's own view is that the individual cannot know what he is except through his deeds, through the whole course of his life. Through introspection you always get a distorted view of yourself. You have no terms of comparison.

In the sequel he develops his doctrine of monarchy, the need for government independent of all arbitrariness. And here Hegel says this is the simple solution, which he developed at length in his *Philosophy of Right.* Let us turn to page 427.

Mr. Reinken:

The State must have a final decisive will: but if an individual is to be the final deciding power, he must be so in a direct and natural way, not as determined by choice and theoretic views, etc. Even among the free Greeks the oracle was the external power which decided their policy on critical occasions; here birth is the oracle—something independent of any arbitrary volition.[8]

LS: We must ultimately have something which is independent of all arbitrariness, of all arbitrary will. And as regards the individual who is at the head of the government, the only way to get it is simple birth, because if you make it dependent on any characters, any qualities, that becomes a matter of judgment. Think of Aristotle's perfect king who is so superior to all others. But in practice this is not the case. As Aristotle makes clear, if he were also the most beautiful and the tallest member of the community in addition to being the wisest and most fully virtuous, then it might be; but since he might not be tall and beautiful, there would be a questioning of his authority, the matter of judgment. It must not be a matter of judgment; it must be purely natural. Birth alone would do that. This is the doctrine developed at great length in Hegel's *Philosophy of Right*.

A key institution in the monarchies is of course the standing armies which developed at that time, as he says in the sequel. The decisive development was the subjugation of the hereditary nobility or aristocracy during this century in all the European countries. That was necessary for the coming into being of the modern state; but on the other hand, Hegel is all in favor of there being privileged members of the state, the highest officials.

Mr. Reinken: Page 430, in the center.

> But the aristocracy have a position assigned them, as the support of the throne, as occupied and active on behalf of the State and the common weal, and at the same time as maintaining the freedom of the citizens. This is in fact the prerogative of the class which forms the link between the Sovereign and the People—to undertake to discern and to give the first impulse to that which is intrinsically Rational and Universal; and this recognition of and occupation with the Universal must take the place of positive personal right.

LS: Which was the state of the feudal nobility. Very simply, it had the privileged position by virtue of positive personal right, whereas in the modern state they have this position by virtue of their knowledge and their competence.

Student: I thought I understood you to say earlier that Hegel rejects the notion of patriarchal monarchy and the emphasis upon birth and . . .

LS: But the key point is that he is indeed a monarch by virtue of his birth, but the patrimonial monarchy means that he regards the state as his property. You can see the difference: Louis XIV was surely not a feudal monarch, but rather because he said *l'état, c'est moi*—"the state, that's me"—whereas Frederick the Great said the prince is the first servant of the state. The latter is what Hegel means. The king as a servant of the state or as a part of the state. That is the decisive point. Go on where you left off.

Mr. Reinken:

This subjection to the Head of the State of that intermediate power which laid claim to positive authority was now accomplished, but this did not involve—

LS: "Not yet," he says.
Mr. Reinken:

did not yet involve the emancipation of the subject class.

LS: "Of the serfs." In other words, this was still a great defect of the enlightened monarchy of the seventeenth and eighteenth centuries.
Mr. Reinken:

This took place only at a later date, when the idea of right in and for it-self arose in men's minds. Then the sovereigns, relying on their respective peoples, vanquished the caste of unrighteousness.[9]

LS: Who is the caste of unrighteousness?
Student: The French noblesse.
LS: The hereditary nobility all over Europe. You see, Hegel was very far from being in favor of the *ancien régime*.

Another characteristic of the monarchy of the seventeenth and eighteenth centuries concerns foreign relations. The principle becomes conquest. There is no longer any possibility of the unity of Christendom, as there was in the Middle Ages, however questionable it was there. And the only help against conquest was the balance of power. That is on page 431. Let us read the remark on page 432, line 14 from the end.
Mr. Reinken:

The pretensions of Louis were founded not on extent of dominion (as was the case with Charles V) so much as on that culture which distinguished his people, and which at that time made its way everywhere with the language that embodied it, and was the object of universal admiration: they could therefore plead a higher justification than those of the German emperor.[10]

LS: It is more Spain than Germany which he has in mind. In other words, their claim to universal empire based on the higher rank of civilization is not simply rejected by Hegel, as you see by this remark. We turn now to the question of Protestantism. On the center of page 435.

Mr. Reinken:

For in the State there must be government, and Cromwell knew what governing is. He therefore made himself ruler, and sent that praying parliament about their business.

LS: You see how secular Hegel is.

Mr. Reinken:

With his death however his right to authority vanished also, and the old dynasty regained possession of the throne.

LS: In other words, that was no way to a stable government, the revolution.

Mr. Reinken:

Catholicism, we may observe, is commended to the support of princes as promoting the security of their government—a position supposed to be particularly manifest if the Inquisition be connected with the government; the former constituting the bulwark of the latter. But such a security is based on a slavish religious obedience, and is limited to those grades of human development, in which the political constitution and the whole legal system still rest on the basis of actual positive possession.

LS: Meaning not on rational grounds.

Mr. Reinken:

But if the constitution and laws are to be founded on a veritable eternal Right, then security is to be found only in the Protestant religion, in whose principle Rational Subjective Freedom also attains development.[11]

LS: We know this by now from Hegel, but these passages suggest that you can have a reasonable state only on a Protestant foundation, and we see that this conclusion is not drawn by Hegel. In the immediate context he draws our attention to the fact that Frederick the Great—the hero of Protestantism, as he is called—understood the Protestant principle from its worldly angle and therefore was led to religious tolerance, not to say indifference.

Now let us turn to page 438, because here the question of Reformation and Enlightenment comes up.

Mr. Reinken:

Protestantism had introduced the principle of Subjectivity, importing religious emancipation and inward harmony, but accompanying this with the belief in Subjectivity as Evil—

LS: And the corruptedness of the will.
Mr. Reinken:

and in a power whose embodiment is "the World." Within the Catholic pale also, the casuistry of the Jesuits brought into vogue interminable investigations, as tedious and wire-drawn as those in which the scholastic theology delighted, respecting the subjective spring of the Will and the motives that affect it. This Dialectic, which unsettles all particular judgments and opinions, transmuting the Evil into Good and Good into Evil, left at last nothing remaining but the mere action of subjectivity itself, the *Abstractum* of Spirit—Thought. Thought contemplates everything under the form of Universality, and is consequently the impulsion towards and production of the Universal. In that elder scholastic theology the real subject-matter of investigation—the doctrine of the Church—remained an ultra-mundane affair.

LS: "A beyond." Why not leave it simply at that, namely, something beyond thought, suprarational?
Mr. Reinken:

In the Protestant theology also Spirit still sustained a relation to the beyond. For on the one side we have the will of the individual, the spirit of man, I myself, and on the other the grace of God, the Holy Ghost; and so in the wicked, the Devil. But in thought, self moves in the limits of its own sphere; that with which it is occupied, its objects, are as absolutely present to it. For in thinking, I must elevate the object to universality. This is utter and absolute freedom, for the pure ego, like pure light, is with itself alone. Thus that which is diverse from itself, sensuous or spiritual, no longer presents an object of dread, for in contemplating such diversity it is inwardly free and can freely confront it. A practical interest makes use of, consumes the objects offered to it: a theoretical interest calmly contemplates them, assured that in themselves they present no alien element.

LS: "Alien to it."
Mr. Reinken:

Consequently, the *ne plus ultra* of Inwardness, of Subjectiveness, is Thought. Man is not free, when he is not thinking; for except when thus engaged he sustains a relation to the world around him as to another, an alien form.

LS: Not only to the world. It would also be in the case of God. If he does not think, he is related to something else, to something other, whereas if he thinks, understands, it becomes his own.
Mr. Reinken:

This comprehension—the penetration of the Ego into and beyond other forms of being with the most profound self-certainty—directly involves the harmonization of Being.

LS: No, "the reconciliation." In other words, the reconciliation which was formerly sought in the grace of God. It is evidently available in thinking.
Mr. Reinken:

For it must be observed that the unity of Thought with its Object is already implicitly present, for Reason is the substantial basis of Consciousness as well as of the External and Natural. Thus that which presents itself as the Object of Thought—

LS: "Vis-à-vis." How do you translate *gegenüber?*
Mr. Reinken: External?
LS: Say, "the object is no longer a beyond."
Mr. Reinken:

not of an alien and grossly substantial nature.[12]

LS: "Not of another substantial nature." It has the same substantial nature. What does he mean? In the Protestant view from which he starts, the emphasis is stronger than in Catholicism, according to Hegel, on the corrupted nature. Man is completely corrupt, the will is in the grips of sin. The world, as distinguished from the inner grace, belongs to the devil; therefore, naturally the longing for the beyond.

Now how is the situation with Catholicism? In Catholicism what is decisive is the good will, not specific actions. This interpretation is of course based on a very special form, namely, on the doctrine of probability as developed by the Jesuits and as polemically presented by Pascal. This is simply presupposed. What Hegel has in mind is the attempts of some Jesuits. What this means is very controversial. According to Gilson,[13] these were not more than scholastic exercises, whereas Pascal and the Protestants took them to be very serious directions of the conscience. I cannot enter into this subject. But the question was this, for example. Dueling is forbidden. But then some of these Jesuit teachers said: It depends; when you kill in a duel but do not do it with the intention to kill, but with the intention to save your honor as a nobleman or officer, then it is not blamable. In other words, everything depends on the intention. The intention, Hegel says, the inner thinking. This is a very summary argument which wants to show that both for modern, seventeenth-century Catholicism and for Protestantism, the emphasis shifts entirely on the inner. And Hegel says that if this is properly understood, it means it shifts onto thought. The evidence in the history of philosophy of course would be Descartes's *Cogito ergo sum*, which he has in mind.

Now here comes the key point. Now the sphere is discovered—and fully discovered and laid bare—within which reconciliation is possible, namely, thought. And why? Because thought knows no beyond. This is the meaning of the thesis that thought is free. As Hegel understands it, thought is never dependent on something other than thought. Therefore, here the conflict, the disharmony between thought and nonthought which primordially exists and which is the root of all human problems, theoretical or practical, is overcome. Thought recognizes itself in every sphere. Now what does Hegel have in mind by that? It seems simply to be a fantastic assertion. If we read on we will get some enlightenment from the sequel.

Mr. Reinken:

Thought is the grade to which Spirit has now advanced.

LS: Did it not advance to that in Plato and Aristotle? Why not?

Mr. Shulsky: It was directed towards nature, which wasn't the same thing; it was something external.

LS: One can put it this way, but more simply and obviously: this society, the political order, was the Greek city with all its qualifications— slavery, Greekness, particularism, and so on. "Thought contains." Go on.

Mr. Reinken:

It involves the Harmony of Being in its purest essence, challenging the external world to exhibit the same Reason which Subject possesses.

LS: First of all, it is only a demand, a postulate. Thought turns now to the external demanding that it exhibit its reasonableness in itself.

Mr. Reinken:

Spirit perceives that Nature—the World—must also be an embodiment of Reason, for God created it on principles of Reason.

LS: This is then the theological, popular version of the thought. But we will soon find what this means in a speculative, nonpopular manner.

Mr. Reinken:

An interest in the contemplation and comprehension of the present world became universal.

LS: The present world—the world which we can see and observe— just as the presence was the key problem of Christianity from the very beginning and a certain misunderstanding of the presence, as we have seen, led to the Crusades. Do you remember that?

Mr. Reinken:

Nature embodies Universality, inasmuch as it is nothing other than Sorts, Genera, Power, Gravitation, etc.—

LS: "Force," one should translate, instead of "power." So in other words, that nature is rational is shown by the fact that nature embodies universals. Species and genera, forces of nature, gravity, and so on.

Mr. Reinken:

phenomenally presented. Thus Experimental Science became the science of the World.

LS: He says, "Experience has become the science of the world." Experience which is always present experience.
Mr. Reinken:

For experience involves on the one hand the observation of phenomena, on the other hand also the discovery of the Law, the essential being, the hidden force that causes those phenomena—thus reducing the data supplied by observation to their simple principles.

LS: In other words, modern natural science, experimental science discovers laws of nature, and laws mean rationality. It discovers the rationality of nature.
Mr. Reinken:

Intellectual consciousness was first extricated from that sophistry of thought, which unsettles everything, by Descartes. As it was the purely German nations among whom the principle of Spirit first manifested itself, so it was by the Romanic nations that the abstract idea (to which the character assigned them above—viz., that of internal schism, more readily conducted them) was first comprehended. Experimental science therefore very soon made its way among them (in common with the Protestant English), but especially among the Italians.

LS: "Especially" should be at the beginning of the sentence. What he wants to make clear is that the discovery of thought is not peculiar to the Protestants, but common to Catholic and Protestant nations.
Mr. Reinken:

It seemed to men as if God had but just created the moon and stars, plants and animals, as if the laws of the universe were now established for the first time; for only then did they feel a real interest in the universe, when they recognized their own Reason in the Reason which pervades it.[14]

LS: When they recognized *their* reason in *that* reason, the reason of nature, that is the basis of rationalism which Hegel simply accepts. Nature is the system of the laws of nature, and therefore nature is reason. Thought knows no beyond, as we see already at this point. Let us turn to the bottom of page 440. The application of that to moral-political matters.

Mr. Reinken:

Right and Morality came to be looked upon as having their foundation in the actual present Will of man—

LS: Again, present—no longer reliance on tradition or authority. The present will of man is the basis of everything.

Mr. Reinken:

whereas formerly it was referred only to the command of God enjoined *ab extra,* written in the Old and New Testament, or appearing in the form of particular Right in old parchments, as *privilegia,* or in international compacts. What the nations acknowledge as international Right was deduced empirically from observation (as in the work of Grotius); then the source of the existing civil and political law was looked for, after Cicero's fashion, in those instincts of men which Nature has planted in their hearts—

LS: "Which nature was believed to have planted in their hearts." Hegel does not accept that.

Mr. Reinken:

the social instinct—

LS: He says "for instance" because he knows of course that there were people who denied the social instinct, men like Hobbes. But fundamentally it is the same character.

Mr. Reinken:

next the principle of security for the person and property of the citizens, and of the advantage of the commonwealth—that which belongs to the class of "reasons of State."

LS: That is a very rough description of the moral political science of the Enlightenment. Very rough, but clearly Hegel knew what he was talking about.

Mr. Reinken:

On these principles private rights were on the one hand despotically contravened, but on the other hand such contravention was the instrument of
carrying out the general objects of the State in opposition to mere positive
or prescriptive claims.

LS: The word "despotically" is deliberately chosen. It is enlightened
despotism. It is despotism. It rides roughshod over all acquired rights,
over all traditional rights, but on the basis of this allegedly rational science
of right and morality.
Mr. Reinken:

Frederick II may be mentioned as the ruler who inaugurated the new epoch in the sphere of practical life—that epoch in which practical political
interest attains Universality, and receives an absolute sanction. Frederick II
merits especial notice as having comprehended the general object of the
State, and as having been the first sovereign who kept the general interest of the State steadily in view, ceasing to pay any respect to particular
interests when they stood in the way of the common weal. His immortal
work is a domestic code—the Prussian municipal law. How the head of
a household energetically provides and governs with a view to the weal
of that household and of his dependents—of this he has given a unique
specimen.

LS: This would be also a subject of critical attention, I suppose. But
Frederick II is for Hegel the most obvious example of Enlightenment policy based on Enlightenment moral teaching. Let us read the first sentence
of the next paragraph.
Mr. Reinken:

These general conceptions, deduced from actual and present
consciousness—the Laws of Nature and the substance of what is right
and good—have received the name of Reason.[15]

LS: "Laws of Nature" does not of course mean here the moral laws of
nature, but it means Newtonian laws and this kind of thing. Founded
on the present consciousness. Here is this double meaning: we see it or
understand it with our own minds, not depending on any extraneous
sources, and secondly, the mind as it has now become. The historical
meaning of "present" is clearly implied. Yes?

Student: I was just wondering whether the connection between "despotism" and "household" and the phrase "have received the name of reason" is meant to be a deliberate reference back to Aristotle's ideas about household relationships.

LS: No, I don't think so. You are quite right by drawing our attention to the domestic, to the paternal character. This is in Hegel's view of course still a defect of the old order, the paternalism. That is one of the key points of the great attack of old liberalism of the late eighteenth century, based on Rousseau, against the enlightened despotism of such people as Frederick II which Hegel shares. That is not yet the rational state. Therefore he says "one has called reasonable," meaning that is not yet true reason but it is relatively rational.

At the end of the paragraph which you just began he speaks of the difference between the Enlightenment and Luther explicitly.

Mr. Reinken:

> But the import of that which is to take place in him—what truth is to become vital in him, was taken for granted by Luther as something already given, something revealed by religion. Now, the principle was set up that this import must be capable of actual investigation—something—

LS: "A present one" and not one which goes back to the past. More particularly, where you have to read the Bible in order to become aware of it without necessarily seeing that it is necessarily so. "That this content is a present one."

Mr. Reinken:

> of which I can gain an inward conviction—and that to this basis of inward demonstration every dogma must be referred.

LS: "Everything must be referred," not "every dogma." In other words, Luther could never see, say, that the Incarnation was evidently necessary. He could only see that it was transmitted to him and that it gave him a sense of being saved. But he could not see that it had to be so necessarily. That alone is reason. Page 442 in the third paragraph.

Mr. Reinken:

> This formally absolute principle brings us to the last stage in History, our world, our own time.

LS: Yes. The end. That is one of the passages which are in favor of the view that there is an end.

Student: The mention of Luther, does it imply a rejection of revelation?

LS: Of revelation, as revelation theologically understood, yes. Because this is only in the element of what Hegel calls *Vorstellung* in German, a "representation" would be the literal English translation. But representation means not present, re-presented. Or, disregarding all etymology, representation is not thought, is not rational thought. And Christianity is true if rationally understood, but then it is no longer what you would find in any dogmatic statements, Catholic or Protestant, and would be radically different.

But what is now the last stage which transcends the Enlightenment? He speaks of that in the following paragraph.

Mr. Reinken:

Secular life is the positive and definite embodiment of the Spiritual Kingdom—the Kingdom of the Will manifesting itself in outward existence. Mere impulses are also forms in which the inner life realizes itself. But these are transient and disconnected, they are the ever-changing applications of volition. But that which is just and moral belongs to the essential, independent, intrinsically universal will, and if we would know what Right really is, we must abstract from inclination, impulse and desire as the particular; that is, we must know what the will is in itself. For benevolent, charitable, social impulses are nothing more than impulses, to which others of a different class are opposed. What the will is in itself can be known only when these specific and contradictory forms of volition have been eliminated. Then will appears as will in its abstract essence. The will is free only when it is does not will anything alien, extrinsic, foreign to itself—for as long as it does so, it is dependent—but wills itself alone, wills the will. This is absolute Will—the volition to be free.[16]

LS: That is the key point which embodies Kant's criticism of all earlier morality. The Enlightenment sought the source of right and morality in man's natural urges or inclinations, in this respect not different from the old tradition. The difference between the Enlightenment and, say, Thomas Aquinas or Aristotle in this respect we cannot discuss here because in this respect there is agreement. There are natural ends, ends which do not originate in the will but are accepted by the will, imposed on it by nature. And, therefore, the will is not free. The will is dependent on something, be it the will of God, be it nature. The truly free will wills nothing but itself, because otherwise it would be dependent on something, i.e., the truly free will wills nothing but its freedom, its self-determination. This radical criticism by Kant of all earlier moral philosophy is simply accepted here.[17]

Hegel criticizes Kant, as he intimates partly in the sequel, by raising the question which he does here immediately afterwards. The next question is: How does the will become determined if it cannot be determined from without by God or by nature? He feels the defect of Kant is that Kant's formal ethics don't show a way towards any content of the will. Let us turn to page 447, line 3.

Mr. Reinken:

> Moreover, because the government as the concrete centre of the power of the State, could not adopt as its principle abstract individual wills, and reconstruct the State on this basis; lastly, because it was Catholic—

LS: He is speaking of the French Revolution here.
Mr. Reinken:

> and therefore the Idea of Freedom—Reason embodied in Laws—did not pass for the final obligation, since the Holy and the religious conscience are separated from them.

LS: In other words, if there is something holy which is not identical with the rational, then the rational cannot acquire its full power. That is the relatively nonpolemical expression of what Hegel has in mind. The holy must be identical with the rational, not higher than the rational. And this has very grave and obvious implications.

In the sequel Hegel develops what he means by "objective freedom." The freedom which Kant has brought out is subjective freedom. The will must not be determined by anything outside of itself. But there is also an objective freedom, and these are the determinations of the will stemming from the will. Hegel gives here only the result of that, on the same page in the next paragraph.

Mr. Reinken:

> The two following points must now occupy our attention: 1st. The course which the Revolution in France took; 2nd. How that Revolution became World-Historical.

1. Freedom presents two aspects: the one concerns its substance and purport—its objectivity—the thing itself; the other relates to the Form of Freedom, involving the consciousness of his activity on the part of the individual; for Freedom demands that the individual recognize himself in such acts, that they should be veritably his, it being his interest that the result in question should be attained.

LS: This subjective freedom, to repeat, is what Kant has provided for us, and the other which he has not. And what is that? The objective or real freedom.

Mr. Reinken:

The three elements and powers of the State in actual working must be contemplated according to the above analysis, their examination in detail being referred to the Lectures on the Philosophy of Right.

1) Laws of Rationality—of intrinsic Right—Objective or Real Freedom: to this category belong Freedom of Property and Freedom of Person. Those relics of that condition of servitude which the feudal relation had introduced are hereby swept away, and all those fiscal ordinances which were the bequest of the feudal law—its tithes and dues, are abrogated. Real liberty requires moreover freedom in regard to trades and professions—the permission to everyone to use his abilities without restriction—and the free admission to all offices of State. This is a summary of the elements of real Freedom, and which are not based on feeling—for feeling allows of the continuance even of serfdom and slavery—but on the thought and self-consciousness of man recognizing the spiritual character of his existence.

LS: Here you see the importance of the difference between feeling—sentiment—and reason. Feeling is wholly insufficient to bring out the full meaning of freedom. Only thought can.

Now the second point concerns government. Read only the last sentence of this paragraph.

Mr. Reinken:

The Few assume to be the deputies, but they are often only the despoilers of the Many.

LS: In other words, the men who claim to be the representatives of the people.

Mr. Reinken:

Nor is the sway of the Majority over the Minority a less palatable inconsistency.

LS: That is the great question of government which we have discussed before. Hegel simply rejects the democratic implication. In the center of the following paragraph.

Mr. Reinken:

There may be various opinions and views respecting laws, constitution and government, but there must be a disposition on the part of the citizens to regard all these opinions as subordinate to the substantial interest of the State, and to insist upon them no further than that interest will allow; moreover, nothing must be considered higher and more sacred than good will towards the State; or, if Religion be looked upon as higher and more sacred, it must involve nothing really alien or opposed to the Constitution.[18]

LS: I.e., the minimum demand is that the state be as sacred as religion. In order to show how alien Hegel is to democracy, we read on page 449, bottom.

Mr. Reinken:

The first Constitutional form of Government in France was one which recognized Royalty; the monarch was to stand at the head of the state, and on him in conjunction with his Ministers was to devolve the executive power; the legislative body, on the other hand, were to make the laws. But this constitution involved from the very first an internal contradiction; for the legislature absorbed the whole power of the administration: the budget, affairs of war and peace, and the levying of the armed force were in the hands of the Legislative Chamber. Everything was brought under the head of Law. The budget, however, is in its nature something diverse from law, for it is annually renewed, and the power to which it properly belongs is that of the Government. With this, moreover, is connected the indirect nomination of the ministry and officers of state, etc. The government was thus transferred to the Legislative Chamber, as in England to the Parliament.[19]

LS: That shows perfectly clearly that Hegel didn't have any regard for parliamentary government even on a nondemocratic basis. Government and subjects are radically different. Then he comes to speak about the solution which was achieved in England, with which he has a certain sympathy, but England doesn't live up to his standards of excellence. That is on page 453, line 8 from bottom.
Mr. Reinken:

England, with great exertions, maintained itself on its old foundations; the English Constitution kept its ground amid the general convulsion, though it seemed so much the more liable to be affected by it, as a public Parliament; that habit of assembling in public meeting which was common to all orders of the state, and a free press, offered singular facilities for introducing the French principles of Liberty and Equality among all classes of the people. Was the English nation too backward in point of culture to apprehend these general principles? Yet in no country has the question of Liberty been more frequently a subject of reflection and public discussion. Or was the English constitution so entirely a Free Constitution—had those principles been already so completely realized in it—that they could no longer excite opposition or even interest? The English nation may be said to have approved of the emancipation of France; but it was proudly reliant on its own constitution and freedom, and instead of imitating the example of the foreigner, it displayed its ancient hostility to its rival, and was soon involved in a popular war with France.[20]

LS: In the next paragraph Hegel develops that the English had one thing which was very important, and that is the local self-government and this kind of thing. The criticism comes in the following paragraph.
Mr. Reinken:

Parliament governs, although Englishmen are unwilling to allow that such is the case.

LS: Because they are loyal monarchists.
Mr. Reinken:

It is worthy of remark, that what has been always regarded as the period of the corruption of a republican people, presents itself here; viz. election to seats in parliament by means of bribery. But this also they call freedom—the power to sell one's vote, and to purchase a seat in parliament. But this utterly inconsistent and corrupt state of things has nevertheless one advantage, that it provides for the possibility of a government, that it introduces a majority of men into parliament who are statesmen, who from their very youth have devoted themselves to political business and have worked and lived in it. And the nation has the correct conviction and perception that there must be a government, and it is therefore willing to give its confidence to a body of men who have had experience in governing; for a general sense of particularity involves also a recognition of that form of particularity which is a distinguishing feature of one class of the community—that knowledge, experience and facility acquired by practice, which the aristocracy who devote themselves to such interests exclusively possess. This is quite opposed to the appreciation of principles and abstract views which everyone can understand at once, and which are besides to be found in all Constitutions and Charters.[21]

LS: So in other words, Hegel would prefer the British order to the simply democratic order introduced by the French Revolution with such chaos.

I think that it is fitting that we should conclude this seminar—and we must now come to an end—with Hegel's statement on the French Revolution. Page 446.

Mr. Reinken:

The principle of the Freedom of the Will, therefore, asserted itself against existing Right. Before the French Revolution, it must be allowed, the power of the grandees had been diminished by Richelieu, and they had been deprived of privileges; but like the clergy they retained all the prerogatives which gave them an advantage over the lower class. The political condition of France at that time presents nothing but a confused mass of privileges.[22]

LS: Turn to page 447, line 6 or thereabouts. After having finished his description of prerevolutionary France, he goes on to say—

Mr. Reinken:

The conception, the idea of Right asserted its authority all at once, and the old framework of injustice could offer no resistance to its onslaught. A constitution, therefore, was established in harmony with the conception of

Right, and on this foundation all future legislation was to be based. Never since the sun had stood in the firmament and the planets revolved around him had it been perceived that man's existence centres in his head.

LS: No. "That man stands on his head." Hegel deliberately chooses a paradoxical expression. "He stands on his head," that is to say, on his thought, and builds actuality according to it.
Mr. Reinken:

Anaxagoras had been the first to say that *Nous* governs the World; but not until now had man advanced to the recognition of the principle that Thought ought to govern spiritual reality. This was accordingly a glorious mental dawn. All thinking beings shared in the jubilation of this epoch. Emotions of a lofty character stirred men's minds at that time; a spiritual enthusiasm thrilled through the world, as if the reconciliation between the Divine and the Secular was now first accomplished.[23]

LS: Hegel reproduces here the feelings he himself had as a young man. He was nineteen years old when the French Revolution started, and he was at a Protestant theological institution in Tübingen. And he and his friends celebrated it, planted a tree of freedom and other things. And this is still a late expression of the expectations which, as Hegel put it, "all thinking beings had at that time." And Hegel is not blind. Of course, he also went through the disappointment, but this is part of the story. We now have to conclude this seminar.

Notes

INTRODUCTION TO THE TRANSCRIPT

1. The transcripts for the 1958 course, along with the audio for the 1965 course, can be found at the Leo Strauss Center website: http://leostrausscenter.uchicago.edu/. The full 1965 transcript will be available on the website two years after this publication.

2. For accounts of Strauss's interpretation of Hegel, mainly as mediated by Kojève, see Sara MacDonald and Barry Craig, *Recovering Hegel from the Critique of Leo Strauss* (Lanham, MD: Lexington Books, 2014), chap. 1; Robert Pippin, "Being, Time, and Politics: The Strauss-Kojève Debate," *History and Theory* 32 (1992): 138–61. MacDonald and Craig refer to Strauss's lectures on Hegel but focus primarily on his published works. In "Kojève's Hegel, Hegel's Hegel, and Strauss's Hegel: A Middle Range Approach to the Debate about Tyranny and Totalitarianism," Waller Newell brings out the differences between Strauss's reading of Hegel and Kojève's; see *Philosophy, History, and Tyranny: Reexamining the Debate between Leo Strauss and Alexandre Kojève*, ed. Timothy Burns and Bryan-Paul Frost (Albany: SUNY Press, 2016), 237–44.

3. See Leo Strauss, *Hobbes's Critique of Religion and Related Writings*, trans. and ed. Gabriel Bartlett and Svetozar Minkov (Chicago: University of Chicago Press, 2011).

4. See the final paragraph of Strauss's "Comments on Schmitt's *Der Begriff des Politischen*," in *Spinoza's Critique of Religion*, trans. E. M. Sinclair (New York: Schocken Books, 1965). See also *The Political Philosophy of Hobbes: Its Basis and Its Genesis*, trans. E. M. Sinclair (Chicago: University of Chicago Press, 1952), preface and introduction.

5. See Heinrich Meier's introduction to Strauss, *Hobbes's Critique of Religion*, 5; also Strauss's December 1933 letters to Gerhard Krüger, Jacob Klein, Karl Löwith, and Gershom Scholem, cited on 5n15.

6. Strauss, *Political Philosophy of Hobbes*, 58n1.

7. Strauss, *Political Philosophy of Hobbes*, 56–58, 122–23. See also Strauss to Hans-Georg Gadamer and Gerhard Krüger, 12 May 1935, in *Hobbes's Critique of Religion*, 159–63.

8. Strauss, *Political Philosophy of Hobbes*, 93–94, 104–7, 130, 150–52.

9. Kojève did write a letter to Strauss on 2 November 1936 in which he thanked Strauss for his Hobbes book and offered some of his own views on the Hobbes-Hegel relationship; reprinted in Leo Strauss, *On Tyranny*, rev. ed., ed. Victor Gourevitch and Michael S. Roth (New York: Free Press, 1991), 231–34.

10. Strauss, *On Tyranny*, 26–27. Strauss first previewed these ideas on Xenophon's rhetoric in "The Spirit of Sparta and the Taste of Athens," *Social Research* 6 (1939): 502–36.

11. Strauss, *On Tyranny*, 78–79, 85–91.

12. Strauss, *On Tyranny*, 147–69.

13. Strauss, *On Tyranny*, 191–92. In his letter to Strauss of 19 September 1950, Kojève comments on this aspect of Strauss's argument: "You appeal to moral conscience to refute my criterion argument. But the one is as problematic as the other" (*On Tyranny*, 255). Similarly he writes on 29 October 1953: "Regarding the issue, I can only keep repeating the same thing. If there is something like 'human nature,' then you are surely right in everything" (*On Tyranny*, 261).

14. Strauss, *On Tyranny*, 207–10.

15. See Strauss's letters of 22 August 1948 and 11 September 1957 (*On Tyranny*, 236–39, 291–94). In these letters, Strauss also questions whether Kojève can do without Hegel's philosophy of nature.

16. Kojève to Strauss, 19 September 1950 (*On Tyranny*, 255). See also Kojève's famous footnote in *Introduction to the Reading of Hegel: Lectures on the Phenomenology of Spirit*, ed. Allan Bloom (Ithaca, NY: Cornell University Press, 1980), 161–62.

17. Strauss, *On Tyranny*, 210–11. For more on the Strauss-Kojève debate, see the essays in Burns and Frost, *Philosophy, History, and Tyranny*; Emmanuel Patard, introductory remarks to "'Restatement' by Leo Strauss (Critical Edition)," *Interpretation* 36 (2008): 3–27; Pippin, "Being, Time, and Politics"; Michael Roth, "Natural Right and the End of History: Leo Strauss and Alexandre Kojève," *Revue de Metaphysique et de Morale* 3 (1991): 407–22; Victor Gourevitch, "Philosophy and Politics, I–II," *Review of Metaphysics* 22 (1968): 58–94, 281–328; George Grant, "Tyranny and Wisdom: A Comment on the Controversy between Leo Strauss and Alexandre Kojève," *Social Research* 31 (1964): 45–72.

18. Leo Strauss, *Natural Right and History* (Chicago: University of Chicago Press, 1953), 278–79.

19. Leo Strauss, "What Is Political Philosophy?," in *An Introduction to Political Philosophy: Ten Essays by Leo Strauss*, ed. Hilail Gildin (Detroit: Wayne State University Press, 1989), 51–56; Strauss, "The Three Waves of Modernity," in *Introduction to Political Philosophy*, 90–92.

20. Leo Strauss, "On a New Interpretation of Plato's Political Philosophy," *Social Research* 13 (1946): 358.

21. A translation of the introduction to *The Philosophy of History*, based on Johannes Hoffmeister's 1955 revision of Lasson's edition, was published in 1975; see *Lectures on the Philosophy of World History: Introduction*, trans. H. B. Nisbet (Cambridge: Cambridge University Press, 1975). An English critical edition of the lectures, based on all the available transcriptions, is currently in the process of being published; see *Lectures on the Philosophy of World History*, vol. 1: *Manuscripts of the Introduction and the Lectures of 1822–23* (Oxford: Clarendon Press, 2011). The editorial introduction to the latter volume contains a good account of the publication history of the lectures in both German and English.

22. G. W. F. Hegel, *Introduction to the Philosophy of History*, trans. Leo Rauch (Indianapolis: Hackett, 1988), 13.

23. Hegel, *Introduction to the Philosophy of History*, 14.

24. Strauss's other courses are cited parenthetically by year and session number.

25. Hegel, *Introduction to the Philosophy of History*, 35.

26. Strauss insists on Hegel's antirelativistic rationalism throughout his lectures. When a student asks whether Hegel's critique of the Enlightenment involved a rejection of the reason and certainty that belonged to it, Strauss responds: "Oh no. According to Hegel's claim, he is much more rigorous than the Enlightenment was" (chapter 11, 247). In his 1958 lectures, he states: "You must not forget one thing: Hegel's rationalism is unsurpassed and unrivaled; as far as universal certainty goes, he wouldn't cede in any way to mathematics" (1958: 2).

27. This characterization of Hegel's political philosophy also appears in some of Strauss's published writings; see "An Introduction to Heideggerian Existentialism," in *The Rebirth of Classical Political Rationalism*, ed. Thomas L. Pangle (Chicago: University of Chicago Press, 1989), 39; also the preface to *Spinoza's Critique of Religion*, 2.

28. G. W. F. Hegel, *The Philosophy of History*, trans. John Sibree (New York: Dover, 1956), 452. This passage appears in Hegel's rather hurried account of the last stage of history, that of his own time. Strauss comments rather humorously on why Hegel abbreviates his narrative at the end of *The Philosophy of History*: "Hegel is much briefer on the later history not because he did not regard it as important but because this is one of the failings of professors. Hegel was a professor, after all, and he took so much time at the beginning that he did not have the time to speak with equal detail about the end. That is really true that this happens generally, and Hegel is no exception" (1958: 10). Strauss knew whereof he spoke, since he commits the same professorial sin in his own lectures.

29. See G. W. F. Hegel, *Elements of the Philosophy of Right*, ed. Allen Wood (Cambridge: Cambridge University Press, 1991), 295 (§270R).

30. This suggests the danger of simply assimilating Strauss's interpretation of Hegel to that Kojève—a danger not always avoided, for example, by MacDonald and Craig in *Recovering Hegel from the Critique of Leo Strauss*, chap. 1. Again, see Newell, "Kojève's Hegel, Hegel's Hegel, and Strauss's Hegel," 237–44, on the differences between Strauss's reading of Hegel and Kojève's.

31. With respect to this claim to finality, Strauss says of Hegel in another place that he "was not an arrogant man at all. When you read his more personal statements, it is absolutely amazing, the noble selflessness. He is not a boaster at all" (1958: 5).

32. Hegel, *Introduction to the Philosophy of History*, 90.

33. In both this course and the 1958 course, Strauss quotes a passage in the German text that does not appear in the English translation to prove his point that Hegel did not envisage anything radically new occurring in America (chapter 4, 100; 1958: 6). The passage reads: "The totality consists in the union of the three principles, and this union takes place in Europe" (G. W. F. Hegel, *Die Vernunft in der Geschichte*, ed. Johannes Hoffmeister [Hamburg: Felix Meiner, 1955], 212).

34. Collingwood's denial that Hegel believed history ended in the present and precluded future progress is found in *The Idea of History* (Oxford: Clarendon Press, 1946),

119-20. Strauss wrote an extremely critical review of this book: "On Collingwood's Philosophy of History," *Review of Metaphysics* 5 (1952): 559-86.

35. As he does in his private correspondence. In a letter to Kojève on 11 September 1957, Strauss writes: "My general reaction to your statements is that we are poles apart. The root of the question is I suppose the same as it always was, that you are convinced of the truth of Hegel (Marx) and I am not" (Strauss, *On Tyranny*, 291).

36. Leo Strauss, "Political Philosophy and History," in *What Is Political Philosophy and Other Studies* (Chicago: University of Chicago Press, 1988), 58.

37. I use quotation marks because, as one student in the class, Catherine Zuckert (née Heldt), told me, there were thirty to forty students in it.

CHAPTER ONE

1. The first edition of Hegel's lectures on the philosophy of history, edited by Hegel's former student Eduard Gans, appeared in 1837. A second, expanded edition, edited by Karl Hegel, appeared in 1840. The Sibree English translation that Strauss uses in this course is based on Karl Hegel's edition. Georg Lasson published a four-volume edition of the lectures in 1917-20, which Strauss from time to time quotes from; see G. W. F. Hegel, *Vorlesungen über die Philosophie der Weltgeschichte*, ed. Georg Lasson (Hamburg: Felix Meiner, 1988). Finally, in 1955 Johannes Hoffmeister published a revised version of Lasson's first volume, containing Hegel's introduction to the lectures; see Hegel, *Die Vernunft in der Geschichte*. Hoffmeister is the "more recent editor" Strauss refers to above, and at several points in the course he quotes from his edition.

2. F. H. Jacobi (1743-1819) published *Briefe über die Lehre Spinozas* (*Letters on the Teaching of Spinoza*) in 1785, thus inaugurating the so-called pantheism controversy in Germany.

3. President Lyndon B. Johnson's State of the Union Address, January 4 1965.

4. Presumably Strauss's translation. The translation of the passage from the preface that he quotes does not correspond to either of the English translations extant at the time, S. W. Dyde's or T. M. Knox's. See Hegel, *Elements of the Philosophy of Right*, 23.

5. There was a change of tape at this point. Apparently a student asks whether Hegel's theoretical posture at the end of history has any practical implications.

6. In *The Holy Family*. See Karl Marx, *Writings of the Young Marx on Philosophy and Society*, ed. and trans. Lloyd D. Easton and Kurt H. Guddat (Indianapolis: Hackett, 1967), 383.

7. This is Marx's famous eleventh thesis on Feuerbach. See *Writings of the Young Marx*, 402.

8. In his 1958 course, Strauss also points out that Hegel is by no means unusual among philosophers for claiming finality for his teaching: "Hegel was not an arrogant man at all. When you read his more personal statement[s], it is absolutely amazing, the noble selflessness. He is not a boaster at all. But he would say in all humility, in all modesty ... Someone else, Spinoza for example, makes occasionally the remark that he *knows* that he knows the truth; and Hegel would claim that for himself without any question. But does not every philosopher make such a claim? I am not now speaking of professors of phi-

losophy; that is a very respectable profession, but it is not philosophy itself—that would be a gross miscarriage of justice. One would do gross injustice if one would say they are philosophers—that is a very difficult and long question. But does not every *philosopher* raise that claim? Even if you take Kant, who says that the most important questions are not answerable, that is in itself a most important answer. No, surely Hegel would raise this claim" (session 5).

9. See Hegel, *Elements of the Philosophy of Right*, 21; also Hegel, *Die Vernunft in der Geschichte*, 95.

10. Charles Edward Stuart (1720–88), commonly known as "Bonnie Prince Charlie," was defeated at the battle of Culloden in 1745.

11. Boroughs are administrative divisions within the United Kingdom; "rotten" boroughs were ones that had declined in population but still elected a parliamentary representative, usually a wealthy landowner. The Reform Act of 1832 introduced changes to the electoral system that abolished such boroughs and increased the electorate.

12. G. W. F. Hegel, *Phenomenology of Spirit*, trans. A. V. Miller (Oxford: Clarendon Press, 1977), par. 37.

13. John Selden (1584–1654), English jurist and legal scholar.

14. In his 1958 course, Strauss states: "You must not forget one thing: Hegel's rationalism is unsurpassed and unrivaled; as far as universal certainty goes, he wouldn't cede in any way to mathematics" (session 2).

CHAPTER TWO

1. Strauss responds to Mr. Bruell's paper, read at the beginning of the session. The reading was not recorded.

2. Hegel, *Philosophy of History*, 6.

3. At the battle of Cannae, which took place in 216 BCE during the Second Punic War, the army of Carthage under Hannibal defeated the much larger army of the Roman Republic.

4. Hegel, *Philosophy of History*, 9.

5. Hegel, *Philosophy of History*, 13–14.

6. Hegel, *Philosophy of History*, 15.

7. Hegel, *Die Vernunft in der Geschichte*, 45.

8. Hegel, *Philosophy of History*, 16.

9. Hegel, *Philosophy of History*, 17.

10. Hegel, *Die Vernunft in der Geschichte*, 61.

11. Strauss appears to be summarizing the German text here; see Hegel, *Die Vernunft in der Geschichte*, 64–67.

12. Hegel, *Die Vernunft in der Geschichte*, 71.

13. In the *Phenomenology*, par. 437, Hegel quotes the following lines from *Antigone* about the unwritten laws of the gods: "They are not of yesterday or today, but everlasting, / Though where they came from, none of us can tell."

14. In his 1958 course, Strauss develops this theme of the interconnection between science and societal corruption at some length:

World history shows how the mind gradually comes to a consciousness and to a willing of the truth. The truth dawns on man, he discovers the main point, and at the end he comes to perfect consciousness. The human mind necessarily arrives at full consciousness, and this has now happened in Hegel. Now what is the difficulty occurring in Hegel himself? We are not now speaking of the difficulties which might arise from the outside. Hegel gives the schema of what happens in every stage: first you have a community, what he calls "a nation," which then posits, outside of itself, its world. For example, the Greek pantheon, the Greek notions of justice, and the general character of their notions of law and government, are the world which the Greek mind has posited. And then, when it has completely objectivated itself, it has reached its peak. Then what happens afterward? Up to the peak inclusive, it lives fully within the world. In more specific terms, the Greeks believed in the gods and these gods are objectivations of the Greek mind, but they were not known to be objectivations of the Greek mind; they are thought to be living and thinking beings with proper names. Then, after this objectivation has been completed, after the tragedians, for instance, have given the most perfect objectivation of the Greek mind, after this, then thinking proper begins. The Greek mind becomes aware of its gods being the Greek mind, objectivation[s] of the Greek mind. But what does this mean for the Greeks? This happens of course only in some special individuals which are loosely called "sophists," or "philosophers"; but what does this mean? At this stage the sciences begin, sciences at all levels, including philosophy. Hence the sciences and the corruption and decline of a nation always go together. In this moment philosophy begins; in the moment the nation becomes aware of its not being subject to its gods but the creator of its gods, the corruption begins. Corruption, of course, has not the meaning in which we see corruption in certain parts of the municipal government of Chicago, but it means, really, the loss of orientation, the complete loss, the decline of a nation! Always!

Those of you who have read Rousseau's *Discourses* will see that Hegel agrees with Rousseau at this point. Rousseau has written a whole discourse on this subject of how science and corruption are inseparable from each other. Now in that of course we must make an application to Hegel, naturally, because Hegel has said in a well-known passage of his *Philosophy of Right* that he has applied the same principle to his times. "The Owl of Minerva—that is, wisdom—begins flight in the dusk." That is to say, when night approaches, when the society declines and there are no longer any great tasks, then wisdom begins. Spengler's *Decline of the West* lets the cat out of the bag, because as Spengler sees it, it means the decline of the West. Of course as Spengler sees it, that [means] the decline of mankind, because the Western civilization is the last civilization, as you know. That is the end of any meaningful human life. It is one of the greatest difficulties of Hegel that one does not really know whether Hegel was fully aware of what he clearly implied: that with the fulfillment, with the completion of world history, there is now the beginning of a final decay, a final corruption of mankind. This is a problem which we shall later raise in the form of the "last man," where people no longer have any tasks, and where all great social tasks have been solved, and where we have the perfect society. After all really important intellectual tasks have been solved, and when the truth is known in the final system, what will happen then? Triviality? There can be no genuine heroism anymore; and whether and to what extent Hegel saw that is, as far as I can see, impossible to decide.

Strauss goes on to contrast Hegel with Marx with respect to the difficulty just sketched:

> But Marx, as far as I know, never had this difficulty which Hegel has in virtue of his agreement with Rousseau's *First Discourse*. What Marx took over from Rousseau included the complete disregarding of all complications. Yes? Rousseau's doctrine is very complex; it is much more sophisticated than people are inclined to think. The German Idealists, Kant and Hegel especially, try to give a harmonistic solution; whereas Rousseau felt unable to give one, and he knew it! And yet certainly Hegel—not Kant—accepted this crucial thesis of the *First Discourse*, where there is a fundamental disharmony between the peak of society and the peak of knowledge. I mean, Rousseau used very simple images like Sparta: the perfect *polis*; or early Rome: no philosophy, no art; Athens: the incarnation of art and intelligence, but corrupt. Yes? I mean one can easily question these, but that doesn't dispose of the fundamental point, the fundamental problem. And Hegel accepts this ... But I think one cannot mention Marx and Hegel in the same breath as far as these questions go, because Marx is infinitely less philosophic than Hegel was.

Finally, Strauss points out that in Hegel's rational state there will no longer be any need for heroic virtues or great individuals:

> In Hegel's sense, I think we can say there will no longer be historic individuals. There will be more or less good administrators, but no longer any historic individuals. I repeat this sentence: "Science and the corruption of a people are always inseparable from each other." [. . .] Still, the question is whether in the absence of great [individuals] what Hegel understands by corrupting can be prevented. That is the question. I mean, I don't think that question, which is absolutely crucial for Hegel and for any other reasonable criticism of Hegel, can be settled on the basis of this passage, but I wanted to mention that this is really the great problem of Hegel: What is the end of history, and what does this mean? Is it possible to live on that basis? One could say that this was the beginning of Nietzsche's criticism of Hegel. (session 3)

15. There was a change of tape at this point.

16. Hegel, *Philosophy of History*, 20.

17. Alexander Pope, "An Essay on Man" (1733), line 16.

18. Bernard de Mandeville (1670–1733) was a Dutch writer who won European fame with his work *The Fable of the Bees* (1714).

CHAPTER THREE

1. Strauss responds to Mr. Hewitt's paper, read at the beginning of the session. The reading was not recorded.

2. Hegel, *Die Vernunft in der Geschichte*, 91.

3. Hegel, *Philosophy of History*, 28–29.

4. Hegel, *Die Vernunft in der Geschichte*, 95.

5. Hegel, *Philosophy of History*, 29.

6. Hegel, *Philosophy of History*, 33–34.

7. Hegel, *Philosophy of History*, 34.

8. In his 1958 course, Strauss treats Hegel's view of the limits of the moralistic approach to politics quite sympathetically:

Hegel has a very deep contempt for political moralizing. That is quite clear. He has contempt for men who pass moral judgment while sitting on the back seat with no responsibility, or maybe having responsibility but not knowing what responsibilities are. I think the most striking example of what Hegel means which I have experienced in my lifetime was the British Labour Party in the '30s with their "Resist aggression and resist rearmament." That was such a beautifully thought-through policy [. . .] What Hegel says, in a way, is that it is really much more immoral and downright political immorality, and it is dangerous because of its pretenses. Another formula is, of course, "Trust in public opinion." That is another version of what Hegel had in mind as really immoral if you want to use more judgment. This means, as a pupil of Hegel put it, to expect others to do what one is too lazy to do oneself. The public opinion taker doesn't take care of anything, whether it is national or international.

That is, I think, an important political point which Hegel makes throughout his work. Whether the Hegelian remark has posed all of the difficulties of a conflict between morality and politics is an entirely different question. But the point is, I think, how much irrelevance is hidden behind a merely moralistic criticism. I take an example from Burke. Burke discusses in one of his writings ["Thoughts on the Approaching Executions"—ed.]—I am not sure which—this question: There has been a rebellion, and that is grave, a capital crime. What about punishment of that crime? From a strictly moral point of view, everyone should receive punishment, a punishment fitting the crime. In many cases this is a capital punishment. Governments do not do that. Why? Because they weigh the legal consideration against the broader consideration of what law is for, namely, the existence, preferably on a higher level, of political society as a whole. And therefore such practices as the Romans' decimating a legion instead of killing everyone is approached. This indicates what Hegel means: the political considerations, the broad considerations are the truly moral considerations as far as these grave and all-encompassing questions are concerned. These kinds of moralists take it very easy, they don't face the complexity of the problem. One cannot say that Hegel is an immoralist. In spirit he is very far from that. Needless to say, Hegel is helped in this presentation by his certainty that a radical breach of law, what we call a revolution, is the victory of a higher concept of justice over a lower concept of justice. In the moment this premise becomes doubtful, one will become somewhat hesitant to accept Hegel's proposition. (session 5)

9. Hegel, *Philosophy of History*, 37.

10. In his 1958 course, Strauss argues that Hegel would not have defended the actions of Stalin and similar murderous rulers: "I think Hegel was the most powerful critic of the moralistic attitude toward the great political issues. The question, for example, of Napoleon who gets the . . . wholly illegally and has him shot. You know that was really against all international law, and I am sure Hegel would never have defended that. There was no justification for that. But let us take the 'murder,' as they say now, of twenty million peasants by Stalin—innocent flowers, we understand—what about that? Hegel could not argue from a moral point of view in the strictly narrow sense, but I think he would take a broad political view and say that a regime that establishes itself in this way, against such powerful resistance—and at a certain point numbers become meaningful . . ." (session 3). Ellipses occur in the original transcript and probably indicate that portions of the audiofile were inaudible.

11. Thomas Carlyle, *On Heroes, Hero-Worship, and the Heroic in History* (1841).

12. In his 1958 course, Strauss develops Hegel's notion of positive freedom versus Lockean negative freedom:

Freedom must not be understood to be the securing of the private sphere. That is the decisive point. Or as Hegel develops it later in an explicit discussion of the notion of a state of nature: Man is not primarily free in the state of nature and does not enter society on this condition; I mean the condition that he is willing to abandon part of his natural freedom in order that he be secured in the most important part of that natural freedom by this self-limitation. That is rejected by Hegel. Hegel says that freedom must be reasonable freedom, and this reasonable freedom must not consist in doing what one likes, be it only in this private sphere; but freedom consists in doing the reasonable, i.e., in obeying, for example, as reasonable law, positively. Now in this point I wouldn't think of Rousseau; another thinker is more obviously used here by Hegel, although he used a somewhat different language: Aristotle. He says the general will must not be a means for the private will; in Rousseau it is fundamentally that the general will is the means for the private will. It is complicated in Rousseau, I grant that, but fundamentally this is so. For Aristotle's thesis the *polis* is prior to the individual, and that is what Hegel means. Only in the membership in the civil society does freedom possibly consist, not by getting a guarantee of a certain private sphere, for example—that is negative freedom. Positive freedom is membership in civil society, and this membership means to regard your obeying, your living for the laws, as your true freedom.

I read to you another passage which is not translated in the English edition, on page 115 in the German [Hoffmeister's edition of *Die Vernunft in der Geschichte*]: "Only the will which obeys the law is free, for only that will obeys itself and therefore is free." In other words, if you do what you like, you follow your subjective will and caprices, and then you are not free, you are a slave of your whim. You are truly free only if you follow what is reasonable in itself, and that you can do only if you obey the law. If the subjective will subjects itself, subjects events, to the law, the opposition of freedom and necessity disappears. Necessity is the reasonable and the substantial, and we are free if we recognize it as law and follow it as the substance of our own beings. The objective and the subjective wills are then reconciled and are one and the same. Here you see clearly the formulation of Rousseau in this later passage. Yes? I mean that only the will which obeys the law is free.

Strauss goes on to develop the differences between Hegel's and Rousseau's notions of the general or rational will: "Now let us look for a moment at the relation between Hegel and Rousseau—I mean in a very general way. This statement which I read to you is simply taken from Rousseau: 'The will which obeys the law is free because it obeys itself'—*Social Contract*, book 1, chapter 8, and other passages as well. What is the difference between Hegel's concept of law and Rousseau's concept? Why is Rousseau so certain that you obey yourself when you obey the law?" A student answers: "Because you have a hand in making the law." Strauss responds: "Absolutely! In other words, the legality of the law is guaranteed by your having a say in the making of the law. Yes? And this is completely refused by Hegel. Hegel denies this very principle of democracy. So in other words, Rousseau also had the possibility of which he availed himself to say that there are unreasonable laws. Yes? He went so far as to say that practically all the laws of Europe of his time were not laws at all because they were imposed by monarchs and not adopted by a freely voting citizen body [. . .] Now both Aristotle and Rousseau, however much they differ among themselves, take it for granted that 'is' will be different from the 'ought.' Somehow Hegel assumes the convergence of the is and the ought, and this assumption is proven as sound by his philosophy of history because it proves that history is rational. The absence of a philosophy of history in Aristotle as well as in Rousseau is the reason for the fundamental difference between them and Hegel. Another example which shows that Hegel's philosophy of history is absolutely critical for his political philosophy in particular" (session 5).

13. Strauss criticizes this misunderstanding of Hegel as a deifier of the state in several places in his 1958 course (see sessions 4 and 9).

14. Hegel, *Die Vernunft der Geschichte*, 121.

15. In his course "Introduction to Political Philosophy," offered in the same quarter (winter 1965), Strauss taught Comte's positive philosophy in sessions 1 and 2.

16. Ruth Benedict (1887–1948), American cultural anthropologist and author of *Patterns of Culture* (1934).

CHAPTER FOUR

1. Strauss responds to Mr. Shulsky's paper, read at the beginning of the session. The reading was not recorded.

2. In his 1958 course, Strauss stresses this fundamental premise of Hegelian historical methodology:

Any intelligent historian is distinguished from the unintelligent historian in that he knows how to distinguish between the important and the unimportant. Everyone admits that; even the unintelligent must admit that. In other words, they have to admit something they really don't understand. But the question is: What is meant by important and unimportant? There is a rough commonsense understanding, of course, which shows that certain questions are silly and only an unintelligent man would bother with them. But Hegel then says that he determines what is important and unimportant in the most objective way possible, especially when the historian treats human beings other than himself. Why? He regards as most important what a human society regards as most important.

Now people would say that Marilyn Monroe is the most important individual in this country, and you might even get a majority. Hegel would say that this is nonsense. He does not want to know what silly individuals think; he wants to know what this society, properly assembled as a society, thinks. Then one would look at the United States Constitution and authentic interpretations of that, and so on, and so get a view. Or take another, more primitive society: he would raise the question of what these people bow to. I mean, when things become serious in war, and when confronted with death, then I see what is important to them. I have been told by certain Chinese that the Chinese travelers in olden times, when they came to witness one of the tribes at the borders of China, the first question they ask is: "How do they bow to their kings or gods or whatever may be?" That is of course a very intelligent approach. It is only a bit misleading in that they raise the question of how they bow instead of first raising the question to whom or what. That is a point—I mean, they have a direction. That is what Hegel means. Hegel contends that in this way he gives states in Europe, in central Africa, the Aztecs, the Greeks, the Chinese, the Jews, the Christians, the Catholics and the Protestants, an opportunity to make their speech—yes?—their assertions regarding the most important things. And then he says that if he goes over these most authentic statements and reads them as thoughtful men should, then he gets a sequence of increasing rationality, say from the African statements up to the Protestant statements. That is what Hegel contends. (session 5; see also session 8)

3. Friedrich von Schlegel (1772–1829) was a German writer and critic considered to be the originator of many of the ideas that inspired the early German Romantic movement.

4. Hegel, *Philosophy of History*, 63–64.

5. Hegel, *Philosophy of History*, 65.

6. Hegel, *Philosophy of History*, 66–67.

7. Hegel, *Philosophy of History*, 69.

8. Hegel, *Philosophy of History*, 86–87.

9. Hegel, *Die Vernunft in der Geschichte*, 210.

10. See Hegel's letter to Baron Boris von Üxküll of 28 November 1821, in *Hegel: The Letters*, trans. Clark Butler and Christiane Seiler (Bloomington: Indiana University Press, 1984), 569. Tocqueville's comments about America and Russia appear in the conclusion of the first volume of *Democracy in America*.

11. Hegel, *Die Vernunft in der Geschichte*, 212.

12. In his 1958 lectures, Strauss makes clear that it is Collingwood's view that he is taking issue with here; see R. G. Collingwood, *The Idea of History* (Oxford: Clarendon Press, 1946), 119–20. There, too, Strauss cites the quote from Hoffmeister's German edition to prove that "Collingwood's interpretation is absolutely wrong," that Hegel did not believe that in the future, in America or elsewhere, any fundamentally new principle would emerge (session 6; see also sessions 5 and 11).

13. Hegel, *Philosophy of History*, 75–76.

14. Hegel, *Philosophy of History*, 77.

15. Hegel, *Die Vernunft der Geschichte*, 180–81.

16. Hegel, *Philosophy of History*, 81.

17. See Hegel, *Die Vernunft in der Geschichte*, 200. Alexander von Humboldt (1769–1859), was a naturalist and explorer and a major figure in the classical period of physical geography and biogeography.

18. See Kant, *The Contest of the Faculties*, in *Kant's Political Writings*, 2nd ed., ed. Hans Reiss (Cambridge: Cambridge University Press, 1991), 184–85.

CHAPTER FIVE

1. Strauss responds to a student's paper, read at the beginning of the session. The reading was not recorded.

2. Hegel, *Die Vernunft in der Geschichte*, 218.

3. Hegel, *Die Vernunft in der Geschichte*, 219–20.

4. Hegel, *Philosophy of History*, 93.

5. Hegel, *Die Vernunft in der Geschichte*, 221.

6. Mircea Eliade (1907–86), a Romanian scholar of myth and religion who taught at the University of Chicago.

7. Strauss here refers to G. W. F. Hegel, *Die Vernunft in der Geschichte*, ed. Johannes Hoffmeister (Hamburg: Felix Meiner, 1955).

8. Since Strauss's course on Hegel, Hoffmeister's edition has been translated; see G. W. F. Hegel, *Lectures on the Philosophy of World History: Introduction*, trans. H. B. Nisbet (Cambridge: Cambridge University Press, 1975).

9. Francis Bacon, *The New Organon*, ed. Lisa Jardine and Michael Silverthorne (Cambridge: Cambridge University Press, 2000), 24, 33.

10. Hegel, *Philosophy of History*, 94.

11. Hegel, *Philosophy of History*, 95.

12. Hegel, *Die Vernunft in der Geschichte*, 225.

13. Hegel, *Die Vernunft in der Geschichte*, 226.

14. Vladimir Lenin, *State and Revolution* (1917), chap. 5, "The Economic Basis of the Withering Away of the State."

15. Hegel, *Philosophy of History*, 99.

16. Hegel, *Philosophy of History*, 103.

17. Hegel, *Philosophy of History*, 104.

18. Hegel, *Philosophy of History*, 108.

19. There was a change of tape at this point. The recording resumes with Mr. Reinken reading the next passage.

20. Hegel, *Philosophy of History*, 115.

21. Hegel, *Philosophy of History*, 117.

22. Hegel, *Philosophy of History*, 120–21.

23. See Max Weber, "Politics as a Vocation," in *The Vocation Lectures*, trans. Rodney Livingstone (Indianapolis: Hackett, 2004), 80–92. Here the two ethics are translated as "responsibility" vs. "conviction."

24. Hegel, *Philosophy of History*, 123.

25. Hegel, *Philosophy of History*, 128.

26. Strauss alludes to this story in his 1958 course (session 7) and attributes it to Nietzsche; see *Daybreak: Thoughts on the Prejudices of Morality*, trans. R. J. Hollingdale (Cambridge: Cambridge University Press, 1982), aph. 199.

27. Hegel, *Philosophy of History*, 130.

CHAPTER SIX

1. Strauss responds to a student's paper, read at the beginning of the session. The reading was not recorded.

2. The Sung or Song dynasty ruled China from 960 to 1279.

3. The Tang dynasty ruled China from 618 to 907.

4. In his 1958 course, Strauss makes a similar point about interpretive charity: "But what . . . I am not a Hegelian; I do not defend my own position; but we must try to understand what Hegel means" (session 6).

5. Strauss here refers to Carl Schmitt (1888–1985), who was labeled the "crown jurist of the Third Reich." Strauss refers to this quote by Schmitt several times in his 1958 lectures, always with a view to denying that there is any connection between Hegel and the Nazis. Thus: "[U]nder no circumstances is it possible to make a case for the Nazis on the basis of Hegel. That is true — I mean up to this point! The most intelligent Nazi of whom I know, Carl Schmitt, a German public lawyer, said it very succinctly; he said that on the 31st of January, 1933, Hegel died. Meaning that the Hegelian tradition was still of immense power, and not only at the universities but also as far as the German state was concerned, up to this moment" (session 7). And: "You know, Hegel was throughout his life opposed to democracy, there is no question about that. But this has nothing to do with Hitler, it would be absolutely stupid to mention that in the same words [. . .] If one wants a single formula indicating what Hegel's philosophy of right stands for, it would be 'rights of man' plus a wholly independent civil service [. . .] I recalled to you on a former occasion a remark which later was made by a Nazi that on the 31st of January, 1933, which was when Hitler came to power, that 'Today, Hegel died!' That is absolutely true, as far as Germany goes, the intellectual rule of Hegel lasted until that moment — watered down, modified in many things, but fundamentally the old ruling people thought in Hegelian terms and it played a decisive role" (session 10).

6. Clovis (466–511) was founder of the Merovingian dynasty. Raised a pagan, he converted to Christianity and according to tradition was baptized by the bishop of Reims in 496.

7. Hegel, *Philosophy of History*, 131.

8. Hegel, *Philosophy of History*, 132. Strauss is apparently translating from the German.

9. Hegel, *Philosophy of History*, 132.

10. I Ching.

11. Hegel, *Philosophy of History*, 133.

12. Hegel, *Philosophy of History*, 135–36.

13. Hegel, *Philosophy of History*, 137–38.

14. Hegel, *Philosophy of History*, 158.

15. Hegel, *Philosophy of History*, 139.

16. Hegel, *Philosophy of History*, 141.

17. Hegel, *Philosophy of History*, 142–43.

18. Strauss probably means the Mughals (or Mongols), who conquered India in the sixteenth century.

19. Hegel, *Philosophy of History*, 144.

20. Hegel, *Philosophy of History*, 144.

21. There was a change of tape at this point. The editor has supplied the passage read by Mr. Reinken. The recording resumes with Strauss's comment.

22. State of the Union Address, 1954.

23. Hegel, *Philosophy of History*, 145.

24. Hegel, *Philosophy of History*, 147.

25. Hegel, *Philosophy of History*, 148.

26. That is, the student paper read at the beginning of the class session.

27. Hegel, *Philosophy of History*, 148.

28. Hegel, *Philosophy of History*, 149.

29. Hegel, *Philosophy of History*, 150–51.

30. Hegel, *Philosophy of History*, 152.

31. Hegel, *Philosophy of History*, 153.

CHAPTER SEVEN

1. Strauss responds to Mr. Franke's paper, read at the beginning of the session. The reading was not recorded.

2. See note 4 in chapter 6 above.

3. In the battle of Leuctra, fought in 371 BC, the Boeotians led by the Thebans defeated the Spartans.

4. Hegel, *Philosophy of History*, 154–55.

5. Hegel, *Philosophy of History*, 155.

6. Hegel, *Philosophy of History*, 161.

7. Hegel, *Philosophy of History*, 166–67.

8. Hegel, *Philosophy of History*, 168.

9. Hegel, *Philosophy of History*, 170–71. There was a break in the tape at this point.

10. Hegel, *Philosophy of History*, 173.

11. Hegel, *Philosophy of History*, 174.

12. Hegel, *Philosophy of History*, 178–79.

13. Hegel, *Philosophy of History*, 181.

CHAPTER EIGHT

1. Strauss responds to Mr. Barber, who read a paper at the beginning of the session. The reading was not recorded.

2. Ferdowsi (940–1020 CE), a Persian poet who composed the *Shahnameh*, the national epic of Persia.

3. Hegel, *Philosophy of History*, 187.

4. Hegel, *Philosophy of History*, 191–92.

5. Hegel, *Philosophy of History*, 192.

6. Hegel, *Philosophy of History*, 194.

7. Hegel, *Philosophy of History*, 194.

8. Hegel, *Philosophy of History*, 195.

9. Hegel, *Philosophy of History*, 195–96.

10. Hegel, *Philosophy of History*, 196.

11. Hegel, *Philosophy of History*, 197.

12. Hegel, *Philosophy of History*, 198.

13. Hegel, *Philosophy of History*, 198–99.

14. Hegel, *Philosophy of History*, 199–200.

15. Hegel, *Philosophy of History*, 206.

16. *Timaeus* 21d ff.

17. Hegel, *Philosophy of History*, 206.

18. This quote comes from the epistle dedicatory of Hobbes's *Elements of Law*. See Hobbes, *Elements of Law: Natural and Politic*, ed. J. C. A Gaskin (Oxford: Oxford University Press, 1999), 19.

19. Hobbes, *Elements of Law*, 19.

20. See Kant, "On the Common Saying, 'This May be True in Theory, but it does not Apply in Practice,'" in *Kant's Political Writings*, 74.

21. In his 1958 course, in response to a student's question about Strauss's claim that Hegel would have opposed both communism and fascism, Strauss states that "for Hegel the recognition of the rights of man—and that implies among other things, surely, a fair and independent judiciary—is absolutely essential to a civilized and respectable state. That couldn't exist under either of these conditions. Hegel was in this sense a constitutionalist." Strauss goes on to claim that, given that Hegel wrote a book entitled *Natural Right and Constitutional Law* [*Elements of the Philosophy of Right: Or Natural Law and Political Science in Outline*], he "of course admitted natural right. What he would say is, for example, that the principles of property, the principles of the inviolability of the person, all this kind of thing, are things which do not depend on human arbitrariness or legal enactment but are the truly natural, rational principles which, for Hegel, cannot have been known always [. . .] Hegel is not a relativist; on the contrary, he is a big bogey for all

relativists—you know, the absolutist par excellence!" (session 4). For Strauss's denial that Hegel deifies the state, see note 13 in chapter 3 above. For his denial that Hegel's political teaching has anything to do with National Socialism, see note 5 in chapter 6.

22. Warren Hastings (1732–1818) was the first governor-general of India. After his return to England he was charged with crimes and misdemeanors by a group of MPs that included Edmund Burke. The trial lasted for seven years. Hastings was acquitted.

23. In his 1958 course, Strauss praises Kojève's book on Hegel: "The only form in which the Hegelian sort of government survives today is that by a French scholar of Russian origin [Alexandre Kojève] who wrote probably the best book on Hegel in this generation. Unfortunately it is not available in English. He wrote a book called *Introduction to the Study of Hegel*, which is a kind of running commentary on Hegel's *Phenomenology of the Mind*, and for those who can read French it is really valuable. It is the most valuable one on Hegel of which I know" (session 5).

24. Hegel, *Philosophy of History*, 206–7.

25. Hegel, *Philosophy of History*, 208–9.

26. Hegel, *Philosophy of History*, 211–12.

27. Hegel, *Philosophy of History*, 213.

28. Hegel, *Philosophy of History*, 214.

29. There follow several questions about the figure of the Sphinx, Oedipus, and Xenophon's criticism of Persia, concluding with a student reading Yeats's poem "The Second Coming." This portion of the transcript has been deleted.

CHAPTER NINE

1. Strauss responds to a student's paper, read at the beginning of the session. The reading was not recorded.

2. Hegel, *Philosophy of History*, 215.

3. Hegel, *Philosophy of History*, 215.

4. Hegel, *Philosophy of History*, 218.

5. Hegel, *Philosophy of History*, 221.

6. Hegel, *Philosophy of History*, 221.

7. Hegel, *Vorlesungen über die Philosophie der Weltgeschichte*, 527.

8. Hegel, *Philosophy of History*, 223.

9. In his 1958 course, Strauss makes a similar comment about the alleged necessity of Alexander's early death:

I think [this] is a very clear example of the limitations of Hegel's philosophy of history. His general thesis is that history is rational; but in order to maintain that, Hegel is compelled, just as the Marxists are, to make a distinction between the essential and the accidental. That there is in history things which are merely accidental, Hegel admits, just as Marx did; but the question is, of course, how to draw the line. Here we see an interesting example: if Hegel sees that all the characteristic Greek institutions—slavery, oracles, republics, manyness of cities, the Homeric gods—are all forming an essential unity, then he is admirable. One would have to check to see that in each case the item

is really true, but his ingenuity in finding this necessity is not only unsurpassed but unrivaled. But here we have another example: a part of this Greekness, as he understands
it, is this use of the human mind; and therefore it finds its expression in Achilles at the
beginning of Greek culture and in Alexander at the end. Now in the case of Achilles at
the beginning it makes some sense, because Achilles is a poetic figure and is therefore
the work of the Greek mind. But the fact that Alexander died—I have forgotten of
which disease—at age 32 or 33, and to link this up with the workings of the world mind
borders on superstition. (session 9)

10. Hegel, *Philosophy of History*, 226.

11. See p. 137 above and accompanying note.

12. Leo Strauss and Joseph Cropsey, eds., *History of Political Philosophy* (Chicago: University of Chicago Press, 1963). Strauss wrote the volume's chapter on Plato.

13. Hegel, *Philosophy of History*, 227–28.

14. James Baldwin (1924–87) was an American essayist, novelist, and playwright who
wrote extensively on race in the United States in the 1950s and 1960s.

15. Hegel, *Philosophy of History*, 231.

16. Strauss asks Mr. Reinken to read a passage on 235 and then says, "Let us drop
this" and turn to the passage later when Hegel speaks about the *Iliad*. This portion of the
transcript has been deleted.

17. There was a break in the tape at this point. The passage that follows refers, of
course, to the *Odyssey*.

18. Hegel, *Philosophy of History*, 236–37.

19. Hegel, *Philosophy of History*, 238.

20. Hegel, *Philosophy of History*, 239.

21. Hegel, *Philosophy of History*, 239–40.

22. Here Strauss takes questions from students. Both the questions and Strauss's responses have been deleted from the transcript.

23. Montesquieu, *Spirit of Laws* 2.2 and 3.3.

CHAPTER TEN

1. Strauss responds to a student's paper, read at the beginning of the session. The
reading was not recorded.

2. *Republic* 439e–440a. The man is Leontius.

3. Hegel, *Philosophy of History*, 241.

4. Hegel, *Philosophy of History*, 242.

5. A marble statute that depicts the god Apollo as archer. Discovered in the sixteenth
century, it is thought to be a copy of a lost Greek bronze. The statue influenced generations of artists, including Dürer and Bernini. It resides in the Vatican.

6. Hegel, *Philosophy of History*, 244.

7. Hegel, *Vorlesungen über die Philosophie der Weltgeschichte*, 575.

8. Hegel, *Vorlesungen über die Philosophie der Weltgeschichte*, 578–79.

9. Hegel, *Philosophy of History*, 249–50.

10. Hegel, *Philosophy of History*, 244.

11. Hegel, *Philosophy of History*, 247.

12. Hegel, *Vorlesungen über die Philosophie der Weltgeschichte*, 599.

13. Hegel, *Philosophy of History*, 252.

14. Hegel, *Philosophy of History*, 251.

15. Hegel, *Philosophy of History*, 252.

16. Hegel, *Vorlesungen über die Philosophie der Weltgeschichte*, 604.

17. Hegel, *Vorlesungen über die Philosophie der Weltgeschichte*, 607.

18. Pisistratus (608−527 BC) was a tyrannical ruler of Athens who unified Attica and contributed to Athens' increasing prosperity.

19. Hegel, *Philosophy of History*, 254−55.

20. Hegel, *Philosophy of History*, 261.

21. Hegel, *Vorlesungen über die Philosophie der Weltgeschichte*, 627.

22. Hegel, *Vorlesungen über die Philosophie der Weltgeschichte*, 628.

23. Hegel, *Philosophy of History*, 268.

CHAPTER ELEVEN

1. Strauss responds to a student's paper, read at the beginning of the session. The reading was not recorded.

2. Nietzsche, *Beyond Good and Evil*, sec. 291.

3. See note 14 in chapter 1 on Hegel's rationalism.

4. Plato, *Timaeus* 40d−41a. Strauss reads from the translation by R. G. Bury in the Loeb Classical Library edition of 1929.

5. Xenophon, *Apology* 28. The "disciple" is Apollodorus.

6. Hegel, *Vorlesungen über die Philosophie der Weltgeschichte*, 646. In his 1958 course, Strauss quotes this same passage and comments: "This sentence is quite striking. You see how far Hegel was from any totalitarianism. That is absolute nonsense. For Hegel, totalitarianism was Robespierre: the inquiry into the intention of the individual—'Are you one hundred percent loyal?' You know? Virtuous, as Robespierre put it—and those who were suspect were already condemned [. . .] [For Hegel] there is no possibility of any inquisition and any treatment of suspicion" (session 9).

7. Hegel, *Elements of the Philosophy of Right*, 295 (§270R) and 303 (§270A).

8. In his 1958 course, after quoting from paragraph 270 in the *Philosophy of Right*, Strauss points to the same contradiction:

> The state has nothing to do with the content of any profession of faith; it is concerned only that every citizen belong to a religious community, because if a citizen is not a member of a religious community, then he lacks that binding element in himself which alone can make him a real citizen. The conclusion which we draw from his remarks that only Protestants can belong is not Hegel's opinion. He goes into some detail here and says that the strong state can be rather liberal in this respect and can disregard details which do not concern it and can even tolerate congregations—if they are small in number—which even reject the direct duties of the state on religious grounds. He

is thinking of Quakers and Baptists and so on. Hegel does not like these people, but he says that a sufficiently powerful state can afford them. He quotes a remark made in the United States Congress when the abolition of slavery was discussed by a deputy from the Southern states—he says "the southern provinces"—who said, "Grant us the Negroes and we grant you the Quakers." In the sequel he defends absolutely the citizenship of the Jews against the view which was then common in Germany. So that is very strange. There is a certain difficulty in Hegel because on the one hand he would seem to concede, by force of the emphasis on the importance of religion and significance of the differences of religion, that it was Protestantism which made possible the rational state—to favor a Protestant establishment and to have some doubt about the citizenship of anyone who was not a Protestant. In fact, he is amazingly liberal. The question is whether this does not lead to a difficulty. How would he have talked himself out of that difficulty? (session 5)

9. Strauss presumably refers here to G. W. F Hegel, *Sämtliche Werke: Jubiläumsausgabe in zwanzig Bänden*, ed. Hermann Glockner (Stuttgart: Fr. Frommann's Verlag, 1928). There is now an English translation of Hegel's *Lectures on the Philosophy of Religion*, ed. Peter C. Hodgson (Berkeley: University of California Press, 1984), though it is constructed on very different editorial principles from Glockner's *Jubiläumsausgabe*. The material cited by Strauss from volume 15 can be found in volume 1, pp. 451–60 of the English translation. The material cited from volume 16 can only very roughly be found in volume 3, pp. 339–47.

10. In his 1958 course, Strauss dilates on this problem of the effect of the growth of irreligion on the masses:

On the basis of Hegel's remarks regarding religion as the bond, what takes the place of religion? Now we have seen that there is a great ambiguity in Hegel already. Why emphasize the fact that the basis of society is religion, and of the rational society the Protestant religion? He also says that the state must demand from all its members adherence to a religious community but it doesn't make any difference what community that is [. . .] Either religion means something, and then religious differences mean a lot, or religion means nothing, and then why should the state demand adherence to any religious community? There is a great ambiguity here already in Hegel. Now I suppose a Hegelian would say the bond of rational society is not religion but reason, and I am sure that is what Hegel means because Hegel understands by religion an inferior form of awareness to philosophy. Still, reason is and can be actual, according to Hegel, only in institutions: if this is a rational society it will reasonably be actual in these institutions and in a few individuals. Hegel had no delusions that the *Logic* would ever become—I don't say a paperback edition—but a kind of reading for every family all over the globe. In brief, what happens to the mass of men if religion is to be the bond of society?

Hegel was thinking very much of an influence of the true philosophy on a large group of people, the educated people. That happened to [some] extent in Germany in his time and the generation after him. The high school teachers, the clergy, the lawyers, the public officials were influenced to some extent by Hegel. Hegel tried occasionally in one of his smaller writings to give this picture: perfect clarity at the top, whether in Hegel or in one close to him, and then it becomes dimmer and dimmer while you go down, but it is still the same substance all the way down. But that is not sufficient; you have also to see how it looks for the simple people, for the mass of people. Now Hegel still assumes the mass of the people will be religious Christians who go to church—in Prussia chiefly Protestants. And these people believe the old catechism and they believe pretty much what the Lutheran songs say. And then their pastor will have gone to the university. Yes? And at the university he will have gotten some very diluted theologically acceptable Hegelianism, so he will no longer be the same thing as his predecessor, who didn't get that at all. You see? That is easily intelligible. It will be diffused into the society. Most of the members will participate in philosophy only by way of deference to more or less Hegelianized people. But you have to think that if this civilization changes radically, if you can no longer assume that the whole citizen body is predominantly Protestant, then Protestantism will no longer be the bond of society. You know? And then the situation is completely altered. In Hegel's language, how do these people that can partake of reason only via religion still partake of reason when religion is no longer there as the most socially potent force? Think of the simple fact which was pointed out after Hegel by a certain critic that if the newspaper takes the place of the daily prayer, it empties the society completely. I think there is no provision for that grave problem in Hegel or in anything which today is inspired by Hegel. (session 5)

11. Johann Jakob Brucker (1696–1770) was a German historian of philosophy.

12. Thomas Stanley (1625–78) was an English poet, translator, and the first English historian of philosophy.

13. Pierre Bayle (1647–1706) was a French philosopher whose writings challenged orthodox Christian beliefs.

14. Averroes (1126–98) was an Islamic philosopher and commentator on Aristotle who, according to some, practiced esoteric writing.

15. Proclus (410–85) was a Greek Neoplatonic philosopher.

16. António de Oliveira Salazar was prime minister of Portugal from 1932 to 1968.

17. Hegel, *Philosophy of History*, 271–72.

18. Hegel, *Vorlesungen über die Philosophie der Weltgeschichte*, 649.

19. Hegel, *Philosophy of History*, 272.

20. Hegel, *Philosophy of History*, 273.

21. See p. 211 above and accompanying note.

22. Hegel, *Philosophy of History*, 278.

23. Hegel, *Philosophy of History*, 279.

24. Barthold Georg Niebuhr (1776–1831), *The History of Rome* (1812–32). The first English translation was published in 1827.

25. There was a break in the tape at this point.

26. Hegel, *Philosophy of History*, 292.

27. Hegel, *Vorlesungen über die Philosophie der Weltgeschichte*, 680–81.

28. Hegel, *Philosophy of History*, 294.

29. Hegel, *Philosophy of History*, 281.

30. Hegel, *Philosophy of History*, 296.

CHAPTER TWELVE

1. Strauss responds to a student's paper, read at the beginning of the session. The reading was not recorded.

2. Hegel, *Philosophy of History*, 298.

3. The 1832 Reform Act.

4. Hegel, *Vorlesungen über die Philosophie der Weltgeschichte*, 693.

5. Hegel, *Vorlesungen über die Philosophie der Weltgeschichte*, 698–99.

6. Hegel, *Philosophy of History*, 304.

7. Hegel, *Philosophy of History*, 308.

8. Hegel, *Philosophy of History*, 309.

9. Hegel, *Philosophy of History*, 310.

10. Hegel, *Philosophy of History*, 311.

11. Theodor Mommsen (1817–1903), a German historian most famous for his work *Römische Geschichte* (*The History of Rome*).

12. Cicero's *Republic* was discovered in the Vatican Library in 1819 by Cardinal Angelo Mai and first published in 1822.

13. See *Hegel's Aesthetics: Lectures on Fine Art*, trans. T. M. Knox (Oxford: Clarendon Press, 1975), 2: 1062.

14. In his 1958 course, Strauss comments on Kojève's rewriting of Hegel:

The most intelligent contemporary I know who says he is a Hegelian [. . .] implies that Hegel's *Philosophy of Right* is not the last word of Hegelianism; the last word of Hegelianism is what he calls "the universal homogeneous society." Universal means here a world state; and homogeneous means no discrimination, to use this famous term, on any grounds of nature, i.e., of birth. This is, you know, the old Napoleonic principle that "Every soldier carries the marshal's baton in his knapsack"—provided he is good enough, that is clear; but reasons of birth or caste do not play any role. This could also be enlarged to abolish the legal difference between the two sexes. That is easy! Sure! Provided it is perfectly understood that this is a considerable change from Hegel's explicit teachings! You could at least try to show that it follows from the spirit of Hegel, and that Hegel, simply in virtue of the practical impossibility of a thing like that at his time, simply didn't draw a logically necessary conclusion. Yes? [. . .] Now, still, this up-to-date Hegelianism of which I spoke, the author of it is a M. Kojève, whose name is now quite well known among students of Hegel. He wrote a very good book on Hegel's *Phenomenology of the Mind* which is of course half Marxist, there is no question, but the decisive difference between Marxism and this kind of Hegelianism is, in the first place, that the economic interpretation of history is not the basis, it is really the history of the mind; and secondly, there is no prospect of the abolition of the state, a withering away of the state is completely out. This also fits Hegel. The question is whether there are not essential reasons for leaving it at the nonuniversal state. You know? In other words, the possibility of war—whether that is not a question into which one would have to go. (session 7)

15. Hegel, *Philosophy of History*, 315.

16. Friedrich Nietzsche, *Thus Spoke Zarathustra*, prologue, section 5.

17. Hegel, *Philosophy of History*, 317–18.

18. Hegel, *Philosophy of History*, 318–19.

19. Hegel, *Philosophy of History*, 319.

20. See Kant, "Conjectures on the Beginning of Human History," in *Kant's Political Writings*, 221–34.

21. Hegel, *Philosophy of History*, 320–22.

22. Hegel, *Philosophy of History*, 326.

23. Hegel, *Philosophy of History*, 327–28.

24. Hegel, *Philosophy of History*, 335.

25. See p. 252 above and accompanying note.

26. See Baruch Spinoza, *Ethics*, trans. Samuel Shirley (Indianapolis: Hackett, 1992), part 2, proposition 47: "The human mind has an adequate knowledge of the eternal and infinite essence of God."

27. For passages in the 1958 lectures relevant to the difficulty Strauss points out here, see notes 8 and 10 in chapter 11.

28. Friedrich Schleiermacher (1768–1834) was a German theologian, preacher, and classical philologist who is widely recognized as the founder of modern Protestant theology.

CHAPTER THIRTEEN

1. Strauss responds to Miss Heldt's paper, read at the beginning of the session. The reading was not recorded.

2. Edward Gibbon, *The History of the Decline and Fall of the Roman Empire*, vol. 5 (1788), chap. 52.

3. According to a legend now largely discredited by historians, Caliph Omar ordered the burning of the library of Alexandria in 640 CE. Hegel quotes Omar as saying: "These books either contain what is in the Koran or something else: in either case they are superfluous" (*Philosophy of History*, 359).

4. Max Weber, "The Nature of the City," in *The City*, ed. and trans. Don Martindale and Gertrude Neuwirth (New York: Free Press, 1958).

5. Lucretius, *De rerum natura* (*On the Nature of Things*).

6. See Strauss's discussion of Hobbes in *Natural Right and History* (Chicago: University of Chicago Press, 1953), esp. 173–74.

7. See note 18 in chapter 8 above.

8. There are many expressions of this notion; perhaps the first in English was made by Isaac Newton in a letter to Robert Hooke.

9. See p. 252 above and accompanying note.

10. See notes 8 and 10 in chapter 11 for relevant passages from the 1958 lectures.

11. J. W. Goethe, *Zahme Xenien aus dem Nachlass*, in *Sämtliche Werke nach Epochen seines Schaffens*, ed. Karl Richter et al. (Munich: Carl Hanser Verlag, 1985–), 18.1: 76.

12. *Hegel's Aesthetics: Lectures on Fine Art*, 1: 10–11.

13. In his address at the dedication of the Eisenhower Presidential Library in Abilene, Kansas, in 1962, Eisenhower questioned: "When we see movies and the stage, and books and periodicals using vulgarity, sensuality, indeed, downright filth, to sell their wares, you think that our spirit—do you say America has advanced as much as we have materially when we see our very art forms so changed that the works of Michelangelo and Leonardo da Vinci are scarcely spoken of in terms of a piece of canvas that looks like a broken down tin lizzie loaded with paint has been driven over it? Now what has happened to our concept of beauty and decency and morality?" *New York Times*, May 2, 1962. Khrushchev famously visited the thirtieth anniversary of the Moscow Artist's Union in 1962, where he saw and criticized abstract paintings by Ernst Neizvestny and Eli Beliutin. The exhibition was subsequently closed.

14. Max Weber, "Science as a Vocation," in *From Max Weber: Essays in Sociology*, ed. and trans. H. H. Gerth and C. Wright Mills (New York: Oxford University Press, 1946).

15. The tape was changed at this point.

16. A student poses a largely inaudible question about Marx here, to which Strauss responds, "not even Hegel has that," and carries on with the point about Kant at which the transcript resumes here.

CHAPTER FOURTEEN

1. Strauss responds to a student's paper, read at the beginning of the session. The reading was not recorded.

2. Hegel, *Philosophy of History*, 336.

3. This is Strauss's version of what appears on page 338 of the Sibree translation of the *Philosophy of History*.

4. Hegel, *Philosophy of History*, 341.

5. Hegel, *Philosophy of History*, 342.

6. Hegel, *Philosophy of History*, 342–43.

7. Hegel, *Philosophy of History*, 345.

8. Hegel, *Philosophy of History*, 346.

9. Hegel, *Philosophy of History*, 350.

10. See note 12 in chapter 4.

11. Hegel, *Philosophy of History*, 353–54.

12. Hegel, *Philosophy of History*, 355–56.

13. Hegel, *Philosophy of History*, 358.

14. Hegel, *Philosophy of History*, 359.

15. Hegel, *Philosophy of History*, 363–64.

16. Hegel, *Philosophy of History*, 368–69.

17. Hegel, *Philosophy of History*, 370–71.

18. G. W. F Hegel, "The English Reform Bill," in *Hegel's Political Writings*, trans. T. M. Knox (Oxford: Clarendon Press, 1964).

19. Hegel, *Philosophy of History*, 379–80.

CHAPTER FIFTEEN

1. Strauss responds to Mr. Reinken's paper, read at the beginning of the session. The reading was not recorded.

2. Karl Barth (1886–1968) was an influential Swiss Protestant theologian who rejected the liberal theology characteristic of the nineteenth century.

3. Hegel, *Philosophy of History*, 389–90.

4. Chinese communist government forces invaded Tibet in 1950. Tensions between Tibet and China flared with particular intensity during the National Uprising in 1959, when the Dalai Lama went into exile in India. The International Commission of Jurists reported brutal suppression and the destruction of thousands of monasteries from 1959 to 1961.

5. Hegel, *Philosophy of History*, 390–91.

6. Hegel, *Philosophy of History*, 391.

7. Hegel, *Philosophy of History*, 391.

8. Hegel, *Philosophy of History*, 393.

9. Hegel, *Philosophy of History*, 394.

10. Hegel, *Philosophy of History*, 399.

11. On 5 March 1965, Circuit Court Judge George Leighton of Chicago dismissed charges against two men accused of resisting arrest by two police officers and assaulting one of the officers with a broken beer bottle.

12. In 1960, French Togo became fully independent from France and assumed the name Togo.

13. Hegel, *Philosophy of History*, 402.

14. Hegel, *Philosophy of History*, 403.

15. Winston Churchill, *The Gathering Storm* (Boston: Houghton Mifflin, 1948), 165.

16. *The Prince*, chap. 7.

17. André Gide, *Strait Is the Gate*, trans. Dorothy Bussy (New York: Vintage Books, 1952).

18. Hegel, *Philosophy of History*, 409.

19. Hegel, *Philosophy of History*, 410.

CHAPTER SIXTEEN

1. Strauss responds to Mr. Schaefer's paper, read at the beginning of the session. The reading was not recorded.

2. Frederick II, or Frederick the Great (1712–86) was king of Prussia from 1740 to 1786.

3. In July 1930 the Bourbon monarch Charles X was deposed and succeeded by Louis Philippe, duke of Orléans, whose eighteen-year reign was known as the July Monarchy.

4. Hegel, *Philosophy of History*, 451–52.

5. In his 1958 course, Strauss denies that this passage indicates that Hegel still sees unsolved fundamental problems: "The last remark [on p. 452 of the *Philosophy of History*] must not be understood to mean that there is still an unsolved problem in the decisive respect, that it is not yet the end of history. It simply means that in the Catholic countries, where the principle of the sound solution is not known, there has to be found a way between liberalism and Catholicism, which they have not yet found. In the Protestant countries, especially blessed Prussia, the situation is, according to Hegel, different" (session 14).

6. Strauss elaborates on Hegel's distinctive emphasis on the rights of man combined with expertise in government in his 1958 course:

> What Hegel means by rationality is not difficult to say in concrete terms in a general way. I have said it before and I will repeat it: the rights of man—the absolute impossibility of slavery or anything of that sort […] So Hegel means the rights of man, but also government which is not derivative from the atomic multitude. That is equally important. If you want to state it in historical terms, he means the Bastille, the seizure of the Bastille, supplemented by Napoleon, by a ruler of the state who is capable of keeping the rights of man, say, as embodied in Napoleon's civic code.
>
> You know, Hegel was throughout his life opposed to democracy, there is no question about that. But this has nothing to do with Hitler, it would be absolutely stupid to mention that in the same words […] If you say that Hegel believed in bureaucracy, you do not speak nonsense, but it must be properly defined—the actual government in the hands of the very well trained and very well educated and conscientious people. And the formal support for that is a hereditary monarch—it may be nonhereditary, but at any rate something which was exempt from the approval of the multitudes.
>
> That was his notion of government, and it was certainly not the rule of a party in any manner or form. Hegel was a liberal but not a democrat. This thing existed in former times. Of course there are great objections, but Hegel would probably say that the guarantee depends in critical periods on the existence of a few very able and correct men in the right spot, but this problem exists in every regime—even democracy and communism needs them. But to the extent that something can be arranged by human provision of institutions, this is the proper thing to do—not Chinese mandarins who devote too much time to empty formalism like beautiful style, but people properly trained and educated and filled with the right kind of spirit and sense of honor—this is the best you can do. That is what Hegel meant. Bureaucracy, all right!—but sensible bureaucracy. And the supplement to that is surely the rights of man; there is no question about that. We have seen what he said about such a relatively innocent thing as whipping as a punishment. After all, if that is legally applied, and the heaviness of the whip is determined by law, and there must be a medical examination of the culprit before the whipping is applied, this would be an infinite improvement on what is done in a number of so-called totalitarian countries today. And Hegel even rejected that as being incompatible with the dignity of man […]
>
> If one wants a single formula indicating what Hegel's philosophy of right stands for, it would be "rights of man" plus a wholly independent civil service. And the connection,

in his case, would be via monarchy. But the monarchy is only for the sake of these other two elements; these are the two pillars of the state, there is no question about that. (session 10)

7. Hegel, *Philosophy of History*, 424–25.
8. Hegel, *Philosophy of History*, 427.
9. Hegel, *Philosophy of History*, 430.
10. Hegel, *Philosophy of History*, 432.
11. Hegel, *Philosophy of History*, 435.
12. Hegel, *Philosophy of History*, 438–39.
13. Étienne Gilson (1884–1978) was a French Christian philosopher and historian of medieval thought.
14. Hegel, *Philosophy of History*, 439–40.
15. Hegel, *Philosophy of History*, 440–41.
16. Hegel, *Philosophy of History*, 442.
17. In his 1958 course, Strauss gives an even fuller account of Hegel's indebtedness to Kant for his concept of will and freedom:

The decisive step is that made by Kant. In Kant there is one formula which says everything: "Practical reason and will are the same, identical." The traditional view, the commonsense view, is this: In order to act rightly you must really *choose* the right action; for example, if you are compelled to behave like a decent man by someone standing over you and slapping you if you behave indecently, then you are not a decent man. You must really freely choose the right behavior. But on the other hand, this freedom of choosing requires a content; and this content is not supplied by the will, but by the reason, more specifically the practical reason [. . .]

Now let us see what Kant has done. Kant raises this question: "Where does this content come from?" The tradition answers that man has natural inclinations toward self-preservation, society, knowledge, and whatnot. Yes? Natural inclinations! These natural inclinations in a way supply the content. The inclinations precede your will; you are by nature inclined toward something, and this is the basis on which you choose. But then the will is absolutely derivative, because you do not choose your inclinations. Yes? You only choose something on the basis of your inclinations. Differently stated, you are at all times under the tutelage of nature; nature directs you toward something, so you are not truly free. Kant stated the problem as follows. The traditional notion assumes that the natural inclinations are good. How do we know that? We would have to know what is good in order to say that the natural inclinations are toward the good. Where do we get this knowledge of the good? It must be from some other source; and that can only be reason, if it is to be rational knowledge. But on what is the declaration of reason based? If it is on nature, then we are back in the old predicament of presupposing the goodness of nature. So it can only be reason itself in its purity which can teach us what is good. But reason in its purity is purely formal; it tells us only that in order to be rational our will must be of such a kind as to will what is in itself susceptible of being universal. Yes? In Kant's formula of the categorical imperative, we act in such a way that the maxim of our actions is susceptible of being given the form of a universal law [. . .]

Now Hegel doesn't believe that Kant succeeded, but he asserts that Kant's beginning is the right beginning. You see, you have here as the ultimate fact, not reason in the sense of a faculty perceiving certain eternal relations or whatever, but "will." But will, however, does not mean desire. That is understood. Will means, really, that act in which I am willing. If I desire, it may very well be, and as a matter of fact it is so, that I have not chosen the desire. Yes? Something urges and pushes me, but it is not I that do this. Therefore, with will, I must have really chosen it and I must have chosen it as something susceptible of universality—only then do I will. Will can only will itself, Hegel says, the will as will is nothing but the choosing of will, i.e., of a universal rule of action. Kant drew one conclusion from this which Hegel does not deny: if this is the deepest in man, that on which his humanity depends, then the dignity of man consists alone in his thus willing, in willing strictly speaking. From this it follows, however, that, reversely, there is an essential dignity of man; because man as man is capable of willing, and this is true of every man; and therefore freedom and equality of all men is implied in this notion of willing. And Hegel imputes, wrongly—but that is uninteresting and really also it is uninteresting for Hegel—that this Kantian notion of freedom was the motivation for the French Revolution; whereas it was really a much more old-fashioned notion of freedom which animated the French people. That could easily be shown by a study of Rousseau. The Rousseauean concept of freedom is not the Kantian concept but rather a minor and purely antiquarian thing. (session 14)

18. Hegel, *Philosophy of History*, 447–49.
19. Hegel, *Philosophy of History*, 449.
20. Hegel, *Philosophy of History*, 453–54.
21. Hegel, *Philosophy of History*, 455.
22. Hegel, *Philosophy of History*, 446.
23. Hegel, *Philosophy of History*, 447.

Index

www.ingramcontent.com/pod-product-compliance
Lightning Source LLC
Chambersburg PA
CBHW022131020426
42334CB00015B/842